Reflective Planning, Teaching, and Evaluation for the Elementary School

With a Foreword by Benjamin S. Bloom

Judy W. Eby
De Paul University

Merrill, an imprint of
Macmillan Publishing Company
New York

Maxwell Macmillan Canada
Toronto

Maxwell Macmillan International
New York   Oxford   Singapore   Sydney

Cover art: Leslie Bakshi
Editor: Linda James Scharp
Production Editor: Mona M. Bunner
Art Coordinator: Lorraine Woost
Cover Designer: Robert Vega
Production Buyer: Pamela D. Bennett

This book was set in Caledonia by Carlisle Communications, Ltd. and was printed and bound by R. R. Donnelley & Sons Company. The cover was printed by New England Book Components.

Macmillan Publishing Company
866 Third Avenue
New York, NY 10022

Macmillan Publishing Company is part of the
Maxwell Communication Group of Companies.

Maxwell Macmillan Canada, Inc.
1200 Eglinton Avenue East, Suite 200
Don Mills, Ontario M3C 3N1

Library of Congress Cataloging-in-Publication Data
Eby, Judy W.
    Reflective planning, teaching, and evaluation for the elementary
school / by Judy W. Eby.
        p.   cm.
    Includes bibliographical references (p.) and index.
    ISBN 0-675-22043-2
    1. Teaching.   2. Thought and thinking.   3. Educational tests and
measurements.   4. Education (Elementary)   I. Title.
LB1025.3.E29   1992
372.12'6 — dc20   91-4169
                                                                                      CIP
Printing: 1 2 3 4 5 6 7 8 9   Year: 2   3   4   5

THIS BOOK IS DEDICATED TO BENJAMIN S. BLOOM

. . . A MASTER TEACHER who has modeled reflective thinking throughout his career. From his observation of classroom events, he has contributed some of the most reflective and productive educational questions of our time.

In the 1950s, he asked, "What are all of the possible educational objectives that can be taught in schools?" The result was the *Taxonomy of Educational Objectives*, which now guides reflective elementary teachers to plan educational experiences that stress high-level thinking processes.

In the 1960s, in *Stability and Change of Human Characteristics*, he asked, "Are human characteristics such as intelligence and achievement fixed at birth or modified by experience?" As a result of his studies and findings on this question, programs such as Head Start have been designed to maximize children's potential for growth and success in school in the early years.

In the 1970s, he asked, "How is aptitude in school related to the time a student needs to learn a subject?" His studies in response to this question led to the individualized teaching strategy known as *mastery learning*, in which students work at their own rate to achieve mastery of a subject.

In the 1980s, he asked, "What teaching methods could approximate the effect of one-to-one tutoring in a classroom of 30 children?" In response to this question, Bloom and his colleagues proposed a teaching process that enhances each student's initial cognitive entry prerequisites at the beginning of a course of study. When this process is combined with mastery learning, students achieve gains similar to those they might attain in one-to-one tutoring.

In the 1980s, he also asked, "What are the processes by which individuals reach the highest level of accomplishment in their chosen fields?" In *Developing Talent in Young People*, Bloom and his colleagues describe their study of 150 eminently talented young adults in six fields. This study led to the identification of many common expectations and behaviors exhibited by the parents and teachers of young people who were subsequently able to attain the highest level of accomplishment in their fields.

After many decades spent studying educational practices and processes, Professor Bloom still reflects on each classroom event he observes with a fresh perspective and the belief that he can make a difference. In the Foreword to this book, you can read about the questions he is asking now and those that he encourages classroom teachers to consider as they begin their careers in teaching.

THIS BOOK IS intended to initiate and encourage a voyage of self-discovery on the part of beginning teachers or those who are committed to improving their classroom performance.

The voyage begins with an analysis of how teachers think and how they may begin to think more systematically and productively about classroom events and student behaviors. Teachers are encouraged to reflect upon their own moral principles and recognize how their own values and beliefs are likely to be translated into actions that affect student achievement and satisfaction with school.

The remainder of the book focuses upon the development of a repertoire of planning, teaching, and evaluation strategies that go far beyond the ordinary and conventional behavioral objectives, teacher-centered instruction, and fill-in-the blank tests. The strategies that are highlighted in this book are those that develop critical and creative thinking and encourage success rather than failure.

If you believe that teaching is a profession that requires extensive self-understanding and commitment to diagnosing and meeting students' affective as well as cognitive needs, this book can assist you in translating that belief into caring, creative classroom learning experiences through reflective planning, teaching, and evaluation.

——◢ ACKNOWLEDGMENTS

I WOULD LIKE to express my appreciation for the many contributions of ideas, materials, curriculum plans, and personal experiences made to this book by practicing professional classroom teachers, students, school administrators, and principals. These include:

Keith Anderson, Third-Grade Teacher, Lincoln Elementary School, West Harvey Dixmore School District No. 147, Harvey, Illinois

Bill Attea, Superintendent, Glenview School District No. 34, Glenview, Illinois (for the use of the Glenview Report Cards)

George "Rick" Bailey, Learning Disabilities Teacher, Crystal Lake School District No. 47, Crystal Lake, Illinois

Virginia Bailey, First-Grade Teacher, Woodland School, Barrington Community Unit School District 220, Barrington, Illinois

Karen Carlson, Principal, Prescott School, Chicago Public School District, Chicago, Illinois

Jim Cosme, Principal, Otis School, Chicago Public School District, Chicago, Illinois

Tim Curbo, Second-Grade Teacher, Hawthorne School, San Francisco Unified School District, San Francisco, California

Tom Eber, Principal, Our Lady of Mercy School, Chicago Archdiocese, Chicago, Illinois

Robert Guercio, Principal, Agassiz School, Chicago Public School District, Chicago, Illinois

Judith Kell, Principal, Hawthorne School, San Francisco Unified School District, San Francisco, California

Monica Lyons, Student, De Paul University, Chicago, Illinois

Jean Malvaso-Zingaro, Sixth-Grade Teacher, Monroe Middle School, Rochester School District, Rochester, New York

Roxanne Owens, Fifth- and Sixth-Grade Teacher, Our Lady of Mercy School, Chicago Archdiocese, Chicago, Illinois

Pamela Patterson, Student, De Paul University, Chicago, Illinois

Herb Price, Principal, Woodland School, Barrington Community Unit
School District No. 220, Barrington, Illinois

Lori Shoults, Second-Grade Teacher, Seth Paine School, Lake Zurich
School District Community Unit School District No. 95, Lake Zurich,
Illinois

Jane Stevens, Sixth-Grade Teacher, Dunn Elementary School, Arlington
Independent School District, Arlington, Texas

Andrew Tinich, Seventh- and Eighth-Grade Teacher, Lincoln School,
Chicago Public School District, Chicago, Illinois

Judy Yount, First-Grade Teacher, Woodland School, Barrington Community Unit School District No. 220, Barrington, Illinois

I also acknowledge the support I received from my colleagues, Sandra
Jackson, John Lane, and Sister Frances Ryan, at De Paul University, for the encouragement they gave me in the writing of this book and for their many suggestions of
resources and ideas that I included throughout the book.

Finally, I would like to express my appreciation to my son, Peter R. Eby,
who drew many versions of the graphic figures and drawings as I formulated them.

▗▌ F O R E W O R D

AS A BEGINNING TEACHER, you are launching into one of the most gratifying and satisfying professional careers. You ask yourself, "How can I help each student feel that he *can* learn, prove to himself that he *has learned*, and that he feels *good* about himself as a *learner?* You have selected an excellent book to guide you.

Let me start with a frequent misconception made by beginning teachers. They often take it for granted that the amount of energy, time, and preparation for a lesson is equal to the amount of learning that takes place in the classroom. Most of us have had this unsettling experience. We all need evidence of the amount of learning actually taking place.

In this book you will find suggestions regarding the planning, teaching, and evaluation of a teaching-learning experience. I will comment on each of these.

PLANNING

Education and learning in the schools are built on sets of prior learnings, largely cognitive in nature. For each learning task there are some prerequisite learnings that are required if the student is to attain mastery of the task. We have chosen to call these prerequisite learnings *entry behaviors*.

We believe it is impossible for a learner to achieve mastery on a learning task if he does not possess the essential entry behaviors for it.

Motivation to attempt a new learning task is in part determined by the individual's perception of his success or failure with previous learning tasks that he believes to be similar or related. Such motivation is largely predicated on the student's belief that the new learning task is in some way related to previous learning tasks he has encountered. It is the student's perception of his history with related learning tasks that is of importance—even though the new task may be in no way related to previous learning tasks he has experienced. Over a period of time, the learner acquires relatively fixed notions about his competence with such learning tasks, and these determine the efforts he will make, the degree of confidence he has in the effectiveness of his efforts, and what he will do when he encounters difficulties or obstacles in the learning.

We regard the affective entry characteristics as a compound of interests and attitudes toward the subject matter of the learning task, and of attitudes toward the school and schooling, as well as more deep-seated self-concepts and personality characteristics. Some of these components may be highly changeable, while others may be relatively stable; this is in part a function of age and previous experiences. While it is not impossible for a learner to achieve mastery on a learning task if he has negative affective entry characteristics, it is very difficult. We believe that it is sometimes possible to present a learning task so that the student will regard it as independent of previous learning tasks and may approach it with positive or even neutral affect. Operationally, what is sought is an openness to the new learning task, a willingness to make the effort required, and, hopefully, sufficient confidence in the self to strive to overcome real or imagined obstacles in the learning.

The main point to note is that affective characteristics are largely perceptual phenomena arising from the *student's* perception of how well he is learning, and that this is usually based on the evidence and judgments he receives from his teachers, his parents, and his peers in the school or class.

In our research, we found that spending the first week of the semester *enhancing* the diagnosed necessary prerequisites resulted in statistically significant improvement in achievement. In Chapters 3 to 6, Judy Eby explores the methods of diagnosing the necessary prerequisites for success in learning.

TEACHING

Teachers are frequently unconscious of the fact that they are providing more favorable conditions of learning for some students than for others in the same class. Generally, teachers are under the impression that all their students are given equality of opportunity for learning. As a beginning teacher, you will find that Judy Eby makes many excellent suggestions in Chapters 7 to 10 on specific procedures that will make your interaction with your students and their interaction with each other most effective.

We would especially emphasize the importance of the teaching of the higher mental processes in almost every learning experience.

In some countries, the national curriculum centers place great emphasis on problem solving, application of principles, analytical skills, and creativity. Such higher mental processes are emphasized because they enable the student to relate his learning to the many problems encountered in daily living. These abilities are also stressed because they are retained and utilized long after the individual has forgotten the detailed specifics of the subject matter taught in school. These higher mental processes are regarded as a set of essential characteristics needed to continue the learning and to cope with a rapidly changing world. Some curriculum centers regard the higher mental processes as important because they make learning exciting, constantly new, and playful.

Five of my graduate students have done studies on the teaching and learning of higher mental processes. In all of these studies, it became apparent that as more time and emphasis were devoted to teaching the higher mental processes, it was found that with each gain in the higher mental processes, there was a corresponding gain in the lower mental processes.

In the past, teachers had little hope that the majority of their students could learn the higher mental processes, since they had so many difficulties in mastering the lower mental processes. We believe that these studies all point to the fact that students can learn both the higher and lower mental processes, and that every effort to improve instruction by the use of mastery learning and problem solving, as well as other approaches, ensures that students will learn both types of mental processes to a high degree.

EVALUATION

In most classrooms, achievement tests are used for summative purposes. The summative test evidence is primarily used to classify the student or judge the extent to which he has learned the content and objectives set for the course. The students' scores on each test are converted into school marks or other indices that compare each student with a set of norms or standards set by the teacher or the test makers. Typically, once the student has taken a test, he is marked; rarely is he given opportunities for correcting his errors or being retested. In general, the basic notion is that the students have all had an equal opportunity to learn the subject over a defined period of time and are then to be judged on what they have learned. This process is repeated again and again during the school year.

It is frequently assumed that test results and school marks are the primary motivators for learning in the school. Marks based on tests are also assumed to be sound estimates of the quality of learning, as well as a proper index of the quality of the learners. Such marks eventually become the basis for many decisions about the learners, including school programs and further education.

If carefully made standardized tests are used over a number of subjects, the correlations over a 5-year period or longer tends to be $+.80$ or higher. That is, the ranks of the students in a school remain very constant over many years of schooling. It is assumed that the student and his background explain this remarkable stability of achievement and that the causes or remedies are not to be found within the school. It is the student who has failed (or succeeded), and the teacher, the instruction, the curriculum, or the school are not to be held responsible.

In contrast to tests used for grading and judging is the use of tests and other evidence as an integral part of the formation of learning. Formative tests are used primarily for feedback purposes in order to inform the student about what he has learned well and what he still needs to learn. When the feedback is provided in relation to procedures to help the student correct the learning, then, with additional time and help, most students do reach the standard of achievement set by the teacher. Typically, a parallel formative test is used to determine when the student has completed the corrective process to achieve the set standard.

Periodic formative testing and corrective procedures can provide one way of ensuring that excellent learning is taking place. However, in the long run, the basic problem of group learning is to find ways of providing feedback-corrective processes as an integral part of the classroom teaching-learning interactions.

In her book, Judy Eby gives many excellent suggestions for evaluation in Chapters 11 and 12.

In conclusion, you as teachers must have a deep belief that every child *can learn* and communicate that belief to each child. Share your ideas and techniques with other teachers. Learn from each other and support each other.

The school is a community. Mothers and fathers are crucial to the success of schools. Share expectations with them.

To quote Roger Mudd recently,

No calling is so demanding,
No calling is more selfless,
No calling is more central to a democracy.

Judy Eby has done an excellent job of delineating the *favorable learning conditions* and the *procedures to be followed* to strengthen the teaching-learning processes. Her well-organized and insightful suggestions will help you be a powerful influence on the lives of your students.

Benjamin S. Bloom
Professor Emeritus,
University of Chicago

▼ CONTENTS

▼ FIGURES

C H A P T E R
1

How Reflective Teachers Think

FROM THE MOMENT they walk into the school building in the morning, teachers face a continual stream of questions that need immediate responses, decisions that affect the well-being of their students, value judgments that may conflict with others' points of view, and complex problems that need elegant solutions.

Lori Shoults began her teaching career in August 1990 at Seth Paine Elementary School in Lake Zurich, Illinois. To illustrate the complexity of the beginning teacher's role and responsibilities, here is a brief account of some of the issues she faced during her first 3 months in the classroom.

▼ ————————————————————————————

When I first walked into my empty classroom in August, I was greeted by a big box of textbooks. But I had been hired by this school district because of my interest in and enthusiasm for the whole language approach to teaching reading and writing. So I had the freedom to create my own curriculum rather than rely on the texts. With that freedom came a lot of hard work.

It was very hard to plan before knowing my students, especially in the first year, when I didn't even know what second graders were like. I wanted the curriculum in my classroom to be fully integrated. I wanted science and social studies to be a part of reading and writing. What I did was to take all the textbooks and go through them in great detail. I made lists of skills that were taught in the English, phonics, and spelling books. From the science, social studies, and reading basals, I looked for topics. I divided the year into 2- to 3-week integrated units on topics such as plants, weather, light, magnets, dinosaurs, animals, and safety.

Within these units, I taught my reading and English skills every morning in a new poem that was related to the unit's theme. I distributed a poem to the children, and they glued it into their folders. We read the poem once just to enjoy its ideas and sound. Then each day I asked the children to look for examples of phonics rules, word structures, types of sentences, and types of punctuation. I focused on two or three new skills each day.

Because I used the whole language approach, the children chose their own reading materials from the books in our room or in the library. To encourage them to read, I decided to use a reading incentive program to give credit or rewards for the number of books each child read. But when I considered this idea, it had a lot of drawbacks. Children who read short, easy books would appear to get more credit than those who read long, challenging books. I talked to other teachers to find out what they had tried. One teacher told me about a system of having students keep track of the number of minutes they read rather than the number of books. When I considered this approach, I concluded that it was more productive than focusing on the number of books read because my goal was for the children to read longer stories and books rather than just counting books. It is also fairer because students at different achievement levels read books of different lengths. This system gives equivalent credit to each child for time spent reading, no matter at what level the child is reading.

The social studies textbook focused on the concepts of community and geography. I decided to have an overall theme of community, which I implemented by establishing a simulated community in the classroom. We had a teacher, a sheriff, a mayor, a meteorologist, a banker, and a gardener. Students signed up for the jobs they wanted, and they rotated every week. The learning stations in the class were community sites such as a post office (letter-writing center), a greenhouse (science center), a newspaper stand (writing center), a telephone company (listening center), a library (reading center), a toy store (learning games), and a computer lab.

My organizational problems were growing more difficult each day. At the beginning of the year, I tried to do it all at once. In addition to my regular reading, writing, and math programs, I set up five rotating math enrichment stations, the community stations, a geography program, and literature circles where children discussed books they were reading on their own. I wasn't able to get to all of these things as I had planned. I kept running out of time during the day. The children were confused. They were always asking when we were going to do different things.

So I sat down and planned for one special activity each day. On Tuesdays we would do community stations, on Wednesdays we had literature circles, and on Fridays we had math enrichment stations. I thought it would be better to have a consistent schedule. The children wanted to know what to expect, and I felt better knowing when to plan for each activity.

For math, I examined the basal text and believed that I could cover the skills in more interesting ways. I wanted to teach with more hands-on activities and use fewer math pages. I decided to use the Everyday Mathematics program (Bell, 1990) for teaching concepts and to use the textbook for practice and review. I also gave the tests from the math book. After using this approach for several months, I found that the students were able to do the textbook tests successfully. More important, they were enthusiastic about math. Even my lowest-achieving students felt confident about participating in math activities.

After 3 months of teaching, I felt that I was beginning to think like a teacher. At the beginning of the year, my schema for teaching and learning was rudimentary, leading me to make most decisions by trial and error. But later, I felt that I had expanded my knowledge and experience base to the point where, when I reflected on a decision, I had a much better understanding of the consequences of my actions.

REFLECTIVE THINKING

As Lori's account shows, teachers are faced with a multitude of complex issues and judgments. Each decision point requires a thoughtful response. But *thought* is an abstract and multifaceted concept, and *thinking* is a relatively mysterious process. In order to solve the mystery of thinking, many cognitive psychologists have proposed a theoretical framework known as *information processing* to help us understand how we think.

Processing Information

According to cognitive psychologists, thinking is, first, a perceptual process. As shown in Figure 1–1, each new bit of knowledge from the environment enters the consciousness of an individual through one or more of the five senses. For example, a new fact stated by a teacher is taken in by an individual's sense of hearing. A new idea read in a book enters through the sense of sight, and a new skill such as operating the clutch and stick shift on an automobile enters our consciousness through the sense of touch. The senses register these new bits of knowledge in one-quarter of a second, and within that instant, an executive function of the brain selects some bits of knowledge for retention in its *working memory* and discards other bits of knowledge entirely. This process, known as *selective perception*, is extremely important to the thinking and learning processes. We experience it simply as an initial awareness of a new fact, term, idea, or other sensation.

Why are some bits of knowledge discarded, while others are sent to working memory? That question is too complex to be answered fully here, but you can certainly recognize that we reject some stimuli when too many are bombarding us at one time, and we reject other stimuli because they are so foreign to our experience that we think of them as unintelligible.

A thought, fact, or skill that reaches the working memory stays there for less than 10 seconds. "Working memory is the 'place' where conscious mental work is done" (Gagne, 1985, p. 10). The obvious analogy of working memory is the computer. In fact, the term *information processing* was originally coined in the field of computer technology, but it is currently used to describe human thinking as well. Cognitive psychologists also use the term *cognitive processing* to describe the concept of the human mind perceiving, sorting, organizing, storing, and recalling knowledge and information.

The stream of new information that is acted upon in working memory is again directed by an executive function of the brain into the *long-term memory* or is rejected and forgotten. A statement made by a teacher, a fact read in a book, or a process such as adding two numbers is either selected for retention in long-term memory because it is perceived as important, useful, and comprehensible, or it is discarded as unimportant, useless, or incomprehensible. Another possibility is that the material is discarded simply because working memory has a small capacity and cannot process many bits of knowledge at the same time.

What we call *learning* occurs after the information is processed. It refers to the retention of knowledge in long-term memory in such a way that it can be retrieved at will. This retention process is analogous to storing the information on a computer disk using the "save" command.

Another part of the thinking process occurs during the *retrieval* of information that is stored in long-term memory. When we call up a fact or idea from long-term memory, it moves back into working memory for further processing and

FIGURE 1–1
Model of How the Brain Processes Information

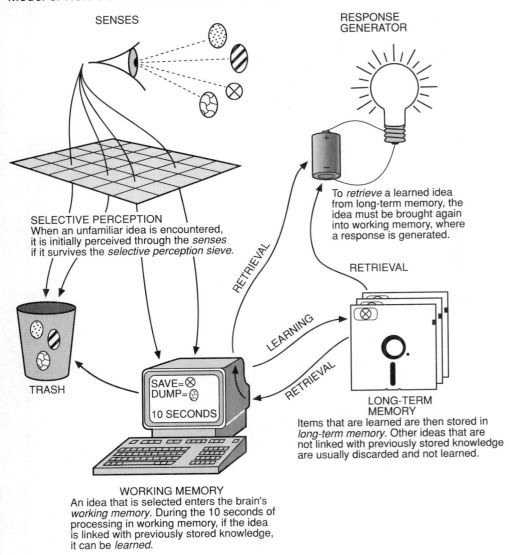

SENSES

RESPONSE
GENERATOR

SELECTIVE PERCEPTION
When an unfamiliar idea is encountered,
it is initially perceived through the *senses*
if it survives the *selective perception sieve.*

RETRIEVAL

To *retrieve* a learned idea
from long-term memory, the
idea must be brought again
into working memory, where
a response is generated.

RETRIEVAL

LEARNING

RETRIEVAL

TRASH

SAVE=⊗
DUMP=🌀

10 SECONDS

LONG-TERM
MEMORY
Items that are learned are then stored in
long-term memory. Other ideas that are
not linked with previously stored knowledge
are usually discarded and not learned.

WORKING MEMORY
An idea that is selected enters the brain's
working memory. During the 10 seconds of
processing in working memory, if the idea
is linked with previously stored knowledge,
it can be *learned.*

Reprinted by permission of Peter R. Eby.

then moves to a *response generator,* where the individual considers an array of possible responses and selects the one that seems to be most suitable in the given situation. The selected response is then performed.

This thinking or information processing model is applicable to all kinds of thinking. Students use it when they learn new facts and skills in the classroom. Teachers use it when they assess the needs of their students and consider how best to explain the new skill they are teaching.

Teachers who understand the process of acquiring and processing information can apply this knowledge in countless ways to the benefit of their students. They can reduce external stimuli so that the important bits of knowledge are perceived by the short-term memories of their students. They can pace the delivery of new information to give students sufficient time to process one bit of knowledge in working memory before introducing another. They can phrase questions in such a way that the questions provide the appropriate cue to retrieve the stored information from long-term memory.

How Teachers' Thinking Affects Students' Learning

The information processing model implies that all human beings think alike—that one brain is as much like another as two computer terminals are. Of course, we know that this is not true. Human personalities, values, and philosophies must be taken into account to fully understand the thinking process.

As a beginning teacher, you are undoubtedly interested in how teachers think, and you are probably even more interested in beginning to assess your own thinking attributes. Are you a systematic and deliberate thinker? A meditative ponderer? A quick, dynamic speculator? A moderate, calm calculator? A creative, original hypothesizer?

Before answering, you may want to know which of these styles of thinking is best suited to the teaching profession. But, alas, there is no research or data to support an accurate response to this question. Successful and effective teachers come in both genders and in all shapes, sizes, ages, and races, and display a wide variety of temperaments, personalities, and teaching styles.

There is, however, a growing body of knowledge that supports the point of view expressed in this book: that successful and effective teachers tend to reflect actively and productively about the important things in their lives, including their careers, their students' needs and educational goals, the school environment, and their own professional abilities.

How will you recognize whether you are a reflective thinker with the potential of becoming a reflective teacher? This book is designed to assist you in making that assessment. You will be confronted with many dilemmas and ambiguous situations that will require you to use your thinking processes. You can monitor your own responses and processes to gain a better understanding of your capacity for reflection. You will also be provided with a model of reflective thinking that may aid you in developing your reflective thinking abilities.

The guiding assumption of this book is that reflective teachers deserve the opportunity to select from a repertoire of ideas rather than accept and duplicate a single pattern. Therefore, this book provides you with a wide-ranging repertoire of curriculum planning ideas, teaching strategies, and evaluation methods that can be applied in elementary classrooms.

This does not mean that all elements presented here are in agreement with each other. Because this book emphasizes the right and the responsibility of the teacher to make informed decisions, conflicting and competing theories and ideas are frequently presented in this text, so that you may reflect on them and make your own judgment. Underlying the ideas presented in this text is the high value placed on encouraging you, the beginning teacher, to use reflective thinking as you consider the alternative modes and methods of teaching.

Definitions of Reflective Thinking and Action

In *How We Think: A Restatement of the Relation of Reflective Thinking to the Educative Process,* John Dewey (1933) defined reflective thinking as the "active, persistent, and careful consideration of any belief or supposed form of knowledge in light of the grounds that support it" (p. 9). An analysis of this carefully worded statement provides a clear description of the reflective thinker and correlates very well with the notion of a reflective teacher.

The first descriptive adjective, *active,* indicates one who voluntarily and willingly takes responsibility for considering personal actions. The reflective teacher is one who actively engages in an energetic search for information and solutions to problems that arise in the classroom. In contrast, there are many passive teachers who fail to consider issues that confront them and their students.

Dewey's use of the word *persistent* implies a commitment to thinking through difficult issues in depth, continuing to consider matters even though it may be uncomfortable or tiring to do so. While some teachers may begin to seek knowledge and information, they may be satisfied with easy answers and simple solutions. The reflective teacher is rarely satisfied, but is continuously and persistently seeking more knowledge and better ways to teach and to manage the classroom.

The *careful* thinker is one who has concern for both self and others. Reflective teachers care deeply about ways to improve their own classroom performance and how to bring the greatest possible benefit to the lives of children. Caring teachers create positive, nurturing classroom environments that promote high self-esteem and concern for each other among their students. Less careful teachers are likely to consider their own needs and feelings to be of greater importance than those of the children. Because they do not reason with care, they may make unreasonable demands on their students.

Dewey's phrase *belief or supposed form of knowledge* implies that little is known for sure in the teaching profession. The reflective thinker maintains a healthy skepticism about educational theories and practices. While a less reflective teacher might be persuaded that there is only one right way to teach, the reflective teacher observes that individual children may need different conditions for learning and a variety of incentives in order to be successful. While a less reflective teacher might adopt each new educational innovation without questioning its value, the reflective teacher greets it with an open but questioning mind, considering whether it is valuable and how it can be adapted to fit the needs of the class.

The final phrase in Dewey's definition, *in light of the grounds that support it,* directly relates to the reflective thinker's practice of using evidence and criteria in making a judgment. While the less reflective teacher may quickly jump to conclusions based on initial observations or prior cases, the reflective teacher gathers as much information as possible about any given problem, weighs the value of the evidence against suitable criteria, and then draws a conclusion and makes a judgment. Once a decision is made, the less reflective teacher may stick to it rigidly, but the reflective teacher is willing to reconsider decisions and judgments whenever new evidence or information becomes available.

But reflective thinking, even when it is persistent and careful, does not automatically lead to change and improvement. Dewey also acknowledged the importance of *translating thought into action* and specified that attitudes of openmindedness, responsibility, and wholeheartedness are needed for teachers to translate their thoughts into reflective actions.

How does a novice teacher learn to be reflective about personal decisions and actions? The process must begin in the courses that prepare teachers to teach, such as the one you are taking now. Cruickshank (1987) notes that "Literally, to reflect is to think. However, reflection is more than merely bringing something to mind. Once one brings something to mind, one must consider it" (p. 3). Drawing on Dewey's work, Cruickshank suggests that "Rather than behaving purely according to impulse, tradition, and authority, teachers can be reflective—they can deliberate on their actions with openmindedness, wholeheartedness, and intellectual responsibility" (p. 8).

This means that as teachers make any choice or take any action in the classroom, they reflect on how their choices and actions affect their students. For example, at the end of a social studies lesson, the teacher may consider whether to state an assignment aloud or write it on the chalkboard. In this example, the teacher may begin by telling the students to "read chapter 6 and write an essay summarizing the main idea." But as the teacher is saying these words aloud, an inner voice reminds the teacher that many children may not remember hearing this assignment; some children need visual reminders, and some children may not be listening. So, as a reflective action, the teacher follows the spoken words by writing the assignment on the chalkboard, perhaps stating in more detail what the essay should contain. The goals of this reflective thinking and action are to meet the varied needs of the students and to enhance the likelihood that the students will be successful in the assigned classroom task.

Donald Schon (1987) concurs with Dewey's emphasis on action as an essential aspect of the reflective process. He defines the reflective practitioner as one who engages in "reflection-in-action," an interior observation and criticism of personal actions:

> Reflection gives rise to on-the-spot experiment. We think up and try out new actions, . . . test our tentative understandings of them, or affirm the moves we have invented to change things for the better. . . . On-the-spot experiment may work, . . . or it may produce surprises that call for further reflection and experiment. (pp. 28–29)

A Moral Basis for Reflective Thinking

While reflective thinking and reflection-in-action may appear to be quite valuable and defensible concepts, several researchers raise a serious question about the value of reflective thinking unless it is done according to a set of moral and ethical principles. Tom (1984) proposes a vision of teaching as a "moral craft" in which the decisions made by teachers are based on moral criteria. Bullough (1989) agrees that, taken by itself, reflectivity is an unfinished concept. "For example, one might carefully weigh a number of alternative forms of punishment and choose to paddle a student because it 'gets results' and never ask the question of whether or not paddling is an ethical action" (p. 16).

Kohlberg (1987) describes *moral judgments* as decisions that are based on values rather than facts. In his studies of the development of moral reasoning, he found that each individual has a set of beliefs about what people ought to do in various situations and what each of us considers to be right and wrong. The teacher who paddles a child may value compliance with authority over respect for children's feelings of self-esteem.

Kohlberg made the study of moral reasoning and development his life's work. His well-respected theory focuses on the concept of *justice*, which includes how people view rules, authority, fairness, and the social contract that binds individuals to society.

In *In a Different Voice*, Gilligan (1982) accepts Kohlberg's conception of justice as one important basis for moral reasoning but asserts that it represents a predominantly male view of moral development. She proposes that the feminine concepts of caring and responsibility are also essential elements of moral development.

Kohlberg acknowledges Gilligan's view that the concepts of caring and responsibility are important elements of moral development. He believes that both caring and justice concerns are adequately addressed in his comprehensive description of three levels (encompassing six stages) of development that individuals may achieve during their lifetime (1987, pp. 18–19).

One way of understanding the three levels of development is to think of them as three different types of relationships between the self and society's moral rules and expectations (see Figure 1–2). From this point of view, Level 1 (preconventional) is a perspective from which rules and social expectations come from some external source and are followed in order to avoid punishment. In Level 2 (conventional), rules and expectations have been internalized by the self and are followed because the individual recognizes the value of a social order that is governed by rules. At Level 3 (postconventional), the individual recognizes the value of society's rules and expectations and, at the same time, upholds a distinctive set of self-selected ethical principles (1987, p. 16).

As you consider your own view of rules, expectations, and what you view as justice, where do you fit on Kohlberg's scale? Consider also how teachers' thoughts, judgments, and actions in the classroom are influenced by their own moral development.

Imagine the types of decisions and actions that are likely to be made by classroom teachers who are operating at a preconventional level of moral development. They are likely to consider all classroom events only from their own point of view, disregarding the needs and feelings of their students. They are likely to act impulsively and inconsistently from minute to minute, depending on their own self-centered and immediate interests.

Teachers at the conventional level of moral development are likely to employ consistent rules and expectations based on the principle of mutual benefit and gain. They are likely to set a model for their students of following society's rules and expectations so that the individual can get ahead and so that the societies of the

FIGURE 1-2

Kohlberg's Six Stages of Moral Development

Level 1 **(preconventional)**	*Stage 1*	Egocentric—Doesn't consider the needs or interests of others. Follows rules to avoid punishment.
	Stage 2	Individualistic—Acts to meet own needs and interests but recognizes that others have different needs. Follows rules that are in one's own immediate interests.
Level 2 **(conventional)**	*Stage 3*	Golden Rule—Recognizes the needs and interests of others as well as one's own. Follows the Golden Rule and complies with society's laws.
	Stage 4	Member of Society—Recognizes that society benefits when individuals comply with its rules and laws.
Level 3 **(postconventional)**	*Stage 5*	Principled—Has a set of moral principles. Recognizes that these may vary from society's rules. Usually chooses to obey laws that are part of the social contract.
	Stage 6	Universal Ethical Principles—Holds principles that respect the worth and dignity of all humanity. May choose not to comply with laws that conflict with own principles.

classroom and the nation can flourish. If your goal is to operate at a conventional level of moral development, you may begin by clarifying which of society's rules are most important to you and then establish classroom procedures modeled on these rules.

One example of a moral principle that a conventional teacher may value highly and want to include is the notion of developing a sense of community or democracy in the classroom. To do this, each choice you make in the classroom needs to enhance communication and develop a shared sense of purpose. There will be many decision points throughout the day about whether students must work alone or can work together on projects, or about whether to take time to listen to students' interests and concerns or keep working to finish a chapter by the end of the week. The reflective teacher who chooses to base judgments on the principle of building a sense of community will need to consider that value in these and many other decision points throughout the day.

If your principles include a high priority on the development of academic excellence, then each time you plan a unit of study or assign an academic task, you will want to make sure that it is as challenging as possible. Instead of assigning all children to do the same page in the same text or workbook, you will consider what academic task is appropriate for various students in the class. You may assign an exploratory, hands-on task to students who need concrete experiences to develop the concept you are teaching, and a more challenging and abstract task to students who have mastered the fundamentals but need to apply what they've learned to other situations.

Teachers who operate at the postconventional level of moral development are likely to have a highly personal and unique set of principles that guide their decisions regarding right and wrong, justice, fairness, and human rights. From time to time, highly principled teachers may find that their values conflict with the rules and expectations imposed upon them by the school administration or the larger society.

If your goal is to become a highly principled teacher, then you are likely to want to analyze many relative and conflicting values, and to select and clarify the ones that matter most deeply to you. You must be willing to act on these values even if your actions result in conflicts with others who hold a different set of values.

An example of a value held by a highly principled teacher might be to encourage and support students' creativity, even when their creative efforts or ideas differ from the norms of society. If you hold this view, then you will want to reflect on how to plan lessons that encourage divergent responses. If you value independence and initiative over compliance with authority, then you will want to consider how to schedule time and plan learning experiences that call on students to work independently and be responsible for much of their own learning.

These are just a few of the many important moral principles and values that reflective teachers may hold. Since many are important, it is vital for you to clarify the principles that you hold and then consider these priorities when you have to make a choice on an issue that may bring more than one principle or value into conflict. For example, in the choice between academic excellence and developing a sense of community, there are likely to be many decision points on whether to push students toward accomplishing challenging academic tasks or to listen to their fear that the task is too difficult. At this point, the reflective teacher considers which of these priorities are most important in this case and takes the appropriate action as a result.

A book such as this one is greatly influenced by the moral principles and values of the author. This work is no exception. In it you will find that the selection of what research to include and exclude, theories of how teaching and learning occur, suggestions of strategies for planning, and teaching and evaluation of learning are all greatly influenced by my own moral principles. I share Gilligan's view that caring and responsibility are essential priorities in moral development. I care deeply about teaching well and about meeting the self-esteem needs of my students. I believe that I have a responsibility to plan engaging and interesting learning experiences and to give my students honest critical feedback about their progress and accomplishments so that they know how to succeed.

At times, my principles have clashed with the conventional rules and expectations of my school settings. For example, if recess were to be eliminated in my school (as it has been in many schools) to save money or to shorten the school day, I would object very strongly and take my students to the playground at least once a day.

You will also find a strong commitment in this book to the moral principles of developing a sense of community in the classroom and of developing planning, teaching, and evaluation strategies that promote success rather than failure among students at all achievement levels. My principles about caring, responsibility, community building, and success are the criteria that I used to select the classroom management strategies, discipline models, teaching methods, examples of classroom materials, and experiences and methods of evaluation for this book.

Translated into action, this book presents a model of reflective teaching, planning, and evaluation based on a set of clarified moral principles in the hope that education students will view reflection and clarification of their moral principles as one of the first and most important steps in becoming a teacher. Accepting this challenge will not be easy. It represents an enormous responsibility with very important consequences. As Schon (1987) suggests, many teaching actions lead to surprising outcomes, some that are successful and others that produce negative or unpleasant results. Reflective teachers are able to reflect on both positive and negative classroom experiences productively, considering what they can learn from each event, gathering information to make better judgments, considering how their actions reflect their moral priorities, and then selecting and implementing the best possible strategy under the circumstances.

Throughout this text, you will be presented with situations similar to those that teachers confront every day in their classrooms. You will be urged to consider these situations and ask yourself how you would react, what you would decide or choose to do in each case. You will be asked to write journal entries examining your own beliefs and defending your own point of view. You will be asked to observe and analyze classroom events, hypothesize cause-and-effect relationships, and look for evidence to test your hypotheses. You will be asked to debate and argue about educational issues with your classmates, take a stand on complex questions, and propose solutions to multifaceted problems. You will be asked to make a decision and predict its consequences or to take an action and examine the consequences, looking for ways to improve the outcome.

By taking an active, persistent, open-minded, and intellectually responsible role in your present educational experiences, you can become a reflective teacher, a lifelong learner, and an agent for growth and change in your educational community.

A MODEL OF REFLECTIVE TEACHING

Reflective thinking may occur spontaneously. Faced with a classroom dilemma, such as a child who refuses to turn in classwork or a class that challenges the teacher's grading of a test, most teachers are likely to reflect on the conditions that brought about this trouble and to consider possible actions to take to improve the situation.

Faced with a child who refuses to turn in classwork, the teacher may think that the contributing factors to this problem stem from the child's home environment, previous school experiences, or lack of readiness to learn the new material. The teacher may decide to talk to the child's parents about the problem or to have the child tested by the school psychologist.

Confronted by a class of angry students who disagree with the grades they have received on a recent test, the teacher who values honest feedback is likely to reflect back on the quality of the teaching and the amount of preparation the students had prior to the test. The teacher who values student success may also reconsider the suitability of the test items and the system used for determining grades. After thinking about these matters, the teacher may decide to allow students to retake the exam, to rescore the present test, or to stand firm on the grades as given.

In these examples, teachers are reflecting, making decisions, considering moral principles, and taking actions as a result. But is spontaneous reflection adequate in the face of the hundreds of important dilemmas and decisions teachers must make every day? Are teachers' personal observations and insights adequate to make informed judgments, or is there a need to gather information from other informed sources?

The process of considering cause and effect can be improved by a more systematic inquiry. There are certain skills that teachers can learn to improve their own reflective thinking.

Pollard and Tann (1987) have provided a very useful model of reflective teaching based on the work of John Dewey. Their analysis of Dewey's work has resulted in the identification of four essential characteristics of systematic reflective teaching:

1. Reflective teaching implies an active concern with aims and consequences, as well as with means and technical efficiency.
2. Reflective teaching combines enquiry and implementation skills with attitudes of openmindedness, responsibility, and wholeheartedness.
3. Reflective teaching is applied in a cyclical or spiralling process, in which teachers continually monitor, evaluate, and revise their own practice.
4. Reflective teaching is based on teacher judgment, informed partly by self-reflection and partly by insights from educational disciplines. (pp. 4–5)

In their analysis of these four characteristics, Pollard and Tann suggest a model of reflective teaching that teachers can learn to apply to almost any classroom situation. The inquiry skills they have identified as essential to the process of reflective teaching include:

Empirical skills. These relate to the essential issue of knowing what is going on in a classroom or school. They are concerned with collecting data and with describing situations, processes, and causes and effects with care and accuracy. Two sorts of data are particularly relevant. Objective data—such as what people actually do, their behavior—are important; but so are subjective data, which describe how people feel and think—their perceptions. The collection of both types of data calls for considerable skill on the part of the investigators, particularly when they may be enquiring into their own classroom practice.

Analytical Skills. These skills are needed to interpret descriptive data. Such "facts" are not meaningful until they are placed in a framework which enables a reflective teacher to relate them, one with the other, and to begin to theorize about them.

Evaluative Skills. Evaluative skills are used to make judgements about the educational consequences of the results of the practical enquiry. Evaluation, in the light of aims and values, enables the results of an enquiry to be applied to future policy and practice.

Strategic Skills. Strategic skills take us directly into the realm of planning for action and anticipating its implementation, following the analysis which a reflective teacher carries out. . . .

Practical Skills. Here we are directly concerned with the skills which are involved in action itself. A reflective teacher is one who is able to link analysis and practice and ends and means to good effect. To be highly analytical but ineffectual in practical matters is not a satisfactory balance, any more than the reverse situation would be.

Communication Skills. Communication skills are necessary because reflective teachers are concerned about aims and consequences as well as means. They are likely to need and to want to communicate and discuss their ideas extensively with others. They are likely to need to establish their legitimacy and to gain the support of others in the processes of development in which they engage. Thus, they should be effective communicators. (p. 7)

Figure 1–3 on page 14 provides a graphic representation of this model of reflective teaching that illustrates the cyclical or spiralling process in which teachers continuously monitor, evaluate, and revise their own practice.

To show the contrast between a teacher who actively uses this reflective teaching model and one who does not, let us consider the classroom event of cheating. The scene is familiar to all of us. The teacher asks students to put everything away except for a sharpened pencil. The teacher then distributes a two-page vocabulary test in which students must write the definition of twenty words and give a sentence using each word correctly. The classroom is hushed as the students begin working. The teacher walks around to see that everyone is starting the exam and then sits down at the desk to correct the morning's math papers. After a few moments, a rustling sound calls the teacher's attention to the back of the room. It is made by a child unfolding and looking at a piece of notebook paper and then writing on the test paper.

Teachers will vary greatly in their response to this situation. One teacher might deal with it almost reflexively, giving little or no thought to the appropriate response. Such a teacher might immediately walk to the student's desk and tear up the exam, saying in a harsh voice, "You'll take an F on this test for cheating." In this case, the teacher has moved from considering a classroom event to putting a plan into action without using any of the intervening, reflective thinking steps of the model.

A second teacher might ask the student to bring the notebook paper and the exam up to the desk. After examining the notebook paper and finding that it contains a list of the vocabulary words and their definitions, the teacher might make a judgment that the child is cheating. The teacher might then consider two or three strategies for dealing with the matter, including yelling at the child, tearing up the paper, giving the child a failing grade, and calling the child's parents to discuss the situation. Valuing the principle of building self-esteem among the students, the teacher chooses the alternative of calling the parents and quietly tells the child to expect the call that evening.

In the second example, the teacher is applying elements of the reflective teaching model. By asking to see the notebook paper and comparing it to the test, the teacher is gathering information before making a judgment. In this case, the teacher has considered several strategies and has applied the criterion of developing self-

FIGURE 1–3
A Model of Reflective Teaching

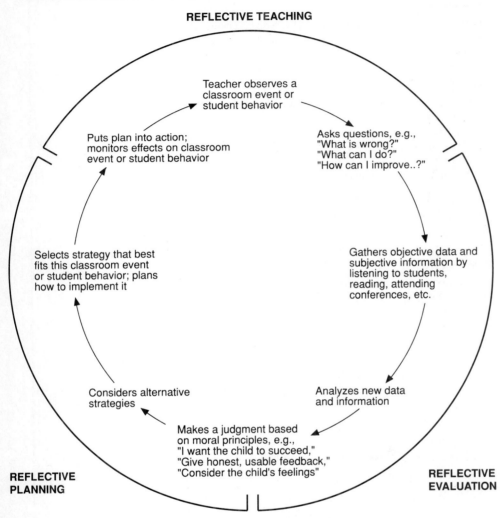

REFLECTIVE TEACHING

Teacher observes a classroom event or student behavior

Puts plan into action; monitors effects on classroom event or student behavior

Asks questions, e.g., "What is wrong?" "What can I do?" "How can I improve..?"

Selects strategy that best fits this classroom event or student behavior; plans how to implement it

Gathers objective data and subjective information by listening to students, reading, attending conferences, etc.

Considers alternative strategies

Analyzes new data and information

Makes a judgment based on moral principles, e.g., "I want the child to succeed," "Give honest, usable feedback," "Consider the child's feelings"

REFLECTIVE PLANNING

REFLECTIVE EVALUATION

Reprinted by permission of Judy W. Eby, Sarah Tann, and Andrew Pollard.

esteem in selecting a strategy. When the teacher puts this plan into action later in the day, there will be more opportunities to gather information from the parents about the child's home life, feelings about school, expectations of success and failure, and other factors that might have contributed to the observed event.

With a highly reflective teacher, the same event might generate a much more in-depth response. On seeing the child with the notebook paper, the teacher might take the child outside the classroom to discuss the observed event. Asking the child the purpose of the paper might result in conflicting information. Perhaps the child will reply that it was on the floor, but the teacher recognizes that the handwriting is the same as that on the exam paper. The reflective teacher might try to investigate several issues embedded in the observed event by asking the student questions about motives, fears, and needs.

Reflective teachers do not make hasty decisions. In this case, the teacher may decide that there is not enough information to make any judgment about the situation. Perhaps the vocabulary words were too difficult for this child, who, rather than fail, cheated to save face. The teacher may review the student's past performance, give a nongraded placement test to test the child's present achievement level, or telephone the parents to find out what information they may have to add before making a judgment. After discussing the case with others, the teacher may consider a dozen different strategies before creating a plan and putting it into action.

When reflective teachers observe nonproductive behavior in children, it often causes them to examine their own classroom practices. In this case, the reflective teacher might consider what strategies could be employed to prevent the need for such cheating in the future. The teacher might use the moral principle of enhancing self-esteem and building self-discipline in children, and might decide that prior to the next vocabulary test children will be allowed to select words that they do not know from the books they are reading for literature, science, and social studies. In this way, all children have an opportunity to select words appropriate to their present level of achievement and be successful in learning how to incorporate these words into their own vocabularies.

Of course, this new classroom strategy may generate new difficulties and issues. When the next test occurs, the reflective teacher will actively consider the effects of allowing students to choose their own words and compare the results from the previous tests as a means of gathering data about the new practice. The spiral of observation, reflection, gathering data, considering moral principles, making a judgment, considering strategies, and putting a plan into action continues without end in the classroom of a reflective teacher.

A Classroom Teacher Reflects on a Classroom Event

In the Perspective on page 16, Virginia Bailey, known as Ginny to her friends and colleagues, illustrates the thinking processes of a highly reflective teacher. She plans each learning event so that students are able to process and learn new ideas by eliciting both their existing knowledge and their interest in learning about an unfamiliar idea.

As teachers often do, Ginny plans learning events with a variety of goals. In this brief lesson, she is teaching children about polar bears, but she also demonstrates many of the attributes of the reflective teaching model. She considers each classroom event, such as this lesson on polar bears, carefully. She gathers information about what her students already know so that she can aim her new teaching at the level that is challenging and interesting for them. She is also guided, in her planning and her interaction with students, by her highly valued principles of teaching children how to process information effectively, how to listen for information, and how to monitor what they have learned and determine what they still need to learn. She

INTRODUCING VIRGINIA BAILEY
First-Grade Teacher, Woodland School, Carpentersville, Illinois

PROVIDING MEANINGFUL EXPERIENCE FOR A CHILD WITH LEARNING DIFFICULTIES

Virginia (Ginny) Bailey teaches first grade in a suburb of Chicago. She has taught for 16 years in primary grades in suburban school systems. After teaching for 10 years, she began to take graduate courses to earn a master's degree in curriculum and instruction. She is currently pursuing a certificate in school administration.

Her philosophy of education is a developmental one. She believes that children learn best when they are presented with materials and experiences that are developmentally appropriate for them at the time, regardless of their grade level. She feels that children learn best when they meet success through their learning. Here, in her own words, is a story that illustrates her philosophy in action.

We were beginning to study polar bears as part of a unit on mammals in my first-grade classroom. One day I planned to read aloud a picture book about polar bears.

Before I began to read, I wanted to assess the students' previous knowledge, and at the same time help them get ready to think and learn about polar bears. I used a comprehension technique called K-W-L. The initials stand for Know, Want to Know, and Learned.

The first step was to ask them "What do you already know about polar bears?" They knew that polar bears lived in cold places, that they were mammals, and that they had white fur. I wrote these ideas down on a large sheet of paper.

The next step was to ask "What do you want to know about polar bears?" They wanted to know what polar bears eat, exactly where they live, why it is cold there, where they go to have their babies, and how big the babies are.

Then I read the book aloud. Afterward, I asked "What did you learn from this book about polar bears?" They reconfirmed that polar bears are mammals. They also learned that they spend a lot of time in the water, that they eat seals, and that their babies are born in snow caves.

Some of their original questions had not been answered by this book, so I went to other sources to get information about the unanswered questions, such as how big the babies are at birth. I used a map to show where polar bears live, and we discussed why it is colder in the northern latitudes.

Using this technique allows me to assess what students know so that I don't repeat what they have already learned. It also allows children to formulate questions and bring their previous knowledge about a topic to bear (no pun intended) on the new topic. I also find that students show much more interest in listening or reading for information when they have asked questions about the subject beforehand.

---

selects teaching strategies that put these principles into action. After each lesson, she considers what was gained and what the students want and need to know next. Her subsequent planning is guided by these considerations.

Today, if you visit Ginny's classroom, you will find an environment in which students are active seekers of knowledge, constructing their own ideas and pursuing many of their own goals, and evaluating their progress with their teacher to decide what they need to learn next.

A Classroom Teacher Describes How Her Team Uses Reflective Thinking

Often teachers work as teams to plan their curriculum. This system has the advantage of providing a support system for individual teachers as they encounter difficult choices and have decisions to make. Jane Stevens plans with other upper elementary teachers at Dunn Elementary School in Arlington, Texas, where she teaches the sixth grade. In the Perspective on page 18, she describes the way her team reflects on a new year in their planning sessions.

Lori Shoults, Ginny Bailey, Jane Stevens, and several other experienced teachers whose ideas and methods you will encounter throughout this text exemplify the growing number of teachers who show a strong commitment to searching for answers and solutions to difficult school-related problems through reflective thinking and action.

School Climates That Nurture Reflective Teachers

Ginny Bailey has grown and developed into a highly reflective teacher because of a strong commitment to meet the needs of her students. She has also continued to grow professionally by taking graduate courses and workshops as a means of updating her fund of information about teaching and the learning processes. But Ginny also gives credit to her school principal, Herb Price, for supporting her development as a reflective teacher.

As a principal, Herb allows and encourages the teachers on his staff to take risks and try new strategies if they can demonstrate that the new strategies are developmentally sound for young children. Since the time Ginny first expressed interest in experimenting with new reading methods, he has fully supported her investigations of the language experience and the whole language approach because he believes that these strategies are beneficial to both the affective and cognitive development of children.

"I label my administrative style the three '-ates,' " states Herb Price. "I facilit*ate*, particip*ate*, and celebr*ate* with the teachers and the students in my school over the accomplishments they are able to make. I also encourage teachers when they need it. For example, Ginny had many moments of wondering whether she was doing the right thing during her transition from using the basal reader to the whole language approach. I encouraged her to keep trying because we were both convinced that the whole language approach was developmentally sound."

Educational decisions and judgments such as this one, which was made by a teacher and supported by the principal, is an example of school reform in action. Many educational researchers now believe that the school is the basic unit of change and improvement. School districts in many parts of the country are being restructured to shift responsibility for decision making from central office administrators to the school faculty, with support and guidance from the local school community.

What effects do schools have on their students? This is a major question that researchers are now debating. While some believe that the school cannot overcome the effects of poverty and other debilitating home/community influences, Schulman and Sykes (1983) believe that schools can make a difference and that the

INTRODUCING JANE STEVENS
Sixth-Grade Teacher, Dunn Elementary School, Arlington, Texas

HOW REFLECTIVE THINKING AND DISCUSSION BUILD TEAMWORK

Jane has taught both primary and upper elementary grades in three states. She currently serves as a team leader for the sixth-grade teachers at Dunn Elementary School. Throughout her career, she has conducted inservice workshops for teachers in several states on a variety of topics. She is currently very proud of her involvement with the Drug Abuse Resistance Education (DARE) program. In this program, police officers visit sixth-grade classrooms to train students on how to resist drugs. They use many teaching strategies, including videotapes, lectures, discussions, role playing, and pantomime. Jane provides inservice training for the police officers on how to teach and manage a classroom.

Like many other elementary teachers, Jane is a generalist. She enjoys teaching and learning about mathematics, literature, writing, social studies, and science. Her goal is to make her classroom and her school a good place where children can experience success. To accomplish this, she says, requires the involvement of all members of the school community, especially classroom teachers. In Jane's view, a good teacher is one who knows the curriculum, thinks vertically as well as horizontally, incorporates a variety of methods and materials in teaching strategies, takes individual learning styles into account, and builds on success so that every child in the classroom feels like a winner.

In her own words, Jane describes the ways her team works together to make these goals come true.

Working with large grade-level teams (five to nine members) provides many opportunities for reflective thinking. Prior to the beginning of school each year, our team meets to plan for the coming year. We are responsible for considering how to group our students and assigning teachers for each class. To do this harmoniously, I allow teachers to discuss openly their preferences, likes and dislikes, and strengths and weaknesses, and together we determine the class assignments and the units of work for which each member is responsible.

We must also make adjustments to our curriculum to meet changes in state or district mandates, and we always discuss new methods of classroom management or discipline strategies that we have read or heard about since the last year. When new teachers join our group, we try to get acquainted with them, discover their interests and strengths, and encourage them to share these with the rest of us. We try to nurture new teachers for the first few years by sharing our time-tested strategies, materials, and knowledge about the learning process itself.

Our reflective thinking is probably most apparent as we try to keep up with the latest research and update our own teaching methods and materials as new, more promising ones become available. In adopting new methods and materials, we also have to choose what to omit and discard. We want to weed out the less effective materials, but we don't want to discard strategies and activities just because they are old. We spend many hours discussing the relative values and merits of old versus new methods and materials. As a team, we like to keep the best of the old tried and true methods, but we want to stay open to new ideas so that we can stay fresh and excited about teaching year after year.

type of school attended is "enormously consequential," especially for less able children (p. 4).

But consequential in what ways? Some of the possible beneficial effects being studied are increased scholastic achievement, attentive classroom behavior, a positive attitude toward learning, lower rates of absenteeism, continued education, higher employment rates after leaving school, and lower rates of delinquency.

While no studies yet exist that demonstrate a one-to-one correlation between a school characteristic and a beneficial effect, most researchers agree that a school is a unit of organization with a particular "ethos" or "culture" and that some of these cultures are clearly more beneficial than others. For example:

> Set in the heart of Miami's Liberty City, where crack, drug-related violence, and poverty are a fact of life, Charles Drew Elementary School is an oasis. Given every excuse to fail, Drew students instead earn high marks on achievement tests, studying everything from basics to ballet. Every Saturday, nearly 200 students troop in for extra help or enrichment.
>
> Thanks to Drew's participation in one of Dade County's two school-based management/shared decision making (SBM/SDM) pilot projects, teachers there help make decisions such as the one that created Saturday classes. (O'Neil, 1990, p. 4)

Sergiovanni (1984) observes that it is difficult to define excellence in schooling but that it is readily recognized when we see it. In excellent schools, "a sense of purpose rallies people to a common cause; work has meaning and life is significant; teachers and students work together and with spirit; and accomplishments are readily recognized" (p. 4).

Many of those who are currently studying school *effectiveness* have limited the definition to "basic skill learning," according to Sergiovanni. He believes that we should expand our vision of effectiveness and study schools that do much more than develop fundamental academic competence. We should include "developing a love of learning, critical thinking and problem-solving skills, aesthetic appreciation, curiosity and creativity" (pp. 4–5).

Sergiovanni observes that important and recognizable differences exist among incompetent, competent, and excellent school leaders. Incompetent principals do not get the job done. Their schools are characterized by malaise, conflict, inefficiency, low achievement, and high absenteeism. Competent principals get the job done in a satisfactory way. Excellent principals exceed expectations by providing a sense of vision and purpose for the entire school community. The result is that "students in excellent schools accomplish far more and teachers work much harder than can ordinarily be expected" (p. 7).

In California, it is the curriculum that is being restructured. In the late 1980s, under the direction of State Superintendent of Public Instruction Bill Honig, committees made up of teachers, administrators, and subject area specialists created new curriculum frameworks that describe literacy in the subject and define the student performance expectations that will lead to literacy (Kierstead & Mentor, 1989).

While many curriculum documents are seen as finished products, to be implemented by teachers without question, the California curriculum frameworks encourage teachers and principals to translate the general framework and standards into a specific local vision with local plans and goals. Through this dynamic process of curriculum shaping at the school level, teachers are encouraged to use reflective thinking and see themselves as valued members of a team effort.

In the following Perspective, Judith Kell, an elementary principal in San Francisco, describes her role in encouraging her staff to develop into reflective teachers.

A highly motivating principal like Judith Kell and a stimulating environment like that of Hawthorne School have a beneficial effect on both students and teachers. Ms. Kell expects a great deal of hard work and effort from her teachers, and in return she gives them a great deal of support and respect. She encourages their creativity and grants them the autonomy that professionals deserve.

But is teaching a profession?

In many ways, the answer to this question is up to you.

The potential for teaching to become a profession has never been stronger than at the present time. Linda Darling-Hammond (1988), director of the Education and Human Resources Program at the RAND Corporation's Center for the Study of Teaching, contends that professionalization of an occupation occurs if and only if those who enter the field have an adequate understanding of the current knowledge base and continue to grow in experience throughout their careers.

At present, you are in the midst of gaining an understanding of the knowledge base on human development and learning, teaching methods, and classroom management strategies. It is likely that your teacher education program itself has recently undergone curricular reform to upgrade its expectations of student teachers. The teacher certification standards you must pass are becoming more rigorous each year.

School restructuring is providing a variety of increased opportunities for collegiality, shared decision making, and active leadership roles for teachers, and these new roles are transforming teaching into a more professional career. Teachers' unions and organizations, including the National Education Association (NEA), the American Federation of Teachers (AFT), the Association of Supervision and Curriculum Development (ASCD), and many smaller groups of subject matter specialists are redefining the job descriptions of teachers to include greater responsibility and accountability.

Reflective teachers are responding to these opportunities by thinking and acting with professionalism. They recognize the value of the service they perform in educating our nation's young people. Through continuing education, they increase their knowledge and skills in teaching and learning throughout their careers. They reflect on the decisions they make and take responsibility for the consequences of their actions. They work with their teachers' associations or school committees to develop standards for professional competency and growth.

This is an exciting time to be a teacher. As a career, teaching offers individuals the opportunity to fulfill their own needs for achievement, recognition, and a meaningful contribution at the same time that they meet the needs of the students they teach. Teaching is also among the most creative of all careers. Teachers create new learning experiences, materials, organizational systems, and interactions every day of the school year.

INTRODUCING JUDITH KELL

Principal, Hawthorne School, San Francisco, California

*HOW A PRINCIPAL EMPOWERS TEACHERS
AND CREATES A HEALTHY SCHOOL CLIMATE*

*Judith (Judy) Kell, the principal of Hawthorne
School, is credited by her staff and school
administrators with turning this school into a
vibrant multicultural community of learners.*

To say that being the principal of a large inner-city school is a varied task is the understatement of the century. Instructional leadership is vital, especially keeping abreast of new directions, tempering new ideas with what works, and making sure that teachers have time to consider curricular changes. However, I also have to worry about getting that hole in the blacktop repaired, getting the syringes and drug paraphernalia off the playground before school starts, having the toilets flushing and clean, and arguing with the food services people about the number of free lunches being served.

It doesn't end there. I must also coordinate all our budgets and funds, deal with parents who speak eight different languages, and be available for the 72 adults and 700 children in the school. What is an urban principal's job like? I'd say it is part cheerleader, part orchestra leader (you have to be acutely aware of the critical function of each instrument), and part caretaker, with endless amounts of patience, perseverance, and a strong sense of purpose.

I believe that developing a healthy school climate was the critical element in our quest for excellence at Hawthorne School. When I arrived, more windows were broken than whole, the plumbing was not functioning, graffiti covered every square inch of the playground wall, and the population of mice outnumbered that of the students. Tackling the problem of environment was a must before curricular matters could be addressed.

The creation of a strong discipline policy was a critical part of the turnaround too. I made sure that our discipline policy was jointly developed by the staff and the parents. This caused the parents to "buy in," and we were able to count on their support as we implemented the new program. These policies have become known as the *Hawthorne STAR (Success Through Acceptable Responsibility) Program.*

In order to empower my faculty to take responsibility for important curricular decisions, I give released time to faculty members to consider how and what we are teaching the students. As a result, they have been able to create a fluid and flexible system of grouping that allows each student to learn the vital concepts and skills at an appropriate level. They have also developed our Language Acquisition Program (LAP), which features targeted teaching in all aspects of language arts instruction. Our oral language program for non-English-speaking students provides for a flexible grouping of students as they develop proficiency with English. As a result, their test scores show more than 1 year's growth each year in language, reading, and math.

What makes the difference? Of course, it is hard work. Most of us work on school matters at least a few weekend days per month, and many teachers are here until late in the evening.

As problems arise, we work them out jointly. I consider input from my staff to be vital, and they know this. Our communication has become more open and trusting over the years.

We have a sense of mission and commitment at Hawthorne School, and more than anything else, we know that we are making a difference. What we are doing is enabling our students to be able to live productive, worthwhile lives. My job is to enable the teachers to enable the students. That seems to sum up what an effective principal must do.

OPPORTUNITIES FOR REFLECTION

▼ Reflective Essay: My Own Reflective Thinking

Consider the teachers you have had in your own school experiences. Describe one who was a reflective thinker. Give an example of a classroom event in which the teacher used reflective thinking. How did the teacher demonstrate this thinking? What decision or action resulted? What was the outcome or result?

Describe an incident in which you used reflective thinking to solve a problem or confront a puzzling issue. How did you gather information? Describe whether you were then able to translate your thinking into action. What was the result?

What is your assessment of your own reflective thinking at this time? What are the moral principles that guide your judgments? What do you need to work on and develop in order to become a more reflective thinker?

▼ Classroom Visit: Reflective Observation

Observe and describe how the teacher uses space in the classroom. How are the students' desks arranged? Where is the teacher's desk? Does the room feel crowded or spacious? Are there activity spaces? If so, for what purpose are they used?

Observe and describe the use of light, color, and decorations. What feeling did you have when you walked into this classroom? Would you like to be a student in this room? Why or why not?

Draw a map of the classroom. Draw another showing how you would prefer to arrange the room.

REFERENCES

BELL, M. (1990). *Everyday mathematics first grade teachers' manual*. Evanston, IL: Everyday Learning Corp.

BULLOUGH, R. (1989). Teacher education and teacher reflectivity. *Journal of Teacher Education, 40*(2), 15–21.

CRUICKSHANK, D. (1987). *Reflective teaching*. Reston, VA: Association of Teacher Educators.

DARLING-HAMMOND, L. (1988). The futures of teaching. *Educational Leadership, 46*(3), 4–10.

DEWEY, J. (1933). *How we think: A restatement of the relation of reflective thinking to the educative process* (rev. ed.). Lexington, Ma: D.C. Heath.

GAGNE, E. (1985). *The cognitive psychology of school learning*. Boston: Little, Brown.

GILLIGAN, C. (1982). *In a different voice*. Cambridge, MA: Harvard University Press.

KIERSTEAD, J., & MENTOR, S. (1989). Translating the vision into reality in California schools. *Educational Leadership, 46*(2), 35–40.

KOHLBERG, L. (1987). *The measurement of moral judgment: Vol. 1. Theoretical foundations and research validation*. London: Cambridge University Press.

O'NEILL, J. (1990). Piecing together the restructuring puzzle. *Educational Leadership, 47*(7), 4–10.

POLLARD, A., & TANN, S. (1987). *Reflective teaching in the primary school.* London: Cassell.

SCHON, D. (1987). *Educating the reflective practitioner.* San Francisco: Jossey-Bass.

SERGIOVANNI, T. (1984). Leadership and excellence in schooling. *Educational Leadership,* *41*(5), 4–13.

SHULMAN, L., & SYKES, G. (Eds.). (1983). *Handbook of teaching and policy.* New York: Longman.

TOM, A. (1984). *Teaching as a moral craft.* New York: Longman.

—▼ *C H A P T E R* ▼
2

Planning for a Healthy Classroom Environment

WHEN YOU WALK into a classroom, you can sense a particular climate or environment within a few moments. A multitude of sensory images enter your consciousness: sights, sounds, and smells for the most part. The way the room is arranged, the messiness or neatness, the wall decorations, the movements and noises made by the children, the smell of chalk dust or an animal cage all combine to form a unique flavor or climate in this classroom. The behavior, body language, and facial expressions of the teacher and students give you the most important clues about what life is like in this classroom. You may sense healthy elements such as excitement, energy, joy, cooperation, and pride, or you may sense debilitating elements such as fear, aimlessness, frustration, and tension. These are all components of the classroom environment, which is largely established by the teacher during the first days and weeks of the school year.

This chapter describes in some detail what reflective teachers think about and how they make decisions to promote a healthy classroom climate that is supportive of student achievement and satisfaction. It also describes how reflective teachers think about the psychosocial environment of their classrooms, and how they carefully structure classroom expectations and incentives to promote enduring patterns of achievement and interest in school.

A GOOD BEGINNING FOR THE SCHOOL YEAR

Studies show that it is the teacher who establishes the particular climate of each classroom (Emmer, Evertson, & Anderson, 1980). Given identical classrooms in the same school, identical materials and resources, and the same clientele, each teacher creates a unique learning environment based on a unique set of expectations, beliefs, attitudes, knowledge, effort, and repertoire of teaching strategies and skills. You have experienced the power of the teacher for many years as a student. It is likely that you still enter every classroom on the first day of a new course hoping that the teacher will be interesting, fair, knowledgeable, and caring.

Many people think that inner-city schools serving lower-income children are deadly and sterile, while suburban schools are vital and stimulating. But, in reality, within each school there is a great variety of classroom environments. Talented, caring, and reflective teachers in inner-city schools can and do make learning a joyful experience, and their classrooms shine with good will, understanding, wit, and creativity. There are, on the other hand, just as many careless, nonreflective teachers in rural areas and in the suburbs as there are in the inner cities who give little thought to their job or to their classrooms, which are dull with anxiety, disorder, anger, and despair.

Unfortunately, great social and economic disparities exist in our country. Children, who have not created these differences, are their victims. Historically, school has been the great equalizer, the means of rising out of poverty, the chance to make the most of one's potential. Reflective, caring, and creative teachers know that they can make a significant difference in children's lives, and they work especially hard to create a positive, healthy classroom environment to counteract the effects of poverty, discrimination, and neglect.

Organizing the Physical Environment

The classroom appearance makes a statement about the extent to which the teacher cares for the environment in which the class lives and works. It may be untidy, neat, colorful, drab, filled with objects, plants, animals, and children's art, or left undecorated. No two classrooms are alike; each has its unique environment. However, some classrooms (and their occupants) bloom with health, vitality, and strength, while others appear sickly, listless, and debilitated.

Studies of teacher planning (Brophy, 1983; Clark, 1983) show that during the days immediately preceding the school year, teachers are primarily concerned with setting up the physical environment of the classroom. Reflective teachers come to school several days before their contracts call for them to be there. They hang posters, decorate bulletin boards, and carefully consider ways to arrange the students' desks, tables, bookcases, and other furniture to fit their curriculum plans and the needs of their students. Less reflective teachers are likely to show up on the first day of school and use the classroom as it was left by the custodial staff after the summer cleaning. We know from the many years we spent in classrooms as students that a bright, colorful, cheerful, and stimulating classroom causes us to believe that school is interesting and that this teacher celebrates life and learning. We also know that drab, undecorated spaces cause us to expect dullness and boredom from school.

How to arrange the desks is a complex issue. Often there are many more desks than the room was designed to hold comfortably. The number of children in a classroom may vary from 15 to 35, and the precise number of children is not known until the last minute, making preplanning difficult. But, generally, teachers know approximately how many students they will have in their classrooms, and they set about arranging the desks in a way that uses space economically and strategically. Their plans are governed by an image of themselves and their students in teaching and learning experiences. While arranging the classroom, teachers are envisioning the "activity flow" of the classroom throughout the coming school year (Joyce, 1978–1979). Teachers envision themselves teaching and can see an image of how the classroom will look filled with children. This imaging helps teachers decide how to arrange the furniture in the room.

Such decisions are not easy to make, as each possible arrangement has both advantages and disadvantages. Desks can be arranged in rows, circles, semicircles, and small groups. Each arrangement has an impact on how children work and how they perceive their environment. Rows of desks provide an advantage in keeping order but leave little space for activities (Figure 2–1). A large circle of desks can be used if the teacher envisions teaching and learning experiences taking place in the center of the circle, but it will be difficult for all students to see the chalkboard (Figure 2–2).

Doyle (1986) reports that open (nonrow) arrangements result in students spending "more time working together, initiating their own tasks, and working without teacher attention than students in traditional rooms" (pp. 402–403). Clusters of four desks are used by teachers who value cooperative group learning experiences over teacher-centered learning experiences (Figure 2–3).

Jones (1987) recommends organizing the classroom into shallow concentric circles no more than three rows deep (Figure 2–4). In this setting, the teacher can maintain eye contact with all students and is able to move quickly to the side of any student who needs assistance or a reminder to pay attention. Physical proximity is thereby increased and facilitated, and the teacher can circulate more easily to provide individual help.

Activity and work spaces can be arranged by using bookcases and room dividers, or simply by arranging tables and chairs in the corners of the room. Some teachers bring in comfortable furniture and rugs to design a space just for quiet reading. Others may create space for science projects and experiments. Computer spaces are appearing in more and more classrooms. Room arrangement and the use of space are highly individual decisions. Each teacher makes these decisions to fit a personal image of what a classroom should be, as well as the curriculum and grade level of the class.

Reflective teachers also consider the effects the physical arrangement of the room will have in developing a healthy classroom environment. Rows of desks connote order and efficiency but do little to build a sense of community. Clusters of desks promote cooperation and communication among groups of students. Large circle or concentric circle arrangements encourage communication and sharing among the entire class. Many reflective teachers change their room arrangements, depending on the goals of a particular learning experience, and thus create a variety of classroom environments to fit a variety of purposes.

The First Day of School

The physical environment and schedule of the classroom may lead students to expect certain things about the way teaching and learning are going to occur during the school year. These expectations are reinforced even more strongly during the first few minutes of the first day of school. For example, consider the experience of the elementary students on their first day of school in the four hypothetical classrooms illustrated in the Perspective beginning on page 32.

You can probably recognize the teachers in these opening day scenarios, and can give them different names and faces from your own experiences in school. You have all been exposed to a variety of teaching styles, methods, attitudes, and philosophies as consumers of education. Now you will soon become teachers yourselves. What style will

FIGURE 2–1
Elementary Classroom Arrangement: Rows of Desks

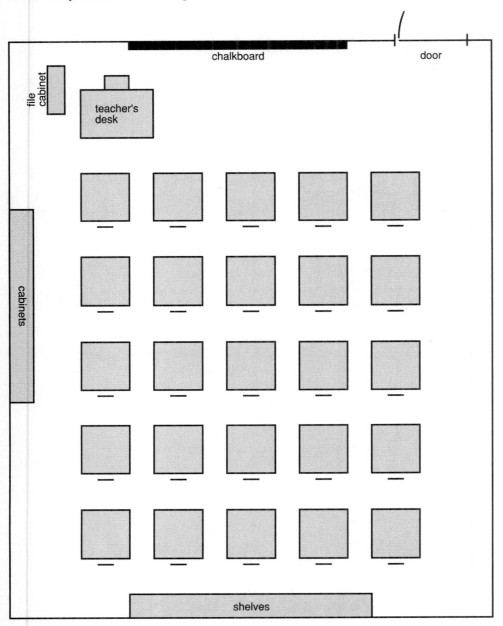

you have? How will your students perceive you? How will they respond to you? How will they feel when they walk into your classroom on the first day of school?

Each of the scenarios presented in the Perspective depicts a variation of what is termed *teaching style*. A teaching style is a highly individual and complex concept made

FIGURE 2–2
Elementary Classroom Arrangement: Circle of Desks

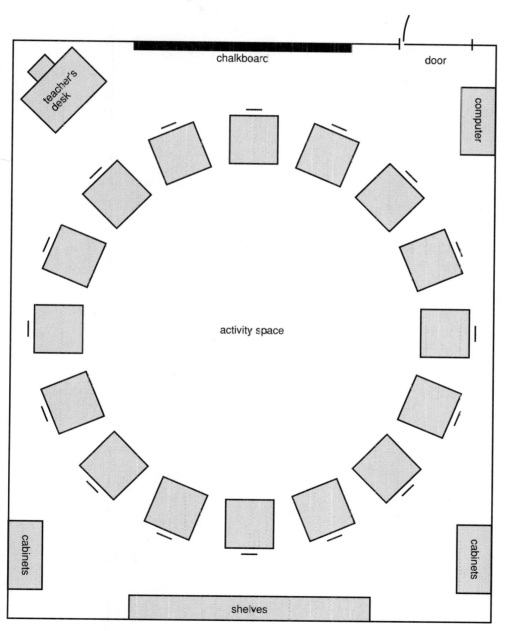

up of personality, philosophy, values, physical and emotional health, past experiences, and current knowledge about the effects of a teacher's behavior on the classroom environment.

Perhaps you may be considering the important question "Is it possible to control and decide on my teaching style, or is it simply a function of my personality?"

FIGURE 2–3
Elementary Classroom Arrangement: Clusters of Desks

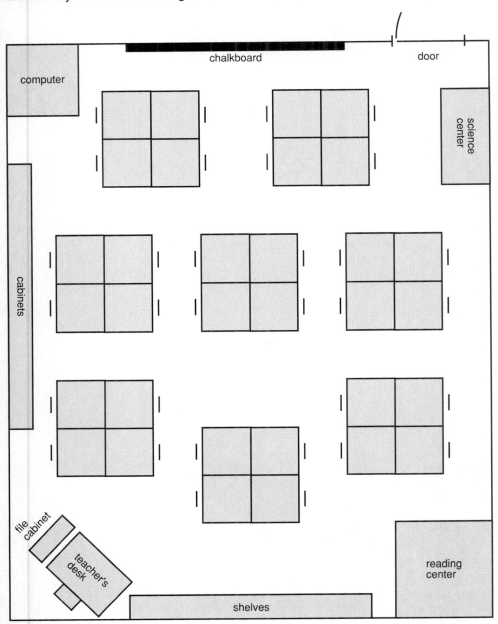

The more information you can gather about how teachers create healthy climates for learning, the more power you have to gain self-understanding and control over this and other important matters pertaining to teaching and learning. Evertson (1989) has demonstrated that when teachers develop effective classroom man-

FIGURE 2–4
Elementary Classroom Arrangement: Concentric Semicircles

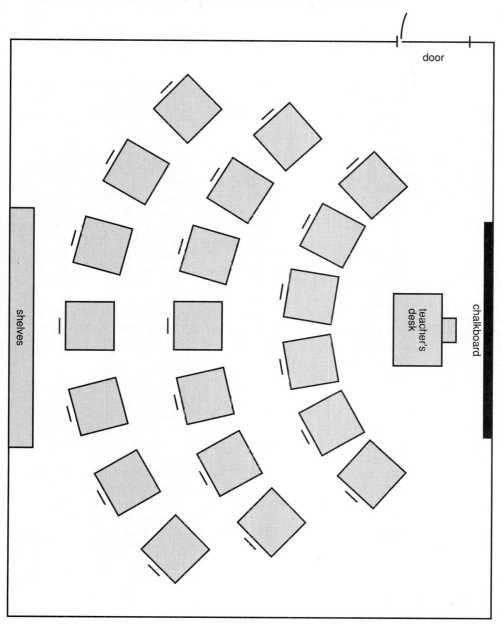

THE FIRST DAY OF SCHOOL

The scene is an elementary school. It is the first day of the new school year. In one corridor, several classroom doors are open. We see and hear four teachers greet the students in their classes.

ROOM 101

Miss Adams is standing at the doorway. As children walk in, she says, in a calm, even-toned voice, to each of them, "You'll find your name on a desk," as she gestures toward six clusters of desks. "Sit at that desk and wait quietly." The children obey, and the room is quiet. When all the children have entered, Miss Adams goes into her classroom and quietly shuts the door behind her. The beginning bell rings at precisely that moment.

ROOM 102

Mr. Baron is nowhere to be seen. Children enter the classroom looking for him, but when they don't see him, they begin to talk and walk around the room. The desks are arranged haphazardly in ragged rows. Two boys try to sit at the same desk, and a scuffle breaks out. The beginning bell rings. Suddenly Mr. Baron comes running down the hall, enters the room yelling, "All right, you guys, sit down and be quiet. What do you think this place is? A zoo?"

ROOM 103

Mr. Catlin is standing at the door wearing a big smile. As each child enters, he gives the child a sticker with his or her name on it. "Put this sticker on a desk that you like and sit at it," he says. The children enter and quickly claim desks, which are arranged in four concentric arcs facing the front of the room. They talk with each other in the classroom. When the bell rings, Mr. Catlin enters, leaving the door ajar for latecomers.

ROOM 104

Mrs. Destry is sitting at her desk when the children enter. Without standing up, she tells the children to line up along the side of the room. They comply. When the bell rings, she tells a student to shut the door.

If we were able to enter the classrooms with the students, this is what we might see, hear, and experience after the beginning bell ceased.

ROOM 101

Miss Adams stands in front of the class. She has excellent posture and a level gaze. As she waits quietly for the children to find their seats, she looks at each child eye to eye. They settle down quickly. When the classroom is perfectly quiet, she begins to talk.

"I see that you have all found your desks. Good. Now we can begin. I like the way you have quieted down. That tells me that you know how to behave in school. Let's review some of the important rules of our classroom."

Pointing to a chart entitled "Class Rules," she reads each one aloud and tells the children its significance. "Rule 1: Students will pay attention when the teacher is speaking. This is important because we are here to learn, and there can be no learning if you do not hear what the teacher is saying. Rule 2: Students will use quiet voices when talking in the classroom. This rule is important because a quiet, orderly classroom is conducive to learning. Rule 3: No fighting, arguing, or name calling is allowed. . . ."

The children listen attentively to all items. They do not ask questions or comment on the rules. After the rules are read, Miss Adams assigns helpers for class jobs. The newly appointed monitors pass out the reading books, and the children begin to read the first story in their books. Miss

Adams walks quietly from desk to desk to see that each child is reading.

ROOM 102

Mr. Baron rushes in and slams some books and papers on the desk. Some of them land on the floor nearby. Stooping to pick them up, he says, "Sit down, sit down, or I'll find cages for you instead of desks." The children sit down, but the noise level remains high.

"Enough! Do you want to begin the school year by going to the principal's office? Don't you care about school? Don't you want to learn something?" Gradually, the noise diminishes, but children's voices continue to interrupt from time to time with remarks to their teacher or to fellow classmates.

Mr. Baron calls the roll from an attendance book. He does not even look up when a child says "Here" but stares intently at the book. He has several children pass out books at one time, resulting in more confusion about whether the children have received all the necessary books. Finally, he tells them to begin reading the first story in their reading books. Some do so; others do not. Mr. Baron begins looking through his file cabinet, ignoring the noise.

ROOM 103

Mr. Catlin walks throughout the room as he talks to the class. From time to time, he stops near a child and puts his hand on the child's shoulder, especially one who appears restless or insecure. This action seems to help the child settle down and pay attention.

"Welcome back to school! This year should be a good one for all of us. I've got some great new ideas for our math and social studies programs, and we'll be using paperback novels to supplement our reading series. But first, let's establish the rules for our classroom. Why are we here?"

A student raises her hand. Mr. Catlin reads the name tag sticker on her desk and calls on her by name. "To learn," she says timidly.

"Exactly!" Mr. Catlin agrees. "And what rules can help us to learn the most we've ever learned in a single year?"

Several children begin to call out responses at the same time.

"Wait a moment, class. Can we learn anything like this?"

A chorus of "No's" is heard.

"Then what rule do we need to solve this problem?"

A child raises his hand, is called on, and says, "We need to raise our hands before we talk."

"What a fine rule," Mr. Catlin says with a broad smile. "How many agree?" The hands of most children go up. Mr. Catlin spots one child whose hand is not raised. He walks over to that child, kneels down next to the child's desk, and says, "Do you agree that this rule will help you learn this year?" "Yes," says the child, and his hand goes up.

After the class has established and agreed upon several other class rules, Mr. Catlin talks about the reading program. He offers the children a choice among five paperback novels, distributes them, and tells the children to begin reading. As they read, he circulates around the room, stopping from time to time to ask questions or make comments about the stories to individual children.

ROOM 104

Mrs. Destry regards the children in their line with an unfriendly gaze. When a child moves or talks, she gives that child a withering stare. From a class list, she begins to read the students' names in alphabetical order, indicating which seat they are to take. The students sit down meekly. No one says a word or makes a sound.

"Now class, you will find your books in your desks. Take out your reading books and begin to read the first story." The children comply, and Mrs. Destry takes out her knitting and begins to knit as she remains seated at her desk.

agement methods, they can learn to examine critically their own practices and behaviors. They can learn to use the more productive and positive classroom practices and discontinue the use of less effective methods.

To identify the most effective classroom management strategies, Emmer, Evertson, and Anderson (1980) conducted a study on how teachers begin the school year and establish their expectations with students. They were especially interested to learn how teachers who are effective classroom managers begin the school year. They hoped to discover some basic principles of effective classroom management that could be taught to beginning teachers. They selected 27 third-grade classrooms in eight elementary schools for their study. Observers were present in each of these classrooms during the first few weeks of school. Using criteria for effective management developed by the team of observers, the 27 teachers were classified into two categories: more effective and less effective classroom managers.

Both groups of teachers had rules and procedures planned for their classes. What distinguished the more effective managers from the others was that they spent the better part of the first day and much time during the next 3 weeks helping their students adjust to their expectations and learn to understand the rules and procedures established for the class. Like Miss Adams and Mr. Catlin, "as soon as most students had arrived, the teachers began describing rules and procedures. In some cases, but not always, pupils were asked to suggest rules. The rules and selected procedures were explained clearly, with examples and reasons" (p. 225).

More effective managers did not rely simply on a discussion of the rules. They spent a considerable amount of time during the first week of school explaining and reminding students of the rules. Many had students rehearse how to follow the procedures, such as how to line up. Most of the teachers taught students to respond to specific signals, such as a bell or another method of calling students to attention. Emmer and colleagues observed that "In summary, the more effective managers clearly established themselves as the classroom leaders. They worked on rules and procedures until the children learned them. The teaching of content was important for these teachers, but they stressed, initially, socialization into the classroom system. By the end of the first three weeks, these classes were ready for the rest of the year" (p. 225).

The reflective teacher, guided by moral principles, will also recognize that it is not simply establishing leadership that is important; the style of leadership counts as well. Both Miss Adams and Mr. Catlin quickly established that they were the classroom leaders, but Mr. Catlin's style of leadership best exhibited the underlying moral principles of caring, consideration, and honesty as he interacts with his students. The result is that students in such an environment return the caring, consideration, and honesty to the teacher and exhibit it in their interactions with each other as well.

In contrast, less effective managers (exemplified by Mr. Baron) did not have well-thought-out procedures. Although most of them had rules, they were somewhat vague, and the teachers tended to quickly tell the class the rules and procedures without spending time discussing and internalizing what they really meant. Like Ms. Destry, the less effective managers in the study moved quickly to academic matters. They seemed to expect the students to be able to comprehend and retain the rules from a single, brief presentation. They did not teach the class routines and procedures.

The second major finding of the study by Emmer and colleagues concentrated on the way the two groups of teachers monitored the behavior of their students. Less effective managers did not actively monitor their behavior. Instead, they busied themselves with clerical tasks or worked with a single individual on a task while ignoring the rest of the class. The study concluded that the consequence of the combination of vague and untaught rules and poor monitoring was "that the children were frequently left without enough information to guide their behavior" (p. 226).

PREVENTIVE DISCIPLINE STRATEGIES

Withitness

Jacob Kounin (1977) also set out to study the differences between well functioning and poorly functioning classrooms. He videotaped classrooms in action so that the characteristics of each could be analyzed. Although he expected to find that smoothly functioning classrooms were correlated with discipline strategies, he found no such relationship. Instead, he found that the best functioning classrooms were those characterized by a high degree of student involvement in work and by a teacher style characterized by a high degree of alertness and the ability to pay attention to two things at the same time.

Kounin labeled the most important teacher characteristic that distinguished good classroom managers from poor ones *withitness*. The good managers he observed knew what was going on in their classrooms at all times. They were aware of who was working and who was not. They were also able to *overlap* their instruction with their monitoring of student behavior. As a result, they were able to alter a presentation at the first sign of restlessness or boredom. If a minor disruption occurred between students, the teacher perceived it immediately and was likely to move a student or otherwise prevent the disruption from growing.

Withitness is expressed more through teacher behavior than through words. Eye contact, facial expressions, proximity, gestures, and actions such as stopping an activity demonstrate teacher withitness to students. These teachers are able to continue teaching a lesson while gesturing to a group or placing a hand on an overactive student's shoulder. These are examples of the concept of overlapping, in which the teacher is able to deal with both the behavior and the lesson at the same time.

Kounin also studied what he calls the *ripple effect*, a preventive discipline strategy that he found to be particularly useful in elementary classrooms. Kounin observed a student in his own college class reading a newspaper during the lecture. When Kounin reprimanded the student, he observed that his remarks caused changes in behavior among the other members of the class as well. "Side glances to others ceased, whispers stopped, eyes went from windows or the instructor to notebooks on the desk" (p. 1). In subsequent observations in kindergarten classrooms, Kounin found that when teachers spoke firmly but kindly to a student, asking that student to desist from misbehavior, the other students in the class were likely to desist from misbehavior as well. When teachers spoke with roughness, however, the ripple effect was not as strong. "Children who witnessed a teacher desist another child with anger or punitiveness did not conform more nor misbehave less than those witnessing a teacher desist another without anger or punitiveness" (p. 10).

Teacher withitness is an essential attribute of reflective teaching. The model of reflective teaching presented in this book begins with observing conditions and gathering information to make good judgments. Withitness raises the quality and level of reflective thinking because it increases the accuracy of teachers' observations and results in more complete collection of information about classroom conditions. Reflective teachers are always monitoring students' reactions to their perceptions, altering them when students show confusion or boredom. Reflective teachers actively monitor students during group activities and independent seat work, looking for signs that students need clarification of the task or have behavioral expectations.

A question of interest to beginning teachers and educational researchers is whether teacher withitness can be learned. Is this quality an inborn trait or personality characteristic that some teachers have and others do not? There is no evidence to answer this question at the present time; however, principals and supervising teachers often note that withitness grows with experience. Few first-year teachers exhibit consistent and accurate withitness, because their attention is focused on monitoring their own performance of tasks and teaching responsibilities rather than students' behaviors. It is probably developed by teachers as they actively reflect on the effects of their actions and decisions on their students' behavior.

For example, a first-year teacher may gradually become aware that the lessons are too long for the students' attention span and, from that time on, can perceive when a lesson is moving too slowly or lasting too long. Another teacher may begin to notice that whenever a student is made to establish eye contact, the student ceases to misbehave; this teacher thus develops the active use of eye contact as part of the repertoire of classroom management skills. A third teacher may notice that using a strong, confident voice causes the children to pay attention, whereas using a tentative, meek voice causes their attention to wander. Active self-reflection is the first step toward developing withitness.

Teachers' Leadership Styles

Leadership style is not a reflection on the teacher's ability to teach; teachers using any style may or may not be effective in teaching the academic subjects they are employed to teach. But leadership style does significantly affect the way students feel about school and, to a great extent, how they feel about themselves and each other.

Although each teacher has a style unique to his or her own personality, behaviors, attitudes, and beliefs, Dreikurs and Cassel (1972) identified one type of leadership style that they labeled *autocratic*. Others have used the term *authoritarian* to denote a similar style. Authoritarian teachers believe that it is their responsibility to plan furniture arrangements to maintain order in the classroom and to plan schedules that seldom vary. In this view, it is the teacher's responsibility to make all class rules and establish the consequences of misbehavior. They believe that the teacher has the knowledge of subject matter and the responsibility to convey it to students through teacher-centered lectures, discussions, and assignments. It is the student's role to obey the rules and do all assigned work satisfactorily. Autocratic teachers are harsh and unyielding.

In the opening day scenario, Miss Adams represents an authoritarian teacher, while Mrs. Destry is quite autocratic. The classroom climate created by this leadership style is often characterized by quiet and orderliness. There is little social interaction in the class. Individuals compete for grades and the teacher's attention. Some children attempt to please the teacher by any means possible, while others tend to revolt and undermine the teacher's efforts to control students' behavior. There is rarely a sense of community in a classroom led by an autocratic teacher; the only sense of community that may develop is a shared sense of rebellion in extreme cases.

Dreikurs and Cassel label a second type of leadership *permissive*, while others have used the term *laissez-faire*. Teachers such as Mr. Baron who employ a permissive style appear tentative and powerless. They make few rules and are inconsistent in establishing the consequences of misbehavior. They accept excuses and seem unable to assert authority over academic work or student behavior. The classroom climate created by such a permissive teacher is characterized primarily by confusion. Students do not know what is expected or how they can succeed. Limits are fuzzy, leading to a constant testing of how much the students can get away with. Little sense of community can develop in a permissive classroom, since students often learn to play one against the other to get their way.

The third type of leadership described by Dreikurs and Cassel is the *democratic* style. Democratic teachers, such as Mr. Catlin, are neither permissive nor autocratic. They are firm and reasonably consistent about their expectations for academic achievement and student behavior. They discuss the need for rules with their students and involve them in establishing specific rules and consequences for the class. From time to time, they may initiate a reevaluation of certain rules to update them and make them more usable and meaningful. Democratic teachers assert their power to make decisions but are willing to listen to their students' reactions, needs, and desires. The result is that the sense of power and ownership is distributed between students and the teacher in the same way that it is distributed in a healthy community.

Establishing Rules and Consequences

In a healthy democratic community, the citizens understand and accept the laws that govern their behavior. They also understand and accept that if they break the laws, certain consequences will follow. Healthy democratic classrooms also have laws that govern behavior, although they are usually called *rules*. In the most smoothly managed classrooms, the students also learn to understand and accept the consequences of breaking a rule from the very first week.

In our hypothetical example of the first day of school, each teacher varied in the way he or she established rules and consequences for the classroom. Miss Adams had established a set of rules beforehand. She read them to the class and told them why each was important. Mr. Baron and Mrs. Destry did not present a set of rules. Their actions indicated that they expected the students to discover the rules of the classroom. These are likely to be quite consistent in Mrs. Destry's classroom, but in the case of Mr. Baron, we suspect that the rules may change from day to day.

Mr. Catlin had planned an entire process for establishing rules. His process involved the students in helping to establish the class rules based on shared expectations and consequences.

Dreikurs and Cassel (1972) described two different types of consequences that are used to guide or shape student behavior. *Natural consequences* are those that follow directly from a student's behavior or action. For example, if a student gets so frustrated while working on an assignment that he rips the paper in half, the natural consequence is that the work will have to be redone from the beginning. If another student wakes up late, the natural consequence is that she misses the bus and has to walk to school, arrives late, and suffers the embarrassment of coming to class tardy. In these cases, there is no intervention on the part of an adult; the consequence grows directly out of the child's own behavior.

Logical consequences are those that are arranged by the teacher to fit the actions of the students, with the intention of causing students to change their behavior. For example, a teacher may decide that the logical consequence of not turning in a paper on time is that the student must stay in for recess or miss another activity period to finish the paper. When the paper is turned in, the logical consequence is that the student may go out to recess.

The difference between a punishment and a consequence is that a consequence is not arbitrary, and it is not dispensed with anger or any other strong emotion. To work effectively, logical consequences must be fully understood by the students. The teacher must describe them and explain the connections between the action and the consequence so that students understand the justification of the consequence. They must be applied consistently to all students who exhibit the behavior.

In many classrooms, teachers write a set of rules on a large piece of posterboard, with the consequences for breaking each rule clearly displayed for all children to see. For example:

Rule	*Consequence*
Wait in line courteously	Go to the end of the line
Turn in assignments on time	Finish late work at recess
Work quietly	Time-out (1, 3, 5, 10 minutes)
No fighting	Time-out (10, 20, 30 minutes)

The Consequence Called Time-Out

A discipline strategy known as *time-out* is frequently used as a consequence for students whose behavior is disruptive to others in the classroom. The child who acts aggressively by fighting or using loud or unacceptable language to gain attention from the teacher or the class is a candidate for this strategy. It requires a quiet, isolated spot in the classroom, perhaps created by arranging large file cabinets or cupboards to block out an area large enough for a single desk and chair. The teacher must describe this procedure to the class so that every child knows what it represents. The teacher must describe it as a consequence rather than as a punishment, and must explain that a time-out is simply an opportunity for the child to go to a quiet area and get back the self-control that was temporarily lost.

When a child breaks a rule, the teacher quietly but firmly states that the consequence is to go to the time-out area and stay there for a specified number of minutes. When a rule is broken more than once by the same child, the number of minutes increases each time, as shown in the preceding list.

The child is expected to stay in the time-out area, without causing any noise or disruption, for a specified length of time. Rimm (1986) suggests that the teacher use a timer and set it only when the child has calmed down and is quietly sitting in the time-out area. When the timer signals that the time has elapsed, the child may quietly return to the group and resume work.

When used with caution and respect for the feelings of the child, this technique can be a powerful way to modify disruptive behavior. It is a strategy, however, that can be very difficult to apply fairly. If the teacher's voice or body language shows anger and vindictiveness when telling the child to take the time-out, it can cause the child to feel embarrassed and to lose rather than gain self-control.

Grandma's Rule

Jones (1987) focuses on preventing discipline problems by helping children to develop self-control. One way to assist this process is through the use of positive consequences or incentives for learning and behaving cooperatively. To this end, Jones has examined familiar and widely used teacher practices, and has recommended ways to refine these practices to make them more effective and to eliminate negative side effects. For example, he examined the familiar incentive systems of grades, gold stars, and being dismissed and discovered that these systems appear to benefit only the top achievers; they are not genuine incentives for students who cannot realistically meet the established criteria.

He also noted that if teachers offer incentives that are not particularly attractive to many students, they will not positively affect student behavior or achievement. Jones uses the term *genuine incentives* to distinguish those that students perceive as both valuable and realistic for them to earn from those that students perceive to be of little benefit or impossible to achieve.

Jones uses the phrase *Grandma's Rule* to describe a familiar teaching practice: "First, eat your dinner; then you can have dessert." Applied to the classroom, this rule requires that students first do what the teacher expects; then they can do something that they genuinely want to do. Examples of genuine incentives that many students prize are learning experiences in art, drama and music, computer activities, films, or free time in which children can choose and play a game in small groups.

If students are to continue to perceive these favored activities as genuine incentives, they must be delivered as promised. Some teachers promise the incentive but then run out of time and do not deliver on their promises. Another counterproductive practice that some teachers use is to continually threaten to reduce or eliminate the incentive if children do not cooperate. Still others deliver the reward even when the work is not done acceptably. When this occurs, the children learn that they can have dessert even if they do not eat their dinner, that is, that they can get the reward without doing their work. This practice can destroy the trust between student and teacher, so that when incentives are established by the teacher, the students do not believe that they will be delivered as promised.

When delivered as promised and as earned, genuine incentives can promote increased achievement among individuals and groups and can cause peer pressure to encourage good behavior. Caring, reflective teachers attempt to understand the real needs and desires of their students and to provide incentives that meet these needs. In the following Perspective, Ginny Bailey describes how she uses Grandma's Rule. Note that she had to add other management strategies for one student when Grandma's Rule was not sufficient by itself to gain his cooperation.

Teachers' Body Language

Jones also found that effective classroom management and control of student behavior depend primarily on the teacher's body language. Strong, effective teachers are able to communicate many important things with eye contact, physical proximity, bodily carriage, gestures, and facial expression.

Consider the *eye contact* of the four teachers in "The First Day of School." Miss Adams had a level gaze and met the students' eyes as she looked at each of them at their first meeting. She communicated that she was aware and in control in a positive, nonthreatening manner. Mrs. Destry gave the children withering stares that probably caused them to feel anxious and fearful about the year ahead. Mr. Baron never met the eyes of his students at all, communicating his own lack of preparedness and confidence to manage the classroom.

Mr. Catlin used *physical proximity* as well as eye contact to put his students at ease and to communicate that he was in charge. Jones recommends the concentric circle arrangement that Mr. Catlin used because it causes students to focus their attention on the teacher and enables the teacher to provide help efficiently by moving quickly to the side of any student who is having difficulty. By moving close to restless students and placing a hand on their shoulders, Mr. Catlin was able to help them allay their fears and focus on the classroom activity. Room arrangement can help or hinder a teacher's ability to control children's behavior. To use physical proximity effectively, the teacher must be able to step quickly to the side of the misbehaving student, as Mr. Catlin did.

The strong, straight posture of Miss Adams reinforced the students' perception that she was an authority worthy of their respect. Good posture and confident *bodily carriage* convey strong leadership while a drooping posture and lethargic movements convey weakness, resignation, or fearfulness (Jones, 1987).

Gestures are also a form of body language that can communicate positive expectations and prevent problems from occurring. Teachers can use gestures to mean "stop" or "continue" or "quiet, please" without interrupting the verbal instruction. When coupled with positive eye contact, physical proximity, bodily carriage, or facial expression, gestures can prevent small disruptions from growing into major behavior problems.

Facial expressions vary greatly among teachers. They can show enthusiasm, seriousness, enjoyment, and appreciation, all of which tend to encourage good behavior; or they can reveal boredom, annoyance, and resignation, which may tend to encourage misbehavior (Jones, 1987). Facial expressions that display warmth, joy, and a sense of humor are those that students themselves report to be the most meaningful.

HOW I APPLY GRANDMA'S RULE

Ginny Bailey, First-Grade Teacher,
Woodland School, Carpentersville, Illinois

My classroom is arranged in five groups of student desks. There are also five different learning stations set up at the perimeter of the room. A group goes to a different learning station each day. At the end of the week, each group has been to each station, and I then change the stations to something new for the next week.

One of the ways that I use the concept of Grandma's Rule in my classroom is by requiring certain things to be accomplished before children are allowed to go to their stations. I list the activities on the chalkboard that the children are to do at their seats before going to a station. Usually they are required to write in their journals and perhaps make some kind of response to a piece of literature. There may also be a phonics skill activity that they are to work on. The students quickly learn to read the list of daily requirements because the last one is always "go to your station," which they all love.

One student, Eric, tended to rush through his work, with little interest in doing a good job. While the other children were still working on their assignments, Eric would wander around the room, bothering others with the news that he was done with his work and was going to his station. Eric's work was sloppy and often entirely inaccurate. I was concerned about this and so were other children, who were aware that Eric always seemed to be done ahead of them.

At that time, I was attending a class on cooperative learning. In small groups, we discussed techniques that teachers had used successfully with children to increase cooperative behavior. A colleague explained her use of a *learning buddy* system that had worked well. This seemed to be a viable solution to my problem with Eric, as well as a positive experience for all the children in the class.

That night, on the way home from class, I mentally paired up my students. For the most part, I tried to pair less mature students with more mature ones or quiet children with outgoing ones. After much deliberation, each child was assigned a learning buddy. From now on, if they had questions about their work or wanted to share their creative endeavors, they were to go to their learning buddy. The learning buddies were to work together to check each other's work, making sure that it was accurate and neatly done before being turned in.

It was amazing how quickly this system influenced Eric's work habits. He did not want to share sloppy work with his learning buddy, especially since this student took great pride in doing neat, accurate work. This system also made the children far less dependent on me and much more so on each other. They learned to come to me with a problem only as a last resort. Often I found it interesting to eavesdrop and hear them discussing their work and evaluating it on their own. Together the learning buddies would go over the list on the chalkboard, making sure they had accomplished everything before going to their stations.

Eric's work improved and so did his self-image. After just a few weeks, Eric realized that he didn't need to hurry through his work just to get to his station. There was plenty of time, and he found new pride in himself for doing a better job.

By observing Eric and his learning buddy, I discovered that often Eric did not understand the directions given and depended on his buddy to do a lot of reteaching. I also noted that his hyperactivity (wandering) was a cover-up for the fact that he didn't understand what he was supposed to do. His learning buddy was a great help, but something more needed to be done. I referred Eric to our special services team, and it was discovered that he had a significant hearing loss. He was fitted for a hearing aid, and this greatly improved his behavior as well as his work habits.

Humor in the Classroom

Csikszentmihalyi and McCormack (1986) recognized the importance of enjoyment in the learning process in a study they conducted on the influence of teachers on their students. When they asked students to tell them who or what influenced them to become the kinds of people they are, 58 percent mentioned one or more teachers, with descriptions such as these:

> Mrs. A. was influential because her [English] class was a lot of fun. . . . After all these years, I found out for the first time that I really *liked* English—it was really fun—and I've kept up my interest even though I'm not doing as well as other kids. (p. 419)

Czikszentmihalyi and McCormack believe that teacher enthusiasm, a sense of humor, and the ability to make learning enjoyable are vitally important in the classroom because they are connected with trust and meaningfulness. "How can young people believe that the information they are receiving is worth having when their teachers seem bored, detached, or indifferent?" (p. 419).

Pam Patterson, a student teacher in Mrs. Theresa Boone's fifth-grade classroom at Beasley School on Chicago's South Side, discovered that a humorous approach can frequently alleviate discipline problems. During class discussions, she was frustrated when many children tried to speak at the same time, calling out responses without being asked to speak. Although the students knew that they were supposed to raise their hands and be called on before speaking, they would raise their hands and begin speaking at the same time. One day, during a disruptive discussion, Pam quietly raised her own hand and stood in front of the noisy class. The noise subsided, and students asked Pam why she had her hand raised. Pam told them that she had something she wanted to say. A child responded, "Okay, Miss Patterson, we call on you!" Everyone laughed at the situation. From that time on, whenever the class got noisy during a discussion, Pam simply raised her hand and the children would say "We call on you" and settle down quietly.

INCREASING INTRINSIC MOTIVATION

The Enhancing Effects of Success

All individuals want to win or succeed. Virtually all children who walk into a classroom on the first day of school hope that this year will be *the year,* and this grade will be *the grade,* and this teacher will be *the teacher* who will make it possible for them to succeed. Some enter secure in the knowledge that they've succeeded before, but they are still anxious to determine whether they can duplicate that success in this new situation. Others enter with a history of failure and harbor only a dim, hidden hope that maybe they could succeed, if only . . .

Winning and success are the most powerful motivations for future effort and achievement that we know of. As Glasser (1969) noted:

> As a psychiatrist, I have worked many years with people who are failing. I have struggled with them as they try to find a way to a more successful life. . . .

From these struggles I have discovered an important fact: regardless of his background, his culture, his color, or his economic level, *he will not succeed in general until he can in some way first experience success in one important part of his life.* Given the first success to build upon, the negative factors . . . mean little. (p. 5)

It is possible to restate Glasser's message as a significant principle of teaching and learning: When an individual experiences success in one important part of life, he or she can succeed in life regardless of background, culture, color, or economic level. Glasser further states that the home and the school are the only two places for children to gain a sense of self-worth (p. 15).

Glasser's work may have caused a significant change in the way schools are managed and the way the curriculum is taught. While change takes place slowly, his landmark book *Schools Without Failure* has caused researchers and practitioners alike to reflect on the fundamental goals of education and to reexamine what students need from the school environment in order to succeed.

Raths (1972) also identified eight emotional needs that people strive to satisfy: the need for love, achievement, belonging, self-respect, freedom from guilt, freedom from fear, economic security, and self-understanding (p. 25). Raths believes that children whose needs are not satisfied will exhibit negative and self-defeating behaviors such as aggressiveness, withdrawal, submissiveness, regressiveness, or psychosomatic illness.

Raths recognizes that teachers cannot expect to satisfy the many unmet needs of all the students in their classrooms. However, he does believe that "children cannot check their emotions at the door and we should not expect them to. . . . If unmet needs are getting in the way of a child's growth and development, his learning and his maturing, I insist that it is your obligation *to try* to meet his needs" (p. 141). His book *Meeting the Needs of Children* contains many specific suggestions about what teachers can do to help meet children's emotional needs so that they are free to learn.

Meeting Students' Affective Needs

In *Motivation and Personality*, Abraham Maslow (1954) first described the human being's *hierarchy of needs*. Maslow recognized that human beings have basic physical and emotional needs that must be satisfied before the individual can attend to the higher needs for achievement and recognition. If the lower needs are not satisfied, the individual is dominated by them, and all other needs become nonexistent or are pushed into the background (p. 373). This explains why hungry or tired students cannot learn efficiently. All their capacities are focused on satisfying their need for food or sleep. To satisfy the hunger needs of many children, some schools provide breakfast, snacks, or milk so that children can pay attention to school tasks.

But what happens when the child has plenty of food and adequate shelter and is well rested? Then "at once other (and 'higher') needs emerge" (p. 375), and these dominate the individual. The needs for safety and security follow basic physiological needs, and the needs for love and belonging follow safety needs. Imagine two classrooms, one that is led by an autocratic or permissive teacher, in which children feel threatened, insecure, and isolated, and the other, led by a democratic teacher, in which children feel safe, secure, cared for, and connected with other members of the class-community. In which setting are students likely to have more of their needs met and therefore be ready and able to achieve greater success in academic work?

The work of Glasser, Raths, and Maslow on recognizing and meeting children's needs has served, in many ways, as the basis of this chapter, which has attempted to describe ways that classrooms can be organized and managed so that students' basic needs for safety, security, love, and belonging are well satisfied. If *and only if* these needs are satisfied, students are able to concentrate a significant portion of their energy and drive on achieving success in school subjects. Maslow's work shows us that intrinsic motivation is something that can be set free and enhanced in school settings. The intrinsic motivation for achievement and recognition for achievement can be released and nurtured by teachers who carefully design a healthy, supportive sense of community in their classrooms.

Community Building

Head Start, the federally funded compensatory program for disadvantaged preschool children, attempts to meet the emotional as well as the academic needs of the children it serves. Eliot Wigginton (1985), a teacher in Rabun Gap, Georgia, tells the story of his own experiences in *Sometimes a Shining Moment*. As a beginning teacher, he mobilized his class to write and publish the *Foxfire* books.

The true story of teacher Jaime Escalante and his students in Watts, Los Angeles, California, that was made into the movie *Stand and Deliver* epitomizes the newer cognitive-mediational view. Escalante refused to believe that learning is predicted by past tests or to act on the commonly held expectation that students from Watts could not learn calculus. He knew that they could learn calculus if he could provide them with the necessary knowledge, skills, and motivation to do so. He also recognized that he had the power and the responsibility to teach them.

Both Wigginton and Escalante worked with their students in such a way that the class became a community with a shared sense of purpose rather than a collection of individuals competing for scarce resources or grades. These well-known examples involved high school classes, but elementary students can also participate in and benefit from a sense of community within their classrooms.

How does a class of strangers or competitive individuals develop into a community? As with all the other important classroom effects discussed in this chapter, the teacher has the power to create a positive, healthy, mutually supportive, and productive classroom environment from the very first day of school. Through furniture arrangement, schedules, the teacher's body language, words of welcome, rules, consequences, and interaction with the class, the teacher demonstrates a unique leadership or teaching style to the students. A sense of community is also achieved through honest and open communication of needs and feelings between students and their teachers. In the following Perspective, Jean Malvaso-Zingaro, a sixth-grade teacher in Rochester, New York, describes how she uses personal diaries to establish a close and trusting relationship with her students.

INTRODUCING JEAN MALVASO-ZINGARO

Sixth-Grade Teacher, School No. 6, Rochester, New York

ESTABLISHING TWO-WAY COMMUNICATION THROUGH STUDENT DIARIES

Jean Malvaso-Zingaro teaches sixth grade in the inner city of Rochester, New York. Ninety-seven percent of the student body at School 6 are drawn from minority groups. Jean has been teaching for 22 years and has generally taught grades 1 to 6.

One of her strongest interests in education is the teaching of writing and English. Her students write every day on topics that are meaningful and important to them. In most years, every student in her class passes the State of New York's writing test. This has caused administrators to visit her classroom to find out what she is doing to have such a powerful effect on her students' writing ability. She is frequently asked to provide inservices for other teachers on the teaching of writing. Throughout this book, you will have opportunities to learn more of Jean's secrets of success, beginning with the following classroom example that illustrates her philosophy of education.

Communication between student and teacher is of the utmost importance to me. On the first day of school, I introduce the students to the activity of keeping a diary. I explain that they are free to write anything they wish. They are given time each day to write. I collect the diaries once a week to read and comment on what they have written. I never correct their spelling or grammar errors.

Through these diaries, I learned, for example, that two girls who had been best friends had had a falling out. I wrote that I understood how terrible it is to lose a friend and suggested that they write a note to each other about it. The following week they wrote in their diaries that they had settled their differences, and they thanked me for my advice.

As another example, a boy in my class did not like school. He was frequently truant and was very unhappy at home. He wrote very little in his diary at first. I asked him to write about himself. A short while later, he wrote that he had been taken away from his mother when he was 8 years old because his mother went to prison. He had been in foster care for 4 years. Now he was back with his mother, but he missed his foster parents. He had formed an attachment to them and was not too sure about his relationship with his mother.

In this case, when I read the boy's diary, I experienced both sadness and joy—sadness because I had no answer or advice for him, but joy that he had trusted me enough to share his private life with me.

One student asked personal questions about my life in her diary. Was I married? What was my husband like? What are some of the things I do in my spare time? I answered each question honestly.

One of the greatest satisfactions I receive as a teacher is to see the students rush into the classroom on Monday mornings to read what I have written in their diaries. The expressions on their faces are of contentment and satisfaction.

Jean's classroom example demonstrates an essential element in creating a healthy classroom environment. Effective communication between teacher and student is based on mutual trust, which grows out of the basic moral principles of caring, consideration, and honesty. Reflective teachers who are guided by these moral principles express them in the classroom by listening empathetically or, as in the case of the diaries in Jean's class, reading empathetically. Listening is one of the most important ways of gathering subjective information about students' needs in order to make informed judgments about why they behave the way they do.

Discussions between teacher and child need to be guided by consideration for the child's feelings and fragile, developing self-concept. There is also a great need for honest, open exchanges of feelings and information among all members of a classroom. A sense of community and shared purpose grows out of a realistic understanding of each other's perceptions and needs.

Classroom Meetings

One method often employed by democratic teachers to build mutual caring, consideration, and an honest expression of opinions and perceptions is to hold classroom meetings to discuss problems confronting the class. The classroom meeting was first described by Glasser in *Schools Without Failure*. Some teachers hold regularly scheduled classroom meetings each week; others schedule them only when necessary. One of the most important effects of a classroom meeting is the sense of community that is created when the students and teacher sit down to solve problems together.

For a detailed account of how to initiate and lead a class meeting, refer to Glasser's *Schools Without Failure*. An abbreviated description is all that can be included in this chapter. The seating arrangement for a class meeting is a single circle of chairs, so that each member of the class can see the teacher and all other members of the class. The teacher has the responsibility of establishing rules and consequences for the meeting. These usually consist of a rule about one person speaking at a time and accepting the ideas and opinions of others without criticism or laughter. When expressing anger or other feelings, class members are encouraged to use "I-statements."

The meeting may be divided into several parts. For example, the teacher may choose to open with an unfinished statement such as "I sometimes wonder why . . ." or "I am proud of . . ." or "I am concerned about . . . ." Going once around the circle, every member of the class is encouraged to respond to this opening statement, which has been chosen by the teacher to encourage communication from every member of the group. While members are encouraged to respond, the teacher makes it clear that any individual who does not wish to speak on that issue can simply say "Pass." Opening the class meeting in this way has the advantage of allowing everyone to speak at least once during the meeting and may bring out important issues that need discussion.

The second part of the meeting can be devoted to students' concerns. The teacher opens this discussion by asking who has a problem to bring up. When a problem is expressed, the teacher moderates discussion on that issue alone until it is resolved. Issues are seldom resolved easily in one meeting, but a problem can be raised, different ideas and opinions can be expressed, and then solutions can be offered by class members. When a reasonable solution is worked out, the teacher's role is to restate the solution, suggest that the class try it for a week, and discuss how it has worked out at the next classroom meeting. Other student concerns can then be expressed.

The third part of the class meeting can address the teacher's concerns. The teacher can bring up a problem by expressing personal feelings or stating expectations for future work. Students' responses can be brought out and discussed and solutions proposed. The sense of community that develops from expressing needs and opinions, hearing other perspectives, and solving problems together is translated into all aspects of life in the classroom. When an argument occurs during recess or when something is perceived by students as unfair, they know that they can discuss it openly and freely in a class meeting. When the teacher needs more cooperation or wants higher-quality work, this issue can be brought up in a class meeting. Mutual understanding, tolerance for opposing views, and a method to resolve conflicts result in a strong sense of ownership and commitment to the academic, social, and emotional goals of the class as a whole. The classroom meeting is also a powerful vehicle for developing ownership of class rules, as Tim Curbo describes in the next Perspective.

Glasser's theories about success causing success and democratic class meetings are methods he recommends to teachers to ensure that these needs can be satisfied in school classrooms. The classroom meeting satisfies students' need for belonging, power, freedom, self-understanding, and self-respect and can diminish students' feelings of fear and guilt. Fun can also be addressed by plans that students and teachers make together to celebrate and enjoy school life.

The Self-fulfilling Prophecy

Children are extremely perceptive beings. They understand and react to subtle differences in adult expectations. As Good and Brophy (1987) have shown in their research, teachers' behaviors communicate to students what the teachers expect of themselves, of the class as a whole, and of individual students.

This effect has come to be known as the *self-fulfilling prophecy* (Brophy, 1983; Rosenthal & Jacobsen, 1968). According to Good (1983), the process appears to work like this: (1) the teacher makes a decision about the behavior and achievement to be expected from a certain student; (2) the teacher treats students differently, depending on the expectations for each one; (3) this treatment communicates to the student what the teacher expects and affects the student's self-concept, achievement motivation, and aspirations, either positively or negatively; (4) if the treatment is consistent over time, it may permanently shape the child's achievement and behavior. "High-expectation students will be led to achieve at higher levels, whereas the achievement of low-expectation students will decline" (Brophy, 1983, p. 54).

Many studies of how teachers' behaviors display their expectations have been done and replicated to show confirmation of the original findings. It has been found that some teachers

1. seat low students far away from the teacher
2. call on lows less often
3. wait less time for lows to answer questions
4. criticize lows more frequently
5. praise lows less frequently
6. provide lows with less detailed feedback
7. demand less work and effort from lows. (Brophy, 1983, p. 55)

INTRODUCING TIM CURBO

First-Grade Teacher, Hawthorne School,
San Francisco, California

ESTABLISHING PUBLIC POLICIES IN CLASSROOM MEETINGS

Discipline begins even before the first child enters the classroom. Two weeks before school begins, I begin setting up my classroom. I've found that the physical environment directly affects student behavior. I group children's desks into three large units because I want my students to interact. I believe that this interaction fosters cooperation, problem solving, and peer teaching and learning.

On the first day of school, we begin with the first of our daily classroom meetings. I do not present a list of rules on the first day. Instead, most of our rules come from a class discussion of problems that arise in the classroom. A fight over a game generates a discussion about sharing, and we develop a common understanding of what we all expect of each other regarding the sharing of classroom materials. I do this because I believe that young children learn best from concrete personal experiences. Our meetings cause the children to generalize a shared value from a concrete example.

Whenever a problem is discussed, I also try to think about how I can modify the environment or my own teaching to facilitate more constructive behavior. In the example of the fight over the game, I may think about how I could place the game somewhere else to make it more accessible, or make a sign telling how many students can play this game. I may think about whether we need more games of this sort so that all of the students can enjoy the participation.

Not all rules can be established in the first week of school. We hold our classroom meeting every day right after lunch. The meeting serves as a forum for setting "public policies" (rules and procedures) and is a time to model and develop problem-solving skills. We place a chair in front of

---

Kerman and Martin (1980) have designed a series of teacher inservices known as *Teacher Expectations and Student Achievement (TESA) Workshops* that are designed to aid teachers in recognizing their own expectations and how these are communicated to their students. In these workshops, teachers are trained to become more observant of the equity and the quality of their responses to various students in their classrooms.

Most teachers enjoy working with high-achieving students, but few are as enthusiastic about interacting with slow, low-achieving students. Reflective teachers realize that teaching is more than telling. They are willing to restate and reexplain concepts and processes to children who do not understand the material the first time. That is one of the most significant challenges of teaching and can be one of the most satisfying and rewarding aspects of the career. If you view teaching slow and low-achieving students as a challenge rather than an ordeal, you will be less likely to communicate low expectations. Reflective teachers often ponder how they can use this knowledge of the self-fulfilling prophecy to their own and their students' advantage.

the room. Six children each day are allowed to share something that they think is important. The number 6 is arbitrary, but it works out to about a 15-minute meeting, which is a realistic amount of time for first graders.

When a student shares a problem, we discuss feelings about the problem. I try to draw in the whole class as much as possible, asking, for example, "How did you feel when you were excluded from the game?" or "How would the rest of you feel?" After dealing with feelings, we discuss solutions to the problem. Too often, our discussion of solutions degenerates into blaming and fault finding. I, as the teacher, try to stress that Billy is not the problem; *hitting* is. We need to decide how we feel about hitting so that our school will be a positive place. Billy is a friend who needs our help in learning another way to address his problems. In discussing our feelings, we establish that hitting is not a good solution to the conflict. Then we move on to what would be a good solution, one that is acceptable to all involved. Out of this process emerges our public policies—*in other words, our class rules.*

My philosophy about discipline is to accentuate the positive. I want to give lots of positive reinforcement to those kids who are modeling good discipline. Sometimes in our class meetings, a student will report a positive interaction. Then we discuss the good feelings that were experienced and heap appropriate praise on our friend who is helping make our school a better place.

As a teacher, I am in the position of enforcing the public policies that are established. Consistency is very important. If we generate a class rule, it must be fairly and evenly applied. We must all be aware of the rule, believe in it, and be committed to enforcing it. I've seen idle teacher threats and uneven application of rules erode classroom discipline.

Clarity is also very important. Many children seem to be crying out for help through their misbehavior. They need a caring adult to help them structure their chaotic life. I've found that the best way to address the needs of these children is to provide them with clear and consistent limits, positive reinforcement, and an opportunity to discuss their feelings and learn new ways of handling their angry feelings.

SCHEDULING TIME FOR ACTIVE LEARNING

How Time Is Spent in Elementary Classrooms

To bring out the best in our students, adequate time must be spent on active learning and teachers must have adequate time to plan. Time is the most important and the scarcest resource in many aspects of our lives. The Beginning Teacher Evaluation Study (BTES) gathered data on the way time is planned and used in elementary classrooms. The research revealed that on the average, "about 58 percent of the school day is allocated to academic activities, about 23 percent to nonacademic activities, and about 19 percent to noninstructional activities such as transitions and class business" (Rosenshine, 1980, p. 123).

The BTES also investigated the amount of time a student spends on teacher-led activities and on seatwork. The average amount of time spent on teacher-led activities (both academic and nonacademic) was only 30 percent of the school day, or approximately 2 of the 6 hours spent in school. The remaining 70 percent of the school day was spent on independent seatwork in the observed classrooms.

The BTES researchers were especially interested in differentiating between the time allocated for learning by the teacher and the time students were actually engaged in academic learning. *Allocated time* refers to the minutes scheduled for a class subject, but within that period, students may or may not engage in academic work. They may daydream, doodle, read a recreational book, sit idly, or cause mischief rather than work. The study showed that "engagement was higher in teacher-led settings (about 84 percent of the allocated time) than in seatwork settings (about 70 percent)" (Rosenshine, 1980, p. 124).

It is important to recognize that these numbers are statistical averages. That means that some teachers spend more time and others less on any one element of the curriculum. What the researchers found was that when teachers spend more than the average time on teacher-led academic lessons, both student engagement and achievement exceeded the average as well. "Teachers with the highest allocated time also had the highest engagement rates" (Rosenshine, 1980, p. 123).

Since seatwork took up so much of the school day, the researchers concentrated their efforts on discovering how student achievement can be improved during this time. They found that engaged time during independent seatwork was raised when teachers (a) gave substantial explanations, responded to students' questions, and gave feedback before the independent work began and (b) actively monitored what the students were doing during the seatwork activities. These two teacher behaviors seemed to create a sense of purposefulness and accountability that students then applied to their seatwork (Rosenshine, 1980, p. 124).

Daily and Weekly Schedules

Teachers at all levels believe that they cannot fit everything they want to teach into the school day. Charles (1983) cites "dealing with the trivial" as one of the teacher's greatest time robbers (p. 243). When teachers simply try to fit everything into the day, they are just as likely to include trivial matters as important ones. A reflective teacher weighs the relative importance of each element of the school program and allocates time accordingly. This may mean eliminating certain items entirely and carefully scheduling the minutes of the day to meet the most important needs of the students.

Schedules differ from grade to grade, depending on the relative importance of the subject at that grade level and the way the school is structured and organized. The most frequently used method in elementary schools is to place students into grade-level *self-contained classrooms* in which one teacher has the responsibility for teaching all the academic subjects. In other cases, students may have a home room but their academic subjects are *departmentalized,* meaning that teachers specialize in one academic area and students move from class to class during the day.

For example, the primary grades are usually structured as self-contained classrooms, and primary teachers often schedule reading and language arts activities for up to one-half of the school day. The intermediate grades may be self-contained or departmentalized, but in either case, math, science, and social studies activities are usually given more time than they are at the primary grades. In junior high school the schedules are likely to be departmentalized, meaning that each teacher specializes in one subject and teaches it to several classes of students during the day.

No two schedules are alike. Teachers in self-contained classrooms are usually allowed great discretion in how they allocate time. Typically, there are state requirements that mandate how many minutes per week are to be allocated to each of several subjects, but teachers make varied plans within those prescriptions. For example, the state may require a minimum of 150 minutes of math per week. Teacher A may schedule 30 minutes per day; teacher B may schedule 40 minutes for 4 days; teacher C may schedule 45 minutes on Mondays, Wednesdays, and Fridays, with brief review periods on other days.

Elementary class schedules may be rigid or flexible. They may be the same every day or vary greatly. They may be governed by bells or by the teacher's own inner clock. Charles (1983) recommends that however it is determined, "the daily classroom schedule should be explained in such a manner that students know what activities are to occur at each part of the day and how they are to work and behave during those activities" (p. 10). When students know the schedule, they can learn to manage their own times more efficiently. Teachers who use a consistent schedule may create a permanent display of the schedule on a bulletin board; teachers who vary their schedule from day to day can write the current schedule on the chalkboard each morning.

The conventional wisdom of teachers is that the most difficult subjects should be scheduled early in the day, when students are most likely to be attentive. Reading/language arts is quite frequently the first subject of the day in a self-contained classroom, followed by math. Science, social studies, art, and music make up the afternoons. This may be the preferred schedule, but often there are school constraints that make it difficult to achieve. Physical education, art, and music may be taught by other teachers in separate classrooms. The schedule for these special classes may affect the classroom teacher's schedule. Some classes must be scheduled for special classes in the morning, causing classroom teachers to adjust their own plans.

Planning Time

Teachers may be annoyed when special classes interrupt their own scheduled lessons, but they appreciate one important side effect: When the class leaves for art, music, or physical education, the classroom teacher has a planning period. Planning time is usually required by the teacher's contract and is designed to provide opportunities for individual or collegial planning. Teachers of self-contained classrooms have complete discretion over their planning time, but departmentalized teachers frequently hold joint meetings during their planning time to discuss how they will jointly plan and deliver their shared curriculum.

Teachers use planning time in various ways, some productive and others less so. Charles (1983) recommends that teachers use this time as efficiently as possible by "prioritizing tasks, giving attention to those that are absolutely necessary, such as planning, scoring papers, preparing for conferences, and preparing instructional materials and activities. Also high on the list should come those tasks that are difficult or boring, leaving for later those that are most enjoyable" (p. 244). Less efficient teachers may use the time for socializing, complaining, smoking, eating, reading magazines, or making personal phone calls. Later they complain that the school day is too short and that they have too much work to do at home.

Charles (1983) states that routine tasks such as watering plants, cleaning the room, feeding animals, or distributing materials should not be done during planning time or by the teacher at all. The teacher who is an efficient time manager delegates as many of these routine tasks as possible to student helpers. This has two effects that contribute to a healthy classroom environment: (a) it reduces the stress teachers feel about time and (b) it provides a sense of responsibility and meaningful accomplishment for the student helpers.

Conclusions

A healthy classroom environment takes an enormous amount of planning. Teachers must consider how to manage and use space, time, and other resources efficiently and effectively.

To prepare yourself for a good first year of teaching, focus especially on the first day and the first 3 weeks of the school year. Formulate a set of rules and procedures that will lead to productive and cooperative student behavior. Then consider how to introduce these rules effectively. Consider the body language and voice quality you want to use to project your self-image as the classroom leader and to convey that you expect your students to view you that way as well.

Allow sufficient time on the first day of school to teach your students what the rules are, the reasons for each of them, and what they mean. Rehearse your cues and routines with the children so that they internalize how to carry them out. During the next week or two, take time to remind students of the rules and expectations. Do not resort to anger if they need to be reminded. The more effective managers in the Emmer, Evertson, and Anderson (1980) study also had to be reminded many times during the first 3 weeks of school. The good managers demonstrated their withitness while monitoring the students' behavior during that time, and dealt with the inattentive or disruptive behavior consistently.

After being guided through the rules and procedures of the class for 3 weeks, students tend to accept them. They come to understand that these rules and procedures are simply the way life is in this classroom, and for the most part, they adapt their behavior to fit the teacher's expectations.

The overarching concern of reflective teachers is to create a classroom in which children can meet their basic human needs for belonging and achievement. To accomplish this, they consider every aspect of the environment as it relates to children's needs. They arrange the furniture in order to meet students' need for a sense of belonging; they create rules and schedule time in order to meet students' need for security; they provide opportunities for children to write about and discuss their other feelings and needs. They do this because they want to create a nurturing sense of community in their classroom as a means of enhancing successful achievement.

The curriculum and evaluation procedures are also critical factors in creating a healthy classroom environment. Glasser (1986) describes classrooms that provide a sense of belonging, allow students to make choices, and contain a variety of interesting learning activities. Classrooms such as these satisfy the needs of most students and encourage them to learn for the satisfaction of learning. The remaining chapters in this book are designed to assist you in developing learning experiences that promote success, develop cooperation, and enhance intrinsic motivation.

OPPORTUNITIES FOR REFLECTION

▼ Classroom Visit: How Time Is Used in Classrooms

Observe how time is used in the classroom you visit. Is a schedule posted or not? If so, is it followed rigidly or flexibly? If not, how is the schedule determined? Keep a record of how much time is spent on academic, nonacademic, and classroom management concerns. Create a schedule that you would use if this were your classroom.

▼ Reflective Essay: Self-Reflection

View the videotape introducing yourself to your class on the first day of school. Write about your reactions to seeing yourself as a teacher. What body language did you use effectively? How does your voice sound? What effect do you think your words will have on your future students? What are your strengths in this video, and what do you want to improve?

REFERENCES

BROPHY, J. (1983). Classroom organization and management. In D. Smith (Ed.). *Essential knowledge for beginning educators* (pp. 42–59). Washington, D.C.: American Association of Colleges for Teacher Education.

CHARLES, C. (1983). *Elementary classroom management.* New York: Longman.

CLARK, C. (1983). Research on teacher planning: An inventory of the knowledge base. In D. Smith (Ed.), *Essential knowledge for beginning educators.* Washington, D.C.: American Association of Colleges for Teacher Education.

CSIKSZENTMIHALYI, M., & McCORMACK, J. (1986). The influence of teachers. *Phi Delta Kappan, 67*(6), 415–419.

DOYLE, W. (1986). Classroom organization and management. In M. Wittrock (Ed.), *Handbook of research on teaching* (3rd ed.) (pp. 392–431). New York: Macmillan.

DREIKURS, R., & CASSEL, P. (1972). *Discipline without tears.* New York: Hawthorn.

EMMER, E., EVERTSON, C., & ANDERSON, L. (1980). Effective classroom management at the beginning of the school year. *Elementary School Journal, 80*(5), 219–231.

EVERTSON, C. (1989). Improving elementary classroom management: A school-based training program for beginning the year. *Journal of Educational Research, 83*(2), 82–90.

GINNOTT, H. (1971). *Between teacher and child.* New York: Macmillan.

GLASSER, W. (1969). *Schools without failure.* New York: Harper & Row.

GLASSER, W. (1986). *Control theory in the classroom.* New York: Harper & Row.

GOOD, T., & BROPHY, J. (1987). *Looking in classrooms* (4th ed.). New York: Harper & Row.

GORDON, T. (1974). *Teacher effective training.* New York: MacKay.

JONES, F. (1987). *Positive classroom discipline.* New York: McGraw-Hill.

JOYCE, B. (1978–1979). Toward a theory of information processing in teaching. *Educational Research Quarterly, 3*(4), 66–77.

KERMAN, S., & MARTIN, M. (1980). *Teacher expectations and student achievement: Teacher handbook.* Bloomington, IN: Phi Delta Kappa.

KOUNIN, J. (1977). *Discipline and group management in classrooms.* New York: Holt, Rinehart and Winston.

MASLOW, A. (1954). *Motivation and personality.* New York: Harper & Row.

RATHS, L. (1972). *Meeting the needs of children.* Columbus, OH: Merrill.

RIMM, S. (1986). *Underachievement syndrome: Causes and cures.* Watertown, WI: Apple.

ROSENSHINE, B. (1980). How time is spent in elementary classrooms. In C. Denham & A. Lieberman (Eds.), *Time to learn* (pp. 107–126). Washington, D.C.: U.S. Department of Education.

ROSENTHAL, R. (1974). *On the social psychology of the self-fulfilling prophecy: Further evidence for Pygmalion effects and their mediating mechanisms.* New York: MSS Modular Publications.

ROSENTHAL, R., & JACOBSEN, L. (1968). *Pygmalion in the classroom.* New York: Holt, Rinehart & Winston.

SKINNER, B. (1971). *Beyond freedom and dignity.* New York: Knopf.

WIGGINTON, E. (1985). *Sometimes a shining moment.* New York: Anchor Press.

3

Diagnosing Students' Needs

IN LATE SUMMER, many teachers make plans and decisions for the coming school year. They may arrange classroom furniture, establish schedules, choose textbooks, consider rules and consequences, and outline major units of study before school begins. But most teachers are aware that these initial plans may need to be modified when the classroom is filled with real live children.

Students have a way of disrupting the most carefully considered plans. They walk in, and suddenly the teacher may see that the desks are much too close together or that some of the larger students don't even fit in their chairs. When the books are distributed, it may become evident that some children will have great difficulty reading and understanding the texts for this grade level. When the rules and consequences are discussed, it may become apparent that some of the rules will need to be spelled out in greater detail and that some of the consequences will need to be strengthened, at least for some children.

The first day of school can be a humbling and disheartening experience for teachers who have invested a great deal of energy and care in their initial plans. Both experienced and novice teachers report that when they meet their students on the first day of school, they often experience feelings of fear and frustration. The actual children seem so much bigger (or smaller), quicker (or slower), more active (or passive) than expected. For experienced teachers who taught the same grade level the year before, part of the jolt comes from their memories of how much more mature and able the class was last year. But, when they consider this more fully, most teachers realize that their memories are based on students at the *end of the year*, who were 9 months older and had become adjusted to life in that teacher's classroom.

GATHERING INFORMATION FOR A DIAGNOSIS

There may be no adequate way to prevent this first day letdown. It occurs primarily because a class is made up of unique individuals with widely varied backgrounds, personalities, and needs. In the first weeks of school, other children reveal their needs to teachers who care enough to look for them. Quiet, orderly children may reveal great deficiencies in math or reading skills. Loud, boisterous children may reveal a deep longing for approval. Shy, withdrawn children are observed to have strong unmet needs for being accepted by peers or adults or both. Some children may simply need breakfast. Others may have language deficiencies that prevent them from learning.

It appears that the number of elementary students with special needs is growing. Recent studies show that "teaching and learning proceed nicely for about half of the students in our schools. For the other half, there are difficulties" (Reynolds, 1989, p. 129). These students have many varied needs. Some have been identified as physically, mentally, or emotionally handicapped; they may receive special services or classes through the growing special education systems that have been created to address their needs. Others may be thought of as economically disadvantaged but have never been formally diagnosed or serviced by special education. Still others may have come from homes where English is the second language or from migrant families who move frequently, resulting in educational disruption.

Can a single teacher, in a single school year, fill all these needs, combat all these inequities, right all these wrongs? No. But can a reflective, caring teacher fill some of these needs, combat some of these inequities, and right some of these wrongs for some children? Yes. Teachers who are willing to diagnose needs and search for solutions to difficult problems can assist some children in getting their needs met and can make a significant and positive difference in the lives of some of the children placed in their classrooms. Moreover, if teachers are able to work with the special education teachers and other professionals in the school system or the community, they can assist children and their families to meet their needs more effectively.

Teachers' Conceptions of How Students Learn

How teachers diagnose their students' needs depends to a large extent upon their conception of how children learn. Through experience and research, teachers construct personal theories of learning that then affect their perceptions and reasoning about what children are able to do and what they need. Anderson (1989) has identified two basic conceptions of learning that she terms the *receptive-accrual* (*R-A*) view and the *cognitive-mediational* (*C-M*) view (p. 86).

The R-A conception is a view that has been held by many teachers over the years. It is based on the assumption that some students have greater ability than others and that those with greater ability are able to receive and accrue knowledge better and faster than those with less ability. Teachers with this point of view tend to diagnose students by categorizing them into groups by ability—highs, middles, and lows.

A growing number of reflective teachers are questioning the R-A view of teaching and learning. They hold the C-M view, which assumes that learning is a function of processing information, and that some children have learned from experience how to process information more quickly and accurately than others. Teachers who hold this view do not diagnose children as having a fixed amount of ability. They reflect on the background experiences of each child they meet and seek information to help them discover what the child needs from the school environment in order to process information more skillfully. The child may need enriched life experiences or training in selecting and applying the appropriate cognitive strategy in order to mediate and improve achievement in school.

Teachers with an R-A conception of learning may diagnose their students' needs before meeting them face to face. This is because they tend to use data such as achievement test scores or ability group placements from the year before to make their decisions about what students are capable of learning. Teachers with a C-M view of learning are likely to wait until they get to know students well before they make a diagnosis of their needs.

Interpreting Data from Students' Cumulative Files

A record of information, called the *cumulative file*, often referred to as a *cume file*, is kept on each child in an elementary school. Each year, the classroom teacher records in the child's file such data as information about the child's family, standardized test scores, reading levels, samples of written work, grades, and notes on parent–teacher conferences. At the end of the school year, the cume file is stored in the school or district office until the next year, when it is redistributed to the child's new teacher.

Obviously, these files contain much useful information for teachers to use in preliminary planning. By studying them, the teacher can make judgments about placement in reading or math groups before meeting the students themselves. Alert teachers may discover information about a child's home environment, such as a recent divorce or remarriage, that can help them in communicating with the child. Some files may reveal little about the child; others may be overflowing with records of conferences and staffings that signal that the child has exhibited a special need or difficulty over the years.

Yet, many teachers resist looking at their students' cume files before meeting the class. Tracy Kidder's *Among Schoolchildren* (1989) provides a realistic look at the entire school year of a fifth-grade class in upstate New York. In the opening chapter, which describes the beginning of the school year, the teacher, Chris Zajac, reflects on the value of cume files as she ponders what to do with a student named Clarence, whose negative attitudes toward school have become apparent on the first day of school:

> Chris had received the children's "cumulative" records, which were stuffed inside salmon-colored folders known as "cumes." For now she checked only addresses and phone numbers, and resisted looking into histories. It was usually better at first to let her own opinions form. But she couldn't help noticing the thickness of some cumes. "The thicker the cume, the more trouble," she told Miss Hunt. "If it looks like *War and Peace* . . . " Clarence's cume was about as thick as the Boston phone book. And Chris couldn't help having heard what some colleagues had insisted on telling her about Clarence. One teacher whom Chris trusted had described him as probably the most difficult child in all of last year's fourth-grade class. Chris wished she hadn't heard that. . . . (pp. 8–9)

While data and observations on students made by former teachers may be a valuable resource for planning, many reflective teachers, like Chris Zajac, are aware of the power of the self-fulfilling prophecy, in which their own expectations may influence the way their students behave or achieve in school. Good and Brophy (1987) define *teachers' expectations* as "inferences that teachers make about the future behavior or academic achievement of their students" and show that the *self-fulfilling prophecy* occurs when "an originally erroneous expectation leads to behavior that causes the expectation to become true" (p. 116).

When cume files contain data and descriptions of low academic achievement or misbehavior, nonreflective teachers may assume that these children are unteachable or unmanageable. On the first day of school, the teacher may place them at desks apart from the rest of the class or hand them textbooks from a lower grade. These teacher behaviors tell the children how the teacher expects them to behave and perform in this class. If these expectations are consistent over time, it is likely to affect the children's own self-concepts and motivations in such a way that they achieve poorly and behave badly. By contrast, consider the possible effects of warm and encouraging teacher behavior on these students. If the teacher builds rapport with these students, includes them in all classroom activities from the first day, and works with them to establish their achievement levels and needs, it is likely that both their behavior and achievement will be improved during the course of the year.

Reflective teachers who understand the great influence of their own expectations on their students prefer to assess the strengths and needs of each student independently in the first few weeks of class. They may read the cume folders at the end of September to see how their own assessments fit with those of the students' previous teachers.

A good case can be made for either point of view: using cume folders for preliminary planning or waiting to read them until the students are well known to you. This is one of those issues that you will need to consider and decide for yourself. Perhaps if you understand the power of teacher expectations, you can find a way to use the information in the files to establish positive expectations and resist the tendency to establish negative ones, as the perspective on page 00 shows.

Interpreting Standardized Test Results

In many ways, the role of the teacher in diagnosing students' needs is quite similar to the role of the medical doctor in diagnosing disease. Doctors get information by observing and talking with patients about their medical histories. Similarly, teachers observe and talk with their students to assess their learning histories. But some important information needed for an accurate diagnosis cannot be observed or discussed. Just as doctors may find that laboratory tests provide them with valuable information about the patient, so teachers may find that achievement tests can provide them with valuable data about their students.

Some tests, known as *criterion-referenced* tests, are created by teachers themselves. They are designed to fit the subject being taught. Questions and problems on the tests are drawn directly from the teacher's lessons, and criteria for success are established by the teacher. For example, after a week of lessons on geometry, the teacher presents the students with a test consisting of 20 geometry problems that are similar to those studied during the week. As criteria for success, the teacher establishes a grading system of A = 90% correct, B = 80% correct, C =

JEAN MALVASO-ZINGARO
Sixth-Grade Teacher

DIAGNOSING STUDENTS' NEEDS FOR RESPONSIBILITY AND SELF-ESTEEM

In dealing with a new class in September, I like to draw my own conclusions and discover for myself what each child is all about. Many times, however, even though I don't peruse the cume files, the previous teachers will tell me about the miserable year they just had with a child who is now in my class. When this happens, I try not to let the teachers' warnings influence my dealings with the child.

One year Tim walked into my class with a bad reputation. His previous teacher told me that he should be classified as "emotionally disturbed." He had failed twice and was very streetwise. He had missed a great deal of school in the past, so I had to give him a reason for wanting to come to school.

I decided to give him both responsibility and trust. On the first day of school, I gave him the job of "keeper of the keys," a position with a lot of status in the classroom. He was responsible for locking and unlocking the classroom door, the file cabinets, and my desk.

Things did not go smoothly for Tim during the year; there were many ups and downs. He began to come late to school, so I assigned him the job of morning Safety Patrol. He treasured his safety belt and began to come on time every day. I also had him work with some of the younger children in a special education class. At first he complained that the children were bad, but he was able to work with them and they enjoyed his help.

Another September, I remember seeing the name Akaby on my class list. The previous year she had been in the class across the hall, and I couldn't forget the day children from that class came running to me for help because Akaby was trying to "beat up" the teacher. Although she was only a fifth grader, she was taller than me and much stronger. I removed her from her classroom and was able to reason with her and convince her to calm down.

Now here was this child's name on my class list. At first, I dreaded the thought of having her in my classroom and hoped she would move to another district. But on the first day of school, there she was.

On the first day of school, I could tell that Akaby was trying to size me up. I waited until she began one of the tirades she was famous for, and then I threw her off base; instead of arguing with her, I asked her to have lunch with me. At lunch, I explained to her that being a teacher was a difficult job and that there are times when I need help. I asked her to help me correct papers and put the daily schedule on the board.

She asked me why she was being asked to do these jobs. I told her it was because I knew that she could handle several responsibilities. She beamed and asked what she had to do to keep the tasks I had assigned. I said to this 12-year-old child, "Just act like an adult and please try not to destroy my classroom." Akaby accepted. She came early and stayed late to correct papers, and during that time we were able to talk; we developed trust and got to know each other well.

The following fall, Akaby returned to tell me that she missed my school. Things weren't working out for her in junior high school. Her reason for this was that she wasn't "important."

70% correct, and so on. From tests like these, teachers are able to determine which students have learned the lessons and which ones need reteaching. Doctors may also employ self-created criterion-referenced tests to determine how well a patient is reacting to a drug or whether the patient is improving after surgery.

A second type of test that is frequently used as a diagnostic tool by teachers is the *norm-referenced* achievement test batteries given to all students in a school district once a year. These test batteries consist of reading, spelling, English, math, science, and social studies exams given over a period of several days. The teacher does not write the questions or establish the criteria to fit a particular classroom. Instead, the items are written to approximate what is taught across the nation in each subject area at each grade level.

Just as in medicine, the information gained from such tests must be standardized to be useful as a diagnostic tool. For example, a doctor who orders a test to measure the time it takes a patient's blood to clot and receives a result of 10 minutes cannot use this information to make an accurate diagnosis unless it is known how this result compares to the clotting time of other individuals on the same test. Similarly, when a teacher receives a reading achievement test raw score of 62 for a student, the score is not useful for diagnosis until it is shown in comparison to the scores of other students in the same grade on the same test.

Test standardization is accomplished by identifying the population for whom the test is written and accumulating a carefully chosen sample of scores from this target population. These sample scores are then arranged from low to high, and an average is calculated. The score of 62 can now be compared with the average score of the sample to determine whether the student is above or below the mean of students in the grade taking that test.

Other statistical calculations provide more precise information about a student's performance. The score may be translated into a percentile or a grade-equivalent score. These interpretations are done by comparing the student's raw score with the raw scores of the sample population. A *percentile rank* tells you what percentage of the people tested scored below a given score. For example, if Joe receives a percentile rank of 78, this means that 78% of the students at Joe's grade level scored below him.

Grade-equivalent scores were created by test publishers especially for use in elementary schools. The results are reported as a function of grade level. For example, if Sally receives a grade-equivalent score of 4.2, this means that her performance is similar to those of students who are in the second month of fourth grade. If Sally is in the fourth grade, her score tells the teacher that Sally is doing about as well as she is supposed to be doing. If Sally is in the second grade, her score tells the teacher that Sally is capable of functioning like students who are 2 years above her present grade level. But if Sally is in the seventh grade, her score alerts the teacher that this student has serious deficiencies and is functioning like students who are 3 years below her present grade level.

There are other score reporting systems for standardized tests, such as age-equivalent scores, stanines, and standard scores. While it is not possible to discuss all of these scores in this text, it is important for you to acquaint yourselves with the tests and scores used in your school system when you begin your first teaching assignment. It is also important for you to realized that the use of standardized tests varies widely from district to district. In some schools, they are used to diagnose learning difficulties of individuals so that corrective measures may be taken.

In other school systems, the test results are published in local newspapers to compare how well students in different schools are doing in the basic skills. This practice is a controversial issue among educators. The tests were not designed to be used as a measure of excellence among schools, but the public believes that they can be used that way. For example, the average test scores on standardized reading achievement tests for each school in a district may be compared. This may lead the public to assume that the school with the highest average reading score is doing the best job of teaching reading. Educators know that there are many other contributing factors, such as the socioeconomic conditions of the families whose children attend each school or the degree to which the items on the test match the curriculum of the school.

Another thing that achievement tests were not designed to do is to show the aptitude for learning or predict the future achievement of any child. Reflective, caring teachers recognize that the teacher's interpretation of a student's low achievement test results could contribute to a negative self-fulfilling prophecy. To avoid that problem, the reflective, caring teacher interprets the information gained on standardized achievement tests with great caution.

Achievement tests were designed, and are useful, in helping you to make a general diagnosis of the current achievement level of your class so that you can plan lessons to begin at that level. These tests can help you pinpoint the children in your class who have low achievement in a certain subject so that you can prescribe a special course of action for them. The tests can also help you identify the children who have mastered the basic skills in one or more subjects so that you can provide them with more challenging learning experiences.

Another form of standardized test that may be given in your school district is the *aptitude* or *ability* test. Individual assessments of ability, known as *intelligence* or *IQ* tests, are given by a school psychologist to one child at a time. The psychologist then interprets the results for the teacher and the child's family. Some test publishers have sought to duplicate these types of measures to accompany their achievement tests. These short, timed, paper-and-pencil tests purport to test the child's innate ability, which is a very different construct from achievement in school. The scores are reported in the same format as IQ tests, with 100 as the mean and a standard deviation of approximately 15. These scores look like IQ scores, but many educators are reluctant to give them that much credence:

> Achievement tests have been defined as measuring what the student *has* learned up to the moment of testing. Aptitude tests, on the other hand, were said to measure the student's *ability* to learn in the future. . . . Achievement and aptitude tests are not all that different. A study of the actual test would show that in format and content they are quite similar. (Wick, 1973, p. 152)

There may be cases where it would be very useful to know whether a child is, using a cliché, "working up to his or her ability." When this information is necessary to make a decision about placing a child in a special program, retaining the child in the same grade, or identifying the child as "gifted," reflective teachers are likely to insist on a full-scale individual IQ score rather than rely on the oversimplified group ability test score given as part of the achievement test battery.

DIAGNOSING STUDENTS' NEEDS IN SCHOOL SUBJECTS

Assessment devices such as tests, essays, reports, performances, and other student products are collectively known as *tools of evaluation*. But evaluation is a very complex and multifaceted concept. When tests are given at the end of a term or unit of study, the purpose is to sum up what each student has learned. For this reason, the process is termed a *summative evaluation*. Grades may be determined by such summative tests, and reports to parents are made on the progress of each student. Summative evaluations are seldom used as diagnostic measures. At the end of the term, it is too late to diagnose students' needs; the lessons have all been taught. But there are two other forms of evaluation that provide important information teachers need, when they need it, to make an accurate diagnosis and set new learning goals.

Formative evaluation is the term given to diagnostic forms of assessment. A formative evaluation may be similar in form to a summative evaluation: tests, oral or written problems to solve, essays, or oral presentations. But, in most cases, formative evaluations are not graded, and students know this. When tests are used prior to the end of the term or unit, their purpose is often to determine how well each student is progressing within the unit of study. When a formative evaluation shows a deficiency in one or more students, the teacher uses this information to plan what needs to be retaught and to whom.

At the beginning of a term or a unit of study, teachers often use *pretests* to determine what skills and knowledge pertaining to the subject students have already mastered. Pretests, which may also be known as *readiness tests*, are designed to determine whether students have the skills and knowledge that will allow them to be successful in the new unit of study.

Some pretests and readiness tests, especially in the area of reading, are provided by textbook publishers to accompany their texts. Others are available separately through test publishers. Kindergarten and first-grade teachers frequently use reading readiness tests at the beginning of the year to determine which students are capable of succeeding in the complex task of learning to read. Certain skills, especially visual and auditory discrimination, have been shown to be essential prerequisites for learning to discriminate between letter shapes and sounds. Students who score very low on a reading readiness test may be provided with a curriculum designed to improve their visual and auditory discrimination skills before they even attempt to learn to read. Readiness tests, then, are designed to prevent children from failing by identifying those who need preliminary experiences to help ready them for the academic curriculum.

Many elementary textbooks, in a variety of subject areas, provide pretests that are matched to the content of the books themselves. Math textbooks may provide an initial pretest, to be used at the beginning of the school year, that covers the material learned in the earlier grades in that series. English textbooks often provide pretests for each unit of study in the book, such as grammar, punctuation, sentences, and organization of paragraphs.

When pretests are not provided by the textbook publishers, they can be created by the teacher to fit virtually any unit of study. For example, prior to introducing a teacher-made unit on molecules and atoms, the teacher may write a brief pretest to determine what the students already know about this subject.

Placement Decisions

The results of standardized tests and subject matter pretests can assist the teacher's diagnosis and planning in several important ways. One decision that may be made as a result of test scores is a *placement decision*. Students with high scores may be placed in a different group from those with moderate or low scores. The groups may be taught separately, using different materials. This conventional strategy, known as *ability grouping*, is used in the teaching of reading, and sometimes math, in many elementary schools. Three reading groups are typically identified in this way, and students are then taught the skills they have not yet mastered at a pace that suits the group of similar or homogeneous students.

Another diagnostic decision that pretests make possible is known as the *mastery learning feedback corrective approach* (Bloom, 1984, p. 7). This strategy is used by teachers who view each student as unique, rather than as part of an ability group. Pretests can be designed to show the specific skills that a student lacks, leading to an individual diagnosis and a corrective plan of action. The teacher, an aide, a classroom volunteer, or a more capable peer can then provide the student with feedback on the deficiencies and show the student how to master those skills. After mastering those skills, the student is then ready to join the class in the regular curriculum.

Studies done by Benjamin Bloom and several graduate students in the early 1980s showed the power of this diagnostic/corrective approach. In one study, Bloom (1984) describes a study in which one of his graduate students worked with high school teachers to develop pretests of essential prerequisites for the courses of Algebra 2 and French 2. The pretests consisted of items from the final exams of earlier courses, Algebra 1 and French 1, that were considered to be essential for success in the advanced courses. The pretests were administered to two French 2 and two Algebra 2 classes.

Students in one French 2 and one Algebra 2 class then had an opportunity to review and relearn the specific prerequisites they lacked:

> The teacher retaught the items the majority of students had missed; small groups of students helped each other over items that had been missed; and the students reviewed items they were not sure about by referring to the designated pages in the instructional material. The corrective process involved about three to four hours of time during the first week of the course. (p. 7)

This review and reteaching was not done for the students in the other two classes. During the 10- to 12-week period of instruction, the experimental classes continued to receive formative evaluations and corrective feedback, while the control group classes received only conventional instruction. At the end of this period, a summative test was given to all four classes. "The average experimental student was above 95 percent of the control students on this examination. There were also attitudinal differences. . . . These included positive academic self-concept, interest in the subject, and a desire to learn more in the subject field" (Bloom, 1984, p. 8).

Although this particular study was done in a high school, Bloom recommends that the process begin in the elementary school in the sequential courses, such as math, spelling, and the skills associated with decoding in reading. If this process is initiated at the beginning of a child's education and is continued in subsequent years, students with learning difficulties are more likely to learn the material targeted for their own grade level from that time forward.

A third decision that teachers may make partly as a result of testing is the creation of cooperative teams or pairs for peer tutoring. To strengthen student motivation and interaction, many teachers employ the cooperative team concept. Cooperative groups typically consist of three to five students who are assigned a set of tasks to complete by cooperating with and assisting each other. In some classrooms, teachers use pretest data to decide which students to assign to each team. Often, teachers use cooperative groups to promote peer coaching and interactive assistance among their students. In this case, a team of four students may consist of one student with very strong performance, two with moderate performance, and one with weak performance in the subject area. Similarly, peer tutoring dyads may consist of one skilled and one less skilled student. These are simply two examples; other types of cooperative group placement decisions, for different purposes, are possible as well.

Diagnosing Underachievement

Teachers who carefully structure their classroom lessons to ensure success are frequently baffled by the tendency of some children to fail even under optimal conditions. As Sylvia Rimm (1986) observes, "Millions of children who are very capable of learning—children with average, above average, even gifted abilities, including those from middle class homes where education is supposed to be valued—are simply not performing up to their capabilities" (p. 1).

Students may underachieve in kindergarten, but most enter school as achievers and gradually or suddenly fall into an underachievement pattern. Standardized test scores may provide dramatic evidence of this decline. Percentile scores on achievement tests may be relatively stable for several years and then suddenly drop 20 or more points. If a student has had math achievement scores in the 80 percentile range for three grades and suddenly drops into the 50 percentile range, the diagnosis of underachievement may be warranted.

A comparison of intelligence (IQ) scores with achievement test scores and grades may offer more reason to suspect underachievement. When a student is tested by a school psychologist and is found to have an IQ score above the mean, but achievement test scores and grades far below the mean, it is likely that the student is underachieving.

There is no single cause for underachievement, nor is there a single cure. There are also no consistent characteristics associated with underachievement. Some underachievers are bossy and aggressive; others are lonely and withdrawn. Some are slow and perfectionistic; others are hurried and disorganized. A few have adopted a behavior pattern of *learned helplessness* because of previous experiences in school, unusually high expectations at home, or a combination of both. These children perceive that they are certain to fail at whatever they try, so they have learned not to try.

Underachievement is a tough diagnosis to make and, once made, an even tougher condition to overcome. Rimm's *The Underachievement Syndrome: Causes and Cures* (1986) provides vivid and realistic descriptions of underachieving children that can assist the teacher in making an accurate diagnosis and creating a management plan to help the child and the parents change this self-destructive pattern.

Diagnosing the Needs of Students with High Achievement

Each school year, teachers discover one or several children in their classrooms who learn extremely easily and rapidly. Some of these children may excel in only one subject area. One child may perform brilliantly in math computation and problem solving; another may write long and complex stories, poems, and essays that express ideas far more mature than those of the child's age or grade level; still another may show a strong sense of leadership and understanding of social interactions among classmates and adults.

To serve the needs of these children, many school systems have established *gifted programs*. The assumption of most gifted programs is that the regular classroom curriculum cannot meet the needs of students with unusually strong ability and achievement. Educators who are specialists in gifted education have designed a number of alternative programs to serve the needs of such children.

Some gifted programs stress accelerated curricula in a subject area such as math. Students with standardized math test scores in the 95 to 99 percentile range are often placed in special programs that allow them to learn advanced mathematical concepts at a rapid pace. Other children may be placed in special enrichment classes focusing on literature and writing. Still others may be placed in special programs that allow them to work with a mentor in a field such as science or government (Cox, Daniel, & Boston, 1985).

In some elementary schools, the gifted programs are not subject-matter specific. They are pull-out programs (meaning that children are pulled out of the regular classroom) that allow children to work on independent studies or group projects that stress higher-level thinking, research skills, and creativity.

As a classroom teacher, you may be asked to assist in the identification of children for the school's gifted programs. You may be asked to nominate children who you believe need the services the program has to offer. In many cases, gifted program coordinators provide a form on which you rate the recommended child's behaviors and characteristics.

Conflicts occasionally arise over the selection of students for gifted programs. Parents may perceive their child to be gifted or may simply want their child to be included in these enriched programs for the educational value they represent. Teachers have varied values and expectations about student behavior and achievement that lead to inconsistent recommendations. One teacher may see a child as clearly gifted because of creative and independent behavior, while another teacher may think that the same child is just an obnoxious troublemaker.

Careful reflection is needed when recommending students for special gifted programs and services. Consider the consequences of labeling some students "gifted." Eby and Smutny (1990) examined the effects of gifted programs on children and concluded that "one effect of labeling a small minority of children 'gifted' is that we are also unwittingly labeling the remaining children in the family or school 'nongifted' " (p. viii). We advocate the elimination of the term "gifted child" in schools because of its negative effects.

In our book, entitled *A Thoughtful Overview of Gifted Education*, we sought to find methods of teaching that provide for the needs of high-achieving and talented children in the classroom without setting them apart from their peers. While many teachers choose the conventional ability groups described above, there are other alternatives that reflective, caring teachers can use to meet the needs of high-achieving students. You can provide enriched materials and activities for any children who finish their regular work. If the materials are interesting and the activities motivating, this strategy has the added advantage of serving as a genuine incentive for completing assignments.

Students with very advanced skills can be allowed to work at an accelerated pace, on suitably challenging material from higher grade levels, by providing them with texts and worksheets from the upper grades and supervising their work on an individual basis. This strategy is known as *mastery learning* because, when students master a certain skill, they are allowed to proceed at their own pace to the next level.

You can team up with your colleagues and allow high-achieving students to learn math and/or reading from teachers in the upper grades. This is sometimes called *walking reading* or *walking math* because the students walk to the classroom for that one subject. It works best when the school has a uniform time for math and reading.

Another strategy is to form children into cooperative groups to assist each other in learning. This strategy does not allow for acceleration, but it does enrich the high-achieving students' self-esteem by allowing them to develop their communication and leadership skills as they assist other students in academic areas. See Chapter Nine for a complete discussion of cooperative group strategies.

DIAGNOSING STUDENTS' AFFECTIVE NEEDS

In conventional classrooms managed by teachers with an R-A conception of learning, much of the diagnosis that takes place centers on the students' cognitive abilities and psychomotor skills. The diagnostic tests that have been widely adopted measure reading levels, math aptitudes, visual and auditory discrimination, and other important cognitive and psychomotor prerequisites for learning. But reflective teachers know that the affective domain of learning is important as well, even though it is more difficult to assess—and they know that it is this domain that encompasses the important concept of motivation.

Identifying Reasons for Problem Behavior

Motivation is that which gives direction and intensity to behavior. It is of utmost concern to teachers because the lack of it seems to be a major obstacle to learning. Some students seem to be bored, others anxious, and still others hostile. Yet these same students, outside the classroom, often seem enthusiastic, calm, and friendly. Why are many students unmotivated in the classroom and yet tremendously motivated in out-of-school pursuits? (Gagne, 1985, p. 302)

Three different theories have been offered to explain student motivation: behaviorist theory, cognitive theory, and Maslow's hierarchy of needs. Briefly, the *behaviorist* theory of motivation, which was derived from experimental research with animals, is that an extrinsic stimulus (e.g., a promise of a gold star or a good grade) provokes or motivates a student response (e.g., studying hard or cheating). When the student's response is reinforced (e.g., by receiving the gold star or the good grade), the student learns to repeat the behavior that was reinforced. Behaviorists believe that when such stimulus-response-reinforcement incidents are repeated, they set up a pattern of similar responses in the student's school career.

In contrast, the *cognitive* theory of motivation, derived from studies of mental processes and information processing, also begins with an initiating stimulus, but here the initial stimulus is a goal. It may be a goal suggested by a teacher (e.g., "Do research on and write an essay on transportation") or it may be self-generated (e.g., "I'd like to know how airplanes fly"). The goal stimulus may cause students to have quite varied responses. Some may begin immediately to do the research and writing, while others may put off the task. Cognitive psychologists recognize that there are a variety of internal responses that play important roles in student motivation. Some of these include uncertainty, curiosity, memories about similar tasks, and expectations of success or failure. These thoughts and feelings contribute greatly to the actions a student takes when presented with a goal stimulus (Gagne, 1985, pp. 302–310).

Maslow's theory of motivation was derived from clinical studies of individuals undergoing psychological therapy combined with research about the physical needs of the body. Maslow believes that the stimulus for most needs is internal rather than external. He believes that humans have unconscious physical and emotional needs that must be met or satisfied before the person is able to pay attention to outside stimuli. Translated into everyday classroom situations, a hungry child's need for food must be met before he can learn multiplication facts; a frightened child must be comforted before she can give her full attention to phonics; a lonely child must have a friend before he can show concern for the environment (Maslow, 1954).

You may consider any one of these theories to be the most useful, or you may find aspects of each one that, when combined, offer you a more comprehensive way to understand the motivation of the children you teach. In making a diagnosis about a child's motivation, most reflective teachers rely on informal assessment strategies: observation and conferences with the student, the parents, and the student's previous teachers.

Informal assessment and diagnostic strategies are quite different from formal testing procedures. In order to be successful, the informal assessment must be handled with genuine caring and interest on the part of the teacher. Taking a child out in the hall and asking, with teeth clenched and finger pointed, "What makes you act like this?" will elicit few illuminating responses. The child is likely to withdraw, lie, or rebel in this situation.

If a conference with a student or with parents is to succeed in discovering the student's underlying needs and motivations, teachers must be willing and able to listen empathetically to the child's (and the family's) fears and hopes. Sometimes a conference in the school setting is not sufficient to encourage children to talk about themselves. American teachers rarely visit children's homes, but such a visit may reveal much more about the child's needs than can be learned in a classroom. I have used, as a neutral ground, a lunchtime or after-school visit with a troubled child to a nearby hamburger stand to find out more about what makes the child behave in certain ways.

Whatever the setting, the informal assessment conference also needs careful planning to be successful. Jot down ideas that you want to discuss, questions that you want to ask, and encouraging remarks that you want to make before you meet with the child or the parents. The conference may reveal some very surprising information, and you will need to follow the lead of the child and the family as to how much of their private lives they wish to reveal to you.

On occasion, you may find that they want to reveal more than you can comfortably assimilate. Difficult issues of poverty, divorce, abandonment, and other damaging social conditions may cause you to feel overwhelmed and helpless to serve the best interests of this child. In cases of severe social and emotional problems, it is recommended that you refer the child to the school psychologist and other school personnel who can assist in making a diagnosis and recommend a treatment plan.

Assessing Students with Special Needs

Students in most elementary classrooms present a wide range of abilities, experiences, motivations, and needs. No class is made up entirely of homogeneous, average, well-behaved children. It is likely that at least some of the children in every classroom have handicaps or needs that are out of the ordinary. Some may have unusual patterns of behavior that cause them to underachieve academically or rebel against authority. Others may have unusual perceptual handicaps that make it difficult for them to distinguish the sounds or symbols required to do school tasks successfully. Others may learn so rapidly and efficiently that they are easily bored with the regular curriculum.

Today most children are screened for handicaps and special needs in preschool. Children found to have *severe intellectual disabilities* are those who "function intellectually within approximately the lowest 1 percent of a naturally distributed population" (Albright, Brown, VanDeventer, & Jorgensen, 1989, p. 60). They have an extreme inability to communicate and respond to learning activities. When a diagnosis of severe disability is made, the child is placed in a full-time special education program rather than a regular elementary classroom.

Children who are diagnosed as being *mildly handicapped* are usually further categorized as having *learning disabilities, mild mental retardation, emotional disturbance,* or *speech handicaps*. These conditions occur with higher frequency than severe handicaps, and the diagnosis is much more difficult to make. Some children are found to have mild handicaps during preschool screening. If so, most school districts provide them with supportive services from kindergarten through high school or until the need has been corrected.

Others may not be identified so early. They enter school without the benefit of special services. In this case, it takes an alert elementary teacher to spot the difficulties and refer the child for special testing and assessment. This is an important responsibility for elementary teachers to consider when they examine the test scores of children in their classes and when they observe a pattern of learning difficulties that no one else has noted in the child's cume file.

A federal law (Public Law 94-142) requires that all states "insure that a continuum of alternative placements is available to meet the needs of handicapped children for special education and services." But the same law also stipulates that the handicapped child must be educated in "the least restrictive environment compatible with his or her educational needs." To meet these requirements, schools provide a variety of services to handicapped children, but for children to receive the appropriate services, teachers must be aware of the alternatives available and alert to the needs of the children in their classes.

When properly diagnosed, children with special needs can receive services from specialists to assist them in overcoming their difficulties or at least in developing coping skills. Each child served by special education programs has an *Individualized Educational Plan (IEP)* designed specifically to meet that child's unique needs. These plans are written by a team including the school psychologist, the special education teacher, and the child's parents. Classroom teachers have an important role in the identification, diagnosis, and treatment plan for children with special needs. They may also be asked to take part in creating a child's IEP, especially if the child is expected to spend at least part of the school day in that teacher's classroom.

A learning disabilities specialist, Rick Bailey, who teaches at West Elementary School in Crystal Lake, Illinois, describes how he interacts with classroom decisions on these important decisions in the Perspective on page 70.

Teachers should not assume that all students in the regular classroom have been properly diagnosed. It is likely that, except for the parents, elementary classroom teachers know the needs of the children in their classroom better than anyone. A fourth-grade teacher may be the first one to observe a child's learning disability; a sixth-grade teacher may be the first one to suspect a child of having a disabling emotional disturbance. When this occurs, the teacher's role is to refer the child to the special education personnel for further testing and assessment. When the testing is completed, the classroom teacher will be part of a group of teachers and parents who make the recommendation for treatment for this particular student.

Chris Zajac, the teacher featured in *Among Schoolchildren* (Kidder, 1989), considers the needs of one student, Pedro:

> Pedro's voice was deep out of all proportion to his size, and his voice had a garbled sound, as if his mouth were full of water, but sometimes perfect lines like that came out and made Chris wonder if Pedro really was, as she'd begun to think, mildly retarded. . . . He didn't often talk. He never misbehaved. He almost always tried to do his homework. It was as another teacher had said: "Poor Pedro. He works so hard to get his F." (p. 80)

In deciding whether to refer Pedro for a *core* assessment for possible services in special education, Chris wonders whether the special education services provided in her school will be better for Pedro than what she can provide for him in her own classroom:

> Chris thought that the wrong children often got, as the saying went, "cored" and sent to the Resource Room, children whose main problem with school seemed to be behavior, not ability. The Resource Room teacher remarked, "It's

---▼| P E R S P E C T I V E |▼

RICK BAILEY
Learning Disabilities Specialist,
West Elementary School, Crystal Lake, Illinois

HOW SPECIAL TEACHERS AND CLASSROOM TEACHERS INTERACT TO DIAGNOSE THE NEEDS OF A STUDENT

A classroom teacher with a child who is not doing well academically refers the child for an evaluation by a school psychologist, social worker, and learning disabilities teacher to see if he or she is eligible to receive special education services. Prior to the evaluation, the teacher meets with these specialists to share information about the child. This information helps the specialists plan the evaluation.

As part of my job as a learning disabilities teacher, I recently participated in two such conferences. Mr. Jones, a first-grade teacher, had referred Tommy for a diagnosis of learning problems. Mr. Jones came to the conference with work samples, which showed very poor handwriting, and an unreadable and incomplete math worksheet. I could see Tommy's weaknesses, but I was also interested in his strengths, so I asked Mr. Jones to tell me about these, as well as about his concerns. Mr. Jones replied, "Tommy has very strong language skills. He can remember everything that I say when I present information orally. He remembers every detail of stories that I read, and he can even spell words out loud when he is asked to. However, when he is asked to read those same words, he cannot. He frequently misspells his own name when he writes it, but never when asked to spell it out loud. When he looks at his own version of his written name, he doesn't realize that it is wrong."

Mr. Jones went on to share information about Tommy's specific reading, phonics, math, and social skills. In addition, he shared some of the special lessons he had prepared for Tommy to try to help him. When the conference was finished, I had a good mental picture of Tommy.

On another occasion, I attended a conference on Sarah, who had been referred by Mrs. Smith. When asked about Sarah, Mrs. Smith said, "Well, she just doesn't seem to learn things. I'm not sure what the problem is. She hasn't got the skills that the other children have. She is in the lowest group, and sometimes she's okay but sometimes she isn't. She's not the best student in my class, but she's not the worst, either." When asked for specific examples of Sarah's learning problems or samples of her work, Mrs. Smith was unable to supply us with much more detail about Sarah's difficulties.

Later, I discussed these two cases with the school psychologist. She said, "I know just how I will proceed in Tommy's evaluation because the information Mr. Jones shared was specific and precise. It showed me areas that I can look at during the evaluation to see if Tommy has a learning disability. However, Sarah's evaluation will take much longer, because I will have to do a lot of preliminary work to discover what she can and cannot do."

When a child is having difficulties in school, reflective teachers observe that child carefully and take notes on specific things that the child can and cannot do. They observe to see how that child learns new tasks, and how the child expresses ideas orally and in writing. They compare the child's performance with their expectations for a typical child at this grade level, and they try to modify their teaching strategies with the child to see if the change in teaching method causes an improvement in the child's skills. When classroom teachers can provide information gained from reflective observation, they are able to help the evaluation team arrive at an accurate diagnosis and an effective treatment plan.

something of a dumping ground. I hate to say it, but it is." Nevertheless, a core was the only remedy available for Pedro. At least the testing might reveal whether or not Pedro really was retarded, and maybe it would give Chris some ideas about what she could do for him. But why hadn't there been a core evaluation of Pedro already? That question really bothered her. Was it because teachers had lost their faith in cores, or was it because Pedro didn't cause any trouble? Teachers had their hands full. Every class had disruptive children. It was easy enough to forget about a child like Pedro. In her time, she had forgotten some. (pp. 81–82)

In keeping with Public Law 94-142, which calls for children to be educated in the least restrictive environment, children diagnosed as having a mild learning disability may spend the school day in the regular classroom, with only occasional services from a learning disabilities teacher. Other, more severely handicapped children may spend most of their day in a special education classroom, with occasional visits to the regular classroom for art, music, gym, or other subjects in which they can succeed.

The beginning teacher should be aware that the process of referring, assessing, and identifying special needs is an imperfect one. Tests and their results may be invalidated by some condition in the testing situation, or the tests themselves may be limited in their ability to predict or measure complex human needs and traits. The size and budget of the school system may limit services to a small percentage of those who could benefit from them. Many teachers experience great frustration when they refer a child for special education testing or services and find that the child has been placed on a long waiting list for such services.

On the other hand, there is growing concern among many educators that students may be labeled as handicapped when no handicap exists. Most standardized tests used in the diagnosis of learning difficulties have been challenged for their tendency to discriminate against students from minority groups. The high percentage of African-American and other minority group children in special education programs is disturbing and has caused some to suspect that they are being inaccurately labeled and placed. "The response of schools to children who are ethnically or racially different illustrates both the use of psychometric testing as a mechanism for interpreting difference as deviance, and the propensity to see school failure as a problem of the child rather than the school" (Sapon-Shevin, 1989, p. 92).

This disturbing phenomenon means that classroom teachers may also need to be willing to take a role in questioning the validity of placement decisions. When special education students are mainstreamed into art, music, physical education, or the regular classroom, teachers should be alert to the possibility that the child labeled "mildly mentally retarded," "learning disabled," "emotionally disturbed," or "behaviorally disordered" may, in fact, be a child with normal abilities but deficient learning experiences, a child who has expectations of failure due, in part, to placement in special education. When a reflective, caring teacher suspects that a child could function normally in a regular classroom environment, this teacher is willing to take responsibility for asking for a reassessment of the child.

Perceiving the Needs of Bilingual and Bicultural Students

When the language, culture, and values of the parents match those of the teachers in school, the child is likely to experience school as satisfying and supportive because the messages received in both settings are congruent. When these important factors are different, the child may experience school as uncomfortable and threatening because the messages may conflict.

When you become teachers, you can expect to teach a class made up of students from many different cultural and ethnic groups, particularly if you choose to teach in a large urban school district. In your own schooling, you have probably witnessed teachers who attempted to "remediate" and prod culturally different children into "adapting" to the majority culture. Reflective teachers, on the other hand, need to consider how to meet the academic, social, and emotional needs of students from cultures different from their own.

At least 10 percent of school-age children in the United States grow up in homes where English is the second language and need assistance in learning English in order to be successful in school. In urban areas, where the concentration of immigrants is highest, a school may have children who each speak one of as many as 25 different languages (Reynolds, 1989, p. 133).

Hispanic children comprise the largest bicultural group and are expected to account for 10 percent of the school population by the year 2000 (Casas & Furlong, 1986). The troubling fact is that Spanish-speaking students have a 50 percent chance of dropping out of school, which suggests that the current educational practices have not had the intended academic benefits.

These current challenges need current solutions, and one advocate for change is Joan M. First, executive director of the National Coalition of Advocates for Students. She believes that solutions need to center on providing culturally diverse students with appropriate *access* to schools and school services. She finds that immigrant children are occasionally "discouraged from attending school" and that the schools they attend are "often short on resources, poorly staffed, badly maintained, and overcrowded" (First, 1988, p. 207). When they enter school, they require access to a comprehensible education. "Estimates of the number of students with limited proficiency in English who are enrolled in U.S. public schools range from 3.5 million to 5.5 million. It is also estimated that two-thirds of them are not receiving the assistance they need to succeed in their studies" (p. 207).

Most experts in bilingual education believe that in order for bilingual children to learn, they require bilingual teachers and instruction that uses their primary language until they learn enough English to function in the regular classroom. Children with *limited English proficiency (LEP)* receive instruction in special classrooms designed to teach them English as a second language and academic skills in their own language. When students attain minimal proficiency in English, they are termed *fluent English proficient* and may be gradually mainstreamed into regular classrooms (Watson, Northcutt, & Rydell, 1989, pp. 59–61).

Diagnosis of the needs of culturally diverse students are very difficult for classroom teachers who do not share the same culture. But, in general, specialists in bilingual/bicultural education state that culturally diverse children need classroom experiences and interactions with the teacher that "stress self-concept, pride in their culture, and academic competence—the three ultimate criteria for any relevant material or curriculum" (Milne, 1982, p. 7).

Many reflective teachers recognize that the presence of bilingual/bicultural children in their classrooms offers exciting possibilities for curriculum development that celebrate and inform all children in the class about the cultural diversity of our world. Culture fairs featuring the crafts, music, food, and language of the many different types of children in the school are excellent ways to meet the needs of children of all cultures, including the need of white, middle-class children to become aware of the contributions and values of others.

Determining Learning Styles

When a child's cultural and developmental patterns differ from those of the predominant white middle class, the child's preferred learning style may also be different. This may cause additional difficulties for culturally diverse students attempting to assimilate to a different set of expectations and patterns than they are used to in their homes.

Learning styles are derived in part from biological and physical characteristics, as in a preference for learning visually, auditorially, or kinesthetically. The preference, in these three cases, may be due in large part to the relative strength of the child's vision, hearing, and motor coordination. But learning styles are also strongly influenced by developmental factors. For example, students exhibit variations in preferences for working alone or working with a group. Given a complex problem to solve and a project to create, some children prefer the challenge of working alone, while others prefer the experience of working with a group. This may be the result of familiar cultural tendencies to work alone or with a group.

One element of a learning style is the need of some individuals for physical activity. This need of many elementary school-age children can be easily misdiagnosed as a behavior disorder. For example, Fadley and Hosler (1979) found that teachers frequently referred children to psychologists for hyperactivity. The teachers complained that the children were unable to sit quietly and pay attention during lessons. The psychologists in the study reported that most of the referred children were not clinically hyperactive at all; they were normal children in need of movement.

Other studies found that when previously restless youngsters were reassigned to classes that did not require passivity, their behaviors were rarely noticed. Teachers report that certain students thrive in activity-oriented classrooms, while others remain stationary despite frequent attempts by teachers to coax them to move (Dunn, Beaudry, & Klavas, 1989, pp. 55–56). This demonstrates the variation among children in learning style preferences.

Learning styles are like fingerprints. No two are alike. Teachers cannot identify all aspects of their students' learning styles, nor can they meet the many diverse needs these styles represent. It would be frustrating in the extreme to attempt to diagnose each child's learning style and provide a unique set of experiences for every child in the class. But what reflective, caring teachers can do is to respect the fact that variations in learning styles exist and be flexible enough to allow children to work in the ways that are most comfortable and productive for them.

Learning style diagnosis and treatment is probably best accomplished by allowing children to make choices. Through self-selection, children can choose to work on a project alone or with a group, read at a desk or in a bean-bag chair, view a filmstrip or listen to an audiotape, or do a measuring project involving movement or one that can be accomplished quietly in one spot. "No learning style is better or worse than another. Since each style has similar intelligence ranges, students *cannot* be labeled or stigmatized by having any type of style. Most children can master the same content; *how* they master it is determined by their individual styles" (Dunn, Beaudry, & Klavas, 1989, p. 56).

Identifying Students' Needs Without Labeling

Diagnosis of students' needs certainly requires reflection on the part of teachers as they consider the many causes of low achievement and plan appropriate school programs for students. But it also requires a great deal of caring as well. Sometimes, noncaring teachers view diagnosis as equivalent to labeling. A quick perusal of a cume file, a glance at a standardized test score, and a few days of classroom observation can lead a teacher to label a child a "slow learner," "behavior-disordered," or an "underachiever," for example. These labels, and others like them, when communicated to the child and parents, can have disabling effects. The implication of these labels—that the child is deficient in some important way—can lead to a self-fulfilling prophecy, as further erosion of self-concept and self-confidence leads the child to experience even more severe learning difficulties.

Students with excellent school performance can also suffer from labeling. Some teachers refer to their most capable and willing students as "overachievers." This pseudoscientific term is attached to children whose standardized test scores are moderate but whose grades and work habits are excellent. The implication is that these children are working beyond their capacity, and this is somehow seen as a negative characteristic by some teachers. The term *overachiever* is usually used by teachers when they are discussing eligibility for school gifted programs.

Children with high scores on standardized tests, especially IQ tests, are frequently labeled "gifted children." This label may appear to be a very positive one; certainly it is sought by many parents for their children. But careful reflection reveals that this label may be as damaging as any other. Rimm (1986) notes that "Any label that unrealistically narrows prospects for performance by a child may be damaging" (p. 84). Being labeled a gifted child tends to narrow the expectations of performance for that child to a constant state of excellence; any performance less than excellent can be interpreted by the child (and the parents) as being unacceptable.

The label "gifted" has many other negative implications. When a small percentage of children (usually 2–5%) in a school are labeled "gifted," the other 95% are unwittingly labeled "not gifted." This has extremely negative consequences for those children who are siblings of gifted children and for those who are excluded because their test scores are a few points below the cutoff score (Eby & Smutny, 1990).

While special programs are essential for the academic success and emotional well-being of many children in schools today, we must find ways of diagnosing students' needs and deciding on appropriate services without the use of damaging labels.

Broader labels can be just as damaging. "The term *minority* itself carries with it a connotation of being less than other groups with respect to power, status, and treatment. Even in situations where a minority group outnumbers other ethnic groups in population size, it may still be relegated to minority status due to the socioeconomic and power structure of the community" (Chinn, 1982, p. 25).

Terms such as *culturally disadvantaged, culturally deprived,* and *economically underprivileged* do not serve any useful purpose and can cause unknown effects when used without regard for the feelings of children and their parents from cultures other than that of the white middle class. Furthermore, these terms do not recognize the intrinsic value and unique contributions of individuals or groups.

Diagnosis of students' needs can take place without reference to stereotypes and labels. Children who need assistance in learning English can be released from the classroom to work with an English as a second language (ESL) teacher or tutor. Children who need a fast-paced math course can travel to another class for math. Children who need practice in visual discrimination and organizing for learning can have this service. But they can all be welcomed back for most of the day to the regular classroom, where they can share their cultural diversity and talents with each other in a community for learning and growing.

OPPORTUNITIES FOR REFLECTION

▼ *Reflective Essay: Ability Grouping*

What is your own experience with ability grouping? Were you in the high, low, or middle reading group when you were in elementary school? What effects did that grouping have on your learning and your self-concept? What will you do to meet the needs of students in your future classroom who are working at very different levels of difficulty?

▼ *Classroom Visit: Learning Styles*

Arrange to interview one child in the class you are visiting. Ask the child questions to learn about his or her preferred learning style. Sample questions are provided here, but you may want to make up your own as well.

> Do you learn easily by reading about something?
> Do you learn well by listening to a teacher explain something?
> Do you need the teacher to write examples on the board?
> Do you learn best by having somebody show you something or by working out the problem by yourself?
> Do you need a quiet room, or can you work and learn when others are talking or when the TV or radio is on?
> Does it bother you when there is movement around you?
> Do you like to sit at a desk or table when you are studying?

You may want to add to your information by telephoning the child's parents to find out what they have observed about how their child learns best. From your interview of this child, write your diagnosis of this child's learning style. Then recommend the classroom conditions that you believe to be important for this child to learn effectively. Share your written study with the classroom teacher to see how well you agree on the diagnosis and the recommendations for classroom conditions.

▼ *Optional Classroom Visit: Special Education*

Arrange to visit a special education classroom. Observe and report on the way this class is similar to and different from a regular class. What effects does class size have on student learning? What are the expectations for success for these students? How does the curriculum compare to that of the regular classroom?

REFERENCES

ALBRIGHT, K., BROWN, L., VANDEVENTER, P., & JORGENSEN, J. (1989). Characteristics of educational programs for students with severe intellectual disabilities. In D. Biklen, D. Ferguson, & A. Ford (Eds.), *Schooling and Disability* (pp. 59–76). Chicago: University of Chicago Press.

ANDERSON, L. (1989). Learners and learning. In M. Reynolds (Ed.), *Knowledge base for the beginning teacher* (pp. 85–104). New York: Pergamon Press.

BLOOM, B. (1984). The search for methods of group instruction as effective as one-to-one tutoring. *Educational Leadership, 41*(8), 4–17.

CASAS, J., & FURLONG, M. (1986). In search of an understanding and a responsible resolution to the Mexican-American educational dropout problem. *California Public Schools Forum, 1,* 45–53.

CHINN, P. (1982). Curriculum development for culturally different exceptional children. In C. Thomas & J. Thomas (Eds.), *Bilingual special education resource guide* (pp. 22–37). Phoenix, AZ: Oryx Press.

COX, J., DANIEL, N., & BOSTON, B. (1985). *Educating able learners.* Austin, TX: University of Texas Press.

DUNN, R., BEAUDRY, J., & KLAVAS, A. (1989). Survey of research on learning styles. *Educational Leadership, 46*(6), 50–57.

EBY, J., & SMUTNY, J. (1990). *A thoughtful overview of gifted education.* White Plains, NY: Longman.

FADLEY, J., & HOSLER, V. (1979). *Understanding the alpha child at home and at school.* Springfield, IL: Thomas.

FIRST, J. (1988). Immigrant students in U.S. public schools: Challenges and solutions. *Phi Delta Kappan, 70*(3), 205–210.

GAGNE, E. (1985). *The cognitive psychology of student learning.* Boston: Little, Brown.

GARDNER, J. (1961). *Excellence: Can we be equal and excellent too?* New York: Harper & Row.

GOOD, T., & BROPHY, J. (1987). *Looking in classrooms.* New York: Harper & Row.

JENCKS, C., et al. (1972). *Inequality.* New York: Basic Books.

KIDDER, T. (1989). *Among Schoolchildren.* Boston: Houghton Mifflin.

LEYTON, F. (1983). *The extent to which group instruction supplemented by mastery of the initial cognitive prerequisites approximates the learning effectiveness of one-to-one tutorial methods.* Doctoral dissertation, University of Chicago.

MAERHOFF, G. (1988). Withered hopes, stillborn dreams: The dismal panorama of urban schools. *Phi Delta Kappan, 69*(9), 633–638.

MASLOW, A. (1954). *Motivation and personality.* New York: Harper & Row.

MILNE, N. (1982). Aspects of dealing with the bilingual special education student. In C. Thomas & J. Thomas (Eds.), *Bilingual special education resource guide* (pp. 3–10). Phoenix, AZ: Oryx Press.

REYNOLDS, M. (1989). Students with special needs. In M. Reynolds (Ed.), *Knowledge base for the beginning teacher* (pp. 129–141). New York: Pergamon Press.

RIMM, S. (1986). *The underachievement syndrome: Causes and cures.* Watertown, WI: Apple.

SAPON-SHEVIN, M. (1989). Mild disabilities: In and out of special education. In D. Biklen, D. Ferguson & A. Ford (Eds.), *Schooling and disability* (pp. 107–177). Chicago: University of Chicago Press.

WATSON, D., NORTHCUTT, L., & RYDELL, L. (1989). Teaching bilingual students successfully. *Educational Leadership, 46*(5), 59–61.

WICK, J. (1973). *Educational measurement: Where are we going and how will we know when we get there?* Columbus, OH: Merrill.

Long-Term Planning of
School Programs

CURRICULUM DEVELOPMENT is among the most important planning responsibility of the professional teacher. The term *curriculum* "derives from the Latin word *currere,* meaning 'the course to be run' " (Eisner, 1985, p. 39). Some educators think of curriculum planning very narrowly as the plan for teaching subjects such as mathematics, language arts, reading, science, and history. Others think of the school curriculum much more broadly, including all the social and emotional experiences a child has in school, as well as the academic learning experiences.

In either case, the curriculum of a school is influenced by many forces, both past and present. History and tradition are powerful influences over what is taught in schools. The three Rs have served as the basis for planning in American schools for over 100 years and will continue to do so for many more. Social and political concerns cause the curriculum to evolve over time as various special interest groups influence state or local school boards to include new programs. Consider the recent additions of drug education and AIDS education programs to the curricula of many schools.

HOW SCHOOL CURRICULA ARE PLANNED

Evaluation and Use of Textbooks

One group who wields an enormous influence on school curricula are textbook authors and publishers, who decide what to include and what to exclude in the texts they distribute nationwide. Their motivation, of course, is to earn the largest possible profits, so they create textbooks that will appeal to the broadest possible market and offend no one. Some critics say that this results in texts that are dull and lifeless. If they are used as is, the curriculum of the school could then become dull and lifeless as well.

Some teachers have little awareness of their own values or their own curriculum orientations and beliefs. They tend to avoid making decisions about the curriculum they teach. In giving up their power to do so, they just follow orders, which are most often given by a source far removed from their own local school system. The orders come from textbooks. As Eisner (1985) observes:

> . . . at present the textbook holds a place of unparalleled importance in influencing what shall be taught in schools. The reasons for its importance are not difficult to determine. Consider the range of subject matters and tasks with which elementary school teachers must deal. The typical teacher teaching, say, the fourth grade in a self-contained classroom is responsible for the following: reading, language arts, arithmetic, social studies, science, music, art, and physical education. In addition to these areas, many elementary school teachers are responsible for health education, career awareness education, human relations education, and environmental education. . . . Given the variety of these demands, is it any wonder that many teachers—perhaps most—would welcome textbooks and other kinds of workbooks that in effect decide for them what children shall study, in what order, for what ends? (p. 31)

When a first-year teacher walks into the classroom, the textbooks are already there, arranged in formidable rows or piled in cumbersome stacks. They are difficult to ignore, especially if the novice teacher's own education was predominantly devoted to reading and reciting textbook material. A nonreflective teacher will, *without thinking*, distribute the textbooks and begin teaching on page 1, with the intent of plowing through the entire book by the end of the year.

Reflective teachers are more inquisitive and more independent in their use of textbooks. They ask questions of other teachers: How long have you been using these textbooks? How were they chosen? Which parts match the school or district curriculum guides? Which parts are most interesting to the students? What other resources are available?

Connie Muther, director of the Textbook Adoption Advisory Service, advises teachers to examine critically the textbooks they use for redundancy of information. Textbooks are usually formatted to present information in a spiraling sequence of increasing difficulty at each grade level. But she finds that most publishers include repetitive material year after year:

> This mindless repetition exists primarily because every teacher at every grade wants to teach, or have available to teach, everything. Therefore, publishers, who usually produce what customers want, include *almost* everything in every book. What happens to sequencing and spiraling when several teachers within a district begin each year on page one and proceed sequentially through the book, completing one-half to two-thirds by June? (Muther, 1987, p. 78)

What does happen? Less reflective teachers tend to think that the "approved" or "correct" curriculum is the one found in textbooks because it is written by "experts." They attempt to deliver the curriculum as written, without questioning its effects or attempting to adapt it to the needs of their students.

Reflective teachers consider decisions about curriculum planning to be within their jurisdiction, their domain of decision making. They consult with others, but they take responsibility for deciding which parts of a textbook to use in order to meet the needs of their own particular class and to match the goals and learning outcomes set by their state and local curriculum committees.

State Curriculum Guidelines

In the United States, each state has a department of education with responsibility for establishing guidelines for curriculum development. In the 1980s, many states revised their curriculum guidelines by inviting representative teachers and administrators to form committees with responsibility for revising the curricular goals for each major subject area. The various departments of education have published and distributed the resulting documents to all school districts they serve.

For example, the California State Department of Education, under the leadership of Bill Honig, has recently created two documents for each subject area. A *Framework* communicates the state committee's basic goals and expectations for each subject area, and a *Model Curriculum Guide* provides details for how the Frameworks can be translated into classroom experiences.

As an illustration of this curricular process, let us examine more closely one of California's Frameworks and Model Curriculum Guides. The *English–Language Arts Framework* was created by a committee of educators drawn from around the state. It was adopted by the California State Board of Education in 1986 and was published and distributed in 1987. It describes "overarching goals" of the curriculum that are:

> To prepare all students to function as informed and effective citizens in our democratic society.
> To prepare all students to function effectively in the world of work.
> To prepare all students to realize personal fulfillment (1987a).

The Framework then specifies eight essential elements of English-language arts programs that include (among others) these three:

> Integrating instruction in the language arts.
> Establishing a literature-based program.
> Learning to read by reading (1987a).

The *English–Language Arts Model Curriculum Guide* interprets these goals pertaining to reading and literature in the Framework by presenting teachers with "representative enabling activities" to use in their classrooms that will accomplish the purposes defined by the state committee. For example, in the primary grades, the *Guide* suggests the following:

> Kindergarten Through Grade Three
> The teacher, with the help of a library media specialist, assembles a classroom library of literary works. . . . Groups of students select from among these works in the classroom library, and each group decides on a method for dramatizing the selected work. Methods such as readers theater, puppetry, pantomime, or choral reading might be employed. Each group presents its selection to the entire class. Some of the selections might then be presented to other classes, parents, or to other audiences, or they might be videotaped for future showings. (1988, p. 7)

As in this illustrated example, the California Frameworks and Model Curriculum Guides emphasize learning experiences that are unusually active, engaging, and creative. The *History–Social Science Framework* (1987b) emphasizes the teaching of history, geography, and democratic values through the use of "new technologies, original source documents, debates, simulations, role playing, or whatever means that will bring the students into close encounters with powerful ideas, great events, major issues, significant trends, and the contributions of important men and women" (p. vii).

The California curriculum Frameworks encourage teachers to take a professional responsibility for creating curriculum. Some teachers find this responsibility to be overwhelming, and prefer to have more specific guidelines to follow and methods and strategies to use in reaching the state goals. Others welcome the opportunity to take a leadership role in the development of a curriculum that meets the needs of their students and communities. When teachers work together, on formal committees or informally as colleagues, they often find that they are able to support each other in interpreting state frameworks, gathering resources, clarifying goals, and making plans for attaining the goals.

How Curriculum Is Transformed in Practice

In response to state mandates or guidelines, school districts usually form committees of teachers and administrators to write or revise the curriculum documents that specify the goals and expectations, that is, the approved curriculum, for each subject and grade level in that district. Often these written curriculum guides also specify textbooks and tests that teachers may use. While some people may believe that these documents are the one and only curriculum in that district, reflective teachers recognize that there are really four different curricula in any school.

The *intended curriculum* is the explicit and approved one; usually it is written in the form of curriculum guides or lesson plans. However, close observation reveals an implicit or *hidden curriculum* that is not written anywhere but is pervasive nonetheless. It varies from teacher to teacher, depending on individual values and interests. In practice, teachers can all use the same lesson plan but teach strikingly different lessons depending on their values, knowledge about the subject, interests, and the time they have allotted to the lesson. The *null curriculum* is whatever the teacher deletes or omits because of lack of time, interest, or knowledge.

When school programs are evaluated, it is usually the documents that make up the intended curricula that are examined. But the actual *delivered curricula* may differ markedly from the intended, planned curriculum. This is because each teacher plans different lessons and delivers the intended curriculum in a unique way. Another transformation occurs as children receive the lessons taught by their teachers. Because each child varies in aptitude, interests, and preexisting knowledge and schema, the *experienced curriculum* is different for every student.

It is the classroom teacher who has both the right and the responsibility to weigh carefully the various elements influencing curriculum decisions, including personal values, interests, strengths, and weaknesses and the needs of the students, in order to plan and deliver a curriculum that meets the guidelines of the state and the school district. This chapter will examine the role of the classroom teacher in planning the curriculum for an entire academic year.

Curriculum Orientations

Most schools have a written curriculum that documents and describes the learning experiences that have been planned for that school by its faculty. Within each subject area, the curriculum may describe which elements should be emphasized and which should be minimized. The curriculum may even specify the methods teachers should use to instruct their students. In some countries, where there is one nationally mandated curriculum, there may be great uniformity from school to school and classroom to classroom. There is no national curriculum in the United States; the curriculum of a school is determined locally, leading to great curricular variations among schools and classrooms.

Curriculum decisions are highly influenced by the values of those who are making the choices. When educators discuss what to include in a course or how to teach a certain subject, several different viewpoints are usually expressed, depending on the values of each individual. For example, should the subject of mathematics emphasize memorization of math facts and formulas, or should it emphasize the logical processes that can be employed to discover mathematical relationships? Should schools teach the religious or the scientific theories of the development of the universe? What types of reading materials are suitable for students to read at various grade levels? These and other curriculum questions cause heated debates, since each individual has a unique curriculum orientation and values.

Eisner (1985) describes five different curriculum orientations in order to provide educators with an awareness of how their own orientation may compare with those of others. He believes that by knowing all five, teachers may be able to expand their own options in curriculum planning. An individual's personal values, experiences, and beliefs about what is important in the world contribute greatly to the type of orientation held. In many ways, one's curriculum orientation is related to one's philosophy of education, as they are both concerned with the goals of education, the relative importance of subject matter, and how teachers and students ought to interact.

Eisner labels one of the oldest and most basic orientations to curriculum *academic rationalism*. Educators with this orientation argue that the goal of education is to teach the basic fields of study and academic disciplines that have traditionally been known as a liberal education. These academic disciplines include mathematics, literature, science, and history. Within these disciplines, academic rationalists believe that the curriculum should consist of "the very best, the most powerful, the most profound, the grandest of man's intellectual works" (Eisner, 1985, p. 68). The role of the teacher is to help students acquire the content, concepts, and ideas of these classic academic disciplines.

In an elementary school, an academic rationalist is likely to believe that the traditional subjects are important and is likely to teach them through lecture, reading, and discussion. Tests and essays are employed to measure what students have learned.

A contrasting curriculum orientation is one that develops students' *cognitive processes*. Teachers having this orientation would not concur with academic rationalists that there is one established content for courses. Instead, their major goal is to help students "learn how to learn" (Eisner, 1985, p. 62). The content of the curriculum is selected for its potential in causing students to use their problem-solving and information-gathering abilities. The role of the teacher is to generate problematic situations for students to investigate and solve.

In an elementary school, teachers with a cognitive process orientation would be likely to combine traditional courses into thematic units, where the major goal is not to teach content but to teach students processes such as the scientific method, research, problem solving, and communication skills. The methods this teacher might employ include experimentation, independent research, and group investigations. While tests might be employed to measure student achievement, these teachers are likely to require students to turn in and report on projects that show what they have learned.

A third orientation is one that emphasizes *personal relevance,* meaning that the curriculum builds on the students' interests. This view is held by educators who believe that learning is a developmental process and that students will learn best from the "inside out" (Eisner, 1985, p. 70). The teacher's role is to construct educational situations that are based on students' present experiences, interests, and needs.

Elementary school teachers who are oriented to personal relevance are likely to provide their students with many opportunities for free choice. Children will be encouraged to select their own reading materials based on their interests. Students may negotiate with teachers about what they want to study and how they will do it. A method of evaluation that is used in this orientation is to have students work on contracts that specify what they are going to do. A completed contract is viewed as a successful school experience.

A *social perspective* in curriculum is an orientation that attempts to develop a critical consciousness among children of the major issues of society. Given this perspective, the curriculum focuses on controversial social issues and is designed to encourage students to take an active role in improving the society in which they live. The role of the teacher using this orientation is to make students aware of the important social issues of their time and culture and to prompt them to debate alternatives, make informed judgments, and act on them.

While this is rarely employed for the entire school curriculum, many teachers with this orientation find ways to incorporate social issues into the conventional curriculum. The elementary teacher with this orientation is likely to select reading materials for their social relevance and is likely to use discussion, class meetings, role playing, and simulation activities. Evaluation is likely to center on the degree to which students show that they have developed mature understanding of social problems and are taking an active role in solving them.

The fifth orientation toward curriculum planning is concerned not with the values and content of the curriculum but with the way the curriculum is constructed. A *technological* orientation stresses a scientific approach using measurable goals and objectives. The role of the teacher is to plan the curriculum in a sequential and orderly manner by specifying a list of sequential objectives with tests that demonstrate the students' mastery of each objective.

Elementary teachers with a technological orientation are likely to emphasize sequential learning of the basic skills in mathematics, reading, grammar, and other curriculum areas. Carefully planned lessons teach new information and skills in small steps, with much opportunity for practice. Pretests and posttests are likely to be used to show how much students have gained from each learning experience.

It is unlikely that teachers have only one of these curriculum orientations. Instead, each teacher may have one that is the most preferred or dominant orientation but can see value in some of the others as well. By recognizing and clarifying your own preferences, you can understand why you make the decisions you do about what to teach and how to teach it. If you understand that other teachers may have different orientations, it is more likely that you will be able to have productive discussions with them even when strongly held differences in values and orientations occur.

Tyler's Basic Principles of Curriculum Planning

Ralph Tyler, an educator who has won unusually high esteem for his work on curriculum planning, observed that in planning educational goals, teachers should first consider the needs of the learners, second the needs of society or what he termed "contemporary life," and then consider the suggestions or recommendations of subject matter specialists. Tyler (1949) observed that "many educational programs do not have clearly defined purposes" (p. 3). To improve this situation, he proposed four fundamental questions that should be considered in planning any curriculum:

1. What educational purposes should the school seek to attain?
2. What educational experiences can be provided that are likely to attain these purposes?
3. How can these educational experiences be effectively organized?
4. How can we determine whether these purposes are being attained? (p. 1)

Reflective educators are very likely to use Tyler's basic principles in planning, organizing, and evaluating their programs, because they are remarkably similar to the process of reflective thinking. Essentially, Tyler is suggesting that teachers consider a classroom event such as curriculum planning by observing the needs of students, gather information from subject matter specialists and others, make a judgment about an educational purpose, consider strategies that are likely to attain these purposes, select and order the strategies to be used, and then begin the process over again by evaluating the effectiveness of the curriculum plan.

While reflective teachers do not memorize these questions word for word, they do carry with them the fundamental notion of each one:

1. What shall we teach?
2. How shall we teach it?
3. How can we organize it?
4. How can we evaluate it?

They ask themselves these questions each year because it is likely that there will be subtle or dramatic changes in their communities, subject matter materials, students, or themselves from year to year that cause them to reexamine their curricula. On reexamination, they may confirm that they wish to continue to teach the same curriculum in the same way or that they wish to modify some aspects of the curriculum. As teachers themselves grow in experience and skills, most greet each new year as an opportunity to improve what they had accomplished the year before. Rather than continue to teach the same subjects the same ways year after year, reflective teachers tend to experiment with new ways of teaching and organizing the curriculum.

An interesting way to think about reflective and nonreflective teachers is that after teaching for 20 years, a reflective teacher has accumulated 20 years of experience, while a nonreflective teacher has had 1 year of experience 20 times. Reflective teachers want to have an active role in the decision-making processes of their schools, and curricular decisions are the ones that count the most. They also display a very strong sense of responsibility for making good curriculum choices and decisions, ones that will ultimately result in valuable growth and learning for their students.

Bloom's Taxonomy of Educational Objectives

Benjamin Bloom, a student of Ralph Tyler's, extended Tyler's basic principles in a most useful way. Bloom and his colleagues Max Engelhart, Edward Furst, Walker Hill, and David Krathwohl (1956) attempted to respond to the first of Tyler's questions as completely as possible. In meetings with other teachers, they brainstormed and listed all the possible purposes of education, all the possible educational objectives that they could think of or had observed over many years of classroom experience. Then they attempted to organize and classify all of these possible objectives into what is now known as the *Taxonomy of Educational Objectives*. Their intent was to provide teachers with a ready source of possible objectives so that they could select the ones that fit the needs of their own students and circumstances. It was also intended to help teachers clarify for themselves how to achieve their educational goals. A third purpose of the Taxonomy was to help teachers communicate more precisely with each other.

The Taxonomy first subdivides educational purposes into three domains of learning: cognitive, affective, and psychomotor. The *cognitive domain* deals with "the recall or recognition of knowledge and the development of intellectual abilities and skills"; the *affective domain* deals with "interests, attitudes, and values"; and the *psychomotor domain* concerns the development of manipulative and motor skills (Bloom, 1956, p. 7).

The cognitive domain is further subdivided into six hierarchical levels of educational objectives that have become very well known and used as the basis for many elementary school curriculum plans. These six levels are shown here and will be described in detail in Chapter Six.

Hierarchy of Educational Objectives
in the Cognitive Domain

HIGHER-LEVEL OBJECTIVES	Level 6: Evaluation (make judgments, opinions)
	Level 5: Synthesis (create an original product)
	Level 4: Analysis (see the relationships among elements)
	Level 3: Application (use concepts in life situations)
LOWER-LEVEL OBJECTIVES	Level 2: Comprehension (understand the main idea)
	Level 1: Knowledge (recognize and remember facts)

As Bloom intended, the Taxonomy has had a powerful effect on planning for teaching. In the 1960s and 1970s, many educators and laypeople observed that in most classrooms, the vast majority of learning experiences were intended to develop knowledge and comprehension, but that fewer experiences caused learners to apply, analyze, synthesize, or evaluate what they learned. Using the Taxonomy as a guide, reflective teachers have actively sought to provide learning experiences at the higher levels as well as the lower ones. They recognize that using high-level learning experiences will better satisfy the needs of their learners to understand fully a subject than mere memorization of facts and comprehension of main ideas alone.

Writing Educational Goals

All three domains are considered to be important in the elementary curriculum because together they support the growth and development of the whole child. In selecting goals for a school or a classroom, it is essential to consider the needs of the whole child and to create goals that are developmentally appropriate for children. The reflective teacher is one who carefully considers what is important for children to learn and writes goals accordingly.

Cognitive goals are expressed in curriculum development as goals to master content or subject matter knowledge. For example, between kindergarten and eighth grade, students are expected to master many of the basic facts and concepts associated with content areas such as literature, math, biology, physics, astronomy, American history, and world geography.

Elementary educators also write many psychomotor goals, including many processes and skills that involve both the mind and the body in the psychomotor domain. For example, elementary students are expected to learn how to read, write, calculate, solve problems, observe, experiment, research, interpret, make maps, and create works of art, music, and other crafts.

Affective goals are viewed by most elementary teachers as auxiliary goals, related more to the development of character than to the skills or intellects of their students. Typically, elementary schools emphasize the affective goals of good citizenship; self-esteem; acceptance of individual and racial differences; and appreciation of art, music, and other aspects of our cultural heritage.

For long-term planning, the clarification of schoolwide goals results in a greater likelihood of accomplishing these goals successfully. This is due to the consistency of experiences that students have in every classroom and with every adult in the school. Many school districts have statements of philosophy and goals written in policy documents, but they may or may not be articulated and applied in the schools themselves. For effective change to take place, the school faculty must consider its common goals each year, articulate them together, and communicate them to the students through words and deeds.

Within a classroom, each teacher has the right and the responsibility to articulate a set of educational goals for the students. Working alone or with teammates at the same grade level or subject area, the classroom teacher may wish to articulate two to four *year-long goals* in each of the three domains that are suited for that particular group of students. Tyler (1949) encourages the teacher to select a small number of highly important goals, "since time is required to change the behavior patterns of human beings. An educational program is not effective if so much is attempted that little is accomplished" (p. 33).

Educational goals vary widely from person to person and from community to community. The goals of private schools affiliated with a church will reflect the values of the religious community it serves. Public school goals vary, depending on the philosophy of its teachers, its administrators, and the surrounding community.

The values expressed in this book are to create a learning environment and learning experiences that enhance students' intrinsic motivation and stimulate their critical and creative thinking. The following are examples of educational goals in the social sciences that fit these values in the three domains described above.

> Cognitive goal: Students will understand the differences and similarities among political and economic systems compared to those of the United States.
>
> Psychomotor goal: Students will be able to use maps and a compass to locate directions and plan a route from one location to another.
>
> Affective goal: Students will be able to express their opinions, make suggestions, and otherwise participate in democratic decision making in the classroom on social and academic concerns.

Classroom Themes to Build a Sense of Community

Some teachers like to express their educational goals through the use of a year-long *theme* or statement of purpose for the entire class. Occasionally an entire school will focus on a single schoolwide theme for a year. As an illustration, the principal of a private school near Chicago introduced the new school year by challenging teachers to find creative ways to apply the theme of "caring and sharing" for a year. Banners and signs with this theme were erected in the halls. Teachers led their students in discussions of how each class could display their caring and sharing to each other, to the environment, and to the community. This theme was actually a schoolwide affective goal carried out in a highly visible way to motivate students to develop caring and sharing attitudes.

Other ways that schoolwide themes can be used successfully are to enlist the cooperation of students in developing school slogans, flags, posters, or songs that express a particular theme or otherwise represent the school in a positive, growth-enhancing manner. We learn from sports competitions that students enjoy thinking of themselves as members of a powerful or winning school, and this sense of power or strength can be developed by any school, in any setting, just by capitalizing on its strengths and building a sense of pride in its academic program as well as its sports program. The result is a schoolwide sense of community that tends to motivate purposeful and responsible behavior among the students.

Even when a school has no common theme, an individual teacher can use the same idea in the classroom. When I was teaching elementary school, I had my students give a name to our class community each year. At the beginning of each year, the class brainstormed and selected such names as Sunshine Valley, Somewhere Over the Rainbow, Prairieville, and Curiosity Corner. Aside from the name, we selected a descriptive phrase that communicated our particular sense of purpose that year. Those that corresponded to the above titles were "Reaching for the sun," "Exploring the yellow brick roads of math, science, reading, and writing," "Digging until we find paydirt," and "Together we'll find out who, what, when, where, why, and how."

I found that the use of such a unifying theme had the effect of developing a bond among all members of the class. The shared sense of purpose worked to eliminate discipline problems and to promote academic motivation.

Translating Goals into Outcome Statements

As described above, an educational *goal* is generally accepted as a general long-term statement of an aim or purpose of education. For example, most schools have a goal of teaching students how to read and write, another to ensure that they understand the cultural heritage of the United States, and another to help them develop attitudes and habits of good citizenship.

But to translate goals into operational plans, it is necessary to specify what *outcomes* are expected as a consequence of being in school and taking part in the planned curriculum. Elliot Eisner (1985) alerts educators to be aware that goals express intentions but that other factors may occur that alter the intentions of the educational process. According to Eisner, "Outcomes are essentially what one ends up with, intended or not, after some form of engagement" (p. 120).

Written outcome statements are used to translate goals into actions. They describe what students will be able to do as a result of their educational program. If educators can envision what it is they want students to be able to do or know after a series of learning experiences, they can plan with that outcome in mind. Learning outcomes generally describe actions, processes, and products that the student will accomplish in a given period of time.

Writing Useful and Appropriate Outcome Statements

The wording of outcome statements must be general but not vague. This is a subtle but important distinction. Some school documents contain goal statements such as "to develop the full potential of each individual." What does this mean to you? Can you interpret it in a meaningful way in your classroom? Can you translate it into programs? Probably not. This goal statement is so general and vague that it cannot be put into operation, and it would be very difficult to determine whether it is being attained or not.

An outcome statement should be general, but it should also describe how you want your students to change over time and what you want them to be able to do at the end of the term of study. Some examples of useful cognitive outcome statements are:

> Students will be able to recognize and name all the counting numbers from 1 to 20.

> Students will demonstrate that they understand how technology has changed the world by creating a time line, graph, chart, or set of models to show the effects of technology on one aspect of human life.

Examples of psychomotor (skill and process) outcome statements are:

> Students will be able to weigh and measure a variety of objects using metric units of measurement.

> Students will be able to compose and edit works on a word processor.

Examples of affective outcome statements are:

> Students will demonstrate that they enjoy reading by selecting books and other reading materials and spending time reading in class and at home.

> Students will demonstrate that they tolerate, accept, and prize cultural, ethnic, and other individual differences in human beings by working cooperatively and productively with students of various ethnic groups.

Yearly outcome statements can be written for only one subject or across several disciplines. Outcome statements can also be written for a shorter period of time, such as a term or a month. They are used as guides for planning curriculum and learning experiences for that length of time. At the end of a given period of time, it is the responsibility of the teacher to assess whether the outcome has been successfully demonstrated by the students. If not, it may be necessary to repeat the same outcome statement or modify it to ensure that it can be met.

Some outcome statements may need to be modified because they are too vague. Compare the original vague statement with the improved second statement:

> *Original Outcome Statement:* Students will be able to demonstrate that they know the U.S. Constitution.

> *Improved Outcome Statement:* Students will be able to describe the key concepts in the articles of the U.S. Constitution and give examples of how they are applied in American life today.

Other outcome statements may need to be modified because they are too difficult for the students. Compare these:

> *Original Outcome Statement:* Fourth-grade students will demonstrate that they know the key concepts of the Bill of Rights by creating a time line showing how each has evolved over the past 200 years.

> *Improved Outcome Statement:* Fourth-grade students will be able to create an illustrated mural showing pictorial representations of each of the articles in the Bill of Rights.

Some outcome statements may need to be improved by adding learning opportunities that will stimulate student interest and motivation to learn the material. Consider the following:

> *Original Outcome Statement:* Students will be able to recite the Bill of Rights.

> *Improved Outcome Statement:* Students will be able to work in cooperative groups to plan and perform a skit showing how the United States would differ with and without the Bill of Rights.

Outcome statements are useful guides for educational planning, but they must be adapted to fit the needs of a particular teacher and class. For this reason, curriculum planning is an evolving process. A curriculum is never a finished product; it is constantly being changed and improved from day to day and year to year.

CURRICULUM PLANNING IN THE SUBJECT AREAS

Long-Term Planning in Mathematics

Mathematics has had a prominent place in the elementary curriculum since the first American schools were founded. It has long been believed that, for students to be able to function in a modern technological society, learning math computation skills is as essential as learning to read. But recently there has been increased awareness of the need for teaching students how to use mathematical concepts in problem solving as well. The National Council of Teachers of Mathematics (NCTM), as noted by Campbell and Fey (1988), recommend the following:

1. Problem solving must be the focus of school mathematics.
2. Basic skills in mathematics must be defined to encompass more than computational facility.
3. Mathematics programs must take full advantage of the power of calculators and computers at all grade levels.
4. The success of mathematics programs and student learning must be evaluated by a wider range of measures than conventional testing.
5. More mathematics study must be required for all students, and flexible curriculums with a greater range of options must be designed to accomodate the diverse needs of the student population. (pp. 53–54)

At the same time, "data from the National Assessment of Educational Progress (NAEP) and from college entrance testing programs reveal a discouraging pattern of mathematics achievement, particularly in problem-solving and higher-order thinking skills. International studies show that U.S. students lag far behind their counterparts in other highly developed countries—those countries we compete with in science, technology, and business" (McKnight, 1987, p. 14).

The challenge to the elementary teacher, then, is to plan a year-long mathematics curriculum that teaches students to carry out arithmetic operations, apply them in problem-solving situations, and use the calculator and computer as problem-solving tools. Teachers must also provide options to fit students' varying capabilities.

Figure 4–1 on page 92 shows an example of the year-long plan used by Jane Stevens in her sixth-grade classroom. Because Jane teaches in Texas, her plan must include the *Texas Essential Elements* that have been mandated by the state legislature.

Long-Term Planning in Language Arts

Two of the original three Rs were reading and writing. In the high school and college curricula, these have been combined in the academic subject known as English. In the elementary curriculum, the term *language arts* or *communication arts* includes reading, writing, speaking, and listening skills. Together these subjects can make up as much as 50 percent of the school day in the primary grades.

P L A N N I N G

YEAR-LONG PLAN IN MATHEMATICS

**by Jane Stevens, Sixth-Grade Teacher,
Dunn Elementary School, Arlington, Texas**

The Texas Essential Elements for sixth-grade mathematics include:

1. Concepts and skills associated with the understanding of whole numbers and the place value system.
2. Basic operations on numbers (addition, subtraction, multiplication, and division).
3. Experience in solving problems by selecting and matching strategies to given situations.
4. Measurement concepts and skills using metric and customary units.
5. Properties and relationships of geometric shapes.
6. The representation of numbers on a line and a graph.
7. The use of probability and statistics to collect and interpret data.

My sixth-grade class is capable of doing grade level work with modification of pacing, length of assignments, and lateral extensions. I meet the state requirements by planning six 6-week units to correspond to our district's reporting periods. Problem solving is one of our district's main concerns, so we build problem-solving activities into each unit. Our textbook provides a 5-point checklist of problem-solving strategies that can be applied to each unit. We also use an additional resource book that is full of stated (word) problems. But what my class enjoys most is writing their own problems with their classmates' names in them. This year I plan to let my students "publish" their word problems by writing them on the computer and distributing them to the class.

Unit One:	Review of Basic Facts and Place Value
	Number Operations (addition, subtraction)
Unit Two:	Number Operations (multiplication and division)
	Begin Fractions
Unit Three:	Fractions, Decimals, Percent, Ratio, and Proportion
Unit Four:	Geometry, Perimeter, Area, and Volume
Unit Five:	Measurement in Metric and Conventional Units
Unit Six:	Graphing and Probability

The teaching of language arts has changed greatly in the last third of the twentieth century. Prior to that time, the elementary curriculum contained subjects named *reading, spelling,* and *grammar.* It was believed that if students learned how to read, spell, and use grammar and punctuation correctly, they would be literate and able to communicate effectively. But research on the developmental learning of language has led to major changes in philosophy and practice in this subject area. Chomsky (1969) demonstrated that children learn to speak as they engage in talk with others around them, gradually comprehending the rule systems in the process. Sulzby and Teale's (1987) investigation of children's early writing revealed it to be a developmental process similar to that of learning how to speak.

Graves (1983) and Murray (1984) have provided models of teaching writing to young children that treat writing as a continuous process of prewriting experiences, first drafts, editing conferences, revising, and sharing. Teachers who use these methods report that children show increased confidence in their ability to communicate in writing.

What has emerged is a commitment by many (but not all) schools to radically restructure their language arts curriculum away from separate rule-dependent subjects of reading, spelling, grammar, and writing toward a holistic, process-oriented approach. In schools with a *whole language curriculum,* children listen to or read literary works, write in journals, participate in editing groups, and speak for a variety of purposes. They gradually assimilate the proper grammar, punctuation, spelling, and other conventions of the English language.

Teachers planning a year-long curriculum in the language arts have a great deal of discretion regarding their methods, procedures, and materials. In many schools, the basal reading, spelling, and English texts are being replaced by children's literature, journals, and class-published stories and poems. Figure 4–2 on pages 94–95 shows the year-long plan of a classroom teacher, Ginny Bailey, who has made the change to a whole language curriculum.

Throughout the 1989–90 school year, Ginny Bailey experimented with using the whole language approach to teaching reading and writing. Rather than rely on basal readers and workbooks, she wanted to use real children's literature, in the form of library materials and paperback books, as her texts. In the summer of 1990, Ginny and Judy Yount, the other first-grade teacher in her school, worked together to translate the State of Illinois Outcome Statements and the school district's written curriculum objectives into a form that would fit their philosophy and the particular needs of the children in their school.

"We began our plan by deciding that we would use thematic units to accomplish the state outcomes," Ginny Bailey said. "We quickly discovered that language arts cannot be separated from science, social studies, and mathematics when you use a unit approach, so we incorporated those areas into our planning. Both of us had attended numerous classes and workshops on using thematic units and had read every book we could find on the subject of using whole language in the classroom. But now it was time to sit down and make our plan for the coming school year. We began by going through the science, math, and social studies curriculum guides to familiarize ourselves with what had to be covered in those areas. We then studied the Language Arts Outcome Statements. Our plan was to teach one or two thematic units a month, depending on the length of the units."

P L A N N I N G

YEAR-LONG PLAN IN LANGUAGE ARTS FOR FIRST GRADE

by Ginny Bailey and Judy Yount, Woodland School, Carpentersville, Illinois, Barrington Community Unified School District

The State of Illinois has six Outcome Statements for Language Arts.

As a result of their schooling, students will be able to:

▼ read, comprehend, interpret, evaluate, and use written material
▼ listen critically and analytically
▼ write standard English in a grammatical, well-organized manner
▼ use spoken language effectively in formal and informal situations
▼ understand how and why language functions and evolves

My teammate, Judy Yount, and I like to use a multidisciplinary approach for our language arts program. We use themes that may be related to social studies, literature, or science, but all of them incorporate and emphasize language activities. In each unit, students read, listen, write, speak, and discuss the way language is used. Our themes change from year to year, but this is a typical example:

September
"Author Study" by Norman Bridwell (Clifford Books)—1 week
"Changes"—3 weeks

1. Butterflies and moths
2. Frogs
3. Colors
4. Apples
5. Seasons
6. Self

October
"Zoo Animals"—4 weeks

November
"Nutrition" (Thanksgiving)—3 weeks
"Five Senses"—1 week

Long-Term Planning in Science

As a subject in the elementary curriculum, science consists of a survey of the basic scientific ideas in the academic disciplines of earth science, biology, chemistry, physics, and environmental studies. Often the subject of health is linked to the science curriculum in elementary schools. There are two sharply different processes by which science is taught at the elementary level: the content approach and the process approach.

December
"Five Senses" (continued) — 3 weeks

      1. Cookies
      2. Christmas

January
"Families" — 4 weeks

      1. Self
      2. Family members
      3. Homes

February
"Earth" — 2 weeks

      1. Day and night
      2. Forces

"Feelings" — 2 weeks

March
"Feelings" (continued) — 1 week
"Farms" — 2 weeks

      1. Rocks
      2. Animals
      3. Spring
      4. Insects
      5. Plants

April
"Farms" (continued) — 3 weeks
"Sun's Family" (planets) — 1 week

May–June
"Community Helpers" — 3 weeks
"Transportation" — 2 weeks

Some textbooks are oriented toward teaching science as a collection of facts, laws, principles, and theories that have been found to be important in each of the science disciplines. When this content-oriented approach is used as the basis for curriculum planning in science, students are expected to read, comprehend, discuss, and take tests to demonstrate their mastery of the subject matter. This academic orientation toward science assumes that content is what students must learn at the elementary level in order to be able to understand science in later schooling.

A very different process orientation toward science emerged in the late twentieth century with widely disseminated school programs such as the Science A Process Approach (SAPA), the Science Curriculum Improvement Study (SCIS), and the Elementary Science Study (ESS). These programs provide elementary students with hands-on experience in investigating scientific principles and relationships.

Project 2061 is an educational study group chartered in 1985 to recommend changes in science education. It is made up of members of the scientific community and supported by the American Association for the Advancement of Science (AAAS), the Carnegie Corporation, and the Andrew W. Mellon Foundation. The initial recommendation of Project 2061 is that the science curriculum should "treat science as a body of developing ideas, a way of thinking and conducting inquiry" (Rutherford & Ahlgren, 1988, p. 85). Project 2061 wants children to experience the methods and processes scientists use to imagine possibilities, speculate on causes, hypothesize effects, gather and weigh evidence, and reach conclusions.

Educators who believe in teaching science processes use fewer textbooks and more laboratory experiences. These teachers believe that students must learn how to *do* science in order to understand it. The curriculum is made up of a series of laboratory and experimental situations in which students observe, hypothesize, experiment, and evaluate their results in each topic of science. They may test rocks or create a model of plate techtonics for earth science. They may observe the moon or simulate an eclipse for astronomy or collect and classify plants and engage in microscopic examinations of pond water for biology. They may build and test simple machines for physics.

Reflective teachers recognize that the process approach provides students with many more opportunities for developing their critical and creative thinking about science than the textbook-centered, content-oriented approach does. While some school districts may provide kits of equipment for each topic in science, others may provide little or no science materials beyond the basic textbook. Many excellent science teachers become adept at scrounging and locating inexpensive equipment at garage sales to make their science programs work.

An example of a long-term plan for a process-oriented science curriculum is shown in Figure 4–3 on pages 98–99.

Tim's long-term plan uses a number of activities taken from the publications of the Activities that Integrate Math and Science (AIMS) Foundation. An example of an AIMS activity is presented in Figure 4–4 on page 100.

Long-Term Planning in Social Studies

As in science, there is a content-oriented approach and a process-oriented approach to the development of the elementary social studies curriculum. Those educators committed to an academic or content-oriented view of social studies believe that students need to know and understand the important facts, persons, events, and sequences in the history of our country and the world. Also important to the academic orientation toward social studies are the important concepts that distinguish various cultures and the basic facts about world geography. Recent critics of American schools have decried the lack of knowledge of history and geography among

American young people. Televised tests and magazine quizzes have demonstrated that many young people lack knowledge about the place names and locations of geographical areas. Content-oriented curriculum planners seek to improve this condition by providing history and geography courses that emphasize knowledge and comprehension objectives to teach facts and concepts.

Process-oriented curriculum planners believe that instead of memorizing facts, names, places, and dates, learners should experience the processes of acquiring information on their own. By teaching students how to do research in social studies and how to use tools such as maps, globes, atlases, charts, graphs, and other resources, they will be able to find information when the occasion demands it. The credo of this orientation toward curriculum development can be summed up in the phrase "Give a man a fish and he will be hungry the next day; teach him to fish and he'll never go hungry again." Process-oriented teachers tend to emphasize the higher-level objectives of Bloom's Taxonomy.

Decision making is also a key focus in the process-oriented approach to teaching social studies. Harlan Cleveland defined social studies as "the study of how citizens in a society make personal and public decisions on issues that affect their destiny" (in Bragaw and Hartoonian, 1988, p. 9). To accomplish this, Bragaw and Hartoonian suggest that the curriculum planner must make sure that students:

1. Develop an information base in the social sciences.
2. Think using the logic and patterns of history and the social sciences.
3. Communicate with others about social science data.
4. Make enlightened personal and policy decisions and participate in civic activities.

The students of Jean Malvaso-Zingaro at School No. 6 in Rochester, New York are involved in the long-term planning for their classroom. For example, in our studies of the Genessee River Valley, the class became very interested in the history of the Erie Canal. They decided to study it in depth. The children did extensive research on the building of the canal and its impact on the development of the city of Rochester, where their school is located.

At the students' urging, the class spent several months visiting locations where the canal was originally located and where it is actually in use today. They took a boat ride on the canal and went through the lock system to experience what the early canal riders experienced. The children learned how the locks worked, what their purpose was, and how the water moved from one lock to another.

As the product of their research, the children decided to put a slide presentation together with a narrative about the history of the canal from its inception to the present day. Heading this project was a girl named Tonjenika. She would come to school very early and stay after school was over to work on this project. She took charge and produced a beautiful finished presentation.

This behavior was in sharp contrast to Tonjenika's first day of school, when she had acted very obstinate and told Jean she didn't want to be in her class. When Jean gave her the opportunity to work on this project, she proved to be a loving and intelligent young lady.

YEAR-LONG PLAN IN SCIENCE FOR FIRST GRADE

by Tim Curbo, Hawthorne School, San Francisco Unified School District

The Guidelines from the California Framework on Science that Tim uses:

First grade students will:

- ▼ Participate in taking care of living things
- ▼ Classify objects according to given criteria
- ▼ Work with simple science equipment in a skillful and safe manner
- ▼ Identify the parts of a plant
- ▼ Identify a variety of animals and some of their characteristics
- ▼ Recognize and use a magnet, a mirror, and a magnifying lens
- ▼ Recognize that energy exists in several forms
- ▼ Recognize that environmental changes are caused by the sun
- ▼ Describe the seasons
- ▼ Recognize the components of good health (rest, exercise, diet, dental hygiene, cleanliness, safety)

I meet these requirements by planning a 2-hour period every Friday morning, using cooperative learning groups for most activities. Many of the activities I plan come from a resource called *Activities Integrating Math and Science* (known as *AIMS*). I divide the year into monthly units as follows:

Sept.: **Bears, Bears, Bears**
Children observe, classify, estimate, predict, collect and record data, measure, compare, and make generalizations and hypotheses about bears.

Oct.: **Other Animals**
Characteristics and Classification (AIMS Animal Crackers)
Zoo field trip

The year-long social studies curriculum for Jean's sixth grade was developed by the team of sixth-grade teachers to focus upon the Genessee River Valley, of which they are a part. The curriculum they developed is outlined in the following perspective. It is structured to develop a knowledge base about eight historical periods of the region and how the geography has affected people's lives in the area. Students are helped to think like social scientists in this study, since the plan is based on a series of questions that the students must try to answer. Students have many opportunities to communicate their findings to each other and to the community as a whole through writings, maps, dioramas, and slide presentations.

Nov.: **Growing Up Healthy**
How Tall Are You? (AIMS)
A Weigh We Go (AIMS)
All Aboard the Nutrition Express (AIMS)

Dec.: **Weather**
A rain machine (water cycle)
Thermometers
Weather Wear (AIMS)

Jan.: **Plants**
Kinds of plants and their needs
Sponge Garden (AIMS)
Seed dissection

Feb.: **The Earth, the Sun, and Beyond**
Earth, our home
The sun by day, the moon by night
Our neighbor planets

Mar.: **Our Senses**

Apr.: **Snails**
My Snail's Tale (AIMS)
Portrait of an Average Snail (AIMS)
The Slime Trail (AIMS)

May: **Dinosaurs**
A dinosaur zoo
Bodysaurus (AIMS)

June: **Magnets and Magnifying Lens**

Creating Time Lines That Fit Your Goals and Outcome Statements

Time is the scarcest resource in the elementary school. Reflective teachers who organize time wisely are more successful in delivering their curriculum than are teachers who fail to consider it. Teachers who simply start each subject on page 1 of every textbook and hope to finish the text by June are frequently surprised. In some cases they finish a text early in the year, but more often the school year ends and children never get to the subjects discussed near the end of the textbook. In math, some classes never get to geometry year after year. In social studies, history after

ANIMAL CRACKERS

from the Activities that Integrate Math and Science Foundation

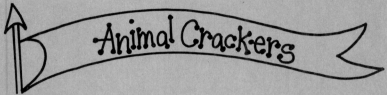

I. **Topic Area**
   Sorting and categorizing

II. **Introductory Statement**
   Students will sort animal crackers into groups. Students will estimate the number of cookies in one box.

III. **Key Question**
   How can we find out how many kinds of animals are in a box of animal crackers?

IV. **Math Skills**
   a. Counting
   b. Estimating
   c. Sorting
   d. Whole number computation

   Science Processes
   a. Observing and classifying
   b. Estimating
   c. Gathering and recording data
   d. Interpreting data

V. **Materials**
   • One box of animal crackers for each group of 6-8 students
   • One estimation sheet for each group (see pattern sheet #1)
   • 16 copies of cages for each group (see pattern sheet #2)

VI. **Background Information**
   Animal crackers vary by brand. Be sure that the animal crackers you plan to use clearly show which animal is being represented.

VII. **Management**
   1. This is small group teacher-directed activity.
   2. Allow about 20 minutes for each group.

VIII. **Advanced Preparation**
   1. Make one copy of estimation sheet for each group. (See pattern sheet #1)
   2. Make 8-10 copies of cages (pattern sheet #2). Cut papers in half so there is one cage per sheet. (These papers can be reused with each group.)

IX. **Procedure**
   1. Show the box of animal crackers to the group. Have the students talk about what might be inside.
   2. Have the students estimate the number of crackers in a box. Record these guesses on the estimation sheet.
   3. Open the box and have the children count the cookies. Record the number on the estimation sheet and circle it. Compare the estimations to the actual amount.

4. Ask the key question: How can we find out how many kinds of animals are in a box of animal crackers?
5. Have the students name the animals they recognize. Write each animal name on a cage and have the students sort the animals into the proper cages.

X. **Discussion**
   1. How many kinds of animal crackers were in the box?
   2. Which cage has the most? The fewest?
   3. Do any cages have the same number of animals?
   4. If we combined the animals in these cages (indicate 2 or 3 cages), how many would there be altogether?
   5. Would another box of animal crackers be exactly the same as this one? What might be different?

XI. **Extensions**
   1. Combine the data from each group and make a class graph that shows how many of each kind of animal were found.
   2. Have the children think of other ways to sort the crackers.
   3. Compare the number of cookies found in each box. Discuss the meaning of the weight shown on the box.

XII. **Curriculum Coordinates**
   Language Arts
   1. Combine this activity with a unit on zoo animals.
   2. Have the students choose an animal they like best and write or dictate a few sentences on why they like it. Make a class book.
   Art
   1. Students can draw or paint pictures of animals. These can be cut out and put into paper cages for a bulletin board display.
   2. Make three-dimensional animals out of construction paper. Roll the paper into a cylinder and staple it. To the cylinder body, add a face, paws, and a tail. Use yarn, pipe cleaners, or paper to add features.
   Music
   1. "Goin' to the Zoo."
   2. Songs about animals.
   Physical Education
   1. Have the students move like the animals do: jump like a kangaroo, run like a tiger, walk like an elephant, etc.

THE GENESSEE RIVER VALLEY PROJECT: YEAR-LONG PLAN FOR SOCIAL STUDIES

by Jean Malvaso-Zingaro, Sixth-Grade Teacher, School No. 6, Rochester, New York

The State of New York Syllabus for Social Studies recommends that the curriculum cover the concepts of change, citizenship, culture, empathy, environment, identity, interdependence, nation-state, scarcity, and technology. Jean and her colleagues at School No. 6 have woven these concepts into a year-long study of local history and geography by studying, in depth, the effects of the Erie Canal on New York State.

September–October
Introduction to the Erie Canal, with a boat trip on the canal and in-depth study of the early history of Rochester

1. Prehistory
2. Early people/woodland Indians
3. Indians, explorers, and settlers

November–December
The purpose of the Erie Canal and the effects of the canal on the Genessee River Valley

1. Visit Erie Canal Village
2. Invite a local historian to speak
3. Visit the Rochester Museum
4. Visit flour mills

January–March
How the canal was constructed

1. Immigrants and ethnic groups involved in construction
2. Field study of canal locks

April–June
Individual research projects
Culminating activity: Slide presentation and student projects

World War I is often crammed into a few short lessons at the end of the year. Stories at the end of basal readers are often missed.

Will you be satisfied if this happens in your classroom? If not, you can prevent it by preplanning the time you will give to each element or subtopic of each subject area you are going to teach. This may seem like an overwhelming task at first, but it can be less threatening if you understand that you are not required to plan every outcome and objective for every subject before the year begins. It is only necessary to give the entire curriculum an overview and determine the number of days or weeks you will allot to each element.

Begin by examining the textbooks in your classroom, looking at the way they are organized. Most books are divided into *units,* each one covering a single topic or collection of related topics within the academic subject. Math books are likely to contain units such as Place Value, Operations, Measuring, and Geometry. History books are divided into units on Exploration, Settling the New Frontier, Creating Government, and others. English books contain units such as Listening, Writing, and Speaking. Units are excellent planning devices because they show children how facts, skills, concepts, and application of ideas are related to each other. The alternative to planning with units is planning a single, continuous, year-long sequence of experiences or planning unconnected and unrelated daily experiences. Units will be used as the basis for planning throughout the rest of this book.

Decide if the units in your school's textbooks are valuable and important, whether you agree with the way they are organized and the quality of the learning experiences they contain. Consider whether using the textbook will result in achieving the outcomes in your school curriculum guide. Will it result in achieving the goals and outcomes you have established for your class? If the textbook learning experiences match your outcomes, you can plan the year to coincide with the sequence of units in the book. If the textbook does not coincide with your planned outcomes or if you disagree with the quality and/or organizational pattern of the book, there are several options. You can plan to use the book but present the units in a different order. You can delete units, or you can use some units in the book as they are written but supplement them with other materials for additional units not covered or inadequately covered in the book. The most adventurous and creative teachers may even decide to use the textbook only as a resource and plan original teaching units for the subject.

In any case, you should carefully consider the amount of time you want to allot to each unit that you plan to teach. Create a time line, chart, or calendar for each subject and use it as you judge how much time to spend on each subtopic. For time-line planning, the school year can be divided into weeks, months, or quarters. For a subject such as math, you may think about the year as a total of 36 weeks and allot varying numbers of weeks to each topic you want to cover during the year. For a subject such as language arts, you may think of the school year as being 8 months long and create eight different units that involve students in listening, speaking, writing, and reading activities. You may divide the year into four quarters for subjects such as science or social studies, with four major units planned for the year. These examples are only suggestions. Each subject can be subdivided into any time segment, or you may combine subjects into interdisciplinary units that involve students in math, science, and language arts activities under one combined topic for a period of time.

Making reasonable and professional judgments about time-line planning depends on having information about your students' prior knowledge and their history of success or failure before the year begins. The pace of your curriculum depends to some degree on the skills and knowledge your class has acquired before you meet them. But your own expectation for their success is also important. You do not want to fall into the trap of reviewing basic skills all year simply because a majority of your students have been unsuccessful in the past. If you expect them to respond to your curriculum with success and be ready to move on to new challenges, it is more likely that this will actually occur.

The time lines you create in September do not have to be rigid and unchanging. They are guidelines based on the best knowledge you have at the time. As the year progresses, you will undoubtedly have reasons to change your original time lines. Students' needs, interests, and success will cause you to alter the pace of the original plan. Current events in the country, your classroom, or your local community may cause you to add a new unit to your plan.

Collegial Long-Term Planning

Long-term planning is an important role for teachers working singly or collegially. If you are teaching in a self-contained classroom, you have the freedom to write your own outcomes as long as they are related to the district and state guidelines. If you are working in a team-teaching school, you will need to articulate your vision of student outcomes to your teammates and adjust yours to include their ideas as well as your own. In either case, the outcome statements you create will improve with experience. As you see the effects of your original outcome statements, you will reflect on them and find ways to improve them with each succeeding year.

Not all teachers take the time to clarify and articulate their educational goals into outcome statements. Not all teachers write learning objectives to fit their outcome statements. Some teachers never think about planning ahead for an entire year. Those who do not use reflective, long-term planning may be reluctant to try it.

When you begin teaching, you may find that you are the one who has to suggest or lead the discussion regarding the articulation of schoolwide, team, or grade-level outcomes. You may be the one to suggest innovative ways of dividing the curriculum into units. While your ideas may be met with skepticism or resistance from some teachers, it is quite appropriate for you to do so, as schools rely on fresh ideas from the newest faculty members with the most recent college or university training to enhance the curriculum and create positive innovations and change.

OPPORTUNITIES FOR REFLECTION

▼ Reflective Essay: Clarifying Your Own Goals of Education

What are your highest-priority educational goals? Write at least one cognitive, affective, and psychomotor goal that you consider to be extremely important in the elementary curriculum.

▼ *Classroom Visit: Observe Goals and Long-Term Plans*

Observe a classroom in action for a few hours and try to infer what the goals are from what you see taking place. Write down your estimates of the major affective, cognitive, and psychomotor goals in effect. Ask the teacher to describe his or her goals and show long-range plans. Write a brief description of the intended curriculum and the hidden curriculum that you observed.

REFERENCES

AIMS EDUCATION FOUNDATION. (1987). *Primarily bears, Book one.* Fresno, CA: AIMS Education Foundation.

BLOOM, B., ENGLEHART, M., FURST, E., HILL, W., & KRATHWOHL, D. (1956). *Taxonomy of educational objectives: Cognitive domain.* New York: Longman.

BRAGAW, D., & HARTOONIAN, M. (1988). Social studies: The study of people in society. In R. Brandt (Ed.), *Content of the Curriculum* (pp. 9–29). Alexandria, VA: Association for Supervision and Curriculum Development.

CALIFORNIA STATE DEPARTMENT OF EDUCATION. (1987a). *English-language arts framework.* Sacramento: Bureau of Publications Sales, P.O. Box 271, Sacramento, CA 95802-0271.

CALIFORNIA STATE DEPARTMENT OF EDUCATION. (1987b). *History-social science framework.* Sacramento: Bureau of Publications Sales, P.O. Box 271, Sacramento, CA 95802-0271.

CALIFORNIA STATE DEPARTMENT OF EDUCATION. (1988). *English-language arts model curriculum guide.* Sacramento: Bureau of Publications Sales, P.O. Box 271, Sacramento, CA 95802-0271.

CAMPBELL, P., & FEY, J. (1988). New goals for school mathematics. In R. Brandt (Ed.), *Content of the curriculum* (pp. 53–74). Alexandria, VA: ASCD.

CHOMSKY, C. (1969). *The aquisition of syntax from 5 to 10.* Cambridge, MA: MIT Press.

CLAY, M. (1977). *Reading: The patterning of complex behaviour.* London: Heinemann.

EISNER, E. (1985). *Educational imagination* (2nd ed.). New York: Macmillan.

GRAVES, D. (1983). *Writing: Teachers and children at work.* Exeter, NH: Heinemann.

ILLINOIS STATE BOARD OF EDUCATION. (1986). *Illinois outcome statements and model learning objectives for language arts.* Springfield: Illinois State Board of Education.

MCKNIGHT, C. (1987). *The underachieving curriculum: Assessing U.S. school mathematics from an international perspective.* Champaign, IL: Stipes.

MURRAY, D. (1984). *Write to learn.* New York: Holt.

MUTHER, C. (1987). What do we teach and when do we teach it? *Educational Leadership,* 45(1), 77–80.

PETERS, W. (1984). *A class divided: Then and now.* New Haven, CT: Yale University Press.

REYNOLDS, M. (Ed.). (1989). *Knowledge base for the beginning teacher.* New York: Pergamon Press.

RUTHERFORD, F., & AHLGREN, A. (1988). Rethinking the science curriculum. In R. Brandt (Ed.), *Content of the curriculum* (pp. 75–90). Alexandria, VA: Association for Supervision and Curriculum Development.

SULZBY, E., & TEALE, W. (1987). *Emergent literacy: Writing and reading.* Norwood, NJ: Ablex.

TEXAS STATE BOARD OF EDUCATION. (1985). *Essential elements for mathematics K–12.* Austin: Texas State Board of Education.

TYLER, R. (1949). *Basic principles of curriculum and instruction.* Chicago: University of Chicago Press.

▼│ *C H A P T E R*
5

▼ *Planning Motivating*
Curriculum Units

EDUCATORS THROUGHOUT THE COUNTRY are currently engaged in a broad-based, comprehensive reexamination of almost all educational policies, curricula, and practices. One of the most productive and practical changes occurring today is the increasingly active involvement of teachers in curriculum development at the state, district, and school levels. Just a few years ago, most teachers relied heavily on textbooks and curriculum guides prepared by distant curriculum specialists. Now teachers are being empowered by state and district administrators to take more professional responsibility for decisions that affect their students. Teachers are taking an active role in examining and selecting textbooks and revising district curriculum guides; they are also proposing new ways of organizing classroom experiences. In California, for example, classroom teachers have taken an active role in the development of new state-sponsored curriculum documents entitled *Curriculum Frameworks* and *Model Curriculum Standards* (Kierstead & Mentor, 1988, p. 35).

At the local school district level, California teachers are encouraged to create original curriculum projects that will translate the vision of excellence described at the state level into practical classroom learning experiences. The word *vision* is carefully chosen in this example because, at the local level, teachers and principals are asked to "develop a common vision" and "shape a mental image of what they want to accomplish with students and how this might look in the various disciplines" (Kierstead & Mentor, 1988, p. 37).

Briefly, the process for creating curriculum that is being used in the California school reform movement involves a local planning group in (1) defining their goals for a particular discipline, (2) describing "performance expectations" (learning outcomes) for their students, and (3) determining the skills and concepts needed to achieve these expectations. They then create a series of learning units that increase in complexity, so that by the end of the year or course, they will have achieved the expectations set out for them (Kierstead & Mentor, 1988, p. 36).

HOW TEACHERS PLAN UNITS

This model of curriculum development involves teachers in an active professional capacity in the planning, teaching, and evaluation of learning experiences. It appeals to reflective teachers who want to be part of the decision-making process and have a commitment to improve the curriculum they are expected to teach. But it also adds greatly to the responsibility of classroom teachers. As curriculum decision makers, teachers must have an excellent knowledge base about the subjects they teach so that the curricula they plan will deliver accurate information. They must also be willing to work with their colleagues to make sure that their individual plans articulate what was covered in earlier grades and what they will learn in subsequent years.

When teachers create their own curriculum, they most frequently use a learning unit to deliver or translate curricular visions into actual classroom experiences. In this chapter, we will examine how teachers decide what units to teach and how they organize the learning experiences in a curriculum unit to ensure that students gain the knowledge, skills, and processes that are intended when a unit is planned.

Deciding on Unit Topics

A single teacher can work alone or with colleagues to translate state and local curriculum outcomes into units of study. Working alone, a single teacher analyzes the state and local outcome statements to be implemented at that grade level in the elementary subjects of math, science, social studies, language arts, and fine arts. The teacher also examines the curriculum materials supplied by the school district, looking for themes or topics. The teacher may choose to look for topics within a subject, such as a math unit on fractions, a science unit on magnets and electricity, or a social studies unit on the electoral process. Other units may be interdisciplinary, that is, they are designed to include information and material from several subjects at one time. For example, the theme of "change" may include learning experiences in science, math, social studies, and literature.

While many teachers choose to work alone, other teachers at the same grade level frequently work together to create units of study. When this occurs, their combined knowledge and ideas are likely to result in a much more comprehensive set of units and a greater variety of learning experiences. Whether working alone or with a team, the first step is to decide on a series of curriculum units that correspond to the major educational goals in a subject or several subjects for that grade level.

Unit topics may be suggested or recommended by the district curriculum guide and the textbooks purchased for the subject area. Teachers can decide to use the suggested topics either in the order presented or in a different order. Teachers may choose to delete or add units to those recommended in order to fulfill the needs of their students.

Teachers may decide not to use units for every subject throughout the year. Instead, they may choose to teach a subject as an unconnected series of lessons. They may use units occasionally to highlight a particular topic in the curriculum. Sometimes teachers are able to plan units that combine more than one subject area, such as language arts and social studies or math and science. No two teachers will use the same units in the same order. Teachers have much discretion in planning units that fit their own strengths and the needs of their students.

When a series of units is planned for a subject, each unit within the series is then developed in planning sessions that may begin in the summer before school starts or take place in after-school meetings during the year. Often teachers plan the first unit during the summer so that it is ready for the fall. Later units are then planned during the school year. Once a unit has been planned, it can be reused in subsequent years, although reflective teachers usually review their older units and revise and update them prior to teaching them the second or third time.

The Process of Creating a Curriculum Unit

When reflective teachers approach the development of a curriculum unit in a subject area, they first consider their long-term goals for that subject. They may begin with the question "What are my major social studies goals this year, and what should I include in each unit of study to accomplish these goals?" Reflective teachers are also likely to monitor each decision point by asking "Why?" Why is it important for children to learn this content? Why am I choosing this method or process? How does it fit with my primary goals for the year?

Practically speaking, the process of developing a curriculum unit also includes the following:

1. Defining the topics and subject matter to be covered in the unit.
2. Defining the cognitive, process, and affective goals or outcomes that tell what students will gain and be able to do as a result.
3. Outlining the major concepts that will be covered.
4. Gathering resources that can be used in planning and teaching.
5. Brainstorming learning activities and experiences that can be used in the unit.
6. Organizing the ideas and activities into a meaningful sequence.
7. Planning lesson plans that follow the sequence.
8. Planning evaluation processes that will be used to measure student achievement and satisfaction.

Analysis will reveal that these statements correspond to Tyler's four questions. Items 1, 2, and 3 pertain to the question "What shall we teach?" Items 4 and 5 relate to the question "How shall we teach it?" Items 6 and 7 respond to the question "How shall we organize it?" Item 8 answers the question "How will we know if we are successful?"

When seen in print, as they are here, these steps appear to depict an orderly process, but curriculum planning is rarely such a linear activity. Instead, teachers find themselves starting at various points in this process. They skip over or go back and forth between these steps as ideas occur to them. For example, a team member may begin a discussion by showing a resource book she has found or describing a particular learning activity he wants to teach as part of the new unit. Discussions may skip from activities to goals to concepts to evaluation to organization.

There is nothing wrong with this nonlinear process as long as teachers are responsible enough to reflect on the overall plan to determine if all of Tyler's questions have been fully and adequately addressed. On a cautionary note, less reflective teachers tend to focus almost entirely on learning activities and materials when planning a unit. They may skip over the planning of goals and outcomes in their eagerness to plan enjoyable or practical learning activities. Their units may be nothing more than a loosely organized collection of games and worksheets, with no planned outcomes or concept development. As an evaluation, they put together a test or do a project, with no real consideration of whether it measures important goals.

Sequencing Learning Experiences in Unit Plans

Unit plans vary widely in types of learning experiences and in the way they are organized. Some subjects, such as math, are very sequentially organized, while others are not. The types of learning experiences also vary greatly depending on the subject, the resources available, and the creativity or risk taking of the teacher.

Some guidelines to consider in the creation of your unit plans are to use the textbook or a district curriculum guide as the basis for planning and as an important resource. *Do not limit yourself, however, to a single textbook as the source of all information in planning your unit or in teaching it*. A good textbook can be a valuable resource for you as you plan and for your students as they learn about the topic, but a rich and motivating unit plan will contain many other elements as well.

Supplementary reading materials from libraries or bookstores might include biographies, histories, novels, short stories, plays, poetry, newspapers, magazines, how-to books, and myriad other printed materials. Other resources to consider are films, videotapes, audiotapes, and computer programs on topics that relate to your unit. Many interesting child-centered computer programs allow your students to have simulated experiences, solve problems, and make decisions as if they were involved in the event themselves. A good example is the computer game called "Oregon Trail," distributed by the Minnesota Educational Computer Consortium (MECC), in which the student travels along the Oregon Trail, making decisions about what supplies to buy, when and where to stop along the way, and how to handle emergencies. This program can enrich a unit on westward expansion by providing more problem-solving and critical-thinking experiences than can ever be provided through reading and discussion alone.

There are many educational games that also provide students with simulated experiences. Some are board games that can be purchased in a good toy or book store. Others are more specialized learning games that must be purchased through educational publishers or distributers. Your school district probably receives hundreds of catalogues from educational publishers. Locate them and find out about the many manipulative and simulation games available on your topic.

Consider field trips that will provide your students with experiences beyond the four walls of the classroom. Which museums have exhibits related to your topic? A simple walk through a neighborhood to look for evidence of pollution or to view variations in architecture can add depth to your unit. If you cannot travel, then consider inviting a guest speaker to speak to your students about the topic. Sometimes parents themselves are excellent resources and are willing to speak about their own careers or other interests.

In thinking about how to organize a unit, many reflective teachers prefer to begin with a highly motivating activity such as a field trip, a guest speaker, a simulation game, a hands-on experiment, or a film. They know that when the students' initial experience with a topic is stimulating and involving, their interest and curiosity are aroused. The next several lessons in the unit are frequently planned at the knowledge and comprehension level of Bloom's Taxonomy to provide students with basic facts and concepts so they are able to build a substantial knowledge base and understanding of the topic. After the knowledge base is established, further learning experiences can be designed at the application, analysis, synthesis, and evaluation levels to ensure that the students are able to think critically and creatively about the subject. This model of unit planning is not universal, nor is it the only logical sequence, but it can be adapted to fit many topics and subjects, with excellent results.

EXAMPLES OF CURRICULUM UNITS

The following sections illustrate the processes used by teachers as they select, order, and create unit plans in several subjects from the elementary curriculum. Since each teacher has a personal curriculum orientation and philosophy, the process of decision making is more complex when teachers plan together than when they plan alone. The first example shows how teachers communicate with each other as they select and pilot a math unit from a published source. The other examples demonstrate how teachers create their own curriculum units and what they put down on paper to record their plans for teaching. You will notice many variations in the way units are created and what they contain, depending on their purposes and the philosophies and values of the teachers who create them.

Adopting a Mathematics Unit

Mathematics is generally thought of as a sequentially ordered subject. For example, students learn the basic skills of addition and subtraction in first and second grades; they learn multiplication and division later. As Piaget demonstrated, math is a subject that requires early experiences with concrete examples and hands-on experiences, allowing students to manipulate materials in order to understand mathematical relationships. Only in the upper intermediate grades can students be expected to understand these same relationships at an abstract level, without the need to "see" them in a concrete way. A third expectation in math is that skillful computation is not sufficient as an outcome or performance expectation; it is also important that students be able to apply mathematical operations to real-life problems and tasks.

Based on these organizational principles, an effective curriculum unit in math is likely to (a) present new skills and concepts in order of difficulty, (b) initiate new learning with concrete manipulative experiences so that students can come to understand the concepts involved, and (c) provide examples, tasks, and problems that call on students to apply their newly learned skills in lifelike situations.

Mathematics is an example of a *spiral* curriculum. This means that certain concepts and skills are taught every year, but in an upward spiral of difficulty. Each year begins with a review of skills from previous years, and then new skills and concepts are introduced. For this reason, the topics of math units are likely to be similar from year to year, but the way these topics are addressed and the complexity of the concepts vary greatly.

To illustrate the processes used in planning a math program, consider the following scenario.

The scene is a first-grade classroom in late August. Three primary teachers are gathered around a table with an array of mathematics books and materials in front of them, preparing to discuss ways to improve their math curriculum.

MR. LOPEZ: I've got something to show you from a workshop I attended this summer. It's a new math program from the University of Chicago called *Everyday Mathematics.*

MS. DILLON: I've heard of that. It's supposed to be very innovative and creates high student enthusiasm for mathematics.

MS. KIM: Yes, but we don't want to jump on any new bandwagons. We need to increase our achievement test scores. Let's not get waylaid by fads. We need to plan more effective ways to get our students to learn and memorize the basic math facts.

MR. LOPEZ: The math facts can be learned in many ways. Memorization is only one important element. They also need to understand the relationships among numbers, and I believe this program does that better than our present text.

MS. DILLON: I agree, and our students don't have many opportunities to play and work with math concepts at home. I think we do need to have more concrete experiences in our curriculum if we want them to understand what the math facts are and how they are used in real life.

MR. LOPEZ: That's what this program is all about. It shows children how math is related to patterns, problems, and relationships in real life. It gets children actively involved in observation and investigation of math principles instead of just doing workbook pages.

MS. KIM: Will this program take a lot of time?

MR. LOPEZ: Yes, it does take time, but if we want our students to improve in math, we are going to have to give it more time.

MS. DILLON: What about materials? Does it use a lot of manipulatives? We don't have a budget for a lot of fancy equipment.

MR. LOPEZ: We do need materials, but most of the equipment is around this school anyway, gathering dust. We just need to collect it. We can substitute beans or buttons for some of the commercial materials, and we can borrow equipment from the science teacher.

MS. DILLON: I'm willing to do that. Let's hear what the program actually does and how it's different from our textbooks.

Mr. Lopez shows the first-grade teacher's manual of the Everyday Mathematics *series to his colleagues and explains the purposes and procedures. He points out that the first-grade curriculum contains 15 math units on topics such as everyday use of numbers, visual patterns and number patterns, measures of length, addition and subtraction facts, fractions, and geometry.*

MS. KIM: I can see why you like this program. It does have more active learning in it than our workbooks do, but I'm reluctant to replace our current textbook until we know for sure that this program is an improvement. I suggest we use the material as a supplementary program this year and then make a decision about adopting it next year.

MS. DILLON: That sounds like a good plan to me. I'd like to do the unit on visual patterns and number patterns in the fall. I think it would help my students understand that math operations are based on patterns and relationships.

MR. LOPEZ: Yes, that unit appeals to me as well. Look at the projects using apples, leaves, and pumpkins. We can collect all of those on our field trip to the pumpkin farm in October.

MS. DILLON: Okay, that is a very relevant unit.

MS. KIM: Great! It can also serve as a fall science project.

MR. LOPEZ: I'm glad you agree with me. I am really looking forward to teaching this unit. I think I'll enjoy it as much as the students do.

Figure 5–1 shows excerpts from the unit on visual patterns and number patterns that this first-grade team decided to pilot test in their math curriculum. While it is impossible to include the whole unit in this context, one representative lesson and the special projects on leaves and pumpkins are shown to exemplify a mathematics unit that is filled with active learning in the form of critical and creative thinking, investigating relationships, concept formation, and problem solving.

Creating a Language Arts Unit

Units created for the language arts curriculum of an elementary classroom are likely to be very different from math units. Since language arts is a composite of the skills and creative abilities related to reading, writing, speaking, and listening, a language arts unit is likely to include a great variety of learning experiences. There are likely to be expected outcomes that call on students to apply basic skills in some form of creative product.

As an example of a language arts unit, let us consider the thinking and planning processes used by a fourth-grade teacher as she created a unit called "What Are Friends For" (Figure 5–2). She decided on the topic because she observed that friendship was a very important element in the lives of her fourth-grade students. She noticed that the students in her classroom who had a number of good friends seemed to enjoy and succeed in school activities better than students with few friends. She knew that it would not be possible to order students to be friendlier to isolated students, but she felt that she could influence the students in her class to become more sensitive to the friendship needs of their classmates.

TEACHER'S MANUAL & LESSON GUIDE

First-Grade Everyday Mathematics

━━━━━━━━━━━━━━━━━━━━━━━━

Unit 3   Visual Patterns and Number Patterns

━━━━━━━━━━━━━━━━━━━━━━━━━━━━━━

The first lesson in this short unit introduces visual patterns of shape, color, and rotation. Through continuous exposure to such patterns, students soon become aware that both simple and complex patterns are a part of our world.

Next, children will extend their knowledge of number patterns to odd and even numbers. They will also explore number patterns for 3, 5, and 10. To help them learn more about number patterns, they will begin to use the Frames and Arrows game.

━━━━━━━━━━━━━━━━━━━━━━━━━━━━━━

Lesson 29   Establishing Visual-Pattern Routines

Objective Introduce visual patterns of shape, color, and rotation.

Materials Activity Sheet 6 (Twelve Diamond Shapes); scissors; crayons; glue; full sheets of construction paper; craft sticks (16 per child); colored chalk.

Math Message Count out 16 craft sticks and put them in your tool kit. *(If children already have craft sticks, have them make bundles of 16 sticks from those in their tool kits.)*

Note. From *First Grade Everyday Mathematics Teacher's Manual* (pp. 61–63, A7, A8, A10) by Max and Jean Bell, 1990, Evanston, IL: Everyday Learning Corporation. Copyright 1990 by Everyday Learning Corporation. Reprinted by permission.

Instruction and Discussion (whole-group)

• Introduce visual patterns.

– Using tape or on overhead projector, display in some pattern two or more of the diamond shapes cut out from Activity Sheet 6. Ask children if they see a consistent pattern. For example,

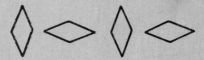

– Ask children what would come next; add the diamond to the pattern.

– Arrange the diamonds in other patterns. Encourage children to describe each pattern and tell what would come next.

Teacher Note At this early stage, children's descriptions of patterns may often be inaccurate or inadequate. Whatever the response, reward the attempt.

– Ask children to attempt a general description of what makes up a pattern. *(2 or more things arranged so that one can predict what comes next)*

– In preparation for the partner activities, tape up displays of a few patterns made with craft sticks or draw attention to the sticks by making "stick" patterns with chalk marks on the board.

• Find patterns in the classroom.

– Explain that patterns (simple or complex) are a part of our world.

– Have children look around the classroom and point out, and perhaps describe, any patterns they observe. *(floor tiles, light fixtures, etc.)*

• Patterns with colored chalk

– Using colored chalk, start a sequential pattern on the board. Have children tell you how to continue it. For example,

> red, white, red, white, red, . . .
> red, red, blue, red, red, blue, . . .

– Ask students to suggest color patterns. Draw them on the chalkboard.

Activity (partners)

• Make a pattern with craft sticks.

– Remind children of partner etiquette. This will help to keep these pattern games from becoming competitive and from having inadequate attempts at describing the patterns ridiculed.

– Keep a classroom pool of extra craft sticks in case some children devise ornate patterns for which they don't have enough sticks.

– Have partners pool their craft sticks. *(Perhaps have them say, 16 + 16 = 32, as you write it on the board.)*

– Partners take turns. One partner starts a stick pattern; the other continues the pattern for two cycles and then tries to describe it.

– For one pattern, have partners take turns continuing the pattern until they run out of sticks.

Independent Activities (individuals)

• Coloring patterns

Children color the diamonds on Activity Sheet 6 using two colors. After they have finished coloring the diamonds, have them cut out the shapes. Tell them to make a pattern by gluing the shapes onto a separate sheet of paper.

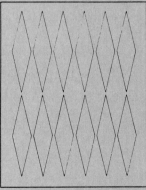

Activity Sheet 6

• Work on some number-writing pages.

• **Math Boxes**

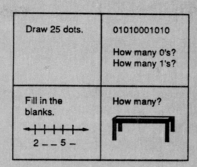

Draw 25 dots.	01010001010 How many 0's? How many 1's?
Fill in the blanks. +—+—+—+—+—+— 2 _ _ 5 _	How many?

Home Link Try to find a pattern in your home. Draw it. If you find a pattern in your clothes, please wear that tomorrow.

Teacher Note Mark calculators with tool-kit numbers and with the letter *R* (*repeat*) on the "=" key for distribution during Lesson 30.

Leaves Project

Objective Collect, observe, compare size, and sort fall leaves.

Materials Fall leaves; chart paper for class graphs; newspaper and cardboard for pressing; inch- and centimeter-grid paper for area activities (*Journal I*, pp. 10-11 or Masters, Appendix pages A28-A29); rulers or tape measures; magnifying lenses; clear material for sealing; yarn or string for mobiles.

Activities (whole-group)

• **Leaf Walk**

– After establishing some ground rules, take the class out for a short walk to collect as many different kinds of leaves as possible. Encourage each child to find only one specimen of each kind of leaf.

  Alternative: Bring to class a bag of assorted fall leaves or ask a parent to do so. Have children collect their sets from these leaves.

– Upon returning to class, several different kinds of class graphs could
   be made by coloring in appropriate squares for each category on a large
   grid sheet.

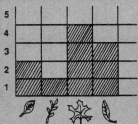
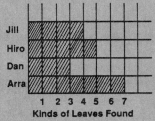

Kinds of Leaves Found

1. *Numbers of kinds of leaves found:* a sample of each kind of leaf
   could be used to label each category. How many different kinds
   of leaves did the class find? Of which kind did they find the most?
   the least? Are there any kinds of which they found the same
   number of leaves? Ask, *How can we find out how many more we
   found of this kind of leaf than that kind? How many less?*

2. *Numbers of kinds of leaves found by each child:* from the graph, is
   it possible to tell the minimum number of different kinds? Does
   each square represent a different kind of leaf? Why not?

Teacher Note Leaves are easier to work with if they have been pressed.
This can be done by having children select a variety to arrange between
double sheets of newspaper labeled with children's names. Stack the
"sandwiches" between a couple of pieces of cardboard and tie together into
a bundle. Apply pressure (weight) by stacking books or heavy objects on
the bundle. It takes several days of pressing to get leaves that are easy to
work with. *(Magnifying leaf details and making leaf rubbings are best done
with fresh leaves, not pressed leaves.)*

• **Magnifying leaves**

– Use sets of leaves to study; compare the structures of the leaves. Have
   children use magnifying lenses to compare such things as

   1. simple, paired, and compound patterns.

   2. shapes and edges of different kinds of leaves.

   3. vein patterns. *(Why do leaves have veins? Do we have veins?)*

   4. size. *(Do the biggest leaves come from the biggest trees?)*

   5. symmetry. *(Can we fold a leaf so that the two halves match?)*

- **Measuring leaves**

  – Compare apparent sizes of leaves; measure width or length.

  – Arrange a typical set of ten or so leaves in order of apparent size. Use visual clues, not measures.

  – Use rulers or tape measures to measure width or length (or both) of a selection of flattened leaves. Ask for some general observations, for example, *Are the widest leaves the largest in area? Do bigger leaves have similar shapes? smaller leaves?*

  – Have children make area estimates of different leaves. Good area estimates can be made by stapling leaves to inch- or centimeter-grid paper and having children carefully rub a crayon or brush or sponge paint around the edges of the leaves, overlapping the paper. A spatter-paint technique also works. Once the paint has dried, have children carefully remove the leaves from the grid paper. Then ask them to count the squares inside the leaf pattern. If half or more than half a square is inside the pattern, tell them to count that square; if less than half a square is inside the pattern, tell them they should not count that square.

  – Have children determine how an ordering of estimates of area made on grid counts compares with a visual ordering.

- **Sort by attributes**

After a brief discussion, let children decide on a rule for sorting their sets of leaves. Obvious rules might be according to size, shape, or color. Less obvious rules might include sorting according to simple-compound leaf structure, vein structure, or edge patterns. Give several children an opportunity to explain their rules for sorting.

- **Leaves in seasons**

Adopt a tree near the school. Sketch or photograph it as it looks now. Watch it throughout the school year, sketching or photographing it again in the dead of winter, in early spring, and just before the end of the school year. Display the pictures. Observe and comment on changes.

Pumpkin Math

Objective Estimate, compare, and count with pumpkins.

Materials Pumpkins *(could be 3 or 4 of different sizes)*; bath scale; tape measure; meter stick; yarn; tape measure for comparing estimates; knife; colander; paper towels; decoration materials, if there is more than one pumpkin, such as yarn braids, markers, colored paper; 100 grids for counting seeds; glue, paper, etc. for seed collage. *Optional:* an oven or other means for roasting or frying seeds.

Math Message *(Put a pumpkin on display.)* Guess the pumpkin's weight. Write your guess on a quarter sheet. Deposit in the Message Box.

Instruction and Discussion (whole-group)

- **Estimating and comparing weights**

  – Using the responses to the Math Message, discuss which estimates might be reasonable. Weigh the pumpkin. Read and record its weight. Compare the actual weight to estimates. Remember to label the number with units when recording. If you have more than one pumpkin, label each so that they can be differentiated. Weigh, read, and record their weights. Use calculators to get the cumulative weight of all the pumpkins.

  – Weigh a child. How many pumpkins would weigh the same? Use pumpkins to show comparisons or equivalents.

- **Estimating and comparing girth** (circumference)

  – Ask several children to estimate how big around the pumpkin is. Have them cut lengths of yarn for their estimates.

  – Tape these estimates onto the chalkboard.

  – Cut yarn of a different color for the actual circumference of the pumpkin. Tape it on the board along with the estimates.

  – *Option:* Measure each piece of yarn with a tape measure. Compare the estimates with the actual circumference.

  – If you have more than one pumpkin, try to relate weight and girth to size.

    – *Does the largest pumpkin weigh the most? have the largest girth?*

    – *Does the smallest pumpkin weigh the least? have the smallest girth?*

This teacher's understanding of child development led her to believe that her students would have a strong interest in the topic of friendship and that they would be more than willing to spend class time reading, writing, speaking, and listening on a topic of such vital social interest to fourth graders. Therefore, she decided to blend her goal of meeting the social needs of her students with her goal of teaching students to listen, think, and read critically and to express their ideas effectively in writing and speaking. The goals and purposes of the unit plan began to take shape in her mind.

Next, she went to the school's learning center and made a list of children's books that had friendship as a theme. A reference book entitled *The Bookfinder*

(Dreyer, 1985) provided her with a long list of books on the theme of friendship, with annotated reviews and appropriate reading levels. She also asked the learning center teacher to recommend her favorites. She purposely chose books with reading levels at, below, and above the fourth-grade level to accommodate the students in her class with varying reading levels. She found that the books themselves suggested learning experiences and activities that used reading, writing, listening, and speaking skills.

She then created a long list of possible activities and began to envision the unit taking place. She could "see," in her mind's eye, the students role-playing scenes from the books they read and writing in journals on their own views of friendship. She tried to envision the class meetings she would hold on the topic of friendship, and how she would introduce the subject to the students to gain their interest and willingness to learn and grow. She silently rehearsed the words she would use to ensure that they understood what she expected of them as they read and discussed their books in cooperative groups and planned their creative products together.

She believed that, if her unit was successful, she would be able to detect an affective change or growth in her students in at least two ways: (1) a greater degree of friendliness toward classmates would occur and (2) individuals would express in their journals or in discussions that they felt more accepted and better liked by their classmates. She also believed that, if her unit was successful, there would be notable changes in the ways students used language in her classroom, including the following: (1) students would choose to read more fiction; (2) they would listen with greater accuracy and empathy; and (3) they would be able to express more clearly their ideas in writing and speaking.

Over a long weekend, the teacher organized her materials, ideas, and learning experiences into a sequence of events that she could envision taking place in her classroom with her students. That sequence of events is presented in Figure 5–2 as an example of a language arts unit plan initiated and created by a single teacher.

This language arts unit contains different elements than the math unit. Outcome statements and projects and performance expectations (instead of objectives) are used as benchmarks for success. The organizational plan is not sequential, but outlines how weekly expectations and learning experiences are combined to develop new attitudes, skills, and abilities in the fourth-grade students for whom it was created. If another teacher were to use this unit plan, it is quite likely that he or she would choose to adapt it, add additional experiences, and organize it differently.

Creating a Social Studies Unit

Social studies in the elementary curriculum combines several academic disciplines, including geography, history, economics, political science, anthropology, sociology, and psychology. The curriculum is designed as an ever-widening circle of ideas, in keeping with the developmental stages of children. In the early grades, the curriculum centers on the home and the community; the middle grades focus on the states and the United States; concepts related to nations and the world are dealt with in the later grades.

Units are the ideal way to deliver a combined curriculum like the social studies. Primary teachers often create units on the community, including maps of the school neighborhood, history of the community, roles of community helpers, economic activities related to stores in the community, and other similar experiences.

WHAT ARE FRIENDS FOR?

A Fourth-Grade Language Arts Unit

DESCRIPTION

A unit in which students read books on the theme of friendship. Discussions, writing, speeches, dramatizations, and other events are planned to allow students to express their views on what they have read.

OUTCOME STATEMENTS

Outcome 1: Students will read at least six books on friendship and demonstrate comprehension, critical thinking, and creative thinking of the books by interacting with others to create an original product related to each book.

Related Projects and Performance Objectives
Students will:

Read: Students will choose and read at least six books (at a reading level appropriate for the student) from the list provided.

Listen: In cooperative groups of students who have read the same book, each student will listen to the opinions and ideas of others in discussions about the book's content and meaning, and to the ideas and suggestions of others about the creation of an original product related to the book.

Speak: Students will take part in a group project to create an original product related to each book and perform or describe it to the entire class.

Outcome 2: Students will express their own opinions, ideas, and suggestions to others in the classroom with clarity, creativity, and supportive evidence.

Related Projects and Performance Expectations
Students will:

Speak: In cooperative groups, students will create an "advertisement" to persuade others to read the book.

Write: Students will write an original story, poem, play, or essay in response to at least one book.

Outcome 3: Students will demonstrate that they recognize, accept, and understand that the need for friendship is important to each member of the class, and that each student has a responsibility to offer support and friendship to other students in the classroom community.

Related Projects and Performance Expectations
Students will:

Read: Students will look for examples of the importance and value of friendship as they read the books they select for this unit.

Speak: Students will contribute opinions about what friendship means during classroom meetings.

Listen: Students will listen to and paraphrase opinions stated by others about what friendship means to them.

Write: Students will choose one classmate and write in a journal about the experience of offering friendship to that person.

ORGANIZATIONAL PLAN

Book Selection: Each week for 6 weeks, students select a book from a list of four, each with a different reading level. Students are encouraged to select books at their own reading levels, but are allowed to select books above or below this level if they have a strong interest in reading that book.

Sustained Silent Reading (SSR): Each day, students spend 45 minutes in SSR of the books they have selected.

Literature Circles: During (or immediately following) SSR, the teacher may call on four students to form a literature circle. The students bring their books and discuss interesting passages from them with others in the circle. The teacher shares his or her book in the same way (idea taken from Hanson, 1987).

Cooperative Groups: Each week cooperative groups are formed by those who have selected a particular book. They must discuss the book, create a plan for advertising the book to the rest of the class, and present their advertisement on Fridays.

Enrichment Plan: Individual students may select additional books to read from the list in response to advertisements. Individuals may work alone or with a partner to create an original project after reading the book.

Classroom Meetings: Weekly classroom meetings on the topic of friendship will be led by the teacher. In these meetings, students will relate the stories they are reading to their own lives and friendships. Suggested topics for the classroom meetings:

Week 1: What are friends for? What are some of the reasons to have friends? What can friends do together that a person cannot do alone?

Week 2: What does it feel like to move away from friends or to lose a good friend?

Week 3: Is it good to have one best friend or many friends? What happens if your best friend chooses another best friend?

Week 4: What happens when friends fight or disagree? How can you make up with a friend after a quarrel? How can you deal with conflict?

Week 5: How can you make more friends or better friends?

Week 6: What can you do if you notice that someone needs a friend? How can you include that person in your activities? How can a class of children make sure that everyone is included and no one is left out? Do we want to do that after all that we've learned about friendship? If so, what will we do differently?

EVALUATION PLAN

Outcome 1 will be evaluated by recording the books each child reads in a cooperative group or independently. Descriptions of the original products are also kept on the checklist. At the end of the unit, the checklist can serve as a means of communicating with the parents what the student has accomplished.

Outcome 2 will be documented by keeping a portfolio of the students' written responses to books they read in the unit.

Outcome 3 will be recorded individually by having students write in their journals following each weekly classroom meeting. They will write their own views on the questions raised in the meeting. The teacher will write at the same time on the same topic.

Middle-grade teachers frequently create units on topics such as American Indians, the explorers, geography of the United States, and U.S. presidents. Upper-grade teachers may offer units comparing countries of the world in terms of geography, politics, economics, and history.

As an example of how a social studies unit may be developed, consider the emphasis on U.S. history at the fifth-grade level. Four teachers who taught fifth grade in the same school district, but at different schools, decided to plan a series of units to cover the major goals and topics of U.S. history. By examining the curriculum materials and textbooks that were available, they identified five major themes and assigned time to each one: the explorers (6 weeks), panorama of the presidents (9 weeks), government and the electoral system (7 weeks), immigration and the melting pot (7 weeks), and economics (6 weeks). Each of these unit topics met some of the outcomes and goals outlined by their state curriculum framework and district curriculum guides.

The unit on history through the eyes of the U.S. presidents was first suggested by one of the four teachers who had read Cullum's (1967) *Push Back the Desks*, describing a project he did in which each student re-created the role of a U.S. president for a day. After describing Cullum's project to her coworkers, the teacher suggested that they adapt the idea to fit their own needs. Her colleagues agreed that it was an efficient way to cover a great deal of history in a short time and would be likely to motivate the students to learn the major historical events in U.S. history.

Together the four teachers decided to adapt Cullum's idea by having each student in the class choose one president to study. Each student would be responsible for researching the major facts about and accomplishments of the president and the historical events that occurred during that president's time in office. This information would be synthesized into a speech that would be written as if that student was the president. At the end of the unit, an all-school assembly was planned in which each student (president) would make his or her speech in chronological order. George Washington would speak first, followed by John Adams, and so on.

The four teachers then wrote down their plan and created some classroom materials to support their students' emerging research skills. Their plan appears in Figure 5–3. It includes an evaluation instrument based on their goals for the unit. They decided to encourage students to develop their own metacognitive skills by asking each student to participate in the self-evaluation at the end of the unit.

A Student Creates a Science Unit

Unit plans, then, are quite varied, depending on the subject matter and the teacher or teachers who create the plan. The unit plans shown above were created by experienced teachers. But you may be required to create a plan as part of this course or in preparation for student teaching. It may be helpful for you to see an example of a unit plan created by an undergraduate student as a course requirement. You may also wish to read about the way she thought about the assignment and some of the steps she took in completing it successfully.

Monica Abramson-Lyons was an undergraduate student at De Paul University taking an introductory curriculum planning course when she was asked to write a unit on a topic of her choice for the elementary grades. In an interview, she reported the reflective processes she used as she created the unit.

"I started out thinking of the units I had been exposed to in elementary school. There were two that I remembered: one on the solar system and one on endangered species. The one I remembered better was the one on the solar system, but I chose the other one because I love animals and want my students to learn to respect the needs of animals, especially those that are endangered. A lot of children have pets, and I thought that animals would be something they would like to talk and learn about.

"I started looking for resources, and interviewed teachers and librarians at the school I had been visiting for clinical experiences. The librarian was very helpful. She gave me pamphlets about the Lincoln Park Zoo and suggested that I visit it to find out about the classes it offers to children and to locate resources at the zoo's library and bookstore. I went to the zoo and talked to people at the information desk and to the manager of the bookstore. They gave me information about adopting an animal and pamphlets about endangered animals.

"I also visited a teacher's store to find resources that would be motivating for children, with hands-on activities. I found flashcards on endangered species. I decided to put them in a learning center and ask students to create additional flashcards on animals they studied.

"After I had gathered about ten resources, I began to think about what is important for children to know about endangered animals. At first, I felt overwhelmed, because this was such a big topic that I didn't really know what direction to take. There are thousands of endangered species. But gradually I narrowed the field. I knew that I wanted to begin by broadening children's schemata about animals that are now extinct, including the dinosaurs. I also wanted them to realize that because of changes in our environment and the expanding population, we are putting many more animals' lives in danger. I thought it was important for them to realize that many animals are sacrificed to produce luxury items such as handbags, fur coats, and cosmetics. I want children to think about how necessary it is to have certain status symbol items when these threaten another living thing.

"Later, when I started to write the unit, I translated these thoughts into my cognitive and affective goals. After that, I began to consider the way I could engage the children in active experiences, such as researching one animal that we don't study in class. These thoughts translated into my skill goals. I want all children to have the experience of being the expert on one endangered animal so they would feel a sense of accomplishment. I believe they need to be able to find information on their own so that they'll be able to make decisions about what they choose to buy and how they treat animals throughout their lives.

"When I wrote the rest of the unit, I tried to visualize myself teaching it, and at first, I thought about the trip to the zoo and making posters about animals. The hardest part was thinking about how to teach what humans do to help and hinder the environment. I wanted to plan experiences that children could really relate to their own lives.

"The evaluation section came surprisingly easy to me. I knew that I wanted to allow different projects, so that there would be many opportunities for children to excel. I also knew that I wanted to have a balance between projects that they chose and overall expectations for the class, so I created four different components, including a cognitive test, a group project, an individual project, and active participation in day-to-day class activities."

The unit Monica wrote is shown in Figure 5–4.

PANORAMA OF THE PRESIDENTS

A Fifth-Grade Social Studies Unit

DESCRIPTION
In this 9 week unit, each student will select one U.S. president to study. Information gathered through independent research will be synthesized into a speech. At the end of the unit, the student will role-play the president and give a speech about the major events that occurred during his presidency in an all-school assembly entitled "Panorama of the Presidents."

PURPOSE
This unit will motivate students to do independent research by gathering facts and information about the lives and historical events of the presidents of the United States. The chronological history of the United States will be covered in a visual and experiential format, enabling students to "see" and "hear" the presidents speak about history.

UNIT GOALS

Cognitive Goals

▼ Students will learn the major events of U.S. history in chronological order.
▼ Students will learn the names and major accomplishments of the presidents of the United States.
▼ Students will develop an understanding of cause and effect as it relates to presidential decisions and resulting historical events.
▼ Students will begin to clarify the concepts of effective versus ineffective leadership.

Psychomotor and Skill Goals

▼ Students will improve their research skills by locating information on their president in libraries and other settings.
▼ Students will improve their writing and organizational skills by summarizing information gained by research in a written speech.
▼ Students will improve their public speaking skills by practicing and delivering a speech to their peers and parents at an all-school assembly.

Affective Goals

▼ Students will gain confidence in public speaking.
▼ Students will gain independence in finding information.
▼ Students will improve their metacognitive skills by participating in a self-evaluation of their own accomplishments during the unit.

TIME LINE OF LEARNING EXPERIENCES

Week 1:   The teacher briefly introduces all U.S. presidents to students. Each student selects several to be studied in depth. The teacher assigns one president to each student. Priority is given to assigning the most well-known presidents to students with the lowest reading levels, so that they can find easy-to-read biographies on their subject.

Week 2: Students begin to locate books and other information on their presidents. They complete Worksheet 1 and report the findings in writing to the teacher and orally to their classmates.

Week 3: Students continue to research the presidents. They complete Worksheet 2 and report their findings.

Week 4: Students conclude their research. They complete Worksheet 3 and report their findings.

Week 5: Students create the first draft of the speeches they will make at the conclusion of the unit. As a group, they begin to plan the assembly, making all arrangements for time, space, and equipment and informing their peers and parents of the event.

Week 6: Students practice speaking from their first drafts in class. Using feedback from the teacher and peers, they work on the second draft of their speeches. In group discussions, students analyze how the decisions made by the president had a cause-and-effect relationship with major historical events of the United States.

Week 7: Students practice speaking from their second drafts in class. The teacher videotapes these practice sessions. Each student views his or her own performance and makes improvements in the third and final draft. In group discussions, students analyze characteristics of the presidents that were associated with effective leadership and other characteristics that were associated with ineffective leadership.

Week 8: Students rehearse their speeches on stage and make final arrangements regarding the use of space, time, and equipment for their final performance. Students take a test on the cognitive goals of the unit.

Week 9: Students take part in the assembly called "Panorama of the Presidents." It may be given once during the day for peers and again in the evening for parents. In the days following the assembly, each student evaluates his or her own accomplishments using the Evaluation Form. This form is then sent home to parents with the quarterly report card.

WORKSHEETS

Worksheet 1: The Early Years

Where were you born?
Who were your parents?
What siblings did you have?
What was your father's occupation?
What was your mother's occupation?
What schools did you attend?
If you went to college, what did you study there?
What was your first job?

Worksheet 2: Becoming President

What other jobs did you have before becoming president?
What important historical events occurred during your early years?
How did you become interested in politics?
What political party did you belong to?
What was your first elected office?
How did you decide to run for president the first time?
Who did you run against?
Who ran as your vice president?
What historical events were most important while you were running for president?
How did the election turn out?

Worksheet 3: My Years as President

What was your first accomplishment on becoming president?
What major historical events occurred during your first term as president?
What were your other important accomplishments in your first term?
What were your mistakes or errors of judgment in your first term?
Did you run for reelection?
Why or why not?
Who did you run against for the second term?
What were the major historical events occurring at that time?
Did you win reelection?
If so, what were your major accomplishments in your second term?
What were your major mistakes or errors of judgment in your second term?
What did you do after leaving the presidency?
How and where did you die?

EVALUATION

This unit consists of an objective test and a subjective evaluation made by both the teacher and the student. The test is designed to assess gains made by the student at all six levels of Bloom's Taxonomy.

COGNITIVE EXAM

List as many presidents as you can remember in chronological order. (Knowledge-level item)

Describe at least one major historical event that occurred during the time of President Washington. (Comprehension-level item)

Describe at least one historical event that occurred during the time of President Lincoln. (Comprehension-level item)

Describe at least one historical event that occurred during the time of President Truman. (Comprehension-level item)

If you were president today, what is a decision you would make and why? (Application-level item)

Describe a decision made by the president you studied and the effect it had upon the history of our country. (Analysis-level item)

Do you believe that the president you studied was an effective or an ineffective leader? Give evidence to support your opinion. (Evaluation-level item)

STUDENT EVALUATION

NAME OF STUDENT _____ GRADE _____ DATE _____

The student completes the left side of this evaluation and then the teacher completes the right side. Afterward, student and teacher discuss the accomplishments made by the student, decide on areas that need to be improved, and plan goals for future learning experiences.

O = Outstanding   S = Satisfactory   N = Needs Improvement
STUDENT EVALUATION   TEACHER EVALUATION

_____ I can now describe many of the major events of U.S. history.   _____
_____ I can name many of the presidents in chronological order.   _____
_____ I can describe how certain presidential decisions affected the   _____
history of our country.
_____ I can give a good rationale for identifying some presidents as   _____
effective leaders and others as ineffective leaders.
_____ I have gained skill in doing research to gather information.   _____
_____ I have improved my writing and organizational skills by summa-   _____
rizing information gained by research in a speech.
_____ I have improved my ability to speak in public.   _____
_____ I have gained confidence in my ability to speak in public.   _____
_____ I have gained independence in working on my own to achieve a   _____
goal.
_____ I am able to evaluate my own accomplishments and identify what   _____
I need to improve with accuracy and honesty.

TAKE A WALK ON THE WILD SIDE!

A Fourth-Grade Science Unit by Monica Abramson-Lyons

DESCRIPTION
This unit will cover the following aspects of endangered wildlife:

▼ Types of animals
▼ Various animals' natural habitats
▼ What extinction means
▼ Animals that are considered threatened or endangered
▼ What humans can do to try to save endangered wildlife

PURPOSE
To stimulate an appreciation and understanding for endangered animals and their habitats. Students will participate in observing, classifying, researching, writing, drawing, exploring, and discussing animals and the environment. Students will examine what individuals can do to try and save some of these precious species from extinction.

GOALS

Cognitive Goals

1. Students will be able to identify the characteristics defining each of the six major animal categories: mammals, reptiles, fish, birds, amphibians, and arthropods.
2. Students will be able to identify where the natural habitats of various animals are located and what they are like.
3. Students will understand the meaning of the words *extinction, threatened,* and *endangered* and why certain animals fall into one of these categories.
4. Students will understand the role animals play in balancing our environment.

Skill Goals

1. Students will be able to use research to identify whether an animal is endangered or not.
2. Students will know how to become involved in supporting conservation organizations.
3. Students will know ways to help preserve our environment, thus giving endangered species a better chance for survival.

Affective Goals

1. Students will show respect and concern for living things and the environment.
2. Students will develop an understanding and a fondness for animals they might have previously been afraid of.
3. Students will understand the difference between killing animals out of necessity and killing them for selfish reasons.

UNIT CALENDAR

Day 1: This day will be an introduction to the unit. Students will receive an outline of the unit, along with a list of projects they will be expected to complete.

Days 2 and 3: These days will focus on animal classification (mammals, birds, fish, etc.). We will also learn what the terms *extinction, endangered,* and *threatened* mean.

Day 4: Field trip to the Lincoln Park Zoo. During the field trip, the class will participate in the Adopt an Animal program at the zoo by adopting an animal from an endangered species and keeping track of it throughout the school year.

Days 5–8: These days will be used to learn about the natural habitats of specific endangered species. We will also discuss the importance of the food chain so that students can begin to see how survival is dependent on many factors.

Day 9: This day will be used to discuss in detail the reasons why specific animals are endangered and what humans can do to help. Students will specify which project they plan to work on.

Day 10: We will review the material learned so far. Then a test will be given asking students to determine an animal's category, identify its locations, and define key vocabulary words. Students who finish the test with time to spare may work quietly on their individual projects.

Day 11: This day will be spent learning about conservation organizations. Students will then be divided into groups of four to begin work on their group projects.

Days 12–14: Students will spend this time preparing their group projects.

Day 15: Projects will be presented.

EVALUATION

Student evaluation for this unit will be based on four different activities: a test, a group project, an individual project, and overall participation in class activities and discussions. Each component is worth 25 points.

UNIT TEST

Fill in the blanks (spelling counts!)

1. I have hair on my body and I drink milk when I'm a baby, so that makes me a _____.

2. I live in water and I have gills, fins, and scales, so I belong to the _____ category.

3. I was born on dry land and I have scaly skin. I am cold-blooded. This makes me a _____.

4. I was born in water. I breathe with gills. Now that I'm grown up, I can survive on land as well as in the water. This makes me an _____.

5. I was hatched out of a hard-shelled egg, and I have feathers. This makes me a _____.

6. I have a hard covering over my whole body and more than four jointed legs. I'm known as an _____.

(Cognitive goal 1)

Asia   blue whale
Africa   bald eagle
Australia   polar bear
Europe   mountain gorilla
The Arctic   panda bear
America   red kangaroo
Oceans and islands   lynx

(First part of cognitive goal 2)

Short-Answer Essays
1. List the five questions the government asks to determine if an animal is endangered.
   (Cognitive goal 3)
   a.
   b.
   c.
   d.
   e.
2. Could a polar bear survive in Africa? Why or why not? (Second part of cognitive goal 2)
3. What is the food chain, and why is it important? (Cognitive goal 4)

GROUP PROJECT
Every student will be expected to participate in the group project.

Students will work in groups of four to create a mock conservation organization that rallies support for a specific endangered animal. Each group will be responsible for giving a demonstration including advertisements for the organization (posters, pins, buttons, signs, etc.) and four 1-minute oral presentations that discuss (a) the type of animal, (b) the animal's natural habitat, (c) why the animal is in danger of becoming extinct, and

Creating a Multidisciplinary Unit

Some units of study cross the boundaries between subjects or disciplines such as math, science, language arts, and social studies. Curriculum plans that include learning experiences from more than one subject area are called *multidisciplinary* or *interdisciplinary* units. For example, the AIMS materials used by Tim Curbo (see the Perspectives in Chapter 4) integrate math and science. The National Wildlife Foundation publishes educational activity books for elementary classrooms on topics such as rain forests, mammals, and weather. The activities in these books develop children's understandings of science, language, and social responsibility.

Figure 5–5 shows Virginia Bailey's and Judy Yount's interdisciplinary unit on changes, with an emphasis on butterflies and moths. This plan incorporates science observations with writing. Children's literature on the topic of butterflies and

(d) what we can do to save it. Finally, there should be an activity that the group urges the class to participate in to show support for the organization (e.g., sign a petition, recycle paper so that fewer trees have to be cut down, etc.).

(Skill goals 1–3,
cognitive goals 1–3,
and affective goal 1)

INDIVIDUAL PROJECT

Each student will pick one individual project to work on and hand in at the end of the unit.

1. Zoos can be a good resource for helping to save endangered species. Build or draw a model of a zoo with at least five different endangered species in it. Show what needs to be provided for each animal to ensure its survival in the zoo. (Cognitive goal 2)
2. Write an original story at least two pages in length describing the cause and the effect of a world without animals. (Cognitive goal 4)
3. Write an essay at least two pages in length answering the following questions: How have stories like "Little Red Riding Hood" shaped our attitude toward the wolf? Is this an attitude we should revise? Why or why not? (Taken from Encyclopedia Britannica Educational Corporation's *Endangered Species Picture Series*, 1976.) (Affective goal 2)
4. Research an animal that we do not study in class and make an "Animal in Danger" flashcard that includes a picture of the animal on the front and five multiple-choice questions about the animal on the back. Use the flashcard to quiz the class. (Skill goal 3)

CLASS DISCUSSIONS AND ACTIVITIES

There will be several discussions and activities throughout this unit that students will be expected to participate in. Overall enthusiasm and involvement in these activities will be evaluated, as well as the students' projects and tests that students will be expected to take.

moths is used during the reading period during this unit. Art activities enrich the learning experiences.

Through their observations of the children they teach, the two teachers learned that, in the minds of first-grade children, reading and writing are very closely related. They decided to develop units that allowed children to read and write and investigate interesting topics such as caterpillars, cookies, and planets. In each unit they selected appropriate children's books of fiction, nonfiction, and poetry that were related to the topic. They located songs on the topic when possible. Skill teaching was embedded in the unit, within the context of the literature, poetry, or music. The science and social studies facts and concepts are easily mastered by children when they are presented in the context of illustrated stories, poems, and songs. Math concepts were introduced by adding counting, measuring, sequencing, and patterning games and activities to each unit.

CHANGES

A First-Grade Multidisciplinary Unit by Virginia Bailey and Judy Yount

This primary learning unit was planned to provide students with a set of varied learning experiences to help them understand the concept of change, with an emphasis on changes in the life cycle of living things.

GOALS

Cognitive Goal: Students will understand that all living things change over time.

Affective Goal: Students will accept change as a natural part of their own lives and environments.

Psychomotor Goals: Students will use observation skills to identify changes. They will use writing and speaking skills to report what they have learned through observation.

ACTIVITIES

Nature Walk

Prior to the nature walk, students are asked to imagine what they might find out about caterpillars and butterflies on the walk. During the walk, they look especially for cocoons. On returning to the classroom, they discuss their findings. They predict whether the cocoons they found will become butterflies or moths. This discussion is followed by writing about what they saw on their nature walk.

Observing Caterpillars

Caterpillars ordered from a science supply dealer arrive in plastic jars. Students observe them climb up to the top of the jar, preparing to form a chrysalis. In just a few days, they begin to spin the chrysalis. They remain in this form for 3 or 4 days and then emerge as butterflies or moths.

As a follow-up activity, students are asked to illustrate the various changes they observe. A strip of 18- by 6-inch paper is prepared for each child. The children fold the paper into fourths and draw each stage of a butterfly's development: (1) egg on a leaf, (2) caterpillar, (3) chrysalis or cocoon, (4) butterfly or moth.

In groups of four, children evaluate their products and check the proper sequence. They then tell stories about their own butterfly to each other.

Color Changes

In a learning center, students experiment to discover how colors change. Using diluted red, blue, and yellow food colors, the children use an empty cup and an eye dropper to mix colors and experiment on their own to create new colors from the original primary colors.

Children's Literature

A variety of picture books related to change are collected by the teacher to be used in the unit. Some books will be read aloud by the teacher and used as a focus for discussion. Others will be selected by the children to read on their own.

Caterpillar/Butterfly Art Activity

Children create a wiggly caterpillar by cutting 12 cups from an egg carton. They make a small hole in the bottom of each cup. They then tie a knot at one end of a piece of yarn, and string the 12 cups together. Finally, they add paper eyes and decorate with crayon or paint.

Children create a butterfly by cutting out 3 of the 12 cups from an egg carton for the body. They then add wings and pipe cleaner antennae.

Gym Shoe Butterfly

The children place their gym shoes on a large piece of pastel-colored paper (arches on the outside). They trace the shoes into a butterfly shape and cut it out. They then add antennae. The children can write a poem inside the butterfly shape.

Days of the Week

Students create a caterpillar with seven circles cut from construction paper. They then copy the name of one day of the week on each circle and glue them to a piece of background paper in the correct order. Afterward, they add a face, legs, and antennae.

How People Change

Students bring in pictures of themselves as babies and put them up on a bulletin board. Current school pictures are also arranged on the bulletin board. Students try to match the baby pictures with the current pictures of their classmates. Discussions focus on how people change, observing differences in size, hair, and other physical features, as well as what people are able to do at different ages. As a follow-up activity, students write in their journals about how they have changed.

Growth Charts

Charts on the students' current height and weight are initiated during this unit. Each student measures and weighs a partner. These data are recorded on a wall graph. These charts are updated three times during the year.

Poetry About Change

Poems about caterpillars and butterflies, seasons, and other changes are distributed frequently during the unit. Students read them, memorize and recite them, discuss them, and illustrate them. The poems are also used to teach language structure and vocabulary skills. A poem is projected on a screen using an overhead projector. Students also have copies of the poem on their desks. Together the students and the teacher look for words in the poem that exhibit certain linguistic features, such as the following:

1. Locate and read words with -y endings.
2. Locate and read words with -ing endings.
3. Locate and read words with -ly endings.
4. Identify compound words.
5. Identify the syllables in the word caterpillar.
6. Locate and read rhyming words.

7. Locate and read short-*u* words.
8. Locate and read short-*i* words.

Art/Nutrition Activity
Children create a caterpillar out of fruit, vegetables, and peanut butter.

Unit Evaluation Activity
Provide students with a piece of paper that has the beginning of three paragraphs (see below). Project a copy on the screen using the overhead projector, and clarify for students how to begin and what is expected.

Because primary students are unable to write all that they know and have observed, this evaluation can be extended by asking children from an upper elementary grade to interview the primary children and write the younger students' responses for them.

This week, I learned about butterflies and moths. First, I learned . . .

Next, I learned . . .

Finally, I learned . . .

Conclusions

The curriculum of any subject or of a combination of subjects may be subdivided into thematic units of study that are often highly motivating to students and a source of pride for the teachers who create them. Teacher-crafted curriculum units are often highly creative and original products. For teachers who choose to create them rather than rely on textbook lessons and content, units are a way of individualizing the curriculum to capitalize on the interests and talents of the teacher and the students.

OPPORTUNITIES FOR REFLECTION

▼ Reflective Essay: Selecting a Unit Topic

List several unit topics or themes that interest you. What are their strengths and weaknesses? Which topics might you be able to use during student teaching? Do you wish to work on your unit alone or with a colleague? Why?

▼ Classroom Visit

While at the school, visit the school library or media center. Locate resources there that you could use in your unit if you taught in that school. Interview the librarian to ask for suggestions for other resources on that topic. Include these materials in your unit resource list.

REFERENCES

BELL, M., & BELL, J. (1990). *First grade everyday mathematics: Teacher's manual and lesson guide*. Evanston, IL: Everyday Math Tools.

CULLUM, A. (1967). *Push back the desks*. New York: Citation Press.

DREYER, S. (1985). *The bookfinder* (Vol. 3). Circle Pines, MN: American Guidance Service.

HANSON, J. (1987). *When writers read*. Portsmouth, NH: Heinemann.

KIERSTEAD, J., & MENTOR, S. (1988). Translating the vision into reality in California schools. *Educational Leadership, 46*(2), 35–40.

NATIONAL WILDLIFE FEDERATION. (1990). *Nature education catalog*. Washington, D.C.: National Wildlife Federation.

Sequencing Objectives in Lesson Plans

6

EDUCATIONAL GOALS, LEARNING OUTCOMES, AND UNIT PLANS are all important elements used in the process of planning curricula to educate our young people. But they are meaningless words on paper unless they are translated into a practical set of logically ordered, day-to-day learning events. Goals, outcome statements, and unit plans are only guides for the real-life classroom encounters between teacher and students. To be successful, when teachers introduce new units in class, they must have a systematic plan for what to teach on Monday, Tuesday, Wednesday, Thursday, and Friday. But, as all teachers know, these plans may need to be flexible enough to fit the particular needs of students in the specific classroom.

This chapter will provide some guidelines for the creation of a sequence of day-to-day learning events, usually referred to by teachers as *lesson plans*. It will also challenge you to consider what to do when the lesson plan goes awry or when students have insufficient skills to master the planned objectives, or when you introduce a topic and find that some students have already mastered that content or skill.

WRITING OBJECTIVES TO FIT GOALS AND OUTCOME STATEMENTS

Goals and outcome statements are the broad, long-term descriptions of how you want your students to grow and develop and what you want them to know, understand, and be able to do over a given period of time. To chart your students' progress toward meeting these long-term goals, it is useful to write a series of objectives that work together to enable your students to show that they are achieving the intended outcomes.

Before we can apply curriculum theories to actual practice, it is necessary to clarify the use of the terms *objective* and *behavioral objective*. Educational *objectives* are short-term, specific descriptions of what teachers are expected to teach and/or what students are expected to learn. As described by Bloom and colleagues in the *Taxonomy of Educational Objectives* (1956), they are intended to be used as an organizational framework for selecting and sequencing learning experiences. Embedded in the goal of teaching children how to read are hundreds of possible specific objectives. One teacher may have an objective of teaching students how to decode an unfamiliar word using phonics and another objective of teaching them how to decode an unfamiliar word using context clues. Another teacher may select and emphasize the objectives of decoding unfamiliar words by using syllabification or linguistic patterns.

Objectives describe the *sequence* of learning events that must take place in order for an outcome statement to be realized. Objectives also allow teachers to chart the progress made by the group or by individuals. Diagnosis of students' needs and deficiencies can be done accurately only if there is a guideline or chart of expected progress with which to compare each student's achievement.

Behavioral Objectives

Over the past several decades, many educators have searched for ways to apply scientific principles of controlling for conditions and measuring outcomes of educational planning. Robert Mager (1962) proposed that teachers plan their lessons by writing *behavioral objectives* that state precisely what the learner will be able to do after successfully completing a learning experience.

Behavioral objectives are distinguished from other types of objectives in that they describe an observable and measurable behavior. They are written in a form that specifies the *conditions under which the learning will take place,* the *newly learned action or behavior,* and the *criteria for success.* As an example, a behavioral objective could be:

> After practice-writing the spelling words five times each, the student
> will write the words when dictated by the teacher, spelling 18 out of 20
> words correctly.

This statement includes a description of the conditions for learning (after practice-writing the spelling words five times each), the behavior (write the words when dictated by the teacher), and the criteria for success (spelling 18 out of 20 words correctly).

Behavioral objectives can have a very positive effect on teaching effectiveness; teachers who use them become better organized and more efficient in teaching and measuring the growth of students' basic skills. When following a planned sequence of behavioral objectives, the teacher knows exactly what to do and how to judge the students' success. The teacher is also better able to explain to the students exactly what is expected and how to succeed with this system of planning.

As with any educational practice, however, overreliance on specific objectives can have a negative result. Critics of behavioral objectives believe that curriculum development has been "reduced to smaller and smaller objectives which too often become ends in themselves. Much of what is worth teaching and knowing becomes trivialized when stated in rigid behavioral form. . . . As with much in life, knowledge and use of objectives can be destructive if used in excess. Beginners should realize that although such knowledge is a useful tool," it is better to emphasize the planning of "coherent, connected learning experiences which facilitate one's goals for the class, as a group and as individuals" (Zumwalt, 1989, p. 178).

Problem-Solving Objectives

Eliott Eisner (1985) observes that when specific skills or competencies are being taught, behavioral objectives can serve as a useful way of visualizing and organizing the appropriate learning experiences. "One must be able to swim four lengths of the pool to be able to swim in the deep end" (p. 117). But, he cautions, "one should not feel compelled to abandon educational aims that cannot be reduced to measurable forms of predictable performance" (p. 114).

As an alternative form, for learning outcomes that cannot be predicted and calibrated, Eisner suggests the problem-solving objective:

> In a problem-solving objective, the students formulate or are given a problem to solve—say, to find out how deterrents to smoking might be made more effective, or how to design a paper structure that will hold two bricks sixteen inches above a table, or how the variety and quality of food served in the school cafeteria could be increased within the existing budget.
>
> In each of these examples the problem is posed and the criteria that need to be achieved to resolve the problem are fairly clear. But the forms of its solution are virtually infinite. (pp. 117–118)

Eisner points out that behavioral objectives have "both the form and the content defined in advance. There is, after all, only one way to spell aardvark" (p. 119). The teacher using behavioral objectives is successful if all children display the identical behavior at the end of the instructional period. "This is not the case with problem-solving objectives. The solutions individual students or groups of students reach may be just as much a surprise for the teacher as they are for the students who created them" (p. 119). As an example, a problem-solving objective might be:

> When given a battery, a light bulb, and a piece of copper wire, the student will figure out a way to make the bulb light up.

This objective describes the conditions and the problem that is to be solved, but the actual behaviors used by the student are not specified. The criterion for success is straightforward but is not quantifiable, and in fact, some of the most important results of this experience are only implied. The teacher's primary aim is to cause the student to experiment, hypothesize, and test methods of solving the problem. This process cannot be quantified and reported as a percentage. Problem-solving objectives, then, are appropriate when teachers are planning learning events that allow and encourage students to think, make decisions, and create solutions. For that reason, they are frequently employed when teachers plan lessons that are designed to develop critical, creative thinking. They are especially valuable when teachers are planning learning events at the higher levels of Bloom's Taxonomy.

Expressive Outcomes

Some lessons are purposely designed to be open-ended experiences. In any of the fine arts, for example, lessons may be designed that have no preplanned or explicit objectives. An example of an expressive outcome is for students to listen to a symphony and draw or paint a response to the music. To expose children to new ideas and experiences, a lesson may consist of a field trip to a museum or through a forest. The teacher may have no prespecified objectives for either event, except to allow the students to discuss their observations afterward. For lessons such as these, Eisner (1985) suggests that the appropriate planning device is the *expressive outcome*, which is intended to "provide a fertile field for personal purposing and experience" (p. 120).

Expressive outcomes are also valuable for including the affective domain in lesson plans. If an affective goal of the unit is to encourage independent thought and action, then lesson plans need to include outcome statements that allow room for exploration and original ideas. If you have an affective goal of increasing cooperation among students, then lessons need to be planned to allow students to work together. If you hope to encourage any form of creative expression, then your lesson plans can reflect and acknowledge the importance of such creative pursuits through the use of expressive outcome statements.

Bloom's Taxonomy

Many teachers use Bloom's Taxonomy of Educational Objectives as the basis for organizing instructional objectives into coherent and connected learning experiences. The term *Bloom's Taxonomy,* as commonly used by teachers, refers to the six levels of the cognitive domain described below. Any curriculum project—a year-long plan, a unit, or a lesson plan—can be enriched by the conscious planning of learning events at all six levels of the Taxonomy:

HIGHER-LEVEL OBJECTIVES	Level 6: Evaluation
	Level 5: Synthesis
	Level 4: Analysis
	Level 3: Application
LOWER-LEVEL OBJECTIVES	Level 2: Comprehension
	Level 1: Knowledge

Knowledge-level objectives can be planned to ensure that students have a knowledge base of facts, concepts, and other important data on any topic or subject. *Comprehension-level objectives* cause students to clarify and articulate the main idea of what they are learning. Behavioral objectives are very useful and appropriate at the knowledge and comprehension levels.

At the *application level,* problem-solving objectives or expressive outcomes can be written that ask students to apply what they've learned to other cases or to their own lives, thereby causing them to transfer what they've learned in the classroom to other arenas. *Analysis-level* objectives and outcomes call on students to look for motives, assumptions, and relationships such as cause and effect, differences and similarities, hypotheses, and conclusions. When analysis outcomes are planned, the students are likely to be engaged in critical thinking about the subject matter. Since the *synthesis level* implies an original response, expressive outcomes are very appropriate. They offer students opportunities to use creative thinking as they combine elements in new ways, plan original experiments, and create original solutions to problems. At the *evaluation level*, students engage again in critical thinking as they make judgments using internal or external criteria and evidence. For these levels, problem-solving objectives or expressive outcomes are likely to be the most appropriate planning devices.

For example, in planning a series of learning events on metric measurement, the teacher may formulate the following objectives and outcome statements:

> *Knowledge-Level Behavioral Objective:* When given a meter stick, students will point to the length of a meter, a decimeter, and a centimeter, with no errors.

> *Comprehension-Level Behavioral Objective:* After a discussion about the uses for each of the following units of measure, the student will write two examples for using the meter, centimenter, liter, milliliter, gram, and kilogram, with no more than one error.

> *Application-Level Problem-Solving Objective:* Using a unit of measure of their choice, students will measure the length and width of the classroom and compute the area.

> *Analysis-Level Problem-Solving Objective:* Students will create a chart showing the relationships among measuring units in the metric family.

> *Synthesis-Level Expressive Outcome:* A group of four students will hide a "treasure" on the playground and create a set of instructions using metric measures that will enable another group to locate the treasure.

> *Evaluation-Level Expressive Outcome:* Students will debate their preference for metric or nonmetric measurement as a standard form of measurement.

In reviewing the six objectives and outcomes for metric measurement, it is clear that the first two differ from the others in that they specify exactly what students will do or write to get a correct answer. In addition, the criteria for success are not ambiguous. These two qualities are useful in ensuring successful teaching and learning at the knowledge and comprehension levels. After successfully completing these first two objectives, students will have developed a knowledge base on metric measurement that they will need to do the higher-level activities. In the problem-solving objectives, students are given greater discretion in determining the methods they use and the form of their final product. In the expressive outcome statements, discretionary power is necessary if students are to be empowered to think critically and creatively to solve problems for themselves.

Although the Taxonomy was originally envisioned as a hierarchy, and although it was believed that students should be introduced to a topic beginning with level 1 and working upward through level 6, most educators have found that the objectives and learning experiences can be successfully taught in any order. For example, in dealing with racial segregation in the United States or in South Africa, a teacher may introduce the topic by asking students to discuss their opinions or attitudes toward segregation (an evaluation-level objective). The teacher may then provide them with knowledge-level data and work back up to the evaluation level, hoping to demonstrate the differences in attitudes that the learning experiences have created among the students. Jane Elliott, the third-grade teacher who divided her class by eye color to teach them to think critically about racial segregation, was beginning with an application-level objective. This story is described in *A Class Divided* by William Peters (1984).

It is often desirable to begin with objectives that call on students to do, think, find, question, or create something and thereby instill in them a desire to know more about the topic. Knowledge- and comprehension-level objectives can then be designed to provide the students with the facts, data, and main ideas they need to know in order to further apply, analyze, synthesize, and evaluate the ideas they are interested in.

Figure 6–1 shows a planning device offering teachers ideas for learning events that correspond to each level of the taxonomy.

SEQUENCING OBJECTIVES IN SCHOOL SUBJECTS

Sequencing Objectives in Mathematics

Some subjects are very sequential in nature. Mathematics is the best example in the elementary curriculum because its concepts and operations can be ordered from simple to complex quite readily. Teachers can very easily organize the teaching of computational skills in the basic operations of addition, subtraction, multiplication, and division. For example, Outcome Statement 1 describes the sequence of presentation of a basic skill (one of the three Rs) that has been part of the elementary curriculum since the establishment of the one-room schoolhouse:

Mathematics Outcome Statement 1: Students will be able to subtract two-digit numbers, using regrouping when necessary.

To accomplish this outcome, kindergarten teachers will introduce the students to the concept of numbers and give them concrete manipulative experiences in adding and subtracting one-digit numbers. First-grade teachers will introduce the concepts of place value and offer students experiences in which they must regroup 1s into 10s and 10s into 1s. With this preparation, students in second grade can learn to write the subtraction problem in a column, determine whether regrouping is necessary, and compute the answer to the problem.

Math textbooks offer a sequence of learning activities and practice using math facts, but reflective teachers find that the textbook must be used flexibly and supplemented with other learning experiences. Prior to planning math lessons for a particular group of students, it is essential for the teacher to pretest their entry-level knowledge and skills. Pretests will reveal that some children have already mastered some of the skills in the sequence and do not need to spend valuable time redoing

FIGURE 6–1
Lesson Planning Using Bloom's Taxonomy

Learning objectives can be planned at all levels of Bloom's Taxonomy. Behavioral objectives are best suited for knowledge and comprehension levels; problem-solving and expressive objectives are best suited for application, analysis, synthesis, and evaluation levels.

Examples of Objectives	*Appropriate Action Verbs*
Knowledge Level Can recognize and recall specific terms, facts, and symbols.	**Knowledge Level** Find, locate, identify, list, recite, memorize, recognize, name, repeat, point to, match, pick, choose, state, select, record, spell, say, show, circle, or underline.
Comprehension Level Can understand the main idea of material heard, viewed, or read. Is able to interpret or summarize the ideas in their own words.	**Comprehension Level** Explain, define, translate, relate, demonstrate, calculate, discuss, express in own words, write, review, report, paraphrase, summarize.
Application Level Is able to apply an abstract idea in a concrete situation, to solve a problem or relate it to prior experiences.	**Application Level** Change, adapt, employ, use, make, construct, demonstrate, compute, calculate, illustrate, modify, prepare, put into action, solve, do.
Analysis Level Can break down a concept or idea into its constituent parts. Is able to identify relationships among elements, cause and effect, similarities and differences.	**Analysis Level** Classify, distinguish, categorize, deduce, dissect, examine, compare, contrast, divide, catalog, inventory, question, outline, chart, survey.
Synthesis Level Is able to put together elements in new and original ways. Creates patterns or structures that were not there before.	**Synthesis Level** Combine, create, develop, design, construct, build, arrange, assemble, collect, concoct, connect, devise, hypothesize, invent, imagine, plan, generate, revise, organize, produce.
Evaluation Level Makes informed judgments about the value of ideas or materials. Uses standards and criteria to support opinions and views.	**Evaluation Level** Appraise, critique, consider, decide, assess, choose, conclude, debate, judge, editorialize, give opinion, grade, rank, prioritize, value.

From TAXONOMY OF EDUCATIONAL OBJECTIVES: The Classification of Educational Goals: HANDBOOK I: COGNITIVE DOMAIN. By Benjamin S. Bloom et al. Copyright © 1956. By Longman Publishing Group. Reprinted by permission of Longman Publishing Group.

what they already know. They need enriched math activities to allow them to progress. Other children may not have the conceptual understanding of number relationships to succeed on the first step. For them, preliminary concrete experiences with manipulative materials are essential for success.

Sample math objectives to fit Outcome Statement 1:

Students will be able to

1. add two single-digit integers.
2. add two double-digit integers.
3. subtract two single-digit integers.
4. subtract two double-digit integers without regrouping.
5. subtract a single-digit integer from a double-digit integer with regrouping.
6. subtract a double-digit integer from a double-digit integer with regrouping.
7. given two double-digit integers, students will be able to subtract one from the other, deciding whether regrouping is necessary.

These sample objectives are representative of the basic knowledge- and comprehension-level skills needed to accomplish the outcome statement. They can be written in behavioral objective form, specifying what percentage of correct answers must be attained to demonstrate mastery.

These objectives emphasize basic computational skills. In keeping with the National Council of Teachers of Mathematics' recommendation to emphasize problem solving over computation, reflective teachers are likely to plan lessons that include many additional math outcomes and objectives at the higher levels of Bloom's Taxonomy to teach students how to apply the math facts to actual problem-solving situations. But this example does illustrate the importance of matching objectives to outcome statements in a logical sequence. Each objective builds on the one before it, as in going up a series of steps on a stairway. If students master each objective, they are continually progressing toward mastery of the outcome statement.

Sequencing Objectives in Language Arts

Not all subjects in the elementary curriculum are as sequential as mathematics. Language arts consists of knowledge, skills, and abilities that develop children's understanding and use of language. Reading, writing, speaking, and listening are all part of the language arts curriculum, and each one can and should have its own outcome statement(s). Outcome Statement 2 suggests one illustration of how the language arts curriculum is designed:

> *Language Arts Outcome Statement 2:* Students will be able to write papers that are spelled correctly, accurate grammatically, and well organized in meaning and form.

Again, this outcome statement will take years to accomplish, but teachers at every grade level are responsible for providing learning experiences that build toward the ultimate goal. The objectives to reach this goal may be similar every year for several years, but written in increasing levels of difficulty. This is known as a *spiral curriculum.*

Sample language arts objectives to fit Outcome Statement 2:

By the end of grade 1, students will be able to

1. write a sentence containing a subject and a verb.
2. use a capital letter at the beginning of a sentence.
3. use a period or question mark at the end of a sentence.
4. review and edit sentences for complete meaning.

By the end of grade 3, students will be able to

1. write a paragraph that focuses on one central idea.
2. spell common words correctly in writing samples.
3. use capitalization and sentence-end punctuation correctly.
4. review and edit a paragraph to improve the organization of ideas.

By the end of grade 6, students will be able to

1. write several paragraphs that explain one concept or theme.
2. use a dictionary to spell all words in a paper correctly.
3. use correct punctuation, including end marks, comma, apostrophe, quotation marks, and colon.
4. review and edit papers to correct spelling, punctuation, grammar, and organization of ideas.

By the end of grade 8, students will be able to

1. write papers with an introductory paragraph, logical reasons and data to support the main idea, and a closing statement.
2. use a dictionary to spell all words in the paper correctly; use a thesaurus to increase the vocabulary of the paper.
3. eliminate fragments and run-on sentences.
4. review and edit papers to correct spelling, punctuation, grammar, organization of ideas, and appropriateness for the purpose.

When teachers are given curriculum guidelines such as these, they must still translate the outcome statements and objectives into actual learning experiences that are appropriate and motivating for their own students. To pretest how well your students use written language when they enter your classroom, plan a writing experience in the first week. Analysis of these writing samples will allow you to plan suitably challenging activities for your students. In this example, the first-grade teacher must decide what topics to have students write about and when to limit students to copying teacher-made examples or allow them to begin to write their own sentences. The third-grade teacher knows that students will not learn all these skills in just one writing lesson. It is necessary to continually provide interesting classroom experiences so that students will have ideas to write about.

The sixth-grade teacher has to plan a series of research and writing experiences so that students will have ample opportunities to synthesize all the skills required at that grade level. The eighth-grade teacher must provide students with a variety of purposes so that they can learn to write differently for different audiences and purposes.

Curriculum planning of subjects such as language arts is a complex undertaking because it contains so many varied outcomes and objectives. The previous example illustrates only a single outcome for teaching students how to write. Teachers must also plan outcome statements and objectives for reading, listening, and speaking. An opportunity to practice this skill in cooperative groups is provided in the Opportunities for Reflection at the end of this chapter.

Sequencing Objectives in Science

As discussed in Chapter 4, the elementary science curriculum should inform students of the basic facts and concepts of science topics, but it should also give students opportunities to experience how scientists work. These dual goals of the science curriculum are often expressed as *teaching both content and process.* An example of an outcome statement in science that covers both content and process is as follows:

> *Science Outcome Statement 3:* Students will be able to name and demonstrate the functions of the various systems of the human body.

Sample science objectives to meet Outcome Statement 3:

The student will be able to

1. draw a human body and label the major organs of the circulatory, respiratory, skeletal, and nervous systems.
2. demonstrate how the heart pumps blood throughout the body.
3. do an experiment to show how the lungs exchange oxygen and carbon dioxide.
4. make a model of how bones are connected at joints.
5. demonstrate how the nerves transport messages from the senses to the brain.

As a method of pretesting students' existing knowledge of each new science topic, the teacher may begin with a preliminary discussion, asking students what they already know about the topic. In this example, the teacher may ask students to describe the functions of various organs. Using the information gained from this preliminary discussion, the teacher can gear the lessons to a level that connects with students' prior knowledge and expand it.

In this example, teachers would plan content-oriented lessons with knowledge- and comprehension-level behavioral objectives that prepare students to identify and accurately label the systems of the body. Subsequent process-oriented lessons would include laboratory experiences in which students work like scientists to gather knowledge through experimentation in order to demonstrate the functions of the various systems.

Sequencing Objectives in Social Studies

Reflective elementary teachers can also see the need for both content and process in their social studies curriculum. They attempt to help their students build a knowledge base in history and geography, but they also give attention and time to teaching students how to acquire information on their own.

An example of an outcome statement in social studies that covers both content and process is as follows:

> *Social Studies Outcome Statement 4:* Students will be able to use a map and a globe to find place names and locations. They will then create a chart listing the countries, major cities, rivers, and mountain ranges in each continent.

Sample social studies objectives to meet Outcome Statement 4:

The student will be able to

1. identify the seven continents on a world map and a globe.
2. interpret the countries' boundaries with a map legend.
3. list the countries in each continent.
4. interpret the symbol for rivers on the map legend.
5. list the major rivers in each continent.
6. interpret the symbol for mountain ranges on the map legend.
7. list the mountain ranges in each continent.
8. create a chart showing the countries, cities, rivers, and mountain ranges in each continent.

In this example, the teacher has planned a set of learning activities that will add to the students' knowledge base about world geography. This set of activities also equips the students to find and interpret information on maps and globes. This social studies curriculum demonstrates that by employing hands-on learning experiences, students are able to learn both content and processes simultaneously, and that they become active rather than passive learners throughout the entire set of activities. An oral or written pretest might consist of having students name or point to certain geographical locations and read and interpret a map legend. The information from the pretest is valuable in planning lessons that use students' existing knowledge and add to it.

Sequencing Objectives in Interdisciplinary Units

The elementary curriculum, especially in the primary grades, is often enriched by incorporating fine arts experiences into the academic subjects. Primary children are often asked to illustrate math examples by drawing one pumpkin plus two pumpkins or to create 10 different pictures using a rectangle. Songs and rhymes frequently accompany learning about historical events and people. Many such events are dramatized as well. Stories and films are often used to augment many aspects of the curriculum.

In the intermediate years, there may be a diminishing emphasis on the fine arts except in special art and music classes or on special occasions and holidays. This is due, in part, to the crowded curriculum that teachers are required to deliver. Given the prevailing culture of the late twentieth century, the fine arts are often deleted to make time for academic and social subjects. But each teacher must consider the place of fine arts in the curriculum. Reflective teachers are likely to consider the importance of the arts in enhancing the joy of living and to make them an integral part of every learning experience. This has the effect of increasing the active involvement, creative thinking, and inventiveness of children.

An example of an outcome statement that includes fine arts with an academic subject is as follows:

Fine Arts/Social Studies Outcome Statement 5: Students will be able to distinguish the important similarities and differences among world cultures by comparing their politics, economies, sports, art, music, literature, and drama.

Sample objectives to meet Outcome Statement 5:

The student will be able to

1. select one country of the world to study.
2. read at least three books or articles about that country.
3. draw a map of the country's geographical boundaries and features.
4. write a fact sheet or chart about the country's political and economic conditions.
5. analyze how the geographical features of the country have influenced its political and economic conditions.
6. draw examples of the country's art and architectural treasures.
7. analyze how the political and economic conditions have influenced the art and architecture of the country.
8. locate a story, poem, or piece of music from that country.
9. create a drama event featuring the stories, poems, and music of all the countries.

This ambitious set of learning experiences demonstrates how well the fine arts can be incorporated into an academic subject. Cognitively, children who take part in this series of experiences will develop a knowledge base of facts, ideas, and concepts about the world. They will also gain the understanding and use of such processes as communication and problem-solving skills. Affectively, they will learn to appreciate and understand differences and similarities among people by sharing the cultural arts of each country.

PLANNING ASSESSMENTS THAT FIT YOUR OBJECTIVES

How does a teacher measure success? Traditionally, the methods that are used most often to assess individual achievement are written quizzes, tests, and essays. When elementary teachers want to determine whether the class as a whole has understood what was taught in a lesson, they frequently use oral responses to questions that usually begin "Who can tell me . . .?" These methods are useful and efficient ways to assess student achievement at the knowledge and comprehension levels of Bloom's Taxonomy, but reflective teachers are seldom satisfied with these measures alone. They seek out other methods that are used less frequently but more appropriate in evaluating learning at the higher levels.

Knowledge-level objectives are tested by determining if the student can remember or recognize accurate statements or facts. Bloom and colleagues (1956) observed that "probably the art of testing has been developed to the greatest extent in the measurement of knowledge. This type of behavior can be measured with great efficiency and economy" (p. 78). Multiple-choice and matching tests are the most frequently used measuring devices.

Comprehension-level objectives are often tested by asking students to define terms in their own words (only knowledge would be tested if the students are asked to write a definition from memory). Another frequently used testing device is a question requiring a short-answer response, either oral or written, that demonstrates that the student understands the main idea. Essays that ask students to summarize or interpret are also appropriate. Multiple-choice tests are also used as tests of comprehension, but the questions call on the students to do more than recall a fact from memory; they ask students to read a selection and select the best response from among several choices.

Knowledge- and comprehension-level objectives are frequently written as behavioral objectives that specify the criteria for success in a measurable form. If the observable behavior is writing an essay, the teacher may need to describe the length, form, and content of a paper that is acceptable. For example, the criteria may be specified as the

> minimum number of correct responses (e.g., 7 out of 10 correct)
> with a minimum of five paragraphs, each describing a geographical feature of the country being studied.

At the *application level*, students are usually asked to apply what was learned in a classroom to a new situation. "If the situations presented to the student to test 'application' are old ones . . ., the student does not have to 'apply' the learning. Rather, he needs merely to recall" (Bloom, Englehart, Furst, Hill, & Krathwohl, 1956, p. 125). For that reason, application-level objectives are usually assessed by presenting an unfamiliar problem that requires the student to transfer what was learned previously to the unfamiliar situation. These types of problems can seldom be quantified into minimums, maximums, or percentages. Instead, success is measured by the extent to which the problem is solved and the means employed to solve it.

To assess application, then, teachers must provide students with challenging problems to solve and a format for tendering their solutions. Essays in which students describe what they would do in the new situation can be used to assess their ability to apply what they have learned. In classrooms where students are encouraged to use manipulative materials and experiment with methods to solve problems, teachers assess the processes used by the student and the end product, such as a hand-drawn or computer-generated design of a new device, a written plan for solving a problem, or a model of a new product. These products may or may not be graded, depending on the teacher's need to quantify or qualify students' success.

Analysis-level objectives may also require the teacher to present the student with unfamiliar material and ask the student to analyze it according to some specified criteria. "The material given for analysis in a test may be a literary passage, a description of a scientific experiment or a social situation, a set of data, an argument, a picture, or a musical selection" (Bloom, Englehart, Furst, Hill, & Krathwohl, 1956, p. 149). In these situations, students may be asked to analyze various elements, relationships, or organizational principles, such as the way elements are categorized, differences and similarities, cause and effect, logical conclusions, or relevant and irrelevant data.

Again, essays may be used to assess analytical behavior, but they must do more than present the main idea (comprehension) and describe how the student would apply previously learned knowledge. Analytical essays must clarify relationships, compare and contrast, show cause and effect, and provide evidence for conclusions. Other student products that are appropriate for assessing analysis are time lines, charts that compare or contrast or categorize data, and a wide variety of graphs that show relationships.

Bloom and colleagues (1956) noted that there were special problems in the assessment of *synthesis-level* objectives:

> A major problem in testing for synthesis objectives is that of providing conditions favorable to creative work. . . . Perhaps the most important condition is that of freedom. This should include freedom from excessive tension and from pressures to adopt a particular viewpoint. The student should be made to feel that the product of his efforts need not conform to the views of the instructor. . . . Time is another important condition. Many synthesis tasks require far more time than an hour or two; the product is likely to emerge only after the student spends considerable time familiarizing himself with the task, exploring different approaches, interpreting and analyzing relevant materials, and trying out various schemes of organization. (p. 173)

The types of student products that demonstrate synthesis are infinitely variable. Written works such as creative essays, stories, poems, plays, books, and articles are certainly appropriate for assessing language arts objectives. Performances are just as useful, including original speeches, drama, poems, and musical compositions. Student-created products may include original plans, blueprints, artwork, computer programs, and models of proposed inventions. Currently, student work may be collected in portfolios to demonstrate growth and achievement in a subject area.

Evaluation of the relative success of synthesis products is a very difficult matter. There may be no objective criteria for judging the value or worth of a student's original product. When students' products are entered in a contest or submitted for publication, other outside judges with expertise in the subject area provide feedback and may even make judgments that are impossible for the classroom teacher to make. "Checklists and rating scales should be especially useful here, but the examiner ought to insure that they do not emphasize elements of the product to the neglect of *global* qualities which, after all, may be more fundamental in any synthesis" (Bloom, Englehart, Furst, Hill, & Krathwohl, 1956, p. 174). Many elementary teachers simply record whether or not a finished product was turned in by the student, rather than attempt to evaluate or grade it.

Bloom and colleagues (1956) describe two quite different forms of *evaluation-level* objectives. One type calls on students to make a judgment based on internal evidence. In this case, all the facts and data needed to make the judgment are provided in the test situation, and the student simply selects and applies them. To test a student's ability to make this type of judgment, the teacher must provide all the needed data, perhaps in the form of charts or graphs, and ask the student to draw certain conclusions from these data.

Another form of evaluation is to make judgments based on external criteria, such as rules and standards by which such works are generally judged. In this case, assessment strategies are designed in which the student is given a situation, makes a judgment, and justifies that judgment by applying the appropriate criteria. For example, students may be asked to make and justify aesthetic judgments of a work of art or to judge the validity of a political theory, stating the appropriate criteria used in making the evaluation. The types of products that students create at this level are critical essays, discussions, speeches, letters to the editor, debates, drama, videotapes, and other forms that allow students to express their points of view.

Like synthesis outcomes, evaluation outcomes and objectives are difficult to grade. A teacher who offers students an opportunity to express their own views usually places high value on independent thinking and freedom of expression. Therefore, the teacher cannot grade a student's response as "right" or "wrong." But the teacher can assess whether the student has used accurate, sufficient, and appropriate criteria in defending a personal opinion. Student work that has cited inaccurate, insufficient, or inappropriate evidence should probably be returned to the student with suggestions for revision.

Affective outcomes may be assessed by teacher observation as students work on various projects. It is also useful to involve students in self-evaluation to monitor their own affective growth in areas such as self-confidence, independence, cooperation, or creativity.

In summary, evaluation of student accomplishment should be directly linked to the lesson's objectives. To assess basic knowledge and skills, behavioral objectives are useful because they state exactly what the student will be able to do and specify the criteria for success. For higher-level objectives, problem-solving objectives may be less precise but they still should describe the type of student behavior or product expected and give some general criteria for success. To assess the growth in the affective domain, expressive outcomes are planned and students can state orally or in writing what they have gained from a certain experience.

When teachers plan by writing clear behavioral, problem-solving, and expressive objectives for their lessons, they are, in effect, clarifying their expectations regarding what students will gain from the lesson and their criteria for success. The evaluation section of a lesson plan is then usually a restatement of the criteria expressed in the objectives. You will see an example of this in the sample lesson plans presented later in this chapter.

VARYING OBJECTIVES FOR STUDENTS WITH SPECIAL NEEDS

Often teachers plan their lessons with a set of objectives for the students in their class whose knowledge and skills are at grade level. The term *at grade level* means the average or typical level of understanding or skill that most children are able to achieve at that age and in that grade. Standardized achievement tests have been normed to provide teachers with information about what average learners should know and be able to do at their grade level in the basic subjects of the curriculum. As teachers gain experience teaching at a grade level, they are able to describe what the typical learner at that grade level can accomplish. Since most children in the class will have skills and knowledge near the average, it makes sense for teachers to plan lessons with difficulty levels conforming to the average.

But reflective teachers also observe that within each classroom, there are likely to be children whose skills and knowledge levels are quite different from the norm or average. *Criterion-referenced pretests* are essential tools in determining what students know and what they are ready to learn. They reveal that some children are able to work more quickly and to understand more difficult material than the average child at that grade level. Pretests reveal that other students do not have the prerequisite skills and knowledge to master the planned objectives. They will learn successfully only if the teacher modifies the lesson to meet their needs. Individual or small-group lessons must be planned to provide them with the vocabulary and skills they lack. For some children to achieve successful growth of skills and understanding, the teacher must be willing to alter the pace of the lesson, the difficulty of the material, and the criteria for success.

For students who learn more slowly, one modification that is needed is to reduce the volume of material in a lesson. If the grade-level lesson calls for the students to complete 20 problems in one class period, the teacher may reduce this requirement to 10 or 15 problems for a student who works slowly. If 20 problems were expected of this child, there would be little chance for success, resulting in frustration for both teacher and child. When the pace is lowered, the child has an opportunity to succeed and is likely to show the increase in motivation that accompanies success.

There are a variety of reasons that a child may have missed or not learned some important basic skills in previous grades. Illness, family problems, emotional difficulties, inferior teaching, or frequent moves may have prevented a child from learning the skills that most children his or her age have attained. In the children's novel *Roosevelt Grady* by Shotwell (1963), a child from a migrant family moves so often that he never learns what "putting into" means:

> This was his question: When you put something into something else and it doesn't come out even, what do you do with what's left over?
>
> What happened yesterday was exactly what had happened at the school where he'd first heard about putting into. The teacher came to where it seemed she must explain it the very next day. And then what? That time it was the beans that ran out. This time it was celery. . . . And same as yesterday, Roosevelt never got back to school to hear what the teacher had to say. (pp. 19–20)

For students like Roosevelt Grady, who have not attained the basic skills necessary for a grade-level task, the modification that is needed is to teach the prerequisite skills first before introducing the new material. When these prerequisite skills have been successfully mastered, the student may be able to proceed at the average pace.

Some children in your classroom may have been identified as *learning disabled*. This label may mean that a child has one or more of a variety of learning disorders, some physical and others social or emotional in origin. When a child has been labeled learning disabled, a teacher who specializes in working with such children will be called on to create an individualized educational plan (IEP) for that child. The classroom teacher will receive some guidance from the IEP on how to modify lessons for that child.

Obviously, children with hearing impairments need lessons that are modified to provide directions and instruction using visual aids. Similarly, sight-impaired children may require extra auditory learning aids. Less obviously, there may be children in your classroom with strong auditory, visual, or kinesthetic learning style preferences. To meet the needs of these children, teachers must modify their lessons to accommodate all three types of learning styles. This is usually accomplished by providing instructions and examples using visual aids to learning such as the chalkboard, books, and written handouts. For auditory learners, the teacher may allow the use of tape recorders to record the instructions and examples given in class. Kinesthetic learners require manipulative materials and hands-on experience in order to make sense of unfamiliar material. When a teacher provides visual, auditory, and kinesthetic learning aids and experiences, students may modify their own lessons by taking in the needed information in the modality that fits their own learning style preferences.

For children who work unusually rapidly and accurately on grade-level material, the task is to provide appropriately challenging learning experiences so that these children are able to continue to make gains even though they have mastered the grade-level requirements. There are two standard methods of meeting the needs of highly able learners: *acceleration* and *enrichment*. While both strategies are valuable modifications, acceleration is appropriate for sequential subjects such as math and enrichment is appropriate for other subject areas. An *inappropriate* modification is to simply give the child more work at the same level. For example, if 20 math problems are required of the students working at grade level, an easy modification to make is to simply require the highly able learner to do 40. This practice is common but does not serve the child's real need to gain new skills and understanding.

Some acceleration strategies that teachers can choose from include ability grouping, curriculum compacting, and mastery learning. *Ability grouping* requires the teacher to modify the curriculum to fit three different groups in the classroom. High, middle, and low groups are created, with variations in material and in expectations for success. Reflective teachers must consider the possible negative consequences of lowered self-esteem and the possible positive benefits of academic fit and organizational efficiency when deciding whether or how to use ability grouping in the classroom.

In some schools, ability grouping may be organized across several grade levels. Subjects such as math and language arts may be scheduled at the same time of day, allowing students who work above or below grade level to leave their own classrooms and travel to another classroom where the instruction is geared to their learning level.

Curriculum compacting can occur in a single classroom. This strategy requires the teacher to pretest students in various subject areas. Those children who demonstrate mastery at the time of the pretest are allowed to skip the subsequent lessons altogether. In this way, the grade-level curriculum is compacted for them. Teachers then provide materials at a higher level of difficulty for these students, who typically work on their own through the more difficult material, with little assistance from the teacher, who is busy instructing the students at grade level.

Mastery learning is a highly individualized teaching strategy that is designed to allow students to work at their own pace on material at their own difficulty level. Pretests are used to place students at the appropriate difficulty level. As each new skill is learned, a posttest is used to demonstrate mastery. This technique will be described in more detail in Chapter 10.

Enrichment strategies vary according to the imagination of the teacher who creates them. The teacher provides students who demonstrate mastery of a basic skill with a challenging application of that skill. Objectives and learning experiences at the higher levels of Bloom's Taxonomy are often used as the basis for enrichment activities. A child who easily masters grade-level material is frequently allowed to investigate or research the topic in greater depth. As outcomes of enriched activities, students typically create an original product, perform an original skit, or teach the class something that has been learned from the research.

Modification of lessons is a continuous challenge to teachers. It is not easy to decide whether a child needs a modified lesson. Reflective teachers struggle with this decision because they know that when they lower their expectations for a child, one of the effects may be lower self-esteem, creating the conditions for a self-fulfilling prophecy that the child cannot achieve at grade level. But they also know that when adult expectations are too high, students experience little or no success, leading to a similar downward spiral. For beginning teachers it is wise to consult with other teachers in the school, especially teachers who specialize in working with learning-disabled, gifted, or handicapped youngsters. Talk over your concerns with these specialists, and make an informed decision about lesson modifications.

WRITING A WELL-ORGANIZED LESSON PLAN

When teachers plan for day-to-day learning experiences, they are creating lesson plans. Usually a lesson plan is created for a single subject or topic for 1 day. Elementary teachers in self-contained classrooms must devise several different lesson plans each day, one for each subject they teach. Teachers in the upper grades who work in a departmentalized setting, where students travel from class to class for various subjects, must still create a different lesson plan for each grade or group of children they teach.

In the university or college courses designed to prepare teachers, the lesson plan is an important teaching/learning device. The professor and experienced classroom teachers can provide the aspiring teacher with models of good lesson plans. As students create their own, they are able to demonstrate the extent to which they understand and can apply the theories and principles they have learned about reflective thinking and planning.

For that reason, many university and college programs require students to create a number of precise, detailed lesson plans. Sometimes students observe that the classroom teachers they know do not write such extensive plans for every lesson. Instead, these teachers write their lesson plans in a large weekly planning book, and that a single lesson plan may consist of "Math: p. 108," "Social Studies: Review Ch. 7," or "Science: Continue Nutrition." While experienced teachers may record their plans with very brief notes, a novice teacher needs to write lessons in great detail in order to be able to know what resources to gather for the lesson. Writing detailed lesson plans also allows the novice teacher to visualize the procedures to be used ahead of time. In addition, by writing lesson plans, novice teachers can communicate their plans to a professor or mentor teacher, who can provide feedback on the plan before the lesson is taught.

Well-written lesson plans have another value. They can be shared. A teacher's shorthand notes that serve as a personal reminder can rarely be interpreted by an outsider. If a substitute teacher is called on to replace a classroom teacher for a day or longer, it is necessary to be able to communicate the daily plans to that teacher in language he or she can understand and use. Teams of teachers often write lesson plans together or for each other. In this case, it is important that they have a common understanding of the lesson's objectives, procedures, evaluation, and resources.

The form may vary, but there are a number of common elements in most lesson plans. Three essential features of a complete, well-organized lesson plan are the objectives, procedures, and evaluation. These correspond to the four questions of curriculum planning formulated by Tyler. Lesson *objectives* specify the "educational purposes" of the lesson. The *procedures* section describes both "what educational experiences can be provided" and the way they can be "effectively organized." The *evaluation* section describes the way the teacher has planned in advance to determine "whether these purposes are being attained" (Tyler, 1950, p. 1).

In addition, there may be several other features in a lesson plan used to identify it and to give the reader a quick overview of its purpose or description. A lesson plan often contains information about the resources needed by teachers as background preparation for teaching the lesson, as well as any materials that will be needed in the actual execution of the lesson.

A suggestion for teachers in this age of computers is to create a basic outline of a lesson plan on a word processor and save it on a disk. Then, whenever you wish to write a lesson plan, you can put the outline on the screen and fill in the spaces. The outline for a lesson plan should contain the elements given in Figure 6–2. This outline can be copied to your computer disk for use in college and beyond.

On rare occasions, a teacher may create a single lesson on a topic such as fire safety, a holiday, or a news item. Usually, however, a single lesson plan does not stand alone in a classroom. It is part of a unit or a year-long plan for a subject in the curriculum. As shown earlier in this chapter, learning events are planned in a logical sequence of lessons designed to gradually increase student understanding and skill in the subject area. In the next three sections, sample lesson plans will be described for

FIGURE 6–2
Model Lesson Plan
            (This model may be entered and saved in your word processor)

Title of Lesson:
Subject Area:
Grade Level:
Date Created:

DESCRIPTION:

OBJECTIVES:
            1.
            2.
            3.

MATERIALS NEEDED:

PROCEDURES (What will you be doing? What will students be doing?):
            1.
            2.
            3.
            4.
            5.
            6.

EVALUATION:

---

four subjects in the elementary curriculum, showing the lesson itself and how it fits into the long-term plan for that subject.

Sample Lesson Plan in Mathematics

Earlier in this chapter, a series of mathematics objectives were described to teach primary children arithmetic computation. Here, again, are three of those objectives:

4. Subtract two double-digit integers without regrouping.
5. Subtract a single-digit integer from a double-digit integer with regrouping.
6. Subtract a double-digit integer from a double-digit integer with regrouping.

Within a math unit on arithmetic, a teacher may plan one or more lessons for each of these objectives. During the second or third week of the unit, after teaching addition and subtraction with single digits, the teacher may plan an introductory lesson on Monday for objective 4, with a follow-up on Tuesday. On Wednesday, the teacher may plan to introduce objective 5, with additional practice on Thursday. On Friday, as an assessment of the first several weeks of the unit, a test will be administered on all the computation skills used up to that point in the unit.

These objectives are representative of what many people refer to as *basic skills*. They may be basic, but they don't have to be boring. Objectives such as these can be written at the higher as well as the lower levels of Bloom's Taxonomy. Figure 6–3 illustrates a sample lesson for Wednesday's introduction of subtraction with regrouping.

The sample lesson plan is an extremely detailed account of a relatively short lesson in mathematics. It is so detailed that you can almost see the teacher and the students as they go through the two learning activities. For learning how to teach, this visualization of a lesson is important. Lesson plans are very similar to *scripts* for the teacher's performance, and allow novice teachers to rehearse their performance before getting up before a class of students.

If this lesson had been planned less thoroughly, the teacher might have been caught unprepared in a number of different ways. Necessary materials may have been missing or instructions may have been less clear, resulting in confusion and misbehavior. In fact, in reviewing this lesson, you may spot errors, omissions, or other problems. You might plan this lesson quite differently. For example, this lesson plan doesn't specify how the objects will be distributed to the pairs of students. You might want to visualize that in your mind and write it down as a separate step. Steps 3 and 4 in this plan could cause difficulty if left in that order. Why? What do you see and hear happening as the coins are distributed and the teacher gives instructions? How would you eliminate this potential trouble spot in the lesson?

Creative teaching takes more organization than rote teaching. This lesson is much more difficult to plan and manage than one in which children match numerals with pictured coins on a workbook page and then compute subtraction problems on a piece of paper. If you hope to be a creative teacher who provides students with a variety of motivating learning experiences, then visualizing and writing down your lesson plans will be especially important to you.

Sample Lesson Plan in Language Arts/Social Studies

Many times a single unit contains learning events in more than one subject, and a single lesson can accomplish objectives in two or more areas at the same time. For example, students can use language skills in a social studies unit or discuss and write about social studies topics in a language arts unit.

Consider the set of objectives described above for language arts that were designed to produce the outcome of writing standard English that is spelled correctly, is accurate grammatically, and is well organized in meaning and form. In the sixth grade, students are expected to be able to

1. write several paragraphs that explain one concept or theme.
2. use a dictionary to spell all words in the paper correctly.
3. use correct punctuation including end marks, comma, apostrophe, quotation marks, and colon.
4. review and edit papers to correct spelling, punctuation, grammar, and organization of ideas.

The teacher may wish to choose a central theme and spend some time on prewriting experiences so that the students will have thought about the topic from

SAMPLE MATH LESSON PLAN

Title of Lesson: Subtraction of two integers with regrouping
Subject Area: Mathematics
Grade Level: Third grade
Date Created: 10/12/91

DESCRIPTION:
Using dimes and pennies, students will regroup and subtract double-digit integers.

OBJECTIVES

1. Knowledge: When given a number from 0 to 50, students will show the correct number of pennies and dimes that correspond to that number.
2. Application: In pairs, students will buy and sell objects from each other, giving correct change when necessary.
3. Comprehension: Students will be able to state in their own words how to regroup dimes and pennies in order to subtract two-digit numbers.

MATERIALS NEEDED

Nine pennies for each pair of students
Five dimes for each pair of students
Household objects each labeled with a price tag ranging from 10 to 49 cents.

PROCEDURES

1. State purpose: To teach subtraction when the bottom digit is larger than the top digit.
2. Pair students and distribute five dimes and nine pennies to each pair.
3. Give instructions for Activity 1: Take turns being the player and the checker. The player will gather the correct coins for each number called by the teacher. The checker will check and help if necessary.
4. Activity 1: Say aloud: 6, 9, 12, 16, 23, 27, 31, 36, 44, 48.
5. Give instructions for Activity 2: Take turns being the buyer and the seller. The seller will choose an item to sell. The buyer will pay with dimes only. The seller will give change. The buyer will check to see if he or she has received the correct change.
6. Activity 2: Allow 5–8 minutes for several transactions.
7. Ask students to tell how to compute the correct change. Show the relationship to regrouping in subtraction, with examples on the chalkboard.

EVALUATION
Call on students of varying achievement levels to describe in their own words how to make change and how making change is similar to regrouping. Five problems using regrouping will be included, and students must compute four of them correctly for mastery.

many different perspectives. The teacher will have developed an interest in it and will have something meaningful to say. Imagine, for example, that the central focus of this language arts unit is "The Law."

Prior to accomplishing any of these objectives, the teacher might show a film in which the central character, perhaps a teenager, has an encounter with the law. Another possibility is a field trip to a courtroom to see a trial. The teacher might create a mock courtroom trial in the classroom. Using "Jack and the Beanstalk" as the court case, the students might be assigned roles as Jack, the giant, various eyewitnesses, attorneys for both Jack and the giant, the judge, the court reporter, the bailiff, and the 12 members of the jury. By rearranging the furniture in the classroom to resemble a courtroom, the students will become actively involved in this learning experience. As they prepare their "cases" or listen to the "evidence," they are likely to care deeply about the outcome of the case.

Following prewriting experiences such as these, the students are likely to care about the quality of the essays they write as well. The students' intrinsic motivation to explain their views on the law will be well established.

Postwriting expectations are just as important as prewriting experiences. To motivate students to edit and improve their writing, it is important to establish a purpose for their essays. If they know that their essays are going to be sent to the local newspaper for possible publication, submitted to a contest, included in a student magazine, or collected and bound as a class collection, they are more likely to take the job of editing seriously.

This set of objectives and the accompanying prewriting experiences will take a number of lessons to accomplish. An example of a lesson that appears in Figure 6–4 occurs after the prewriting experiences, including the classroom trial, have taken place. In this sample lesson, the teacher's plan is to help students consider possible ideas related to the law, focus on a single topic for an essay, and assist them in getting started writing.

Although this lesson contains fewer details in the procedure section than the math lesson did, it still has the same basic elements. One addition here is a notation about the time planned for each section of the lesson. This is a useful strategy because it helps the teacher focus on what is important and what is not. Many lessons have been spoiled by including too much or staying too long on a trivial matter. By visualizing the lesson beforehand and estimating the amount of time each activity will take, the teacher can decide how much to include in each lesson.

When this lesson is actually taught, the teacher may discover that the times allocated for each procedure are inappropriate. The lesson may remain unfinished if the webbing takes longer than planned. If students are unable to focus on topics, the actual writing may have to be postponed altogether. The starting place for the next day's lesson is dependent on how much is completed in this one. For that reason, lesson planning is a flexible, changeable process rather than a rigid and exact system.

Sample Lesson Plan in Science

The lesson plan for science (Figure 6–5) is taken from the unit on endangered animals created by De Paul University student Monica Lyons (see Figure 5–4).

SAMPLE SOCIAL STUDIES/LANGUAGE ARTS LESSON PLAN

Title of Lesson: Law Essay Topic Selection
Subject Area: Language Arts/Social Studies
Grade Level: Sixth
Date Created: 11/9/91

DESCRIPTION

Guided by the teacher, students will brainstorm a list of concepts and topics related to the law on the chalkboard. Students will select one topic from the group list and start on the first paragraph of their essays.

OBJECTIVES

1. Analysis/Synthesis: Students will contribute ideas to a list of concepts about the law and assist in categorizing the ideas that fit together.
2. Application: Students will write the first paragraph of an essay on a topic of their choice.

MATERIALS NEEDED

Chalk and chalkboard
Paper
Pens or pencils

PROCEDURES

1. State purpose: to write a well-organized essay on the law
   Tell expectations: three to four paragraphs, all errors edited and corrected
   Final drafts to be bound together in a book
2. Webbing (15 min.): Write "LAW" in the center of the board. Ask students to provide topics, people, ideas, and examples related to that word. As each student contributes an idea, he or she must state where it goes in relation to other words on the chalkboard. Go around the room once before allowing students to give a second idea.
3. Topic Selection (10 min.): In pairs, students discuss topics, ask each other questions, and write down possible topics that each would like to do. The teacher walks around the room, giving advice as needed on topic selection.
4. Writing (20 min.): Pairs rehearse possible topic sentences for the first paragraph of the essay, followed by quiet writing of the first paragraph.

EVALUATION

Each student contributes at least one idea to the web. Students turn in their first paragraphs at the end of the period for the teacher to review. Editing will take place in groups and in teacher–student conferences as writing progresses.

SAMPLE SCIENCE LESSON PLAN

TAKE A WALK ON THE WILD SIDE!

DESCRIPTION

Students will learn about the mountain gorilla of Africa, analyze its situation, and make a poster of an animal we have studied so far.

OBJECTIVES

1. After studying the mountain gorilla, students will be able to point out Africa on the map and explain what the gorilla's habitat is like. (knowledge for cognitive goal 2)
2. Students will be able to explain in their own words why the mountain gorilla is endangered and what will happen if these contributing factors continue. (analysis for cognitive goal 3 and affective goal 3)
3. Students will work in groups of four to make a poster (with either drawings or cut outs from magazines) of one of the animals we have studied so far, showing the animal and its natural habitat and labeling the poster correctly. We will hang posters on the classroom bulletin board. (application for cognitive goal 2)

PROCEDURES

1. Introduce Africa and have students find it on a map.
2. Explain the climate.
3. Show a picture of the mountain gorilla.
4. Describe the animal's appearance and habits.
5. Go over the reasons for endangerment.
6. Lead a class discussion on what can be done to save the mountain gorilla.
7. Tell about a poster and divide students into groups of four so that they can work on the poster.

EVALUATION

Student evaluation will be based on suggestions they give during the class discussion and on the accuracy of the poster, with attention to neatness and detail.

MATERIALS

Map of the world
Picture of the mountain gorilla
Construction paper
Scissors
Markers
Copies of National Geographic magazine

According to her organizational plan, this is the seventh lesson in her unit. In it she begins a process that will actually take much longer than a single day to complete, as students plant a tree from a seed and record its growth over the next 3 months. Your own lesson plans can vary from these three models, but by creating a standard form with the elements suggested in this chapter, you will quickly learn how to plan a well-organized lesson on paper, and can then translate that practice into planning "in your head" and "on your feet" as you gain experience in the classroom.

Conclusions

Lesson plans are written scripts that teachers write so that they can present a well-organized set of learning experiences for their students. The objectives of the lesson specify the teacher's expectations for what the students will learn or be able to do as a result of the lesson. When teachers plan objectives that specify the criteria for success, they clarify for themselves what the students must be able to do in order to demonstrate mastery of the skill or understanding of the concepts in the lesson.

To plan the procedures of a lesson in advance, many reflective teachers visualize themselves teaching the lesson. They write down what they must do to teach the lesson successfully and what the students will do in order to learn the material actively. Teachers who can visualize the entire process of teaching and learning can write richly detailed lesson plans. When they begin to teach the lesson, they have a supportive script to follow.

As teachers become more proficient and experienced at planning and teaching, their written lesson plans are likely to become less detailed. But for beginning teachers, a thorough, richly detailed plan is an essential element for a successful lesson.

OPPORTUNITIES FOR REFLECTION

▼ Reflective Essay: Adapting Lessons to Fit Individual Needs

What are your views on meeting the individual needs of students in your classroom? With mainstreaming becoming more prevalent, you are likely to have a number of students with special needs in your classroom every year. How will you provide them with appropriate learning experiences and criteria for success that are possible for them to achieve? How will you cope with the fairness issue if other children complain that they have to do more work than a special needs child?

▼ Classroom Visit: Teacher's Lesson Plans

Ask the cooperating teacher to show you his or her lesson plans. How do these plans differ from the ones presented in this chapter? Teachers with many years of experience seldom write detailed lesson plans. Instead, they use a plan book and jot down main ideas for each lesson to be taught.

REFERENCES

BLOOM, B., ENGLEHART, M., FURST, E., HILL, W., & KRATHWOHL, D. (1956). *Taxonomy of educational objectives: Cognitive domain.* New York: Longman.

EISNER, E. (1985). *Educational imagination* (2nd ed.). New York: Macmillan.

MAGER, R. (1962). *Formulating instructional objectives.* Palo Alto, CA: Fearon.

PETERS, W. (1984). *A class divided: Then and now.* New Haven, CT: Yale University Press.

SHOTWELL, L. (1963). *Roosevelt Grady.* New York: Grosset & Dunlap.

TYLER, R. (1950). *Basic principles of curriculum and instruction.* Chicago: University of Chicago Press.

Reflective Classroom Instruction

LEARNING TAKES PLACE almost continuously in our lives. Every new experience has the potential to teach us something that we didn't know before. From the day of birth, individuals learn new responses, skills, facts, and ideas. We learn at home, at the ball park, at a swimming pool, in the woods, and in school classrooms.

Teaching is also a common and natural occurrence. Small children teach each other new words, how to climb trees, and how to make block towers. As we mature, we have more and more occasions to teach others what we have learned from our own experience. Some individuals are referred to as "born teachers." They seem to require no textbooks or courses to instruct them how to teach; teaching appears to come naturally to them. They sense what the learner needs to know, and the language springs easily from their mouths to assist the learner in understanding the new idea or the next step in a process.

As you begin to have opportunities to teach, it is likely that you will begin to develop your own conception or personal theory of how learning is best encouraged in elementary classrooms. Your personal conception of the teaching/learning process will be drawn from your own experiences as a learner, from the values and beliefs you hold about what children ought to know and how they ought to behave, and from your perceptions and reflections about the theories and practices of other classroom teachers that you observe.

CURRENT RESEARCH ON TEACHING AND LEARNING

In order to become a reflective teacher, it is also important that you stay current with the emerging research and knowledge base about teaching and learning. Gathering information from research is an important attribute of a reflective thinker and teacher.

The Cognitive-Mediational Conception of Learning

Anderson (1989a) describes two widely disparate conceptions of learning that affect teachers' perceptions and reasoning about the teaching and learning processes.

"These conceptions do not correspond exactly to formal theories of learning offered in the psychological literature. They do, however, represent two types of common personal theories held by teachers and other adults" (p. 86). Anderson terms one the *receptive-accrual* (R-A) view and the other the *cognitive-mediational* (C-M) view.

Teachers who hold the R-A view believe that each student has innate, immutable individual differences in the ability to learn. Learning itself is defined as a relatively passive act of receiving information and storing it in memory without modification. In order to demonstrate achievement, the student is expected to recall information from memory and display or demonstrate that it was retained accurately. One implication of this view is that while teaching may be a very active process, learning is passive.

Because R-A teachers view learning as the gaining and storing of information, they believe that the best method to assess how much a student has learned is through the use of tests of memorized data and skills. An important derivative of this view is that success in school is believed to be due to a combination of a student's innate ability and the effort to accrue and retain knowledge. This view leads teachers to explain student failure as a result of inherent inadequacies or lack of effort. When failure occurs, teachers who have this view comfort themselves with the conviction that some students are able to learn and achieve success in school, while others are not (Anderson, 1989a, p. 87).

In contrast, teachers who hold the C-M view believe that learning is dependent on the student's cognitive activity. Learning is defined as the act of processing new information through active, selective perception, relating the new information to prior knowledge and storing it in an organized way until it is called for again.

In this view, teachers view success in school as dependent not on ability or effort but on the student's background knowledge and on knowing how to select and apply cognitive strategies appropriately. Teachers with this view explain student failure as most likely a result of the student's having inadequate prior knowledge and/or a need for more training in selecting and using the cognitive strategies appropriate for the task.

Which view do you hold? Your many years as a student in conventional classrooms will strongly influence your belief in the R-A theory. For many years, you have been led to believe that students are either smart, average, or stupid. Since you are now in a teacher education program, it is likely that you were one of the smart ones. You may have observed long-suffering teachers struggling with students in the low reading group or the low tracks in high school, and you may be convinced, as your former teachers were, that these students can't or won't learn.

The C-M viewpoint, then, will be a struggle for you to accept. From experience, you can expect some of your students to be skillful, accurate, and quick in processing new information, while others are clumsy, erroneous, and slow. As a teacher, it is your task to diagnose the reasons for students' failure to process information efficiently and accurately. It is then your responsibility to plan a set of learning experiences that assist students in activating their existing knowledge so that they can comprehend the new information or skill you are teaching.

In practice, the teaching methods selected by teachers with these two contrasting conceptions of learning are likely to be quite different from each other. The teacher with the R-A view is likely to assign a reading or a page of problems and then monitor students by responding to questions, but doing little else to deliberately stimulate the cognitive processes necessary for students to actively construct meaning. From this perspective, the teacher's role is simply to provide tasks and information and then to offer incentives for students to perform these tasks in the form of grades or gold stars. Unfortunately, the R-A teacher may believe that the actual learning of the material is "out of the teacher's power" (Anderson, 1989a, p. 87).

In contrast, C-M teachers believe that they do have the power to mediate in the learning process. This power is not automatic and it is not easily won, but by using the reflective teaching model, C-M teachers observe their students carefully, gathering information about what prior knowledge they possess and what is lacking. They observe students as they work on a problem and listen to them as they read or respond to a question. From this process of gathering information, they plan lessons and select teaching strategies that will fill in the gaps in their students' knowledge and help them to organize what they know into useful patterns and structures, so that they are able to activate the appropriate knowledge and bring it to bear on new learning situations.

Teachers who understand the cognitive process of acquiring and processing information can apply their power in countless ways to the benefit of their students. They can reduce external stimuli so that the important bits of knowledge are perceived by the short-term memories of their students. They can pace the delivery of new information to give students sufficient time to process one bit of knowledge in working memory before introducing another. They can phrase questions in such a way that they provide the appropriate cue to retrieve the stored information from long-term memory.

Schema Theory

The retrieval process is obviously a critical factor in being able to use stored information. Knowledge, concepts, and skills that are learned must be stored in the brain until they are needed. According to the *schema theory,* each subset of knowledge is stored in a *schema,* an outline or organized network of knowledge about a single concept or subject. It is believed that young children develop schemata (the plural form of *schema*) made up of visual or other sensory images, and as language increases, verbal imagery replaces the sensory images (Anderson, 1989a; Anderson & Pearson, 1984; Bransford, 1983).

For example, an infant stores sensual images in the schemata for mother, bottle, bed, and bath. Later, the verbal labels are added. A schema grows, expands, or otherwise changes due to new experiences. If the infant sees and touches a large, round, blue ball, he or she can store sensory images of its size, color, rubbery feel, and softness. At a later encounter, the infant may experience it bounce toward or away from him or her, and can store these images in the same schema. A year later, when the child learns to say the word *ball,* the label is acted on in working memory and stored in long-term memory within the schema for ball.

Children come to elementary school with widely varied schemata. Some children, who have had many experiences at home, in parks, zoos, and museums, and in other circumstances, may enter kindergarten with complex schemata for hundreds of topics and experiences. Other children, whose experience has been severely limited by poverty or other circumstances, are likely to have fewer schemata, and the ones they have are quite sparse. Similarly, if children come from highly verbal homes where parents talk with them frequently, their schemata are likely to contain accurate verbal labels for stored sensory experiences and phenomena. But children who are raised in less verbal homes have fewer verbal components to their schemata. This theory complements Piaget's observations of the stages of development and helps us to understand how a child's vocabulary develops.

Schemata also vary according to their organizational patterns. As children mature, each schema expands to include many more facts, ideas, and examples. In cases of healthy development, the schemata are frequently clarified and reorganized. Learning new information or observing unfamiliar examples often causes a schema to be renamed or otherwise altered. For example, very young children have a schema labeled "doggy" that includes all four-legged and furry creatures. As they see new examples of animals and hear the appropriate labels for each type, the original schema of doggy is reorganized to become simply a subset of the schema "animal." New patterns and relationships among schemata are forming every day of a child's life when the environment is full of unfamiliar concepts and experiences.

The importance of schema theory in the C-M conception of learning is that it helps to explain why some students are able to retrieve knowledge better than others. Children who have many accurately labeled schemata are more likely to have the background knowledge needed to learn an unfamiliar concept. Children whose schemata are richly detailed and well organized into patterns and hierarchies are much more likely to be able to retrieve useful information on request than are children whose schemata are vague and sparse.

There are several other important connections between schema theory and the C-M view of learning. Teachers who believe that it is within their power to help their students improve their cognitive processing recognize that one of the best ways to do this is to stimulate students to actively create more well-developed, accurately labeled, and better-organized schemata.

At the elementary grade levels, teachers recognize that one of their most important responsibilities is to aid students in schema development with accurate verbal labels. At the earliest grades (especially kindergarten), teachers emphasize spoken labels, teaching children to recognize and name objects and concepts such as numbers, letters of the alphabet, and colors. In the primary grades, teachers emphasize the recognition and decoding of written labels as an integral part of the reading program. When students exhibit difficulties in learning to read, the C-M teacher is likely to plan learning experiences that assist them in developing schemata that are necessary prerequisites for reading.

Children who have been raised in environments characterized by few experiences with books are likely to have very underdeveloped schemata for reading and books. Reflective teachers who consider the needs of the whole child are likely to provide their students with many opportunities to hear stories read aloud, to choose from a tempting array of books, and to write their own stories as a means of developing a rich and positive schema for the concept of reading.

Advance Organizers

When teachers want to assist students in retrieving information from their schemata, they provide visual or verbal cues that help the students access the appropriate information efficiently. It is also possible for teachers to provide cues to assist students in accurately and efficiently processing and storing what they read, see, or hear. D. P. Ausubel (1960) proposed that learners can comprehend new material better when the teacher provides a clear statement about the purpose of the lesson and about what type of information the students should look or listen for in advance of the lesson. This introductory statement is known as an *advance organizer.*

When we relate this theory to the information processing theory, it is apparent that what the advance organizer does is to provide the learner with an important cue as to which schema will incorporate this new knowledge. The learner can be more efficient in processing the information in working memory and transferring it to the appropriate schema in long-term memory than if no advance information was presented.

For example, consider what is likely to happen when a third-grade teacher introduces a lesson on long division with no advance organizer. Some students will simply reject the new knowledge as incomprehensible. But if the teacher tells students to watch for how division is similar to subtraction, and how it is the opposite of multiplication, the teacher is providing students with the cues they need to retrieve their subtraction and multiplication schemata in advance of the new learning. In the second case, it is more likely that the new facts will be routed into working memory, where they can be processed using the subtraction and multiplication schemata as a framework.

In follow-up studies of Ausubel's hypothesis, many educational researchers designed experiments that showed the same effects. Therefore, this knowledge has been added to our growing common knowledge base. In fact, this particular study demonstrates the way the knowledge base grows. The original hypothesis and study conducted by Ausubel led others to apply the principle to different types of students and environments. As the hypothesis was confirmed in subsequent studies, the knowledge was gradually accepted as a reliable principle of effective teaching. You yourself probably experience the beneficial effects of advance organizers when your teachers tell you in advance what to listen for in a lecture or what to study for an exam. Now you can learn how to use this principle in your teaching career for the benefit of your students.

Time on Task, Active Learning

Children who are provided with suitably challenging learning experiences, and who are involved in cooperative efforts to solve problems or reinforce skills, are actively involved in learning. But active learning is not as common in classrooms as you might suppose.

A major study known as the Beginning Teacher Evaluation Study (BTES) was conducted in the 1970s by a group of researchers who wanted to identify teaching activities and classroom conditions that foster student learning in elementary schools (Denham & Lieberman, 1980). Fifty classrooms in urban, rural, and suburban school districts were observed during math and reading periods. The observers kept logs of the way the teachers taught math and reading, and they interviewed both the students and the teachers to gather data for the study. They used achievement tests as outcome measures (Rosenshine, 1979, 1980).

Their findings showed dramatic differences in the amount of time that teachers allocated for math and reading. Some allocated 25 minutes, while others allocated 50 minutes for one subject per day. As expected, student achievement was found to be positively related to the amount of time allocated.

But allocated time is not always time well spent. The study revealed that in some classrooms students were engaged in work on classroom tasks during the time allocated to the subject, while in other classrooms they did not pay attention to the task for a portion of the allocated time. Time that is actually spent on learning tasks is known by teachers as *time on task*. This is quite a different concept from allocated time, which may or may not be spent on actual work or learning by students.

Studies such as these, as well as reflective observation in their own classrooms, have caused many teachers to realize that simply allocating time to a subject does not ensure that students will be actively engaged in the task. The BTES study showed that student time on task occurred more frequently in the classrooms of teachers who had a high degree of interaction with their students during the task and gave students a good deal of academic feedback.

Other teacher behaviors found to be highly correlated with student achievement were accurate diagnosis of students' skill levels and the prescription of appropriate tasks so that students were able to have a high success rate during the learning period. These elements suggest that it is not only allocated time or time on task that is important. It is the *active learning time,* the amount of time students spend working at their own levels with a reasonable degree of success in learning something new, that is most important in student achievement.

Barak Rosenshine (1980) analyzed the data from the BTES study to determine what actually occurs during the school day. The data showed that only 58% of the school day was spent on academic activities; 23% was spent on nonacademic subjects such as music, art, and physical education; and about 19% was spent on other activities, such as transitions between classes and class business. Within the time teachers allocated to a subject, he found that "overall, students spent about 30 percent of their time in teacher-led activities and 70 percent of their time doing seatwork" (p. 117). Since seatwork is such a large part of the day in most elementary classrooms, reflective teachers give as much serious thought to planning and managing seatwork as they do to planning and managing other forms of instruction. It is important that seatwork provides students with active learning opportunities rather than busy work.

PRESENTATION SKILLS THAT INCREASE CLARITY AND MOTIVATION

Teaching is more than telling. You have been on the receiving end of teachers' lectures, discussions, and other forms of lessons for many years. You know from your own experience that the way teachers present material has an effect on student interest and motivation, which are both integral aspects of the classroom climate. You may have been unable to understand the beginning of a lesson taught by a teacher who failed to get the full attention of the class before speaking. You have probably experienced a sinking feeling when a teacher droned on and on in a monotonous voice during a lecture. You may have experienced frustration when a teacher explained a concept once and hurried on, ignoring questions or comments from the class. Reflective teachers are not likely to be satisfied with a dull, repetitive, or unresponsive presentation style. Most of them are anxious to improve their presentation skills in order to stimulate interest and motivate student achievement.

Getting the Attention of Your Students

To consider systematically the way you present a lesson, think about the beginning. The introduction to a lesson is very important, whether it is the first lesson of the day or a transition from one lesson to another. As Kounin (1977) found in his study of well-functioning classrooms, transitions and lesson beginnings start with a clear, straightforward message or cue signaling that the teacher is ready to begin teaching and stating exactly what students should do to prepare themselves for the lesson. To accomplish this when you teach, it is necessary to tell your students to get ready for a certain lesson and to give you their full attention. Some teachers use a visual cue for this purpose, such as a finger on the lips or a raised arm. Others may strike a chord on the piano or turn off the lights to cue the students that it is time to listen.

It is unlikely that students will become quiet instantly. It will probably take a few moments to get the attention of every student in the class. While you are waiting, use an erect bodily carriage and direct eye contact with those who are slow to respond. Watch quietly as the students get their desks, pencils, books, and other needed materials ready for the lesson. The waiting may seem uncomfortable at first. You will be tempted to begin before they are ready because you will feel that time is being wasted. Don't give in to this feeling. Wait until every voice is quiet, every chair stops scraping, every desk top stops banging, every pencil stops tapping. Wait for a moment of pure, undisturbed silence. Then quietly begin your lesson. You will have the attention of every student.

Some teachers use a bit of drama to begin a lesson. They may pose a question or describe a condition that will interest their students. Richard Klein, a teacher at the Ericson School on the west side of Chicago, begins teaching a unit on aviation by asking students what they know about the Wright brothers. The students' replies are seldom very enthusiastic, so he unexpectedly asks them, "Then what do you know about the Wrong Brothers?" They show a bit more interest but are still unable to provide many informed responses. So Mr. Klein turns out the lights and turns on a videotape of the Three Stooges in a skit called "The Wrong Brothers." Afterward, partly in appreciation of Mr. Klein's humor, the students show a greater willingness to learn about the real historical events.

Often teachers begin with a statement of purpose, describing how this particular lesson will help their students to make an important gain in skills or knowledge. Still others begin by doing a demonstration or distributing some interesting manipulative materials. Madeline Hunter (1982) calls this technique providing *anticipatory set*, both to gain attention and to motivate students to be interested in the lesson. She encourages teachers to use a variety of anticipatory sets appropriate to the lesson content and objective (p. 29).

In contrast, less reflective teachers begin almost every lesson with "Open your books to page _____. David, read the first paragraph aloud." No presentation skills at all are employed in this example. This nonmethod relies on the material itself to whet the students' interest in the topic. While some materials may be stimulating and appealing, most are not. The message the teacher gives to the students is "I don't care much about anything; let's just get through this." The students' motivation to learn drops to the same level as this message and can best be expressed as "Why bother?"

Once you have gained your students' attention and inspired them to want to know more, you move on to the lesson itself. Presentation skills that you can systematically learn to use in your lessons include

> enthusiasm
> clarity
> smooth transitions
> timing
> variation
> interaction
> active learning
> closure

Enthusiasm

Animation is the outward sign of a teacher's interest in the students and the subject. Enthusiasm is the inner experience. "There are at least two major aspects of enthusiasm. The first is conveying sincere interest in the subject. . . . The other aspect is vigor and dynamics," and both are related to getting and maintaining student attention (Good & Brophy, 1987, p. 479). Outwardly, the teacher displays enthusiasm by using a bright and lively voice; open, expansive gestures; and facial expressions that show interest and pleasure. It is well accepted that salespeople who use animated, enthusiastic behaviors can sell beach umbrellas in the Yukon . . . in January. Why shouldn't teachers employ these techniques as well? You can "sell" long division better with an enthusiastic voice. You can convince your students that recycling is important with a look of commitment on your own face. You can encourage students' participation in a discussion with welcoming gestures and a warm smile.

Is animation something that you can control? Absolutely. You can practice presenting information on a topic with your classmates, using an animated voice and gestures. They can give you feedback, which you can use to improve your presentation. Have yourself videotaped as you make a presentation. When you view yourself, you can be your own best teacher. Redo your presentation with new gestures and a different voice. Repeat this procedure several times, if necessary. Gradually, you will notice a change in your own presentation style. You will add these techniques to your growing repertoire of effective presentation skills.

Clarity

A critical factor in student success is the extent to which the teacher's presentation of lesson directions and content is clear and understandable by students. Brophy and Good (1986) listed the importance of teacher *clarity* as a consistent finding in studies of teacher effectiveness. Their review of research on teacher clarity describes negative teacher behaviors that detract from clarity. These include using vagueness terms, mazes, discontinuity, and saying "uh" repeatedly.

As an example of *vagueness terms* Brophy and Good present the following example, with ambiguous language in italics:

> This mathematics lesson *might* enable you to understand *a little more* about *some of the things* we *usually* call number patterns. *Maybe* before we get to *probably* the main idea of the lesson, you should review *a few* prerequisite concepts. . . . (p. 355)

The vagueness terms in this example have the effect of making the teacher sound tentative and unsure of the content. As an introduction to a lesson, it is not likely to capture students' attention or interest. Clarity can be improved by exchanging the vagueness terms for specific ones, resulting in a simple, straightforward statement: "This mathematics lesson will enable you to understand the concept of number patterns. Before we get to the main idea of the lesson, we will review three prerequisite concepts."

Clarity is also reduced by what Brophy and Good call *mazes:* false starts or halts in the teacher's speech, redundancy, and tangled words. For example:

> This mathematics lesson *will enab* . . . will get you to understand *number, uh,* number patterns. Before we get to the *main idea of the,* main idea of the lesson, you need to review *four conc* . . . four prerequisite concepts. . . . (Brophy & Good, 1986, p. 355)

Even when students attempt to pay attention, they may be unable to decipher the meaning of the teacher's words if the presentation is characterized by the false starts in this example. It is obvious that the way to improve this statement is to eliminate the redundant words. This example is a very simple one. Clarity is also reduced when the teacher has begun to present a lesson, is interrupted by a child's misbehavior or a knock at the door, and then begins the lesson again. Kounin (1977) observed that the most effective teachers are able to *overlap* teaching with other classroom management actions. That is, they are able to continue with the primary task, presenting the lesson to the class, while at the same time opening the classroom door or stopping misbehavior with a glance or a touch on the shoulder. When teachers can overlap their presentations, the clarity of their lessons is greatly enhanced.

The third teacher behavior that detracts from clarity is discontinuity, "in which the teacher interrupts the flow of the lesson by interjecting irrelevant content" (Brophy & Good, 1986, p. 355). This is why lesson planning is so important. Without a plan, teachers may simply begin a lesson by reading from a textbook. As they or the students are reading, the teacher (or a student) may be reminded of something they find interesting. They may discuss the related topic for quite some time before returning to the original lesson. This side discussion may or may not be interesting or important, but it is likely to detract from the clarity of the original lesson.

The fourth detractor from teacher clarity noted by Brophy and Good (1986) is repeatedly saying "uh." It is also likely that other repetitive speech patterns are just as annoying, such as "you know." For the beginning teacher, it is likely that some of these behaviors will occur simply as a result of nervousness or unfamiliarity with the content being taught. It would be interesting to study the hypothesis that these four detracting behaviors decrease as a result of teaching experience; in other words, as a teacher gains experience, the four detracting behaviors are reduced and clarity increases.

Two teacher behaviors that were found to enhance clarity were an "emphasis upon key aspects of the content to be learned and clear signaling of transitions between parts of lessons" (Brophy & Good, 1986, p. 355). To emphasize key aspects of a lesson, teachers may state, "This is important" or "To be able to succeed, you need to understand this concept." To signal a transition clearly, teachers may state, "Now we will move on to the next step."

Smooth Transitions

Just as lesson introductions are important to gain students' attention, *smooth transitions* are essential to maintaining that attention and making the classroom a productive working environment. Transitions occur within a lesson as the teacher guides students from one activity to another. They also occur between lessons as students put away what they were working on in one lesson and get ready for a different subject.

Knowing when to terminate a lesson is an important element of teacher withitness:

> When the group is having difficulty maintaining attention, it is better to end the lesson early than to doggedly continue. This is especially important for younger students, whose attention span for even the best lesson is limited. When lessons go on after the point where they should have been terminated, more of the teacher's time is spent compelling attention and less of the students' time is spent thinking about the material. (Good & Brophy, 1987, p. 245)

Transitions between activities and lessons may require that students move from place to place in the room, such as having one group come to the reading circle while another group returns to their seats. Usually students are required to exchange one set of books and materials for another. These movements and exchanges can have a high potential for noise in the form of banging desk tops, scraping chairs, dropped equipment, and students' voices as they move from lesson to lesson.

Jerky and chaotic transitions are often caused by incomplete directions or vague expectations about student behavior from the teacher.

"Take out your math books" is incomplete in that the teacher does not first specify that the students should put away other material they have been working with. The result may be that the students begin to work on desks cluttered with unnecessary materials.

Often, inexperienced teachers begin to give directions for a transition, and the students start to get up and move around while the teacher is speaking. When this happens, teachers may attempt to talk louder so that they can be heard over the din. A way to prevent this from occurring is to inform students clearly that they are to wait until all directions have been given before they begin to move.

Smooth transitions are characterized by clear directions from the teacher about what is to be put away and what is to be taken out, and about who is to move and where they are to go. Clear statements of behavioral expectations are also important. The same techniques for getting attention that were described above apply to the beginning of each new lesson. After a noisy transition between lessons, it is essential for the teacher to have students' complete attention before beginning the new lesson. Wait until all students have moved into their new positions and gotten all of their materials ready before trying to introduce the lesson.

Use of a signal that the teacher is ready to begin the new lesson is very useful. Raised hands, lights turned off and then on again, or the simple statement "I am ready to begin" will signal to the students that they should be ready for the next lesson. After giving the signal, it is important to wait until the students have all complied and are completely silent before beginning the new lesson.

In considering strategies that result in smooth transitions, teachers do well to reflect on children's need for physical activity. It is unrealistic to expect children to be able to sit still through one lesson after another. Some teachers take 5 to 10 minutes to lead children in singing or movement games between two working periods. Other teachers allow students to have a few moments of free time in which they may talk to friends, go to the washroom, or get a drink of water. Some transitions are good opportunities for teachers to read aloud from a story book or challenge students to solve a brain teaser or puzzling math problem.

Reflective teachers find that when they allow students a respite and a change of pace during a brief transition period, the work periods are more productive and motivation to learn is enhanced.

Timing

Actors, speakers, and comedians give considerable attention to improving the timing of their presentations. Good use of timing engages the attention of an audience, is used for emphasis of major points, and sometimes creates a laugh. Teachers also work in front of an audience, and class presentations can be improved by considering timing and pacing as a means of getting attention and keeping it. The pause for a moment of complete silence before you begin teaching is a good example of a way to incorporate timing into your presentation.

In most instances, students respond best to teachers who deliver information and instructions briskly. Kounin's (1977) research on the most effective classroom managers demonstrated that students are best able to focus on the subject when the lesson has continuity and momentum. Interruptions result in confusion. When teachers forget to bring a prop, pause to consult a teacher's manual, or backtrack to present material that should have been presented earlier, inattention and disruptive behavior are likely to occur (Kounin, 1977). Jones (1987) found that students' attention was improved when teachers gave them efficient help, allocating *20 seconds or less* to each request for individual help or reteaching. When this time was lengthened, the result was restlessness and dependency on the part of students.

However, there are times when a pause in instruction can improve your presentation. When presenting new information, researchers have found that it is important to do it in small steps, with a pause after the initial explanation to check for understanding (Hunter, 1982; Rosenshine, 1979). Students may not respond immediately during this pause because they need a moment to put their thoughts into words. Wait for them to do so. Encourage both questions and comments. Ask for examples or illustrations of the fact or concept being discussed. This pause allows your students to reflect on the new material and allows you to test their understanding.

Variation

Lesson variation is an essential presentation skill for teachers who want to develop a healthy, vital classroom climate. On analysis of classroom videotapes, Kounin (1977) noticed that satiation results in boredom and inattentiveness. If presentations are monotonous, students will find a way to introduce their own variation by daydreaming, sleeping, fiddling with objects, doodling, or poking their neighbors.

Planning for variation is important whenever you plan a lesson that will take 30 minutes or longer. Divide your lesson into several segments. Use a lecture for only a part of the time. For example, include segments of discussion, independent practice, small-group interaction, and making and doing activities. If you cannot break up a single lesson into segments, then plan to use a variety of strategies over the course of a day. Use quiet independent work for one subject, group interaction for another, lecture for a third, and hands-on activities for a fourth. In this way, your students will always be expectant and eager for each new lesson of the day. They will feel fresh and highly motivated to learn because of the variations in the way you choose to present material.

Interaction

Students thrive on interaction with the teacher and with their classmates. Rather than employing a traditional teacher-to-student, student-to-teacher pattern of communication, open up your classroom to a variety of interactive experiences. Cullum's (1967) *Push Back the Desks* encourages teachers to do just what the title suggests and provides dozens of suggestions for learning experiences that result in active and interactive learning in every subject in the elementary curriculum.

Pushing the desks into a large circle encourages open-ended discussion from all students. Arranging the desks into small groups encourages highly interactive problem solving. Pushing the desks aside leaves a lot of space in the middle of the room for activities. Pairing the desks provides opportunities for peer teaching or partnerships of other kinds. Your presentations can include all of these types of activities, and you will find that they are motivating not only to your students, but to you as well. You will feel a sense of expectant excitement yourself as you say, "All right, students, let's push the desks into. . . ."

The need for interaction derives from the powerful motivational need for belonging described by Maslow (1954) and Glasser (1986). When these needs are frustrated or denied, disruptive behavior is likely to occur as a means of satisfying them. When teachers consciously plan interactive learning experiences, they allow students to satisfy their drive for belonging and thereby prevent unnecessary discipline problems.

Active Learning Experiences

The BTES study demonstrated the important differences between the time allocated for learning and the actual time during which students engaged in active learning. Presentations must be designed to engage the student in *active learning;* otherwise, the time allocated to the learning experience may, in reality, result in passivity, rote learning, or even resistance to learning.

Presentations can include many verbal, visual, or hands-on activities and opportunities for active learning. Consider a lecture on a topic such as the closed circuit in electricity. Ho hum. Add a visual aid—a poster or an overhead projection. Students sit up in their seats to see better. Now add a demonstration. Turn off the lights. Hold up a battery, some copper wire, and a light bulb. There is a new sense of interest in your students as they watch expectantly.

Turn the lights back on. All of these techniques are adequate to teach the students a concept, but none of them is as valuable as a hands-on experience for in-depth learning and understanding. Picture this scene instead. After lunch the students come into their classroom to find a battery, a flashlight bulb, and a piece of copper wire on each desk. After getting their attention, the teacher simply says, "Working independently, try to get your bulb to light up." Lights go on all over the room—in children's eyes and in their minds as they struggle with this problem. The motivation to succeed is intense and intrinsic, not tied to any exterior reward. Each child has a sense of power and a need to know.

Closure or Lack of Closure?

In the example above, the teacher can aid the students in comprehending what they've learned by having them share what they did that worked and didn't work. Concepts can be developed by articulating and generalizing what they learned about electricity. For this reason, a teacher-led discussion is an essential part of active, hands-on learning. It provides a sense of closure.

On the other hand, Bloom (1981) described a *lack of closure* as an element of the peak learning experiences he studied. He found that some students responded to the lack of closure with an independent effort to find out more about the subject. Each teacher must reflect on this dilemma and find a reasonable balance. To develop concepts, it is vital to lead a discussion of what the students observed and discovered in the present lesson. To stimulate further independent learning, it is possible to generate some additional unanswered questions and hypotheses purposely at the conclusion of a lesson.

Every lesson or presentation can be improved by giving thoughtful consideration to its ending. It is important to allow time for closure. You may use this time to ask questions that check for understanding so that you will know what to plan for the lesson that follows. You may allow the students to close the lesson with their own conclusions and new insights. A few moments spent summarizing what was learned is valuable in any form. If insight is to occur, it will probably occur in this period. At the close of one lesson, you can also indicate what will follow in the next lesson so that your students know what to expect and prepare for.

SYSTEMATIC CLASSROOM INSTRUCTION

Direct Instruction of New Knowledge and Skills

The curriculum of the elementary school, especially in the lower grades, contains a high proportion of basic knowledge and skills that learners must master thoroughly in order to be successful in the upper grades. Basic language concepts such as letter recognition, phonics, decoding words, writing letters and words, and the conventions of sentence and paragraph construction must be mastered. Basic mathematical concepts such as number recognition, quantity, order, measurement, and the operations used in computation must be learned.

In the 1980s, a number of experimental studies were conducted to discover the effects of various teaching methods on the achievement of basic language and mathematics skills. In these studies, student achievement was compared between untrained teachers using conventional teaching methods and teachers who were trained to use a certain sequence of instructional steps in planning, teaching, and evaluating the progress of their students. From these studies, Rosenshine and Stevens (1986) concluded that the most effective series of instructional strategies for teaching basic sequential knowledge or skills are:

> Begin a lesson with a short review of previous, prerequisite learning.
> Begin a lesson with a short statement of goals.
> Present new material in small steps, with student practice after each step.
> Give clear and detailed instructions and explanations.
> Provide a high level of active practice for all students.
> Ask a large number of questions, check for student understanding, and obtain
>   responses from all students.
> Guide students during initial practice.
> Provide systematic feedback and corrections.
> Provide explicit instruction and practice for seatwork exercises and, where nec-
>   essary, monitor students during seatwork. (p. 377)

When these nine strategies are reviewed quickly, many readers may respond with reactions such as "But isn't that what all teachers do? What is new about these methods?"

It is true that many teachers have used these strategies throughout the history of education in rural, urban, and suburban classrooms. But it is equally true that many teachers have not. We have all observed classroom teachers who take a much less active role than these nine steps describe. For teachers who foster the R-A view of teaching and learning, there are often only two steps: assigning work and correcting it.

Rosenshine and Stevens (1986) refer to the proposed sequence of strategies as *systematic teaching* because of its highly organized and sequential pattern of events. On close examination, these steps are comparable to the C-M view of teaching and learning because they describe methods that would be used by a teacher who expects all students to achieve in school if the teacher takes an active role in helping them process the new information that is being taught.

In selecting appropriate teaching methods and strategies, reflective teachers are likely to look for and discover relationships between various theories of learning and methods of teaching. One such relationship exists between the Rosenshine–Stevens model of systematic teaching and the process of thinking and learning known as *information processing.*

The first step, *Begin a lesson with a short review of previous, prerequisite learning,* is a signal to the learner to call up an existing schema that will be expanded and altered in the new lesson. When the teacher begins a lesson with *a short statement of goals,* it provides the student with an advance organizer that allows the processing to take place with increased efficiency. In practice, these first two steps are often presented together and can be interchangeable, with no ill effects.

Current information processing theories suggest that there are limits to the amount of new information that a learner can process effectively at one time (Gagne, 1985). When too much information is presented at one time, the working memory becomes overloaded, causing the learner to become confused, to omit data, or to process the new data incorrectly. This overload can be eliminated when teachers *present new material in small steps, with student practice after each step.* "In this way, the learner does not have to process too much at one time and can concentrate his/her somewhat limited attention on processing manageable size pieces of information or skills" (Rosenshine & Stevens, 1986, p. 378).

Teachers who *give clear and detailed instructions and explanations* are likely to provide students with the support they need while they are processing new information in their working memories.

Providing students with *a high level of active practice* after each step, and again at the conclusion of a series of steps, is important because the practice enhances the likelihood that the new information will be transferred from working memory to long-term memory, where it can be stored for future use. Each time a new skill is practiced, its position in long-term memory is strengthened.

As teachers *guide students during initial practice* and *ask a large number of questions, check for student understanding, and obtain responses from all students,* they are also encouraging their students to process the information accurately. Learning occurs when schemata stored in long-term memory are expanded, enriched, and reorganized. Effective teacher questions and checks for understanding cause students to think about new ideas from a variety of perspectives and to update their existing schemata accordingly.

Providing systematic feedback and corrections and *monitoring students during seatwork* also increase the likelihood that students will process the important points and practice the new skills in the most efficient manner.

Teacher Modeling and Demonstration

When teachers present new information to students, they must carefully consider the method they will use when they introduce it. For elementary students, it is rarely sufficient for teachers to simply talk about a new idea or skill. A much more powerful method of instruction is to model or demonstrate it first and then give students an opportunity to practice the new learning themselves.

A simple example of this technique occurs in the primary grades when teachers say, "First, I will say the word; then you will say it with me." In the middle grades, the teacher may first demonstrate the procedures used in measuring with a metric ruler and then ask students to repeat them. In the upper grades, teachers may write an outline of a paragraph and then ask students to outline the next one.

Teacher demonstration and modeling is an effective instructional technique for almost every area of the elementary curriculum. It is useful in teaching music: "Clap the same rhythm that I do." It is vital in teaching math: "Watch as I do the first problem on the chalkboard." It can easily be applied to the teaching of creative writing: "I'll read you the poem that I wrote about this topic, and then you will write your own."

When teachers circulate throughout the classroom to monitor students as they practice or create their own work, it is efficient to use modeling and demonstration on a one-to-one basis to assist students in getting started or in correcting mistakes.

Scaffolding

Scaffolding is a variation on the technique of teaching by modeling and demonstrating a new skill. It involves a highly interactive relationship between the teacher and student while the new learning occurs. Anderson (1989b) cites Jerome Bruner's work with mothers and children as the first reference to scaffolding. As a mother reads aloud to a toddler, she may simplify the book to meet the attention span and interests of her child, calling the child's attention to material that is appropriate and eliminating material that is beyond the child's present capacity. She is also likely to allow the child to interact with her as they read and discuss the words and pictures on each page. This flexible and simplified interaction between child and parent allows the child to connect new ideas to existing schemata at his or her own level.

Teachers can apply scaffolding in the classroom by reducing complex tasks to manageable steps, helping children to concentrate on one task at a time, being explicit about what is expected and interpreting the task for the student, and coaching the child using words and actions that are familiar and supportive. When coaching the child during a difficult task, it is important to provide sufficient scaffolding through the use of hints and cues so that the child is able to succeed. As students become more and more skillful, the scaffolding can be reduced and finally eliminated entirely.

Scaffolding is a technique that is especially valuable for the primary teacher, since most young students require supportive interaction and accommodation to their existing vocabularies in order to learn new skills. But scaffolding is also appropriate for upper elementary students when the tasks are complex or the students have difficulty with the language.

Some teachers do not use scaffolding techniques at any level:

> Instead of seeing themselves as supporters of students' constructions of knowledge, many teachers see themselves as presenters of content (especially facts and skills) and as orchestrators of activities that bring students in contact

with that content (i.e. the receptive-accrual view described previously). One result is the predominance of the recitation mode of instruction, in which the teacher asks a question, students offer answers that the teacher confirms or disconfirms and the cycle is repeated. Teachers spend little time in the classroom encouraging students to explain how and what they are thinking, elements that are necessary for scaffolded dialogues. (Anderson, 1989b, p. 107)

For beginning teachers scaffolding may not come naturally, since they may not have experienced it in their own school experiences. This technique can be learned only by reflecting on the needs of students, gathering the latest information on such techniques from reading and talking to experienced teachers who have used them successfully, and gradually adding such strategies to your own repertoire.

Structuring Tasks for Success

Researchers have found that the degree of success students have on school tasks correlates highly with achievement in the subject area (Rosenshine, 1979). This finding supports the well-known maxim that "success breeds success." Both formal research and informal discussions with children reveal that when students experience success on a given task, they are motivated to continue working at it or to tackle another one. The number and type of successful learning experiences students have affect their self-knowledge, leading them to have expectations regarding probable success or failure in future tasks (Anderson, 1989a, p. 93).

In order to structure tasks for success, there must be a good fit between the teacher's expectations, the student's ability, and the difficulty of the task. Sylvia Rimm (1986), who has specialized in assisting underachieving students to reach their potential, describes it this way:

> Children must learn early that there is a relationship between their effort and the outcome. . . . If their schoolwork is too hard, their efforts do not lead to successful outcomes but only to failures. If their work is too easy, they learn that it takes very little to succeed. Either is inappropriate and provides a pattern which fosters underachievement. (p. 92)

When teachers select and present academic tasks to their students, it is important that they reflect continuously on how well the task fits the students' present needs and capacities.

William Glasser (1969) has been committed to improving schools throughout his career. As a psychiatrist, he strongly believes that a person cannot be successful in life "until he can in some way first experience success in one important part of his life" (p. 5). Glasser recognizes that children have only two places in which to experience success: home and school. If they are lucky enough to experience success in both settings, they are likely to be successful in their adult lives. If they achieve success at home, they succeed despite a lackluster school experience. But many children come from homes and neighborhoods where failure is pervasive. For these children especially, it is critical to experience success in school. Glasser's book, *Schools Without Failure,* offers many realistic and practical methods for teachers to develop a classroom environment that breeds success.

Matching Teaching and Learning Styles

In order to fully motivate students to learn new material, it is also important to consider each student's particular *learning style*. Dunn, Beaudry, and Klavas (1989) define a learning style as "a biologically and developmentally imposed set of personal characteristics that make the same teaching method effective for some and ineffective for others" (p. 50). In other words, each person has a particular pattern of needs for optimum learning.

Some children learn best in quiet rooms, while others prefer a certain level of noise. Students have individual preferences for light and dark, temperature, and seating. Learning styles in enormous variety have been described, including preferences for the structure of tasks and the best time of day for learning. While you cannot accommodate all the needs of all students, you will want to become aware of some of the many variations in learning styles so that when a student with an unusual sensitivity or a severe impediment to learning appears in your classroom (and this will happen), you will be able to reflect on this student's particular needs and provide a learning environment or restructure your own teaching style to better match his or her learning style.

A set of learning styles based on sensory preferences is especially useful to elementary teachers. In eight studies in the 1980s, learning style preferences for *visual, auditory,* and *kinesthetic* learning were examined. It was discovered that most learners prefer to receive information either visually (by viewing or reading), auditorially (by hearing), or kinesthetically (by touching, working with, or otherwise manipulating materials). There is a strong tendency for teachers to *teach* using the modality they prefer as a learning modality. Specifically, visual learners who rely on reading and viewing material to learn tend to rely on reading and other visual aids as teachers. Similarly, if you learn best by hearing, you may assume that others do also, and as a result, you may teach primarily by using lecture and discussion. Kinesthetic learners who enjoyed hands-on activities as students tend to provide many of these active learning materials in their own classrooms:

> When youngsters were taught with instructional resources that both matched
> and mismatched their preferred modalities, they achieved statistically higher test
> scores in modality matched, rather than modality mismatched, treatments.
> (Dunn, Beaudry, & Klavas, 1989, p. 52)

At present, there are two major approaches to solving this educational dilemma. One solution requires schoolwide cooperation. At each grade level, teachers may be identified as having visual, auditory, or kinesthetic preferences. Students are then tested and placed in the classroom with the teacher whose style matches their own. But this approach offers few opportunities for learners to improve their weaker learning modalities.

Another approach is for each teacher to conscientiously plan to teach using all three modalities. For example, when presenting a lesson, the teacher will provide visual aids in the form of pictures and reading material; auditory aids in the form of a lecture, a discussion, or tape-recorded material; and kinesthetic aids in the form of models or other manipulative materials. Studies show that providing all three types of learning experiences to all students is likely to result in higher achievement than simply matching one style. "When children were taught with multisensory resources, but *initially through their most preferred modality,* their scores increased even more" (Dunn, Beaudry, & Klavas, 1989, p. 52).

Conclusions

Reflective, caring teachers are likely to value the C-M view of teaching and learning, which holds that students must be active learners rather than passive recipients of knowledge. Using this philosophy, reflective teachers attempt to plan varied and interesting lessons, with many opportunities for students to practice actively what they are learning.

In this chapter, we have discussed some general presentation skills that can engage the learner's interest in the lesson being taught. We have also focused on the strategies that teachers use to instruct a large group of students in the basic skills of a subject. Since the techniques of direct instruction are used frequently in elementary classrooms, it is important for the beginning teacher to become proficient at planning and teaching lessons of this type.

While some teachers may rely on direct instruction of a large group as their major or only teaching strategy, reflective teachers are likely to want to be able to choose from a variety of strategies. The next three chapters offer the beginning teacher a glimpse at a wide range of teaching methods. From these, you may begin to build a repertoire of teaching strategies to expand your own teaching skills and increase your students' motivation for learning.

OPPORTUNITIES FOR REFLECTION

▼ *Reflective Essay: A Successful Teaching Experience*

Write about the time when you were very successful in teaching something to another person. It may have been an informal setting, such as a kitchen or on a ski slope. What made this experience a success? How did you begin the "lesson"? How did you interact with the "student(s)"? What did you do that worked best? Do you believe that you can apply what worked in this lesson to your classroom teaching?

▼ *Classroom Visit: Presentation Skills*

Observe the teaching strategies and presentation skills used by the teacher in the classroom you visit. Look for and describe examples of strategies such as the use of an advance organizer, teacher modeling and demonstration, direct instruction, and teacher-led discussion. What methods does the teacher use to get the attention of students at the beginning of a lesson? What methods are used during transitions? How would you adapt these methods to fit your own style of teaching?

REFERENCES

ANDERSON, R., & PEARSON, P. (1984). A schema theoretic view of basic processes in reading. In P. Pearson (Ed.), *Handbook of reading research* (pp. 255–291). New York: Longman.

ANDERSON, L. (1989a). Learners and learning. In M. Reynolds (Ed.), *Knowledge base for the beginning teacher* (pp. 85–99). New York: Macmillan.

ANDERSON, L. (1989b). Classroom instruction. In M. Reynolds (Ed.), *Knowledge base for the beginning teacher* (pp. 101–115). New York: Macmillan.

AUSUBEL, D. P. (1960). The use of advance organizers in the learning and retention of meaningful verbal material. *Journal of Educational Psychology, 51,* 267–272.

BLOOM, B. (1981). *All our children learning.* New York: McGraw-Hill.

BRANSFORD, J. (1983). Schema activation—schema acquisition. In R. Anderson, J. Osborn, & R. Tierney (Eds.), *Learning to read in American schools* (pp. 23–37). Hillsdale, NJ: Erlbaum.

BROPHY, J., & GOOD, T. (1986). Teacher behavior and student achievement. In M. Wittrock (Ed.), *Handbook of research on teaching* (3rd ed.) (pp. 328–375). New York: Macmillan.

CULLUM, A. (1967). *Push back the desks.* New York: Citation Press.

DENHAM, C., & LIEBERMAN, A. (1980). *Time to Learn.* Washington, D.C.: U.S. Department of Education.

DUNN, R., BEAUDRY, J., & KLAVAS, A. (1989). Survey of research on learning styles. *Educational Leadership, 46,* (6), 50–57.

GAGNE, E. (1985). *The cognitive psychology of school learning.* Boston: Little, Brown.

GLASSER, W. (1969) *Schools without failure.* New York: Harper & Row.

GLASSER, W. (1986). *Control theory in the classroom.* New York: Harper & Row.

GOOD, T., & BROPHY, J. (1987). *Looking in classrooms* (4th ed.). New York: Harper & Row.

HUNTER, M. (1982). *Mastery teaching.* El Segundo, CA: TIP Publications.

JONES, F. (1987). *Positive classroom discipline.* New York: McGraw-Hill.

KOUNIN, J. (1977). *Discipline and group management in classrooms.* New York: Robert E. Kreiger.

MASLOW, A. (1954). *Motivation and personality.* New York: Harper & Row.

RIMM, S. (1986). *Underachievement syndrome: Causes and cures.* Watertown, WI: Apple.

ROSENSHINE, B. (1979). Content, time and direct instruction. In P. Peterson & H. Walberg (Eds.), *Research on teaching: Concepts, findings and implications* (pp. 28–56). Berkeley, CA: McCutchan.

ROSENSHINE, B. (1980). How time is spent in elementary classrooms. In C. Denham & A. Lieberman (Eds.), *Time to learn* (pp. 107–126). Washington, D.C.: U.S. Department of Education.

ROSENSHINE, B., & STEVENS, R. (1986). Teaching functions. In M. Wittrock (Ed.), *Handbook of research on teaching* (3rd ed.) (pp. 376–391). New York: Macmillan.

Discussion and Questioning Strategies to Promote Cognitive Engagement

"A BASIC TENET of the cognitive-mediational perspective on learning is that active processing by the learner is necessary for learning to occur" (Anderson, 1989, p. 108). Researchers in education are currently focusing considerable attention on the phenomenon known as *cognitive engagement,* which occurs when a student becomes actively and enthusiastically interested in thinking about and discussing an idea. Making cognitive engagement a classroom goal is a powerful new concept for teachers to consider when they select teaching strategies for their classrooms. It connotes the opposite of the sterile, passive classroom environment in which students attend listlessly to the lessons and carry out their seatwork and homework with little real effort or interest.

When students are fully engaged in reading, listening, discussion, or creation, the classroom climate is likely to be as lively and stimulating as a thundershower. Can you recall a classroom learning experience so powerful that you had almost total recall of it many years later? When you recall the event, do you feel as if you are reliving it because the memory is still so vividly etched in your mind? Do you think of this event as life-changing? Perhaps it altered the way you think about an issue or caused you to change your career goal or provoked you into making a lifestyle change. These relatively rare classroom events have been described as "peak learning experiences" by Benjamin Bloom (1981, p. 193) and are related to the "peak experiences" described earlier by Maslow (1971).

TYPES OF CLASSROOM QUESTIONS AND DISCUSSIONS

Not all discussions that you plan will be as engaging as a peak experience, but many can approach it and many others can be satisfying and provocative when you take care to plan for full cognitive engagement on the part of your students.

In some classrooms, what passes for discussions are really dull and repetitive question-and-answer periods. Some teachers may simply read aloud a list of questions from the teacher's manual of the textbook and call on students to recite the answers.

As you probably recall from your own school experiences, when this type of "discussion" occurs, many students disengage entirely. They read ahead, doodle, or do homework surreptitiously. They seldom listen to their classmates' responses, and when it is their turn to recite, they frequently cannot find their place in the list of questions.

Reflective teachers value the processes of considering alternatives and debating opinions and ideas. That is how reflective teachers approach the world themselves, and they are likely to want to stimulate the same types of behavior among their students.

Educational literature abounds with terms and systems related to the promotion of high-quality and actively engaged thinking. Teachers are encouraged to promote *higher-level thinking processes* (also known as *higher-order thinking skills*), *problem-solving skills, critical thinking,* and *creative thinking* among their students. These terms and concepts can be confusing and overwhelming for the beginning teacher, since it appears that it is necessary to establish separate programs for each of them.

That is not the case. When you become more familiar with these concepts, you will find that it is possible to discover common attributes among them. You can then plan classroom discussions and other experiences that promote high-level thinking, problem solving, and critical and creative thinking at the same time. One question may pose a problem, another may call for a creative response, a third may be analytical, and a fourth may ask students to evaluate a situation and make a critical judgment. The best (which is to say, the most highly engaging) classroom discussions do all of these in a spontaneous, nonregimented way.

In the following sections, descriptions of various thinking processes will be presented, along with alternatives for planning classroom discussions to promote these processes. As you read these sections, reflect on the similarities and differences; look for patterns and sequences; and consider how you would use, modify, and adapt these systems in your own classroom.

Although these processes can be applied to both academic and nonacademic areas of the elementary curriculum, we will illustrate how classroom discussions are created and managed, using the topic of racial discrimination as a common theme. In this example, the operational goal is to promote understanding of the effects of racial discrimination on the lives of human beings and to generate a sense of respect for individuals who are different from oneself.

Questions That Develop Higher-Level Thinking Processes

Bloom's Taxonomy (Bloom, Englehart, Furst, Hill, & Krathwohl, 1956) is the most well-known and most commonly used system for promoting the use of higher-level thinking processes. Discussion questions can be readily planned at every level of the Taxonomy, just as other learning experiences are planned. The term *higher level* refers to the top four levels of the hierarchy:

HIGHER-LEVEL	Evaluation
THINKING	Synthesis
PROCESSES	Analysis
	Application
LOWER-LEVEL	Comprehension
THINKING PROCESSES	Knowledge

Given any topic, teachers can fashion questions to fit each of these levels. Because the Taxonomy is arranged as a hierarchy, teachers frequently ask lower-level questions first in order to develop a base of knowledge on the topic and then proceed to higher-level questions. In our illustrative example, the teacher has assigned the class to read a biography of Martin Luther King, Jr., and has planned a discussion that includes questions at all six levels:

▼ *Knowledge Level*   At this level, the learners are asked to recall specific bits of information, such as terminology, facts, and details:

When and where was King born?
Who were the other members of his family?
What jobs did King's father do to earn a living?
What jobs did his mother do?
What career did King choose?

▼ *Comprehension Level*   At this level, the learners are asked to describe the main ideas in their own words:

King lived in a ghetto. What does this term mean?
What does prejudice mean?
How did school change King's life?
How did the church affect his life?

▼ *Application Level*   At this level, the learners are asked to apply what they have learned to their own lives or to other situations:

Give an example of prejudice that has affected you.
If King were alive today, what do you think he would be most concerned about? What do you think he would do about it?

▼ *Analysis Level*   At this level, the learners are asked to describe patterns, cause-and-effect relationships, comparisons, and contrasts:

How did Rosa Parks' decision to sit in the front of the bus change King's life? How did her decision change history?
In what ways was King a minister, a politician, and a teacher?

▼ *Synthesis Level*   At this level, the learners are asked to contribute a new and original idea on the topic:

Complete this phrase: I have a dream that one day . . .
If there were suddenly a strong prejudice against people who look just like you do, what would you do about it?

▼ *Evaluation Level*   At this level, the learners are asked to express their own opinions or make judgments about some aspect of the topic:

What do you believe was King's greatest contribution?
Which promotes more social change: nonviolence or violence? Give a rationale or example to defend your answer.

Some teachers find that Bloom's Taxonomy is a useful and comprehensive guide for planning classroom discussion questions, as well as other classroom activities. Others find that the Taxonomy is more complex than they desire and that it is difficult to discriminate between some of the levels, such as comprehension and analysis or application and synthesis. Other systems of classifying thinking processes are available. Doyle (1986) proposes that teachers plan classroom tasks in four categories that are readily applicable to classroom discussions: (1) memory tasks, (2) procedural or routine tasks, (3) comprehension tasks, and (4) opinion tasks.

Classroom questions and discussion starters can be created to fit these four task levels as follows:

▼ *Memory Questions*   Learners are asked to reproduce information they have read or heard before:

King was born?
Who were the other members of his family?

When and where was King born?
Who were the other members of his family?

▼ *Procedural or Routine Questions*   Learners are asked to supply simple answers with only one correct response:

What jobs did King's father do to earn a living?
What jobs did his mother do?
What career did King choose?

▼ *Comprehension Questions*   Learners are asked to consider known data and apply it to a new and unfamiliar context:

King lived in a ghetto. What does this term mean?
What does prejudice mean?
How did school change King's life?
How did the church affect his life?
How did Rosa Parks' decision to sit in the front of the bus change King's life? How did her decision change history?
In what ways was King a minister, a politician, and a teacher?

▼ *Opinion Questions*   Learners are asked to express their own point of view on an issue, with no correct answer expected:

Give an example of prejudice that has affected you.
If King were alive today, what do you think he would be most concerned about? What do you think he would do about it?
Complete this phrase: I have a dream that one day . . .
If there were suddenly a strong prejudice against people who look just like you do, what would you do about it?
What do you believe was King's greatest contribution?
Which promotes more social change: nonviolence or violence? Give a rationale or example to defend your answer.

You will notice that the questions in Doyle's four categories are the same as the ones listed in the Taxonomy's six levels. Questions at the comprehension and analysis levels are both contained in Doyle's comprehension category, and questions at the application, synthesis, and evaluation levels are contained in Doyle's opinion category. Both of these systems offer teachers a comprehensive framework for planning a wide range of thought-provoking questions. The choice of which system to use is entirely up to you.

Problem-Solving Discussions

Much has been written about the need to develop students' problem-solving and decision-making abilities. This can be done by presenting students with a complex problem and providing adequate scaffolding support so that they are able to learn how to solve problems. While some problems must be solved by using paper and pencil or a hands-on experimental approach, others can be solved through classroom discussion.

To create productive problem-solving discussions, the teacher must understand the processes involved in problem solving and then structure the questions to guide students through that process. A problem is said to exist when "one has a goal and has not yet identified a means for reaching that goal. The problem may be wanting to answer a question, to prove a theorem, to be accepted, or to get a job" (Gagne, 1985, p. 138).

According to cognitive psychologists, the framework for solving a problem consists of identifying a goal, a starting place, and all possible solution paths from the starting place to the goal. Some individuals are efficient and productive problem solvers; others are not. An excellent classroom goal for the elementary teacher is to help students become more efficient and more productive problem solvers.

Nonproductive problem solvers are likely to have difficulty identifying or defining the problem. They may simply feel that a puzzling situation exists, but they may not be aware of the real nature of the problem. Students who are poor problem solvers need experience in facing puzzling situations and defining the problem. They also need experience in identifying and selecting worthwhile goals to strive for.

When a problem has been defined and a goal established, it is still possible to be either efficient or inefficient in reaching the goal. Efficiency in problem solving can be increased when students learn how to identify the alternative strategies to reach a chosen goal and recognize which ones are likely to provide the best and quickest routes to success. This can be done by helping students visualize the probable effects of each alternative and applying criteria to help them choose the most valuable means of solving the problem they have defined.

As in the teaching of higher-level thinking processes, there are several useful systems available to teachers who want to teach students to become better problem solvers. Osborne (1963) proposed the technique known as *brainstorming*, which includes four basic steps:

1. defining the problem
2. generating, without criticism or evaluation, as many solutions as possible
3. deciding on criteria for judging the solutions generated
4. using these criteria to select the best possible solution

Brainstorming is an excellent way to generate classroom discussion about a puzzling issue. Rather than formulating a series of questions, the teacher supplies a dilemma or puzzle, teaches the students the steps involved in brainstorming, and then leads them through the process itself.

In discussing the life of Martin Luther King, Jr., and helping students to understand the effects of racial discrimination, the teacher might use a portion of the classroom discussion to brainstorm answers to one of the most perplexing questions. For example, the teacher might use brainstorming to expand the discussion on the following question:

> If King were alive today, what do you think he would be most con-
> cerned about? What do you think he would do about it?

The technique of brainstorming calls for the teacher to pose the question or problem in such a way that it engages the students' interest and motivates them to take it seriously. Since students may not be proficient at discussions of this sort, it is frequently necessary for the teacher to give additional cues and suggestions as a scaffold. In this instance, the teacher might need to pose the original question and then follow it up with prompts such as these:

> "What do you think he'd be concerned about in our community?"
> "What has been in the news lately that might alarm him?"
> "Who are the people in the world who are presently in need?"
> "What about threats to our environment?"

Open-ended questions such as these will generate many more responses than discussions in which they are not used. After recording all of the students' responses on the chalkboard, the teacher leads the students through the process of selecting the most important items for further consideration. This may be done by a vote or a general consensus. When the list has been narrowed to several very important issues, the teacher must lead the students through the process of establishing criteria for judging them.

Since the question is related to Martin Luther King, Jr.'s, own values, one possible criterion is to judge whether King showed concern for the issue in his own lifetime. Another criterion might be the number of people who are threatened or hurt by the problem. After judging the issues by these criteria, the class makes a judgment about which ones would most concern King. Then the process of brainstorming begins again, but this time the problem the class is considering is what King would be likely to do to help solve the problem. Generating responses to the first question, "If King were alive today, what would he be most concerned about?", will help students understand the many aspects of racial discrimination that exist today. By selecting one of these as the main concern and generating responses to the question "What do you think he would do about it?" the students will be reflecting on their own responsibilities to other human beings and on ways to increase tolerance and brotherhood in their own community.

To moderate a brainstorming discussion, the teacher faithfully records every response generated by the students, no matter how trivial or impossible it sounds. The teacher then leads students through the process of eliminating the least important items and finally works through the process of establishing criteria to use in evaluating the best possible solutions.

Brainstorming alone does not solve problems. It merely trains children in thinking productively about problems and considering many alternative solutions. In some classrooms, teachers may wish to extend the hypothetical discussion of possible solutions to an actual attempt to solve a problem or at least contribute to a solution. Teachers who wish to go beyond discussion to action will want to read Joyce and Weil's (1986) descriptions of two models of teaching: group investigation, based on the work of Herbert Thelen (1960), and social inquiry, based on the work of Massialas and Cox (1966). A group investigation or social inquiry may begin with an academic subject or a local issue, but under the teacher's guidance it can become a class project similar to the Erie Canal project carried out by Jean Malvoso–Zingaro's class that was described in Chapter 4. Group investigations of this type involve many highly engaging and interactive discussions as students work together to solve a real problem.

Discussions That Promote Critical Thinking

The term *critical thinking* is not a separate and distinct concept that is different from higher-level thinking processes and problem solving. It overlaps both of them. It is presented here in a separate section because, over the past few years, it has become a field of study with its own literature and suggested classroom processes.

The field of study of critical thinking grew out of the philosophical study of logic, which was a staple in the secondary curriculum in the mid-twentieth century. The principles of logical thinking were meant to train people to think about a single hypothesis deductively in order to arrive at a rational conclusion. But in the late 1960s de Bono (1967) observed that while logical thinkers were prepared to deal with a single issue in depth, they were not prepared to deal with unexpected evidence or ideas.

Using the analogy of digging for treasure, de Bono suggested that in thinking about a hypothesis, a logical thinker might dig a deeper and bigger hole, but if the hole was not in the right place, then no amount of digging would improve the solution. In contrast, de Bono believed that a critical thinker would be more flexible than a logical thinker, and after considering a problem or issue, the critical thinker would be able to select from a tool box of thinking skills that allows the individual to clarify where to dig, select from among alternative digging methods, use a variety of procedures to analyze the contents of the hole, and judge the worth of what is excavated.

Critical thinking, then, is partially defined as a complex set of thinking skills and processes that are believed to lead to fair and useful judgments. Mathew Lipman (1988) defines it as "skillful, responsible thinking that facilitates good judgment because it 1) relies upon criteria, 2) is self-correcting, and 3) is sensitive to context" (p. 39). He points out the strong association between the words *criteria* and *critical thinking*. In this way, the process obviously overlaps the problem-solving technique of brainstorming and applying criteria to select the best solution.

But critical thinking is a much more multifaceted concept than problem solving. Ennis (1985) points out that critical thinking occurs as a result of both dispositions and abilities. "The list of dispositions includes such things as being open-minded, paying attention to the total situation, seeking reasons, and trying to be well informed" (p. 48). This implies that the teaching of critical thinking involves much more than simply training students to use a set of strategies or procedures. It also involves establishing some affective goals for students to support them in becoming more independent and open-minded.

Richard Paul (1988), director of the Center of Critical Thinking at Sonoma State University in Rohnert Park, California, agrees. He describes affective attributes of critical thinking that include independence, avoidance of egocentricity and stereotyping, and suspending judgment until much evidence has been gathered.

Ennis (1985), Paul (1988), and other investigators have also described lists of cognitive strategies that critical thinkers can be trained to use. These include skills involving observation, focusing on a question, distinguishing facts from opinions, distinguishing relevant from irrelevant information, judging the credibility of sources, recognizing contradictions, making inferences, and drawing conclusions. Since almost every specialist in critical thinking proposes a slightly different set of thinking processes and skills that comprise critical thinking, it is necessary for reflective teachers to judge for themselves which strategies to stress in their own classrooms.

Raths, Wasserman, Jonas, and Rothstein (1986) describe a set of thinking operations that they believe comprise critical thinking, and then provide a wealth of practical classroom applications at both the elementary and secondary levels. The operations they emphasize are comparing, summarizing, observing, classifying, interpreting, criticizing, looking for assumptions, imagining, collecting and organizing data, applying facts and principles in new situations, and decision making.

To systematically train students to become better thinkers, Raths and colleagues suggest methods using the whole class or small groups. In classroom discussions, they recommend that the teacher select one thinking operation at a time and tell the class that they will be focusing on improving this thinking skill. The teacher then proposes a discussion topic, listens attentively to students' responses, and records them if appropriate.

In our classroom example focusing on Martin Luther King, Jr., and the effects of racial segregation, the teacher might introduce a *comparison* question such as "Compare the ways black Americans felt discriminated against when King was a boy and when he died." For a *summary* question, the teacher may ask students to summarize the class response to the first question. For an *observation* question, the teacher may propose that students observe instances of racial discrimination for 24 hours and report their observations to the class the next day. The other critical thinking operations can be treated in a similar manner.

Discussions That Enhance Creative Thinking

Can individuals learn to be creative? Perhaps the more important question is, do individuals learn to be uncreative? A century ago, William James (1890) stated his belief that education trains children to become "old fogeys" in the early grades by teaching them to adopt habits of convergent, conformist thinking.

Divergent thinking is the opposite of convergent thinking in that it diverges from common understanding and accepted patterns. J. P. Guilford (1967) contributed a definition of divergent thinking that is still well accepted and has become the basis for E. Paul Torrance's (1966–84) well-known tests for creativity. Guilford describes (and Torrance's test measures) four attributes of divergent thinking: *fluency, flexibility, originality,* and *elaboration.* In other words, a divergent thinker is one who generates many ideas (fluency), is able to break with conformist or set ideas (flexibility), suggests ideas that are new in the present context (originality), and contributes details that extend or support the ideas beyond a single thought (elaboration).

Classroom discussions can be designed to help students develop these four attributes of creativity. Using a technique similar to brainstorming, the teacher can ask students to generate many responses to a single question as a means of helping them to become more fluent in their thinking. For example, given our topic of King's "I have a dream" speech, the teacher may begin the process with the unfinished sentence "I have a dream that someday . . ." I hope that someday . . .

Students may be asked to write their own responses for several minutes before the discussion begins. This allows each child to work for fluency individually. Then the ideas on paper are shared aloud and other new ideas are created as a result of the discussion. To promote flexibility, the teacher may ask students to imagine making their dreams come true and suggest ways that they could do this, using flexible and original strategies rather than rigid and ordinary methods. Finally, to extend the students' elaborative thought, the teacher may select one dream, asking the entire class to focus on it and create a more detailed vision and a more in-depth plan to accomplish it.

Einstein and Infeld (1938) add a further dimension to our understanding of creative thinking: Question answers

* The formulation of a problem is often more essential than its solution, which may be merely a matter of mathematical or experimental skill. To raise new questions, new possibilities, to regard old problems from a new angle, requires creative imagination and marks a real advance in science. (p. 92)

Problem solving, then, is related to creative thinking. It is readily apparent that the methods described for improving problem solving involve critical thinking, and that both involve the use of higher-level thinking processes. Whatever we call it, the goal of aiding students in developing better thinking skills is an integral part of any classroom discussion.

Just as we respect Einstein and Infeld's ability to pose new problems, we should respect and develop our own and our students' capacity to ask questions and suggest new ways of solving age-old problems. Certainly the teaching profession needs people with the capability of regarding old educational problems from a new angle. Often it is the newest and youngest members of a faculty who see things from a helpful new perspective and suggest new ways of dealing with difficult school issues.

Another dimension of creativity involves the production of something useful, interesting, or otherwise valued by at least a small segment of society. Carl Rogers (1954) defines creativity in terms of a process that results in a "novel relational product growing out of the uniqueness of the individual on the one hand and the materials, events, people or circumstances of his life on the other" (p. 251).

In this textbook, the definition of creative thinking is a combination of the concepts described above. That is, a creative thinker is one who poses new problems, raises new questions, and then suggests solutions characterized by fluency, flexibility, originality, and elaboration. The solutions result in a product unique to that individual in those circumstances.

Do schools enhance or discourage these conditions and processes? Do elementary textbooks, curriculum guides, rules, regulations, and expectations support the development of creative thinking and the process needed to create a unique product? Many teachers do, and this book supports those who want to try to assist students in learning to become creative thinkers rather than 9-year-old old fogeys.

THE ROLE OF THE TEACHER IN LEADING DISCUSSIONS

Discussions that promote the use of critical thinking can be exciting classroom events for both students and teachers, but beginning teachers may find it difficult to elicit responses from students who are not used to taking part in such activities. Raths and colleagues (1986) ask:

> "What if you ask a wonderful question and the pupils don't respond?"
> There is nothing quite so demoralizing for a teacher as a lack of response from students.
> "Now boys and girls, how do you think the sound got onto this tape?"
> No response. Interminable silence. Finally the teacher leaps in to break the tension and gives the answer. Everybody, including the teacher, visibly relaxes. Whew! Let's not try that again. (p. 183)

This example of a nondiscussion is more common than is desirable. Students in your classroom may not have had opportunities to think creatively and express their own ideas. If not, they may be very reluctant to do so at first. They may believe that you expect one right answer, just as most of their teachers have in the past. Since they do not know the one right answer, they may prefer to remain quiet rather than embarrass themselves by giving a wrong answer. Your response to their silence will tell them a great deal. If you do jump in with your own response, they will learn that their own responses were not really wanted after all.

Scaffolding is a necessary component of teaching critical thinking and discussion strategies to elementary students. Be explicit about what you expect from them in a discussion. Tell them that there are no wrong answers and that all opinions are valued. If they still hesitate, provide cues and prompts without providing answers. Simplify or rephrase the question so that they are able to answer it. If the question "How do you think the sound got on this tape?" gets no response, rephrase it. "What sounds do you hear on this tape?" "Can you imagine how those sounds were captured on a piece of plastic like this?" "Do you think machinery was used?" "What kinds of machines are able to copy sounds?" These supporting questions provide scaffolds for thinking and talking about unknown and unfamiliar ideas.

Another consideration in leading discussions is to *value silence* rather than fear it. Silence can indicate that students are truly engaged in reflection. By allowing a few moments of silence, the resulting discussions may be much more creative and productive. Students need time to process the question. They need time to bring forward the necessary schema in their working memories and to consider the question in light of what they already know about the topic. Some children need more time than others to see connections between new ideas and previously stored information and to generate a response of their own.

Some teachers consciously use *wait time* by requiring a short period of silence after each significant question is asked. Students are taught to listen quietly, then think quietly for several seconds and not raise their hands to respond until the wait time has passed. Rowe (1974) found that when teachers used a wait time of 3 to 5 seconds, more children were able to generate a response to the question. Without a planned wait time, the same group of fast-thinking children are likely to dominate all discussions. With the wait time, even slower-thinking children will have an opportunity to consider what they believe before hearing the opinions of others.

Lyman (1989) recommends that teachers employ a system called *listen, think, pair, share* to improve both the quantity and the quality of discussion responses. This technique employs a structured wait time at two different points in the discussion. When a question is asked, wait time goes into effect while students jot down ideas and think about their own responses. Students are then expected to discuss their ideas in pairs for a minute. Then a general discussion takes place. After each student makes a contribution, the remainder of the class is expected to employ a second wait time of 3 to 5 seconds to process what their classmate has said before they raise their hands to respond.

The quantity and quality of students' responses may be improved by introducing the questions early in the class period, followed by reading, a lecture, or another type of presentation and then a discussion of the questions themselves. This strategy follows the principle of using the question as an advance organizer. By hearing the question prior to the presentation of new material, the students are alerted about what to listen or read for and have sufficient time to process the information they receive in terms of the question. When teachers use this technique, they rarely experience a silent response.

Another strategy that promotes highly interactive discussions involves the physical setup in the classroom. To facilitate critical and creative thinking, it is important for students to be able to hear and see each other during the discussion. Arranging the chairs in a circle, rectangle, U shape or semicircle will ensure that each student feels like a contributing member of a group.

Meyers (1986) notes that a hospitable classroom environment is the most important factor in engaging students' attention and interest and promoting their creative responses during discussion:

> Much of the success in teaching critical thinking rests with the tone that teachers set in their classrooms. Students must be led gently into the active roles of discussing, dialoguing, and problem solving. They will watch very carefully to see how respectfully teachers field comments and will quickly pick up nonverbal cues that show how open teachers really are to student questions and contributions. (p. 67)

Reflective teachers are critical and creative thinkers themselves. They welcome opportunities to model their own thinking strategies for their students and plan experiences that encourage the development of their students' higher-level thinking processes. They are likely to make even the simplest discussion an exercise in problem solving, reasoning, logic, and creative and independent thinking. They examine the subjects taught in the elementary curriculum in search of ways to allow their students to learn to think and communicate their ideas. They plan discussions involving the creation and testing of hypotheses about science. They promote thinking that avoids stereotypes and egocentricity in social studies. They teach their students to suspend judgment when they lack sufficient evidence in discussions of math problems. They promote flexible and original thinking in discussions of literature. Discussions in every part of the elementary curriculum can be crafted in ways that cause individuals to learn to think reflectively, critically, and creatively.

OPPORTUNITIES FOR REFLECTION

▼ Reflective Essay: Your Own Discussion-Leading Abilities

Write about your own experiences as a participant in discussions. Do you enjoy contributing ideas? What type of support do you need from a teacher or discussion leader to encourage you to take a more active role?

Write about your own experiences in leading discussions. Are you comfortable in the role of leader? Do you tend to ask good questions spontaneously? Do you need to prepare carefully and write questions ahead of time?

▼ Classroom Visit: Leading a Discussion

Ask the classroom teacher for an opportunity to lead a classroom discussion under his or her guidance. The topic can come from the curriculum, or you can plan a topic of your own. Prepare the questions ahead of time, and show them to the teacher for feedback before leading the discussion. Afterward, ask the teacher to provide you with feedback on the discussion itself.

REFERENCES

ANDERSON, L. (1989). Classroom instruction. In M. Reynolds (Ed.), *Knowledge base for the beginning teacher* (pp. 101–115). New York: Macmillan.

BLOOM, B. (1981). *All our children learning.* New York: McGraw-Hill.

BLOOM, B., ENGLEHART, M., FURST, E., HILL, W., & KRATHWOHL, D. (1956). *Taxonomy of educational objectives: Cognitive domain.* New York: Longman.

BRANSFORD, J., & STEIN, B. (1984). *The ideal problem solver.* New York: Freeman.

DE BONO, E. (1967). *New think.* New York: Basic Books.

DOYLE, W. (1986). Classroom organization and management. In M. Wittrock (Ed.), *Handbook of research on teaching* (3rd ed.) (pp. 392–420). New York: Macmillan.

EINSTEIN, A., & INFELD, L. (1938). *The evolution of physics.* New York: Simon & Schuster.

ENNIS, R. (1985). A logical basis for measuring critical thinking skills. *Educational Leadership, 43*(2), 44–48.

EVERTSON, C., EMMER, E., CLEMENTS, B., SANFORD, J., WORSHAM, M., & WILLIAMS, E. (1981). Organizing and managing the elementary school classroom. Austin: Research and Development Center for Teacher Education, University of Texas.

GAGNE, E. (1985). *The cognitive psychology of school learning.* Boston: Little, Brown.

GUILFORD, J. P. (1967). *The nature of human intelligence.* New York: McGraw-Hill.

JAMES, W. (1890). *Principles of psychology.* New York: Holt.

JOYCE, B., & WEIL, M. (1986). *Models of teaching.* Englewood Cliffs, NJ: Prentice-Hall.

LIPMAN, M. (1988). Critical thinking—what can it be? *Educational Leadership, 46*(1), 38–43.

LYMAN, F. (1989). Rechoreographing the middle-level minuet. *Early Adolescence Magazine, IV*(I), 22–24.

MASLOW, A. (1954). *Motivation and personality.* New York: Harper & Row.

MASLOW, A. (1971). *The farther reaches of human nature.* New York: Viking Press.

MASSIALAS, B., & COX, B. (1966). *Inquiry in social studies.* New York: McGraw-Hill.

MEYERS, C. (1986). *Teaching students to think critically.* San Francisco: Jossey-Bass.

OSBORNE, P. (1963). *Applied imagination.* New York: Scribner's.

PAUL, R. (1988). *31 Principles of critical thinking.* Rohnert Park, CA: Center for Critical Thinking and Moral Critique.

PETERS, W. (1984). *A class divided: Then and now.* New Haven, CT: Yale University Press.

RATHS, L., WASSERMAN, S., JONAS, A., & ROTHSTEIN, A. (1986). *Teaching for thinking.* New York: Teachers College Press.

ROGERS, C. (1954). Toward a theory of creativity. In S. I. Hayakawa (Ed.), *ETC: A review of general semantics,* (Vol. 11, No. 4, pp. 249–260). Chicago: International Society for General Semantics.

ROWE, M. (1974). Wait time and reward as instructional variables, their influence on language, logic and fate control: part one—wait time. *Journal of Research on Science Teaching, 11,* 81–94.

THELEN, H. (1960). *Education and the human quest.* New York: Harper & Row.

TORRANCE, E. P. (1966–84). *Torrance tests of creative thinking.* Bensenville, IL: Scholastic Testing Service.

Cooperative Learning Strategies

> The age of cooperation is approaching. From Alaska to California to Florida to New
> York, from Australia to Britain to Norway to Israel, teachers and administrators are
> discovering an untapped resource for accelerating students' achievement: the
> students themselves. There is now substantial evidence that students working
> together in small cooperative groups can master material presented by the teacher
> better than can students working on their own. (Slavin, 1987, p. 7)

MANY REFLECTIVE TEACHERS are reconsidering the traditional practices that emphasized
competition over cooperation in the classroom. Teachers are reevaluating the conventional wisdom that individuals should work quietly, in isolation, hiding their
findings from each other so that no cheating can occur. Instead, many teachers are
experimenting with a wide variety of strategies that promote student interaction and
encourage them to share their skills, knowledge, and understandings.

But experimentation may lead to failure if it is not based on a mature
understanding of the principles and methods that successfully promote cooperative
learning in the classroom. Sometimes teachers will hear about a new strategy and
quickly decide that they like the idea and will use it immediately. Without taking
adequate time to gather the necessary information and evaluate it carefully in light of
the needs of their own students, they may simply try it out the very next day. This
premature adoption of a new teaching method can have disastrous results.

Imagine, for example, that a teacher hears some general ideas about cooperative groups at a conference or reads the first few paragraphs of an article on the
strategy. Thinking that it seems to be an intriguing idea, the teacher may hurry back
to the classroom, divide the class into several small groups, and tell them to study the
Civil War together for a test that will be held next Friday. After a few moments of
discussing what they have (or have not) read about the Civil War, the groups are likely
to dissolve into chaos or, at best, evolve into groups who sit near each other and talk
to each other as each person studies the text in isolation:

> Cooperation is *not* having students sit side-by-side at the same table to talk with
> each other as they do their individual assignments.

Cooperation is *not* having students do a task with instructions that whoever finishes first are to help the slower students.

Cooperation is *not* assigning a report to a group of students wherein one student does all the work and the others put their names on the product, as well. (Johnson & Johnson, 1984, p. 8)

Teachers who wish to become both knowledgeable about and proficient in the use of cooperative learning in their classrooms must take the time to seek out information from books, journals, conferences, and visits to classrooms where the techniques are being used. This chapter provides a cursory overview of this multi-faceted strategy and lists some references for your own follow-up study of the subject.

MODELS OF COOPERATIVE LEARNING

Group Investigation

The strategy or model known as *group investigation* is a good place to begin the search. Joyce and Weil (1986) provide a description of the model, which they attribute to the work of John Dewey. Dewey (1910, 1916) believed that children can learn to live in a democratic society only if their education provides them with actual experiences of democratic decision making and problem solving. He envisioned classrooms in which students participate fully in the democratic process by investigating real problems.

Thelen (1960) adapted Dewey's educational philosophy to the group investigation model for the study and improvement of social issues and concerns. In this model, a class of students encounter or is presented with a puzzling situation that they are encouraged to discuss freely. It is expected that individual views will differ and that values and assumptions will clash. The teacher's role is to facilitate the discussion without being overdirective, and lead the group to make a plan for studying and investigating the issue further. The larger group is divided into smaller study groups with various assignments to gather data and information to present to the larger group. An extended period of time is given to the small-group investigations. Finally, the small groups report their findings and suggest their ideas or solutions to the entire group. This may lead to a resolution of the problem. If it does not, the investigation continues.

An excellent example of group investigation at the elementary level occurred in Jean Malvaso-Zingaro's sixth-grade classroom (see the following Perspective). The students encountered a real problem in their neighborhood. At school the students voiced strong concerns, and their teacher encouraged the discussion and guided their investigation into the matter. She allowed students to take school time to study the matter and, in effect, built the investigation into her social studies curriculum. Guest speakers were invited, field trips were taken, and the class took an active role in proposing a solution to the City Council and defending it with data they had collected.

Sharan (1984) adapted the group investigation procedures to include opportunities for students to participate in all aspects of planning the investigation. In his model, the teacher proposes a general topic for study and asks students to orga-

——▼| P E R S P E C T I V E |▼——————————

JEAN MALVASO-ZINGARO
Sixth-Grade Teacher, School No. 6, Rochester, New York

COMMUNITY ACTION UNIT: A GROUP INVESTIGATION

The curriculum must be meaningful to students. They are concerned with immediate, real problems that touch their own lives. When the curriculum also includes these issues, students want to learn.

As a recent example, a historic church was going to be torn down in the inner-city neighborhood of our school. This was going to happen because it was deteriorating due to lack of maintenance.

The children in my class were alarmed. They didn't want another vacant lot where drug dealers would sell their drugs, the homeless would congregate, and garbage would be dumped. So they wrote letters voicing their concerns to the City Council. The letters were also published in the local newspaper.

The children invited speakers to come to our class to speak on both sides of the issue. Four representatives of various groups came to our school to share with us their reasons for either demolishing or preserving the church. The class also went on a field trip to the church to examine the architecture of the period in which it was built and to assess the extent of the damage. They compared the cost of preserving the church with the estimates of the cost of tearing it down.

We began working with the Rochester Historical Society to have the church declared a landmark. The children brainstormed different ways the church could be used. Finally, the children were asked to speak in front of the City Council. They prepared well for the event, writing and practicing their speeches. Two hundred people were at the Council meeting that night. They spoke with pride about their neighborhood and what they foresaw for the church.

At least in part because of the efforts of my sixth-grade class, the City Council elected to preserve the church and declare it a historic landmark.

---

nize themselves into small, academically and ethnically heterogeneous groups to be responsible for subtopics. The students are allowed more choice in what they study and who they study with, but they are led by the teacher to make responsible choices and ensure that the groups are heterogeneous. By sharing this responsibility, Sharan believes that students will grow in awareness and tolerance of individual differences.

In Sharan's model, students also participate in deciding on the methods they will use in the investigation and the types of products that will be produced by the groups. In studying the human body, for example, the class may decide that they want to produce booklets, charts, and diagrams, or they may decide to produce entirely different products. Teacher and students negotiate to decide on the methods and products that the groups will use. When the final presentations are made, the teacher asks students to assist in evaluating the contributions made by each group to the class as a whole.

Group investigation is a relatively unstructured form of cooperative learning. The role of the teacher is fairly nondirective, and the goals of the learning situations are almost always social or affective rather than academic. Cognitive learning may take place, but it is a by-product of the investigation into the social issue. Recently, educational researchers have been adapting the notion of cooperative learning to include more highly structured models that can be used to teach academic material as well.

Jigsaw

Aronson, Blaney, Sikes, and Snapp (1978) propose a model known as *jigsaw,* which was developed to foster understanding among students from various racial and ethnic groups. In this model, cooperative groups are made up of students from a variety of ethnic groups. Each student is given a different portion of the total task to foster mutual interdependence. Often each student is also given a different portion of the materials or information needed to complete the task.

For example, if the class is studying the human body, the teacher may form ethnically heterogeneous groups of five students to work together. The teacher then assigns each student in the group the responsibility for becoming knowledgeable about a different system in the body. One child studies the circulatory system, another the respiratory system, another the nervous system, another the digestive system, and another the skeletal system. If the group must create a life-sized mural of a human body as their finished product, students in the group take responsibility for drawing and labeling the parts of the body associated with the systems they studied.

As the students work, each child who has studied one system teaches the others in the group what he or she has learned. Because the final exam will cover all the systems of the body, students are dependent on other members of their group for learning about the systems they did not study. This interdependence motivates students to listen carefully to each other and to offer assistance and encouragement as needed (Stallings & Stipek, 1986, p. 749).

Learning Teams

Robert Slavin (1983, 1987) emphasizes the team concept in several variations of cooperative learning that are designed to accompany the regular academic curriculum of the elementary school. In a model called *student teams achievement division* (*STAD*), the teacher presents information to the entire class in the form of lectures, discussions, and/or readings. As a follow-up, students are formed into four- or five-member heterogeneous teams to learn the new material or practice the new skills. The teacher then gives individual quizzes and tests to determine how well the material has been learned. Students are not allowed to help each other on the tests themselves, only during the practice sessions. The individual test scores are then combined to produce a team score.

As a variation on this approach, in Slavin's model called *teams-games-tournaments* (*TGT*), tests are replaced by tournaments and groups work to prepare themselves for the event. In the tournament, individuals from each team compete against others of similar ability, and the results are combined to produce a total team score. This method appeals to teachers who prefer this lively oral assessment of learning to the written testing used in STAD.

Team accelerated instruction (TAI) is a third model created by Slavin. In this approach, cooperative learning is combined with individualized instruction. It was designed especially to teach mathematics to children in grades three through six. TAI students are given placement tests in math, and each student enters a sequential mathematics curriculum made up of many units at the appropriate starting level. Students work individually at their own rates on the math assignments in the sequence. Tutoring teams are heterogeneous, with students at all levels on a single team. Teammates check each other's work using answer sheets, and help each other understand their errors and learn new concepts. On completing a unit, the student takes a unit test. Each week the teacher totals the number of units completed by all team members and gives certificates and other rewards to teams for homework, completed units, and extra points for perfect papers.

Because students are responsible for monitoring and assisting each other, the teacher is free to spend class time presenting lessons to small groups of students drawn from the various teams. For example, the teacher may call together all students in the fraction unit, present a lesson, check on their understanding, and then send them back to their teams to work on their assignments (Slavin, 1987, pp. 10–11).

Cooperative integrated reading and composition (CIRC) is designed to enrich conventional methods for teaching reading and writing in the elementary grades. Pairs of students are assigned to encourage and support each other in their reading and writing efforts. In Ginny Bailey's first-grade classroom, these pairs of students are known as *reading buddies*. While the teacher works with a reading group, pairs of students read aloud to each other, summarizing stories to each other, and writing and editing stories and poems.

THE PURPOSE OF COOPERATIVE LEARNING

Although many variations of cooperative learning have been proposed, Stallings and Stipek (1986) found that most models have a common set of purposes, which, in turn, are founded on certain assumptions and beliefs.

First, cooperative learning is designed to encourage students to help and support their peers in a group rather than compete against them. This purpose is based on the assumption that the perceived value of academic achievement is raised when students are all working toward the same goal. Cooperative groups emphasize the notion of pride in one's "team" in much the same way that sports teams do.

Another major purpose is to boost the achievement of students of all ability levels. The assumption is that when high-achieving students work with low-achieving students, they both benefit. Compared to tracking systems that separate the high achievers from the low achievers, cooperative groups are composed of students at all levels so that the low-achieving students can benefit from modeling and interaction with their more capable peers. It is also believed that high-achieving students can learn to be more tolerant and understanding of individual differences through this type of experience than if they are separated from low achievers.

Third, cooperative teams are believed to be more motivating for the majority of students because they offer a greater opportunity to experience the joy of winning and success. In a competitive environment, it is likely that the same few high-achieving students will win over and over again. But in a classroom divided into cooperative teams, each with its own high- and low-achieving students, the opportunity to succeed is more evenly distributed. To this end, the reward systems do not honor individuals but are contingent on a group effort. As in a sports team, individual performances are encouraged because they benefit the whole team.

Selecting and Adapting Models

After researching the various models of cooperative learning that are being written about and discussed, reflective teachers will need to consider which model fits the goals they have established for each learning experience. Some models are most appropriate when the goal is to develop cooperation and communication skills; other models are more appropriate when the goal is to motivate students to learn cognitive material accurately and efficiently. In many cases, reflective teachers adapt and change the models they read about to fit the unique needs of their own classes.

In *Circles of Learning,* Johnson and Johnson (1984) describe in detail how cooperative learning can be implemented in an elementary classroom, but they do not prescribe a certain set of guidelines or steps for teachers to follow. They believe that, for most teachers, prepackaged programs will not work. Creative teachers may feel too constricted by rigid rules and procedures. Instead, they propose a set of principles that reflective teachers can use as the basis for creating their own models of cooperative learning.

According to Johnson and Johnson, the structure of productive and mutually beneficial cooperative groups contains four basic elements: positive interdependence, face-to-face interaction, individual accountability, and the development of interpersonal skills.

The tasks and goals assigned to the cooperative group must use the skills of all members and require that all members take an active role in completing the job. When this *positive interdependence* occurs, there is a sense that each member of the group is making a valuable contribution to the common goal. To achieve this, it is necessary for the teacher to assign a singular role to each member, or to divide the tasks among the members, or to provide each member with some materials and information needed by the group. Through any or a combination of these means, the teacher engineers the group's perception of "all for one and one for all."

Individual members could conceivably complete their tasks separately and turn them in together. But to encourage the maximum benefit from the cooperative effort, it is necessary for the teacher to allow class time for students to work *face-to-face* with each other. When this occurs, the groups have an opportunity to increase their communication skills, as well as working to achieve other academic goals.

When a well-defined group goal and an incentive are established, cooperative groups tend to resolve differences and follow through to the completion of their tasks. But in addition to the group goal, a system of *individual accountability* needs to be established. Individuals must each be responsible for demonstrating their own mastery of the subject matter by completing and turning in assignments or by performing well on written or oral quizzes and tests. Without a system of individual accountability, what begins as a group effort can turn into the efforts of a few carrying the rest of the group. High-achieving students may become impatient with slower classmates and want to take over the entire task. Low-achieving students may be fearful of making errors or holding the others back, so they pass off their work to be completed by others.

Whenever students are assigned to work in cooperative groups, they need guidance from the teacher in order to recognize, practice, and enhance their *interpersonal skills*. Effective listening and speaking skills need to be employed to work productively together. Students need to learn how to manage conflicts and be assertive. Teachers can help by training students in these skills and designing tasks that encourage their development. When students are initially introduced to working cooperatively, the tasks may be simple so that the groups can be successful. Early experiences will require simple communication and problem-solving skills. But as groups become more experienced and mature, it is possible to increase the complexity of the tasks in such a way that the members continually enhance and develop their communication and problem-solving skills.

HOW COOPERATIVE LEARNING IS USED IN CLASSROOMS

Cooperative groups can be used in the elementary grades in almost every part of the curriculum. Various models may be more appropriate for different subjects and grade levels. The uses and adaptations of the cooperative group strategy are limitless, depending only on the imagination and style of the classroom teacher.

Some teachers may divide students into long-term cooperative groups: pairs or small groups of students who sit near each other and assist each other in all subject areas. Other teachers may prefer to create cooperative groups for a single purpose only, changing the membership of groups for each new project.

In the following examples at each grade level, a typical classroom task will first be described as it would be taught using conventional methods. Then it will be revised to describe how the subject could be taught using cooperative group strategies.

Kindergarten Applications

A major component of the kindergarten curriculum is learning to recognize letters and the sounds that letters make. In a conventional classroom, the day may begin with a large group meeting to discuss the day, the weather, and the season. Students may then be encouraged to share important news with each other in a "show and tell" format. The teacher may then teach the group the shape and sound of the letter *B* and, as a follow-up exercise, ask the students to go to their desks and do phonics worksheets emphasizing this letter.

Because kindergarten classes emphasize socialization as part of their curriculum, it is natural to introduce children to cooperative groups at this early age. The lesson on the letter *B* can easily be adapted to a cooperative venture. When the large group meets in a circle for opening exercises and sharing time, the teacher may initiate a search for things in the room that have the *B* sound. The teacher can then assign students to cooperative groups, taking care to include both readers and nonreaders in each group. In their groups, students are given a stack of old magazines and are asked to work together to find and cut out pictures of objects that begin with the letter *B* and paste them on a large piece of paper. The student with the most advanced skills can then write the name of each object as a label for each picture. Roles that can be assigned to each student in the group include finder, cutter, paster, and labeler. On successive days, these tasks can be reassigned so that all children get an opportunity to perform each task that they are capable of doing.

As a group goal, the task is to find as many objects as possible in a given time. Incorrect items do not count toward the final tally. The group's reward may be a minute of free play for each item or a similar number of grapes or crackers for snack time. As a measure of individual accountability, the teacher may meet with each student separately and have each student "read" aloud the names of the objects on the poster.

First-Grade Applications

At the first-grade level, students may be doing a science lesson on nutrition that could be handled in a similar fashion. The conventional method might be to read and discuss the four food groups, followed by an activity in which individual children search for examples of foods that fit each group. To make the task more interesting, the teacher may choose to assign students to cooperative groups and tell them that each group will be responsible for starting a new restaurant. Their first task will be to name the restaurant. Then they must work together to plan three menus: one each for breakfast, lunch, and dinner.

Given large sheets of construction paper, the groups will create menus that include all four food groups for each meal. The division of labor can be handled by having three students per group, one responsible for each meal. When the menus are completed, the groups can interact by having students role-play the act of visiting each other's restaurants as customers and choosing a well-balanced meal. Individual accountability can be built in by giving a quiz at a later date. Groups can earn certificates of merit if their group menus are accurate and well prepared and if the individuals in their group meet a minimum criterion on the follow-up quizzes.

In an activity-centered math program or a whole language reading/writing program, pairs of learning partners are vital to the success of the programs. By pairing a high achiever with a low achiever as learning partners, the teacher can ensure that students will actively learn each new concept and will get the scaffolding necessary to understand difficult new concepts. For example, in teaching addition without learning partners, the teacher usually models the operation on the chalkboard and asks students to duplicate the process at their desks. As learning partners, students work on their problems and then check each other's work. If there is a difference between the two answers, they redo their work until they both have the correct answer.

Tim Curbo, who teaches first grade at Hawthorne School in San Francisco, California, describes in the following Perspective how he uses cooperative groups to encourage students to develop their language skills, problem-solving skills, and co-operation skills all at the same time.

▼ **P E R S P E C T I V E** ▼

HOW TIM CURBO USES COOPERATIVE GROUPS IN HIS CLASSROOM

At Hawthorne School, students move to different classes for language arts on Monday through Thursday. On Friday they stay in their own classrooms. I use that day for cooperative group activities.

I divide the class into groups of four. Because I have many bilingual students in my class, I make sure that each group has a combination of English-speaking and Spanish-speaking children.

In each group there are four different jobs or roles for children to take. I post the roles on the bulletin board—for example:

Maria — Materials
Jed — Reporter
Carlos — Facilitator
Ana — Writer

The materials person gets all the necessary materials for the task. The facilitator makes sure that everyone is participating and solves any problems that arise. The writer keeps a written record of the activity. As I teach first grade, the writer may just draw illustrations, and as I circulate around the room, I record the other observations of the members of the groups. The reporter gives a report of what the group accomplished. Children get a different role each time we do cooperative group activities.

Before the first task, we talk about the various responsibilities. I usually choose a simple task initially, such as a puzzle. All the students work together to solve the puzzle. Then the writer may draw the finished puzzle, and the reporter describes the process the group used to solve the puzzle.

One of the first tasks of the group is to select a name. This is then posted on the board. The writer's report is posted next to the group's name. Other products can also be posted in this space.

From the very beginning, I turn questions and problems that arise back to the group. I encourage the facilitator to take charge but to involve the others in trying to solve the problems. I tell them, "Four heads are better than one." I keep myself free to circulate, clarifying, extending the activity, and making encouraging remarks.

It's always noisy, and things are bumpy at first. Children aren't sure of their roles. There are personality clashes. We process or talk about all these issues. Most issues are worked out with time. My students enjoy the spirit of cooperation that develops and the social interaction. Through repeated use of this strategy, it becomes evident that cooperation and problem-solving skills are prominent shared values in our classroom.

Second-Grade Applications

The second-grade curriculum emphasizes the concept of community. Reflective teachers recognize that in order to truly understand the concept of community, students need to live it. Using a jigsaw approach, small groups can each study one element of a community and report their findings to the class. Using a group investigation approach, students may discover a controversy in their own community that they wish to study and then take a stand on the issue.

As an example of a cooperative learning unit on communities, the teacher may choose to begin with the local community or neighborhood if the school is located in a large city. Beginning with a walking or bus tour of the commercial area, the entire group discusses the various elements that are needed for a successful community. If possible, some teachers extend the tour to pass by the house of each person in the class. Given a map of the area, cooperative groups can be formed with an initial assignment of depicting on the map the important sites they observed on the tour. Each person in the group can be given the job of locating and recording an equal number of sites on the map.

Later, the same cooperative groups can select one aspect of the community to study, such as the hospital, fire station, police station, city hall, library, churches, or the school itself. With the teacher's help, each group can invite speakers to come to the class to discuss their jobs and responsibilities to the community. Each group can also prepare a short skit (containing all members of the group) that informs the rest of the class about the roles and responsibilities of the community helpers they studied.

After a thorough study of the local community, this unit can be expanded to include a study of very different communities around the world or how one community has changed over time. Again, cooperative groups can each take responsibility for researching one type of community and creating a model of it for others to see. Roles and tasks may have to be assigned to ensure that everyone in the group is actively included in the project. These roles could include reader, writer, builder, and painter.

Third-Grade Applications

At the third-grade level, students are expected to demonstrate mastery of the basic skills taught during the primary grades. Standardized achievement or criterion-referenced tests may be given to document the gains made by the students as a class and as individuals. For example, many third graders are expected to demonstrate that they can meet the school's criteria for computing the basic addition, subtraction, and multiplication facts. In a traditional classroom, teachers may prepare students for this assessment by providing them with daily worksheets for practicing and memorizing the math facts. In an effort to motivate students to improve their skills, conventional teachers may post charts for all to read that display the names of students who have reached the criteria and those who have not.

While this competitive environment may please and motivate the high achievers, it is not likely to encourage the remainder of the class. To modify the process of learning math facts from a competitive to a cooperative experience, teachers could adapt the STAD model to fit the needs of their classrooms.

Using a STAD approach, the teacher would begin by giving a pretest of 100 math facts to the entire class. By sorting the pretests into high, medium, and low scores, the teacher can divide the class into heterogeneous groups with equivalent ability in math facts. Each group would contain one of the top scorers, one of the lowest scorers, and two in the middle range.

How the teacher sets up the conditions and expectations for this cooperative learning experience is very important. The achievement goal and the behavioral expectations need to be clearly explained at the outset. For example, the teacher may state that the groups are expected to practice math facts for a given period of time each day. Worksheets, flash cards, and other materials will be provided, and the teams are free to choose the means they use to practice. The goal, in this instance, is to raise all scores from pretest levels as much as possible. A posttest will be given on a certain day, and each individual will have an improvement score, which is the difference between the correct responses on the posttest and the correct responses on the pretest. The group score will be computed by adding up the individual improvement scores. This method of scoring encourages the group to give extra effort to raising the scores of the lowest scorers because they have the most to gain. Top scorers, in fact, may not gain many points at all, since their pretests may already be near the total. Added incentives for this group may be devised, such as a certain number of points for a perfect paper.

The incentives that will be awarded for success depend a great deal on the class itself. The teacher may choose to offer one reward for the group whose scores improve the most or to reward each group, depending on their gains. For example, a single reward for the most improved group may be tangible, such as a certificate of success or temporary possession of a traveling math trophy. Less tangible incentives are also important to third graders, such as the opportunity to be first in line for a week, go to the library together during a math class, or eat lunch with the teacher. To spread the incentives to all groups, the points that each group earns may be translated into an award, such as 1 minute of free time per point, or may be cashed in to "buy" special opportunities and materials.

When it is time for the standardized tests to be given, these groups are likely to take a considerable interest in assisting and supporting their members in doing well on the math portion of the test. Similar groups could operate to improve spelling, vocabulary, the mechanics of writing, or other basic skills. The members of these groups would be different because students would score differently on pretests for various subjects.

Fourth-Grade Applications

While math computation lends itself to a STAD approach, math problem solving can be enhanced by the extra incentive of working toward participation in a tournament in the TGT model of cooperative learning. Traditional methods of teaching math problem solving involve individual children doing pages of story problems on paper and having the papers corrected and graded. When students have difficulty with story problems, the teacher must work personally with them to help them understand the processes and operations needed to solve the problems.

Using a team approach, pretests or other measures of past performance in math problem solving are used to form heterogeneous groups consisting of high, middle, and low achievers. Textbooks, worksheets, and other practice problems can be given to groups of students to prepare them for tournaments to be held once or twice a week. During a tournament, the groups are divided again so that each student is assigned to a table or station to compete individually against students of similar ability from other teams. Problems can be presented orally or in written form during the tournaments. The difficulty of problems can be varied to match the ability levels of students at each station.

Slavin (1983) recommends that scoring of tournaments be cumulative. The top scorer from each table receives six points, the middle scorer four points, and the low scorer two points. Team scores are then calculated by simply adding the results for the teammates. These scores are added to the team's tallies from previous sessions. Team standings are then publicized in newsletters that go home to parents.

Fifth-Grade Applications

In many classrooms, the conventional approach to teaching science was centered on textbook reading, discussion, an occasional demonstration by the teacher, and written tests of understanding. But more recently, science curriculums have been revised to include many more hands-on experiments and investigations. The current philosophy is that elementary students need to learn how to do science rather than simply learn about it.

Hands-on science is an area of the elementary curriculum that has a natural fit with cooperative group strategies. By participating in cooperative science investigations, students learn how scientists themselves interact to share observations, hypotheses, and methods. While many teachers value these current science goals, they may be reluctant to try them because they are unsure of how to manage the high level of activity in the classroom when science experiments are happening. Cooperative groups can provide the support and structure that are needed in managing successful science investigation in the elementary classroom.

When a topic or unit approach is taken for teaching science, each unit offers opportunities for cooperative learning. For example, the topic of astronomy may be studied by jigsaw groups, each of which studies one planet, creates models and charts of information about their planet, and reports their findings to others.

Investigations into the properties of simple machines, magnets, electricity, and other topics in physics can be designed by establishing a challenge or a complex goal for groups to meet by a given date. Groups may be given a set of identical materials and told to create a product that has certain characteristics and can perform a specific function. For example, given a supply of toothpicks and glue, groups are challenged to construct a bridge that can hold a pound of weight without breaking. Given a raw egg and an assortment of materials, groups work together to create a way to protect their egg when it is dropped from a high window onto the pavement below.

Science groups can be mixed and matched frequently during the year, offering students an opportunity to work cooperatively with most other members of their class. In this way, the principles of social science are likely to be reinforced as well. As Johnson and Johnson (1984) recommend, one interpersonal skill can be learned and practiced during each academic group experience. For example, during the astronomy unit, the emphasis could be on learning how to come together as a group, quickly, quietly, and efficiently when getting started on the day's project. During the bridge-building unit, the groups could practice encouraging everyone to participate, taking time to ask for opinions and suggestions from every member of the group before making an important decision. After each unit is completed, it is recommended that the groups participate in an evaluation of how they worked together and how well they demonstrated the interpersonal skill emphasized during that unit.

Sixth-Grade Applications

The sixth-grade reading curriculum is designed to introduce students to a variety of literary forms. Using conventional methods of teaching reading, three homogeneous reading groups based on ability may still be used at the sixth-grade level. Each group reads stories, essays, poems, and plays collected in a basal reader geared to its reading ability. Discussions of reading materials are led by the teacher, and seatwork is assigned to be done while the teacher works with other groups.

Many upper elementary teachers, however, prefer to use literary materials in their own format rather than as collections in basal readers or anthologies. They believe that students' motivation to read will be increased if they are encouraged to choose and read whole books, novels, poetry collections, and plays. A variety of paperback books in sets of six to eight books apiece are needed to carry out this type of reading program.

At Our Lady of Mercy School in Chicago, Illinois, sixth-grade teacher Roxanne Farwick-Owens has developed a system that allows choice, maximizes cooperative efforts, and holds individuals accountable. Elements of the CIRC, jigsaw, TGT, and Sharan's group investigation models are woven into her unique system.

To maximize student motivation and enjoyment of reading, Roxanne believes that students need to be allowed to choose their reading materials. Each month she provides three or four reading selections, in the form of paperback books, to the class. Students are allowed to choose the book they want to read, and groups are formed according to interest rather than ability level. Roxanne may advise students about their selections and try to steer them to appropriate ones, but in the end, she believes that they have the right to choose for themselves what they will read, especially since she provides only books that have inherent value for sixth graders.

During initial group meetings, students decide for themselves how much to read at a time. They assign themselves due dates for each chapter. Periodically, each group meets with Roxanne to discuss what they are reading, but most discussions are held without her leadership. Usually the groups are held responsible for generating their own discussion on the book. To prepare for this discussion, all members are expected to prepare questions as they read. For example, each person in the group may be expected to contribute three "why" questions and two detail questions per session. Roxanne reviews the questions each day as a means of holding each individual accountable for reading the material and contributing to the group.

Another task is to plan a presentation about the book using art, music, drama, and other media to share with the rest of the class at the end of the month. In this way, books read by one group are introduced to other members of the class, who are then likely to choose them at a later date. One group made wooden puppets and a puppet stage to portray an event from Mark Twain's *Tom Sawyer*. To advertise Judy Blume's *Superfudge*, a group created a radio commercial complete with sound effects and background music. Familiar television interview shows are sometimes used as a format, as are music videos.

About once per quarter, two teams are formed to compete in a game show-type tournament. Questions about the books are separated into categories such as characters, plot, setting, authors, and miscellaneous. Each person is responsible for writing five questions and answers on index cards to prepare for the tournament. One student acts as emcee, while another keeps track of the points. The team with the most points wins the tournament.

Roxanne finds that this cooperative group structure increases her students' social skills, especially their ability to work with others and to find effective ways to handle disagreements. But the primary reason for the program is to help her students learn to see that reading can be enjoyable, and that instead of being a solitary pursuit, reading can have a social aspect. It is Roxanne's belief that many of her students may become lifelong readers as a result of this 1-year experience.

Middle School Applications

In many states, at the middle school or junior high level, students are expected to pass a test on the U.S. Constitution before they graduate to high school. In most classrooms, the study of the Constitution and memorization of key items is seen as an individual responsibility, but it can easily become a very productive cooperative group experience. Study groups can be formed that are similar to those used by law students. The goal is to have everyone in the study group pass the exam and score as well as possible.

Because of the nature of the topic and the age of the students, this task may be best accomplished by using Sharan's group investigation model. After introducing the subject and showing the class an example of the test they will have to pass, the teacher can ask students to help develop a plan of action that will support them in studying and learning the material. The class may suggest a STAD approach to learning the facts, in which teams prepare each other to compete on weekly written quizzes. They may prefer a TGT approach when the weekly quizzes are oral. They may suggest that each cooperative group become expert on one area of the Constitution (the Bill of Rights or the articles dealing with the executive branch, judicial branch, and legislative branch) and prepare study aids for other groups to use.

The class can also take part in the decision making about the incentives they want to work for. Weekly incentives can be used to encourage members to learn enough to do well on the quizzes or tournaments. A whole class incentive can be planned if every member of the class passes the test on the first or second try. When middle school children are invited to participate in the planning of their own learning, they are likely to show interest, energy, and responsibility in handling the task.

CLASSROOM CONDITIONS THAT ENCOURAGE COOPERATION

Cooperative groups are a welcome change of pace for many students. They enjoy the opportunity to interact with their peers for part of the school day. But teachers may be hesitant to try the strategy for fear that the students will play or talk about outside interests rather than work at the task assigned. Cooperative groups can degenerate into chaotic groups if certain conditions are not met.

When the goals of the task are poorly understood by the group, the results of their efforts may be unproductive and frustrating. To prevent this from occurring, it is important that the teacher clearly state the goals and expectations of each group task and provide a copy of them in writing so that the group can refer to them from time to time.

In addition to being clear, the goal or task must have inherent value and be perceived by the group as worthy of their time and effort. When students care about the outcome, they are more likely to take each other seriously and ask each other for help in achieving the goal (Slavin, 1987).

In order to encourage high-quality effort and achievement, there must be incentives that are perceived as meaningful and valuable by the groups. The incentives may be extrinsic, in the form of a certificate, points, grades, a pizza party, or an extra-long recess. In some cases, there may be intrinsic incentives as well, such as enhanced group pride or the good feeling that comes from having contributed to the well-being of other human beings. Each teacher and each school community has different needs and values that must be taken into account as incentives are planned and communicated to the children.

Johnson and Johnson (1984) provide the following suggestions to implement successful cooperative groups. The size of the group may vary from task to task. Generally, groups consist of two to six students, with smaller groups in the primary grades and larger groups in the upper grades. Pairs are excellent for monitoring and checking tasks. Groups of three to six are used for study teams and investigations. The shorter the period of time available, the smaller the groups should be. Small groups can be more efficient because they take less time to get organized, they operate more quickly, and there is more "air time" per member (p. 27).

Assigning students to cooperative groups can be the most difficult part of the process for teachers. The philosophy of heterogeneous grouping is excellent on paper but is difficult to achieve in a classroom where no two children are alike. There are likely to be one or two superstars in a classroom whose ability cannot be matched in some subject areas. Similarly, there may be one or two students with unusual learning difficulties or behavior problems. For most types of learning situations, the teacher must simply make the best judgment about the combinations that are approximately equivalent in ability.

It is advisable to put non-task-oriented students into groups with highly task-oriented teammates so that peer pressure will work to keep them on task. This theory, however, does not always work out in the classroom. Angry or highly restless students may refuse to participate or otherwise prevent their team from succeeding. When this happens, it is believed that the group itself should be encouraged to deal with the problem as a means of learning how to cope with and resolve such occurrences in real life (pp. 28–29).

In arranging the room during cooperative group activities, it is important that each group have comfortable space together, and that members be able to face each other and have eye contact with every other member of the group. Separating the groups from each other is also necessary so that each group can work undisturbed by the conversations and activities taking place in other groups (p. 29).

Materials that are intended for cooperative groups may differ from those used in conventional teaching and learning situations. It is suggested that only one set of materials explaining the task and the expectations be distributed. This causes students in the group to work together from the very beginning. In some cases, each member of the group may receive different information from other members. This promotes interdependence, as each member has something important to share with the others (p. 30).

Interdependence can also be encouraged by the assignment of "complementary and interconnected roles" to group members. These roles will vary with the type of learning and task but might include discussion leader, recorder of ideas, runner for information, researcher, encourager, and observer (pp. 30–31).

Tasks that result in the creation of products, rather than participation in a test or tournament, are more likely to succeed if the group is limited to the production of one product. If more than one product is allowed, students may simply work independently on their own products. It is also suggested that members of the group be asked to sign a statement saying that they participated fully in the development of the group's product (p. 32).

To ensure individual accountability, students must know that they will all be held responsible for learning and presenting what they learned. During the final presentations, the teacher may ask any member of the group to answer a question or describe an aspect of the group's final product or present a rationale for a decision of the group (p. 32).

THE EFFECTS OF COOPERATIVE LEARNING

To compare the academic achievement of elementary students using the cooperative learning methods with those using more conventional approaches, Slavin (1987) compared pre- and posttest scores for students in math, writing, reading, social studies, science, and language arts. "Of 38 studies of at least four weeks' duration comparing cooperative methods of this type to traditional control methods, 33 found significantly greater achievement for the cooperatively taught classes" (p. 10). In addition, positive effects were found on higher-order objectives as well as on the basic skills. But perhaps the most striking effects of cooperative learning are affective rather than cognitive.

In a school setting, children learn in classes generally made up of their agemates. With conventional teaching methods, the relationships among peers in a class are likely to become somewhat competitive, since most students are aware of how well they are doing in relation to their classmates. Grading systems reinforce the competitive nature of school, as do standardized tests and entrance exams.

It is recognized that individual competition can enhance the motivation for high-achieving students who perceive that they have a possibility of winning or being the best. However, the public nature of competitive rewards and incentives leads to embarrassment and anxiety for children who fail to succeed. When the anxiety and embarrassment are intense, children who recognize that they are not likely to win, no matter how hard they work, eventually drop out of the competition in one way or another.

Even when the anxiety over competition is less intense and under control by students with average or high average achievement, they may become preoccupied with grades to the extent that they avoid complex or challenging tasks that will risk their academic standing and grades (Doyle, 1983).

Despite these negative effects of competition, it is difficult to imagine a classroom without some type of competitive spirit or reward system, and despite its obvious flaws, competition does create an energetic response from many students. Slavin's (1984) models of cooperative group structures are designed to maintain the value of competition by adapting it in the form of team competition so that each student is equally capable of winning.

Team competition, then, has motivational advantages for low- and middle-achieving students that individual competition does not. Still, any competitive situation has winners and losers, and Johnson and Johnson (1984) caution that losing team members may blame one another and hold as scapegoats individual members of their team whom they believe to be responsible for the team's loss.

Reflective teachers who undertake some form of cooperative learning will need to be aware of all possible effects and observe for both positive and negative interactions among teammates. When using competitive teams, teachers should take steps to ensure that every team has an equal chance to win and that attention is focused more on the learning task than on who wins and loses. When anger or conflict arises within groups, teachers must be ready to mediate and assist students as they learn the interpersonal and communication skills necessary to learn from their team's losses.

Johnson and Johnson (1984) report that when cooperative groups are well planned and managed, they "promote considerably more liking among students" than do competitive and individualistic structures. "This is true regardless of differences in ability level, sex, handicapping conditions, ethnic membership, social class differences, or task orientation. Students who collaborate on their studies develop considerable commitment and caring for each other no matter what their initial impressions of and attitudes toward each other were" (p. 18).

Slavin (1984) and Sharan (1984) also report that cooperative groups may actually improve race relations within a classroom. When students participate in biracial teams, studies show that they choose each other for friends more often than do students in control groups. Researchers attribute this effect to the fact that working together in a group as part of a team causes students to promote more differentiated, dynamic, and realistic views (and therefore less stereotyped and static views) of other students (including handicapped peers and students from different ethnic groups) than do competitive and individualistic learning experiences (Johnson & Johnson, 1984, p. 21).

Slavin (1984) also reports that cooperative groups have a positive influence on the successful mainstreaming of handicapped children into the regular classroom. Research on the use of cooperative groups to facilitate mainstreaming and meet the needs of remedial readers has found positive effects on both the achievement and the social acceptance of these learners. This is believed to occur because students generalize the concept of helping one another to learn from the team efforts in cooperative groups to become a fundamental principle of classroom organization.

Cooperative learning experiences have also been shown to promote higher levels of self-esteem. Johnson and Johnson (1984) attribute this effect to a relationship between cooperative relationships with peers and basic, unconditional self-acceptance. In contrast, they found that competitiveness promotes conditional self-acceptance and that highly individualistic attitudes tend to be related to self-rejection.

Cooperative learning experiences have also been shown to affect students' relationships with adults in the school. "Students participating in cooperative learning experiences, compared with students participating in competitive and individualistic learning experiences, like the teacher better and perceive the teacher as being more supportive and accepting academically and personally" (Johnson & Johnson, 1984, pp. 21–22).

Slavin (1987) also believes that the effects of cooperative groups can lead to the concept of a cooperative school, in which it becomes the norm for students to help each other and for teachers to coach and support each other as well. Administrators, parents, teachers, and students could work together to develop a community sense that "every student's learning is everyone's responsibility, that every student's success is everyone's success" (p. 12).

OPPORTUNITIES FOR REFLECTION

▼ Reflective Essay: Cooperative Group Experiences

Do you believe in using competition or cooperation to motivate your students to learn? In your own experience with cooperative groups, do you find them to be enjoyable and stimulating or frustrating and discouraging? What type of role do you usually take in a cooperative group? Do you get impatient with others in your group and wish you could work on the assignment by yourself? What could be done to improve the structure of the groups you have participated in? Are you likely to use cooperative groups in your classroom? Why or why not?

▼ Classroom Visit: Cooperation vs. Competition

In the classroom you are visiting, is competition or cooperation more highly valued? Give examples of classroom events or incentive structures that support your observation. How would you alter this balance to create more cooperation? Give an example of a recent classroom event that you observed and tell how you would change it.

REFERENCES

ARONSON, E., BLANEY, S., SIKES, J., & SNAPP, M. (1978). *The jigsaw classroom*. Beverly Hills, CA: Sage.

DEWEY, J. (1910). *How we think*. Boston: Heath.

DEWEY, J. (1916). *Democracy and education*. New York: Macmillan.

DOYLE, W. (1983). Academic work. *Review of Educational Research, 53,* 159–199.

JAMES, W. (1890). *Principles of psychology*. New York: Holt.

JOHNSON, D., & JOHNSON, R. (1984). *Circles of learning*. Alexandria, VA: Association of Supervision and Curriculum Development.

JOYCE, B., & WEIL, M. (1986). *Models of teaching.* Englewood Cliffs, NJ: Prentice-Hall.

SHARAN, S. (1984). *Cooperative learning in the classroom: Research in desegregated schools.* Hillsdale, NJ: Erlbaum.

SHARAN, S., & SHARON, Y. (1976). *Small group teaching.* Englewood Cliffs, NJ: Educational Technology Publications.

SKINNER, B. (1953). *Science and human behavior.* New York: Macmillan.

SLAVIN, R. (1983). *Cooperative learning.* New York: Longman.

SLAVIN, R. (1984). Students motivating students to excel: Incentives, cooperative tasks and student achievement. *The Elementary School Journal, 85,* 53–62.

SLAVIN, R. (1987). Cooperative learning and the cooperative school. *Educational Leadership, 45* (3), 7–13.

STALLINGS, J., & STIPEK, D. (1986). Research on early childhood and elementary school teaching programs. In M. Wittrock (Ed.), *Handbook of research on teaching* (3rd ed.) (pp. 727–753). New York: Macmillan.

THELEN, H. (1960). *Education and the human quest.* New York: Harper & Row.

Developing a Repertoire
of Teaching Strategies

SCHOOL EXPERIENCES can be enjoyable for both teachers and students. One way of heightening the enjoyment is by using a variety of teaching strategies and activities. When learning experiences are varied, students are more likely to become actively engaged in the learning process. Their intrinsic motivation to learn is also likely to be enhanced by the expectation that the skill or knowledge they are learning will be presented in a novel and unusual format. To promote the enjoyment of teaching and learning, many reflective teachers are continuously searching for new methods and strategies that they can employ to motivate and engage their students in the learning process.

Developing a repertoire of teaching strategies is also necessary because students' needs and learning styles are so diverse. For this reason, teachers should be ready to modify lesson plans and prepared to present information in more than one way.

The purpose of this chapter is to introduce you to a repertoire of strategies that you can select from when you teach. An overview of strategies as they relate to Bloom's Taxonomy is presented, followed by more detailed descriptions of some teaching models that are appropriate for elementary classrooms. This book can only provide an overview of the descriptions, illustrations, and examples you will need in order to employ these methods successfully. You will need to search for more detailed descriptions of these strategies in books such as Joyce and Weil's (1987) *Models of Teaching*, in journal articles, or by observing experienced teachers.

As you read about or select a strategy to try out in a laboratory or classroom, you will find that some of them work for you and others do not. You will need to reflect about what works for you and your students and why. As you think about what works for you, it is quite acceptable to combine, adapt, modify, and add your own unique strategies to the ones you read about or observe. Through this process of practice and reflection, you will discover, create, and refine your own unique teaching style.

TEACHING STRATEGIES THAT FIT BLOOM'S TAXONOMY

In this section, brief descriptions of some of the most frequently used teaching strategies will be presented to give you an overview of the rich and varied methods that are available. They are organized within the framework of Bloom's (1956) *Taxonomy of Educational Objectives* so that you can understand the relationship between planning an objective at a certain level of the Taxonomy and selecting a teaching strategy or method to achieve that objective in the classroom. As you will see, some strategies, such as class discussion or cooperative groups, can be used to achieve objectives at several levels of the Taxonomy, depending on what the class is asked to discuss or what task the group is asked to do.

Teaching Strategies That Develop a Knowledge Base

The most common teaching strategies used to help children develop a knowledge base of facts, information, and skills are reading for information and the method known as **direct instruction,** which was described in Chapter 7. Many teachers also employ strategies known as *drill and practice,* which means that students repeat what they have learned in an oral recitation or in written exercises in order to reinforce their understanding of the new facts or skills and commit them to memory.

Drill, practice, lecture, reading, and recitation—are these the only strategies that teachers need to know in order to teach the basic facts and skills that students must master in each content area? These were the traditional teaching strategies used in elementary schools until educational psychologists such as Ausubel (1960) showed that meaningful learning consists of linking new bits of knowledge to already known facts and ideas gained from previous learning experiences. Reflective teachers have learned from cognitive psychology that a key to successful development of a knowledge base is providing rich and *varied learning experiences,* not just relying on drill and practice.

The elementary curriculum emphasizes the learning of basic facts, skills, processes, and concepts in all subject areas. As children experience the complexities of the world they inhabit, they gather many unrelated verbal and numerical symbols, facts, data, concepts, and ideas. When these bits of knowledge are successfully integrated in the brain, they can be stored and recalled on demand. Cognitive psychologists use *schema theory* to explain this process of sensing, storing, and recalling information. Each separate schema is a storehouse of images, sensations, symbols, and words that are somehow related in an individual's mind (Anderson, 1977; Bransford, 1983).

For children to develop a knowledge base on a particular subject, they must first create a simple, rudimentary, or basic schema on that topic through direct or vicarious experience. For example, consider how children learn about animals. Many children have an experience with a dog or cat before coming to school. They store the sensations (furry, barking, wet nose and tongue, four legs, petting, tail) in a schema often labeled "doggy" or "kitty." Images of stuffed teddy bears or goats in story books may be included in the child's schema labeled "doggy" for a time, until the child is able to differentiate among these four-legged creatures.

Children need additional experiences in school that will help them to develop richly detailed and accurate schemata on a wide variety of topics. Several teaching responsibilities are implied by this statement. First, the teacher must choose teaching strategies and plan learning activities that provide students with appropriate experiences so that they gain new bits of knowledge and create new schemata. Second, the teacher must assist students in ordering and classifying the knowledge they have stored so that it is readily accessible.

There are many teaching strategies that teachers can use to provide students with new experiences, sensations, and ideas. Very young children can gain knowledge through vicarious experiences such as listening to the teacher read aloud, while older children can read for themselves. Teachers use films, filmstrips, videotapes, audiotapes, records, and pictures to extend their students' experience and knowledge base. Hands-on activities are also important for schema development in the elementary grades. When children play with balls, rocket ships, measuring cups, dolls, and other objects, they develop increasingly complex schemata for these things. Field trips are especially likely to cause children to create new schemata. Taking children out of their familiar environments to go to a zoo, museum, play, or concert is likely to result in the formation of new schemata.

Teachers assist students in classifying and ordering their existing schemata by planning verbal discussions and explications of what they are seeing and experiencing. Children may develop a schema for "alphabet" by viewing *Sesame Street* or singing the "ABC Song." But teachers must assist their students in making these symbols meaningful by explaining the relationship between a visual symbol and its meaning or use.

Manual tasks such as copying the letters of the alphabet help the child to differentiate among these symbols. Oral exercises make the child aware of the sound each letter represents. Matching pictures of familiar objects with the same sound as the letter helps the child understand the symbol–sound–use relationship. With each new experience, the child's schema for "alphabet" becomes increasingly complex, but also much better organized and accurate.

Drill, practice, memorization, and recitation may help students to strengthen existing schemata, but they cannot replace authentic learning *experience* for schema creation or development.

Teaching Strategies That Promote Comprehension

Is comprehension the same as decoding? "Decoding means cracking a code, and this is exactly the function of decoding processes—they crack the code of print to make print meaningful" (Gagne, 1985, p. 167). Decoding strategies include (1) instructing students to match unknown printed words to their previously learned sight word vocabularies and (2) teaching students to use phonics to sound out unfamiliar words. While these strategies are useful in the literal comprehension of words, reflective teachers know that students need to be taught to comprehend ideas and concepts, not just single words.

To teach comprehension at the level of ideas, teachers often use the strategy of the **advance organizer.** Ausubel (1960) demonstrated that teachers can increase student comprehension by introducing unfamiliar material with a statement showing how the new material is related to knowledge the student has already learned. This introduction allows the student to recall a related schema prior to reading or hearing the new material. When the unknown ideas are encountered, the student has an existing schema in mind that makes the new idea more meaningful.

For example, when asking students to read a passage on the boundaries between nations, the teacher may describe how fences in a neighborhood are used to protect private property and maintain relationships among neighbors. This description uses language and concepts students understand. It allows them to call up an existing schema, "fences," and be ready to construct a new schema called "boundaries." After the passage is read, the teacher may ask students to tell how boundaries and fences are alike. The strategy of following up the reading with a discussion that includes the advance organizer and the new material strengthens the students' understanding of the new concept.

Teachers may also use questions, clues, and suggestions to alert students to look for, listen for, or search for some new, previously unknown element. Madeline Hunter (1976) encourages teachers to use a variety of introductory experiences to motivate students to want to find out more about a subject. This strategy, the use of an *anticipatory set,* creates a positive anticipation on the part of the student. For example, a teacher might preface the reading of a passage on water evaporation by wiping a wet sponge on the chalkboard and drying it with a hair dryer. Students would then be asked to read the passage to discover what happened to the water.

Discussion is an important strategy that teachers use for increasing student comprehension of a new subject. As students state their ideas aloud, they are reinforcing their own understanding of the topic. When teachers respond to a student's idea by showing agreement or by giving useful feedback and clarification, the student's understanding is further enhanced. Class members who listen to their classmates' ideas and the teacher's responses may also gain new perspectives and greater understanding of the subject.

One of the most frequent methods teachers use to evaluate student comprehension is to ask students to state or write the meaning of something in their own words. In the example of water evaporation, a teacher may ask students to summarize in writing how water evaporates. When students are able to do this, the teacher knows that the material has been successfully learned. If the students are unable to state or write a summary of the concept, the teacher knows that the material must be retaught.

In order to reteach, it is necessary to present a subject to students differently than the first time it was taught. When descriptions and explanations of unfamiliar material do not work, many teachers find that the use of *analogies* helps students to understand a difficult new concept by building a bridge between unknown or abstract concepts and known, concrete experiences. The use of the phrase *building a bridge* in the preceding sentence is itself an analogy for the abstraction known as *analogy.*

By describing how a fence is similar to an international boundary, the teacher makes an abstract concept more concrete. In a class discussion or lecture, the teacher may extend this analogy to describe how family loyalty resembles patriotism, how economies of nations are similar to the economies of families, and how the decisions about land use may vary from nation to nation as well as from family to family.

Another teaching strategy that promotes comprehension is to provide graphic examples and illustrations to assist students in interpreting new information.

Just as a picture is worth a thousand words, a graph or a chart can summarize a great deal of data in a form that students can comprehend. Bar graphs show temperature comparisons much better than lists of figures do. Pie charts vividly demonstrate the amount of time or money spent on various pursuits better than paragraphs can. Reflective teachers frequently employ visual or graphic aids in their own teaching. They also ask their students to create illustrations, graphs, diagrams, and charts to demonstrate that they have interpreted data or new concepts successfully.

Teaching Strategies That Cause Students to Apply What They Learn

A well-accepted principle of learning is that "if a student really comprehends something, then he can apply it" (Bloom, Englehart, Furst, Hill, & Krathwohl, 1956, p. 120). These authors noted that the fact that most of what we learn is intended for application to problem situations in real life is indicative of the importance of application objectives in the general curriculum.

Reflective teachers are eager to offer students opportunities to apply what they've learned in most of the subjects in the elementary curriculum. *Discussion,* as a teaching strategy, can be an occasion for application as well as comprehension. For example, a teacher-led discussion on current events may focus on the way the news item affects the lives of the students in the class. Literary discussions are valuable for the exchange of views on how characters deal with situations and how class members might act under those circumstances.

Many teachers employ *simulations* and *role playing* to bring the world into the classroom. These strategies will be described in greater detail later in this chapter, but all have in common the presentation of a puzzling situation and the opportunity to discuss alternatives and generate solutions to problems. Their function is to assist students in clarifying what they know and believe about situations that they may well encounter throughout their lives. These strategies allow elementary students to rehearse difficult decisions in the secure environment of their classroom, so that later in life they will be able to make real decisions with more confidence.

Discovery learning is another strategy that can be successfully used by classroom teachers to cause their students to apply not only what they have already learned, but also what they are currently learning, and thereby to learn by doing. Instead of telling students a rule, principle, or concept, the teacher sets up conditions in the classroom so that students may discover it on their own. Math teachers frequently use this technique when they ask students to solve several equations and then state the rule or algorithm that is discovered in the process. Science processes frequently require that students discover a principle through experimentation. In both of these cases, students are applying known ideas to unknown situations and generating both solutions and insight in the process. This strategy is described in greater detail later in this chapter.

Another application strategy that reflective elementary teachers employ is *model making,* as when students are asked to build or replicate a model of an Indian village, a simple machine, a heart that pumps simulated blood, or a volcano. Teachers also use *cooperative groups* as a strategy to have students apply communication and problem-solving skills to solve problems or do meaningful work together.

Teaching Strategies That Require Analysis

As students apply what they have learned, they often think inductively about the specific cases they are working on and make generalizations about the ideas they are applying. Analysis calls on students to do the opposite: begin with a generalization and break it down into its constituent parts, separating elements and looking for relationships and organizational principles.

Teaching strategies that stimulate analytical thinking include *discussions* that focus on identification of the elements of an argument: assumptions, hypotheses, facts, opinions, inferences, and conclusions. For example, after reading an article on a controversial topic such as the relationship between drugs and gang membership, the teacher may ask students to separate the facts from the opinions in the article and to identify the author's assumptions and hypotheses.

Expanding on the analysis of separate elements, the teacher may then guide students in recognizing how the elements relate to each other. Discussion may then focus on whether the data presented in the article are consistent with the author's original assumptions and how that affects the conclusions. Hilda Taba's (1967) strategy of *concept formation* is a way of training students to analyze concepts in order to refine their understanding. Classroom examples of Taba's method are provided in a separate section later in this chapter.

Analysis of relationships can also focus on comparisons, similarities, differences, and cause and effect. A strategy other than discussion that is appropriate to this level of Bloom's Taxonomy is *independent research* to compare and contrast or show cause and effect. Once the research is complete, teachers usually ask that students prepare written or oral reports on their findings. They may also require students to prepare charts that classify the elements they've studied or graphs showing relationships. As an example, the teacher may assign students (individually or in cooperative groups) to investigate one of the systems of the human body. Those students researching the skeletal system will have to describe, illustrate, and analyze the bones (elements) and how they fit together (relationships). They may also prepare charts that show the cause-and-effect relationship of good and bad nutrition on bone development.

Analytical thinking has much in common with what is now known as *critical thinking*. The discussion strategies to promote critical thinking that were described in Chapter 8 also help students think and communicate with each other in an analytical way.

Teaching Strategies That Encourage Synthesis

Synthesis is another word for creativity; it occurs when students express what they have learned in an original way. According to Bloom and colleagues (1956), synthesis involves "recombination of parts of previous experience with new material, reconstructed into a new and more or less well-integrated whole" (p. 162). Synthesis requires the creation of a unique communication or product by an individual or a group. Criteria are established by the teacher to make sure that the children's products fit the subject and demonstrate that learning has taken place.

In the elementary classroom, synthesis is usually expressed through *art, music, creative writing, storytelling,* and *drama* activities that are related to the subject being taught. Criteria may specify that these products include a number of facts in stories or plays, show realistic details in drawings, or suggest new ways of solving the problems or issues in the subject being taught.

After students study the first Thanksgiving, many teachers allow them to dramatize the event with simple costumes and a real or simulated feast. In a unit on the prairie, a teacher may allow students to create a mural of the prairie along one side of the classroom. Students are allowed to draw and paint their pictures of prairie grasses, animals, and insects on the mural. After reading a story, students may be asked to write a new ending for it or to extend a book by writing a new chapter.

Cullum's (1967) *Push Back the Desks* is a wonderful resource for curriculum that emphasizes synthesis objectives. Cullum contends that "through creative play, imaginative approaches to the curriculum, competitive, yet supportive, games, encouragement of self-expression, and new projects of all sorts children will absorb knowledge and develop the basic skills" (p. 14).

He describes learning experiences in all subjects of the elementary curriculum that call on students' creative expression of ideas. His method of teaching U.S. history centers on the "Parade of the Presidents," in which each student role-plays one of the presidents of the United States and delivers a "State of the Union Address" to the joint session of Congress. Students in his classroom learned grammar by simulating a "Grammar Hospital" where students wearing surgical masks operated on ailing sentences. In his classroom a "poetry pot" bubbled all year long, inspiring students to read and discuss poetry as well as write their own. Students crawled through "King Tut's Tomb" to discover and solve mathematical problems.

The primary reason for including synthesis activities and products in the elementary curriculum is that they emphasize and encourage personal expression rather than passive participation, and independence of thought and action rather than dependence (Bloom, Englehart, Furst, Hill, & Krathwohl, 1956, p. 166).

Teaching Strategies That Generate Evaluation

The highest level of Bloom's Taxonomy is evaluation because it represents an "end process" in the range of cognitive behaviors in which students are asked to make judgments about some aspect of what they have studied. A key part of evaluation is that the students are expected to use criteria in making their judgments, although these criteria can be determined by the students or given to them by the teacher. It is believed that students can make the most informed judgments after experiencing all other levels of the Taxonomy (Bloom, Englehart, Furst, Hill, & Krathwohl, 1956). For example, a unit on economics may begin with preliminary discussions that encourage the children to give their opinions about how to spend their allowances, but it is expected that their opinions will become better informed, and that they will be able to make judgments about money using criteria such as supply and demand at the end of the unit.

Teaching strategies that generate useful and valid evaluations are those that involve students in *discussion, writing, problem solving, debate,* and any other activities in which students express their own views and opinions on a subject. In the elementary classroom, one of the most frequently used strategies is a class discussion after reading a story or chapter in a book. Students are asked to say whether they agree or disagree with the character or the issue and to state why.

Occasionally, older elementary students take sides on an issue and prepare an argument for a class debate. This may require a long-term research project to gather data and information prior to the debate. Debates such as these are likely to be connected with the science or social studies curriculum.

Group problem-solving endeavors on controversial issues may cause students to generate solutions as well as opinions about how to solve a problem. Simulations may be used to illustrate the complex nature of real-life problems. For example, students may be given roles to play in a simulation of where to locate a new city dump. They must use criteria to persuade the group to locate the dump somewhere other than their own backyards.

It is not easy for teachers to evaluate their students' evaluation activities. As free expression of opinions and judgments is expected, perhaps the only fair way to assess students' products is to determine the extent to which the students use evidence and criteria to support their judgments.

ADDITIONAL TEACHING STRATEGIES

The following strategies are offered as alternatives to consider as you develop your own repertoire. These strategies cover a wide range of philosophies and styles. Not all of them will appeal to you, but many of them can be employed to add variety and spice to your classroom curriculum. As you read these brief descriptions, keep in mind that it is necessary to look for more detailed sources of information to truly understand the model and how it can be used.

Taba's Concept Formation Model

Hilda Taba (1967) created a model of teaching social studies to elementary students that emphasizes formation of concepts, interpretation of data, and application of principles to explain new phenomena. The purpose of the model is teach students how to process information with accuracy and efficiency. Each concept is stored in the brain in the form of a schema. As individuals experience and learn more about the world, they add to and reconstruct their schemata. Taba believed that teachers can assist students in the development of their thought processes.

The teacher's role in this strategy is to direct students' observations and thinking about a new concept by asking questions that cause students to see relationships, identify categories, and make inferences about their experience. For example, a teacher may wish to help students differentiate their concept of animals into more specific categories, including those of domestic and wild animals.

The first strategy, known as *concept formation*, begins by listing or showing pictures of many types of animals and asking students to identify categories of animals with similarities. As an illustration, the list might include such animals as the eagle, tiger, horse, robin, rattlesnake, dog, bear, zebra, and cat. Students may identify categories based on color, number of legs, size, or habitat. When a category is identified, the teacher assists students in giving it an appropriate label, such as "birds," "four-legged animals," or "brown animals."

The second strategy, known as *interpretation of data*, includes the thinking processes of interpreting, inferring, and generalizing. To help students form the two unfamiliar concepts of domestic animals and wild animals, the teacher reviews the list or pictures of the animals and directs their observations toward the relationships and patterns associated with the new concepts by asking questions such as these:

> What did you notice about the places where the animals lived?
> What did you see about how they got their food?
> Why do some animals find their own food and others get fed?
> What did you notice about their relationships with people?
> What does this mean about how they prefer to live?
> Which animals prefer to live in the wild?
> Which animals prefer to live near human beings?
> Which animals would you put in a category called "wild animals"?
> Which would you put in a category called "domestic animals"?
> What do you think *domestic* means?
> What do you think *wild* means?

The third task involved in Taba's strategy is called *application of principles*. It involves helping students make hypotheses and predictions involving the concepts they have just learned. In our example, the teacher may ask students to consider what would happen if a tiger were kept as a pet or if a pet cat were lost in a jungle. To verify their hypotheses, students may be asked to carry out research or otherwise investigate the predictions they have made. In our present example, this could lead to a visit to a zoo or an interview with a zookeeper to find out what habitat wild animals need in order to live.

Taba's model teaches students to think inductively, to collect information and make observations, to identify relationships, and to develop relatively sophisticated classifications and categories. It also helps them to develop a verbal vocabulary of accurate labels and improves their ability to speak about complex abstract concepts.

Some teachers may set out to use Taba's strategy for the purpose of improving students' thinking skills, and simply create a list of items and categories as a means of teaching thinking. More often the strategy is used in a content area to develop concepts and thinking about the topic itself. It can also be used to develop affective concepts such as justice, fairness, and tolerance. A more complete description of this model is included in Joyce and Weil's (1986) *Models of Teaching*, as well as in Taba's (1967) *Teacher's Handbook for Elementary Social Studies*.

Discovery Learning

In the 1960s and 1970s, a phenomenon known as the *open classroom* bloomed, mushroomed, and then faded into obscurity. The underlying philosophy of the open classroom was that students would become more active and responsible for their own learning in an environment that allowed them to make choices and encouraged them to take initiative. To this end, the rows of desks in many classrooms were rearranged to provide more space for activity and learning centers. The curriculum of the open classroom was revised to allow students to choose from among many alternatives and schedule their own time to learn what they wanted to learn when they wanted to learn it (Silberman, 1973).

One of the teaching strategies emphasized in the open classroom was known as *discovery learning*. The principle of discovery learning is that students learn best by doing rather than by hearing or reading about a concept. Teachers may still find this strategy to be an excellent addition to their repertoire. It can be used occasionally to provide real rather than vicarious experience in a classroom.

In employing discovery learning, the teacher's role is to gather and provide equipment and materials related to a concept that the teacher wants the children to learn. Sufficient materials should be available so that every child or pairs of children have immediate access to them. Materials that are unfamiliar, interesting, and stimulating are especially important to a successful discovery learning experience. After providing the materials, the teacher may ask a question or offer a challenge that causes children to discover the properties of the materials. Then, as the children begin to manipulate the materials, the role of the teacher is to monitor and observe as the students discover the properties and relationships inherent in the materials, asking occasional questions or making suggestions that will guide the children in seeing the relationships and understand the concepts. The period of manipulation and discovery is followed by a discussion in which students verbalize what they have observed and learned from the experience (Hawkins, 1965).

A simple example at the primary level is the use of discovery learning to teach the concept of colors and their relationships to one another. Rather than telling students that blue and yellow make green, or demonstrating this while students watch, the strategy of discovery learning is to provide them with a brush and small puddles of blue and yellow paint on white paper and allow them to discover it for themselves. In this case, the opening question may simply be "What happens when you mix blue and yellow together?" When this relationship becomes apparent and is verbalized by the children, the teacher can then provide additional puddles of red and white paint and challenge students to "create as many different colors as you can." Experiences can be easily designed to allow students to discover how and why some things float, what makes a light bulb light, how electricity travels in circuits, and the difference between solutions and mixtures.

Math relationships can also be discovered. Beans, buttons, coins, dice, straws, and toothpicks can be sorted according to size, shape, color, and other attributes. Objects can be weighed, measured, and compared with each other. The concept of multiplication can be discovered when children make sets of objects in rows and columns. Many resources in the form of math curriculum projects involving discovery learning are presently being developed for the elementary school. This is occurring because discovery is part of the problem-solving process, a current hot topic in elementary education.

Role Playing

When problems or issues involving human relationships are part of the curriculum, teachers may choose to use role playing to help students explore and understand the whole range of human feelings that surround any issue. This strategy is frequently used to resolve personal problems or dilemmas, but it can also be employed to gain understanding about the feelings and values of groups outside the classroom.

For example, in order to help students understand the depth of emotions experienced by immigrants coming to a new and unfamiliar country, the teacher may ask students to role-play the interactions between family members who are separated or the dilemmas of the Vietnamese boat people or others who want to emigrate to the United States but are stopped by immigration quotas.

There are two major phases to successful and meaningful role playing: the role playing itself and the subsequent discussion and evaluation period. In the first phase, the teacher's responsibility is to give students an overview of both phases of role playing so that they know what to expect. The teacher then introduces and describes a problem or dilemma, identifies the roles that need to be taken, assigns the roles, and begins the action by setting the stage and describing the immediate problem that the actors must confront. Roles must be assigned carefully. Usually teachers select students who are involved in the problem to play the role. In an academic dilemma, the roles may be assigned to students who most need to expand their experience with and understanding of the issue. Those students who are not assigned roles are expected to be careful observers.

To set up the role-playing situation, the teacher can arrange some chairs to suggest the setting of the event to be played out. During the role play itself, the actors are expected to get inside the problem and "live" it spontaneously, responding realistically to one another. The role play may not flow smoothly; actors may experience uncertainty and be at a loss for words, just as they would in real life. The first time a role is played, the problem may not be solved at all. The action may simply establish the problem, which in later enactments can be probed and resolved (Joyce & Weil, pp. 248–249).

To increase the impact of role playing, Leyser (1982) suggests that after a scene is played out once, the actors may exchange roles and play out the same scene so that they grow to understand the other's point of view. Actors may also be allowed to select consultants to discuss and improve the roles they are playing.

In the second phase, the observers discuss the actions and words taken by the initial role players. The teacher helps the observers review what they have seen and heard, discuss the main events, and predict the consequences of actions taken by the role players. Following the initial discussion, it is likely that the teacher will decide to have new class members replay the role to show an alternative way of handling the problem. The situation can be replayed a number of times if necessary. When a role-played situation generates a useful solution or suggests an effective way of handling a problem, the situation can be adapted and subsequent role plays can focus on communication skills that will enhance or improve the situation even further.

Role playing has many applications to both the cognitive and the affective goals of the elementary curriculum. Through role playing, students can experience history by researching the life of a public figure and taking the role in a historical interaction. Each student in the class, for example, can study the life of a U.S. president and be the president for a day. Frequently, teachers ask students to play the roles of characters in books they have read as a means of reporting their own reading and stimulating others in the class to read the book. Students can enact the feelings of slaves and slave traders, the roles of scientists as they are "doing" science, or the interaction between an author and editor as they try to perfect a piece of writing.

Students can also learn new behaviors and social skills that may help them win greater peer acceptance and enhance their own self-esteem. Interpersonal conflicts that arise in the classroom can be role-played as a means of helping students discover more productive and responsible ways of behaving. For example, when two students argue about taking turns playing with a toy in the kindergarten class, the teacher can ask them to role-play the situation in an effort to learn new ways of speaking to each other, asserting their own desires, and creating a plan for sharing the scarce resource. In an upper elementary classroom, the teacher may notice that one child is isolated and treated like a scapegoat by others in the class. The dilemma can be role-played, with the role of the isolated child assigned to be played by some of the children who have been most critical and aggressive toward the child. Through this active, vicarious experience, it is possible that the students will learn to be more tolerant and accepting of each other.

To learn more about becoming an effective director of role playing and to gain a resource of ideas that describe useful role-playing dilemmas, consult Joyce and Weil's (1986) *Models of Teaching*, Shaftel and Shaftel's (1982) *Role Playing in the Curriculum*, or Leyser's (1982) article in *Contemporary Education*.

Simulation

Student drivers drive simulated vehicles before they learn to drive a real car on the highway. Airplane simulators provide a realistic but safe way for student pilots to practice flying in which mistakes lead to realistic consequences but no lives are threatened. In many high school courses on marriage and the family, young people are offered the opportunity to simulate marriage and caring for a newborn baby in the form of a raw egg that they must protect and nurture over a period of several weeks. It is believed that their experiences with the egg may lead them to consider carefully their own life choices.

Simulations usually involve some type of role playing but also include other gamelike features, such as a set of rules, time limits, tokens or other objects that are gained or lost through the action of the simulation, and a way of recording the results of the players' decisions and actions. Simulations almost always focus on dilemmas in which the players must make choices, take actions, and then experience feedback in the form of consequences of their actions. The purpose of simulations is primarily to allow young people to experience tough real-life problems and learn from the consequences in the safe, controlled environment of the classroom.

In the elementary school, there are many valuable academic and social simulations that can be used to enrich the classroom experience and cause children to understand the relationship between their choices, actions, and consequences. Simulation games can be purchased or created by the teacher. A company named *Interact* publishes a catalogue called *Elementary Simulations* in all areas of the curriculum that can be purchased for a relatively small price (see the last section of this chapter for the telephone number of this company). These kits include teacher's manuals describing the rules, time limits and procedures to follow, and a set of student materials that may include fact sheets, game pieces, and record-keeping devices. The titles of some of the simulations include "Zoo," "Dinosaur," "King Lexicon," "Shopping Spree," and "Classroom City."

The role of the teacher during a simulation is to explain fully the conditions, the concepts to be covered, and the expectations at the outset of the event. A practice session may be held to further familiarize participants with the rules and procedures of the simulation. After assigning roles or creating groups that will interact, the teacher moderates, keeps time, clarifies misconceptions, and provides feedback and consequences in response to the actions of the participants. At the conclusion of the simulation, the teacher leads a discussion of what occurred and what was learned by asking students to summarize events and problems and to share their perceptions and insights with each other. At the end of the discussion, it is appropriate for the teacher to compare the simulation with its real-life counterpart and ask students to think critically about what they would do in real life as a result of having taken part in the simulation.

An example of an elementary simulation in economics involves the creation of small companies or stores in which students decide on a product, create the product, set up the store, price and sell the product, and keep records on the transactions. The purpose, of course, is to learn about the principles of supply and demand, as well as the practical skills of exchanging money and making change. Along with the primary goals of the simulation, there are secondary learning experiences. Students are also likely to increase their capacity for critical thinking and to learn about their own actions and decisions regarding competition, cooperation, commitment to a goal, and communication.

Students in an upper elementary classroom may simulate the writing of the U.S. Constitution by writing a classroom constitution. After studying various countries, sixth-grade students may take part in a mock United Nations simulation in which students are delegates to the UN and face daily world problems presented to them by the teacher.

In the language arts, students may establish a class newspaper in order to learn how news is gathered and printed in the real world. They may even establish a number of competitive newspapers to add another dimension of reality to the simulation. Students may simulate the writing, editing, and publishing processes as they create, print, and distribute their own original books.

An excellent example of a classroom simulation that provoked children to think critically and change their views on an important human issue is described in *A Class Divided* (1984) by William Peters. Jane Elliott, a third-grade teacher in Riceland, Iowa, taught her students to think critically about racial prejudice by randomly dividing the class into two groups: those with brown eyes and those with blue eyes. She actively discriminated against the children with blue eyes for a full school day. Mimicking behaviors of people who exhibit racial prejudice, she called the blue-eyed children names, did not let them play on the swings, and criticized their work and behavior. She successfully influenced the brown-eyed children to follow her lead and convinced them to avoid social contact with their inferior blue-eyed classmates.

The next day, she reversed the process and discriminated against the brown-eyed children in much the same way. Blue-eyed children were now considered superior to brown-eyed children in her eyes and their own. At the conclusion of the second day, Mrs. Elliott led a discussion of the effects of the entire learning experience. Twenty years later, at their high school reunion, her students reported that their understanding of prejudice and their attitudes toward people of different races were radically restructured as a result of this classroom experience.

Before the experience, they had not been critical thinkers about racial prejudice. They easily accepted the prevailing notion that some people are superior to others. Afterward, they had grown in empathy, had recognized points of view different from their own, and had become more self-directed or independent in their thinking than they were before the experience.

Simulations may be used either to introduce a unit or as the culminating activity of a unit. They may take a few minutes or the entire year. They may be continued from week to week but played for only a specified amount of time each session. Some may take a full day or longer. Simulations are powerful learning experiences that may change the way students view themselves and the world, as it did for the participants in the blue-eyes, brown-eyes experience.

Mastery Learning

Teaching strategies known as *mastery learning* derive from the philosophy that all students can learn if the task fits their aptitude and they are given sufficient time to master the new skill or concept. The theoretical model for mastery learning was inspired by Carroll's (1963) observation that students with low aptitude for a particular subject could still learn that subject, but that it would take them more time to do so. He proposed that students have different *learning rates* rather than different ability levels.

Bloom (1974) created the practical system for instruction using mastery learning based on Carroll's theoretical model. He observed that most schools are established on the assumption that learners vary in their ability to achieve. Bloom disagrees. Studies conducted under his guidance have shown that 95 percent of the students in our schools can achieve the educational objectives established for them, but because they learn at different rates, some students appear to be better or worse than others.

Bloom (1984) points to cases where students are tutored to prove his point. In a controlled experiment, he demonstrated that "the average tutored student outperformed 98 percent of the students in the control class" (p. 5). He attributes this finding to the fact that a tutor is able to determine what each child knows in a given subject and is then able to plan an educational program that begins instruction at the child's level and proceeds at the child's own pace.

The basic structure of the mastery learning model, including adaptations known as *individually prescribed instruction (IPI)* and *continuous progress*, lend themselves best to the learning of basic skills in sequentially structured subjects. Specific behavioral objectives are written for each unit of study. Pretests are used to assess students' prior knowledge, which then determines the placement or starting level for each student. Working individually, as children master each objective in the sequence of learning, they are able to proceed to the next one. Periodically, unit tests covering several objectives are given to check on the mastery and retention of a whole range of knowledge and skills.

The teacher's role in this process is quite different from that in teaching skills with a whole class approach. The teacher rarely instructs the entire class at one time. Instead, as students work independently, the teacher monitors their progress by walking around the classroom and responding to requests for assistance. In a cooperative version of mastery learning, Slavin (1987) proposes the TAI model (see Chapter 9), which pairs students as monitors and assistants for each other during a mastery learning experience. This frees the teacher to work with small groups of students rather than devoting all the time to responding to individual needs.

The value of mastery learning is that it allows students to actively learn new material and skills on a continuous basis. It is also assumed that motivation to achieve is increased because students work at their own pace and have the prerequisite skills necessary for success. Also, since testing is done individually and opportunities are provided to repeat what they did not learn, students should suffer less embarrassment when making mistakes. The affective goal of mastery learning programs is to help students become independent, self-directed learners.

Contracts for Independent Learning

While mastery learning is appropriate for use only in sequential subjects that require a great deal of independent practice, many teachers are searching for methods of promoting independence and self-directed learning in other subjects as well. An alternative to direct, whole class instruction is the use of independent or group academic learning contracts. A learning contract such as the one in Figure 10–1 is usually created by the teacher at the beginning of a unit of study. The contract specifies one list of required activities, such as reading a chapter in a textbook, finding a library resource and writing a summary of the topic, completing a fact sheet, and other necessary prerequisites for developing a knowledge base on the subject.

A second list of activities is offered as choices or alternatives for students to pursue. This list includes opportunities to do additional independent research or plays, stories, songs, and artwork on the topic. When learning contracts are offered to develop independence, individuals usually select the activities they want to accomplish. A variation on this strategy would be to combine the concepts of cooperative groups and learning contracts and allow each group to sign a joint contract specifying the tasks and products they will complete.

Science investigations, social studies research projects, and creative language arts activities can be presented in the form of learning contracts. The primary advantage of this strategy is that it allows individuals with various levels of ability to work on an appropriate amount and type of work during the unit of study. High-achieving students can select the maximum number of tasks and products, while lower-achieving students can select fewer tasks. The assumption is that both types of students will then actively learn and experience success during the same amount of time.

FIGURE 10–1
Social Studies Learning Contract

Westward Expansion of the United States
Required Learning Activities

Date	Approval	
_____	_____	Read Chapter 6 in the social studies textbook.
_____	_____	Write answers to the questions at the end of the unit.
_____	_____	Locate and read a book on the American West or the Indians.
_____	_____	Write a two- to four-page summary of the book.
_____	_____	Play the computer game "Oregon Trail" until you reach the state of Oregon.

Alternative Learning Activities

Date	Approval	
_____	_____	Imagine that you are a member of a wagon train heading west. Write a series of letters to family or friends back home describing your journey.
_____	_____	Write a play about a meeting between Indians and settlers. Find a cast for your play and be prepared to present it to the class assembly.
_____	_____	Draw or paint a large picture of a scene that you imagine took place during the westward expansion.
_____	_____	Create a song or ballad about life in the West. Be prepared to play and sing it for the assembly.
_____	_____	Create a diorama or a model of a Plains Indian village at this time in history.
_____	_____	Research the lives of the Plains Indians today. Be prepared to give a speech about the conditions in which they live now and how these are related to the westward expansion.
_____	_____	Create your own alternative plan for a learning experience on this topic.

- -

I, _____, agree to complete the following required learning activities by the date _____. In addition, I select two to five alternative activities to pursue on my own. I will present my creative work to my classmates at our assembly on _____.

_____   I have reviewed this contract and under-
           student signature   stand the work my child has agreed to
                                             do. I agree to support this effort.
_____
           teacher signature   _____
                                                        parent signature

Learning Centers

Learning centers or stations are areas of the classroom where children can go to do independent work on a given subject or topic. Learning centers vary enormously in the way they look, the way they are used, and the length of time they are set up. Teachers who use learning centers use them for a variety of purposes and with a variety of expectations.

Some centers may be informal and unstructured in their use. For example, a classroom may have a permanent Science Center containing a variety of science equipment and materials. Students can go to the center to do science experiments in their free time. In the same classroom there may be a permanent Reading Center furnished with a rug, comfortable chairs, and shelves or racks of books where children can go to read quietly.

Other centers may be set up for a limited amount of time and have highly structured expectations. For example, to accompany the unit on westward expansion described previously, the teacher may have set up an area of the classroom as a Westward Expansion Research Center. It would contain a computer, with the MECC computer program called "Oregon Trail" turned on and ready for students to use. It would also contain posters and maps of the western United States and a wide variety of reading materials on the topic. When the unit is finished, the center will be redesigned; new learning materials will replace the ones on the finished unit, and the center will become the focus of a new unit of study.

In some primary classrooms, learning centers are an important adjunct to the reading and language arts programs. Many teachers set up four or five learning centers or stations with different activities each week. Students in small groups travel from one station to another according to a prespecified schedule. For example, Ginny Bailey uses a weekly theme as the basis for her first-grade language arts program. Each week she sets up activities related to that theme in her five stations: art, math, writing, listening, and reading. To accompany her theme of butterflies, students will find books on butterflies to read at the reading station, paper and directions for a writing project at the writing center, paint and brushes to create a picture at the art station, a prerecorded tape to listen to at the listening station, and a math game involving butterflies and caterpillars at the math station.

Ginny uses five centers because there are five days of the week, so that each group can visit each center once each week. A poster on the wall shows the schedule of groups and centers:

Learning Station Schedule

GROUP	MONDAY	TUESDAY	WEDNESDAY	THURSDAY	FRIDAY
BLUE	Art	Math	Writing	Reading	Listening
GREEN	Math	Writing	Reading	Listening	Art
RED	Writing	Reading	Listening	Art	Math
YELLOW	Reading	Listening	Art	Math	Writing
ORANGE	Listening	Art	Math	Writing	Reading

In Ginny's classroom, students can go to their stations only after completing their assignments of daily work. In her system, the stations extend the students' learning experiences on the weekly theme but are also used as an incentive for students to complete their required work.

Computer-Aided Instruction

While some elementary teachers may still be reluctant, based on their fear of the unknown, to use computers in their classrooms, many others believe that having a computer in the classroom is like having another teacher. When computers were first introduced into elementary classrooms in the 1970s, few software programs were available. The first educational goals established at that time involved teaching students how computers function and how to write their own computer programs. This goal contributed greatly to the fear of computers that many classroom teachers still have. Not being computer programmers themselves, they rarely felt comfortable teaching these skills to their students.

In the 1990s, the purposes of computer technology in the classroom are very different and much more reasonable for elementary teachers to accept. The primary computer-education goal has changed from turning children into computer programmers to helping them become efficient and creative computer operators. Operating a computer with a user-friendly software program is a skill that elementary teachers can master readily, and they are then confident in their ability to teach their students how to operate computers as well.

With the growth of the computer software industry, there are now hundreds of computer programs that can be used to accomplish many useful tasks. Computer programs are now available that can diagnose students' skill levels in math, reading, vocabulary, and other basic skills and prescribe lessons at the appropriate level. In "teaching" the lessons, computers make excellent tutors because they are endlessly patient in waiting for a student's response and give the appropriate feedback without emotional side effects. An excellent example is the "Write to Read" program developed by IBM, which teaches primary children how to plan, write, and edit stories and poems.

Some gamelike programs are useful in expanding children's experiences beyond the classroom walls to simulated journeys, laboratories, foreign countries, earlier periods of history, and the future. Many of these programs increase students' decision-making and problem-solving abilities by offering them opportunities to make choices and get immediate feedback on the consequences of their decisions. An example is the MECC program known as "Oregon Trail," which allows students to simulate the experience of a wagon train journey, with full decision-making power over how many supplies to bring, when to stop and restock, and how to deal with emergencies along the way. Poor choices in any of these areas lead to death on the trail. It takes most elementary students many attempts to reach Oregon alive.

Another MECC program known as "Lemonade" plunges students into the economic decision making necessary to market a product in order to make a profit. Students must decide how many lemons to buy, how many glasses to make each day, and how much advertising is needed, and must establish a price based on the weather report. Good choices lead to profits while poor choices lead to losses.

The programs "Oregon Trail" and "Lemonade" are both available to educators through the Minnesota Education Computer Consortium (MECC), which is available in many school districts or libraries throughout the country.

There are many excellent software programs that provide students with a blank slate for creating and composing original works. "Logo" and "Turtle Geometry" are frequently used in elementary schools to allow students to create mathematical patterns and figures. Papert's (1980) *Mindstorms: Children, Computers and Powerful Ideas* and Abelson and diSessa's (1981) *Turtle Geometry: The Computer as a Medium for Exploring Mathematics* are good resources for incorporating these programs into your curriculum.

Word processing programs are probably the most versatile programs available for computers. Early experiences, especially in the primary grades, may be devoted to very simple writing assignments with a dual purpose: composing and learning keyboarding skills. When students master keyboarding skills, they are free to compose many types of verbal products, including letters, stories, poems, essays, reports, and plays. Studies have shown that elementary students write longer pieces on a word processor than they do by hand. The other major benefit is that the editing and revision processes are greatly simplified on the word processor. Students' motivation to write is increased in part because of the novelty of computers, but also because the final products that are printed out are neat and relatively error-free. This provides a strong sense of pride and success related to the writing process (Moore, Moore, Cunningham, & Cunningham, 1986, p. 132).

In addition to student uses, computers can be used by teachers to create classroom materials, keep records, and compute grades. Many teachers use word processing programs to create and store curriculum plans, student worksheets, quizzes, and tests. They may also use them to write reports, proposals, and newsletters. Specialized record-keeping programs are available that allow teachers to record students' achievements. Many of these will compute average grades for report cards.

The major limitations on the use of computers in the classroom are money, availability of high-quality programs, and management concerns. Because of their expense, many schools have only a few computers that must be shared by many classrooms. In some cases, computers are placed on traveling carts that are moved from room to room according to a schedule. In this case, teachers must coordinate their plans to fit the computer schedule. In other instances, the computers are all housed in a single classroom, designated as a computer lab, and teachers must arrange to bring their students to the lab when they wish to incorporate computers into their plans.

Even when there are enough computers for each classroom to have its own, locating high-quality computer software can be difficult. Most software is expensive, and much of it is of low or indifferent value. Many programs that purport to teach math or language skills are little better than workbooks. Teachers must carefully review software before purchasing it. The criteria for selecting programs vary from class to class, but at a minimum, computer programs should be selected only if they are user-friendly and easy to load, start, and understand the directions. They should also be interesting and should actively engage the learner in a meaningful learning experience.

When teachers have access to computers in the classroom, they must learn to manage their use efficiently. In some cases, the computer is available for a variety of student uses, while in others, teachers may dedicate it to a specific purpose for a period of time. Students may work singly or in pairs at a computer terminal. With 30 students, this means that each student gets to use the computer for only a short time each day.

Despite the management problems, computers are valuable tools with many uses in remediation, tutoring, and creative efforts. Additionally, when students are able to use computers frequently for a variety of purposes, they learn to accept and understand the place of computers in society and are more likely to be ready to accept further technological advances of the twenty-first century.

Keith Anderson, a third-grade teacher at Lincoln Elementary School in Dixmoor, Illinois, was one of the recipients of the Golden Apple Award in 1990 from the Foundation of Excellence in Teaching in Chicago. His philosophy is "Never be a textbook teacher; be a teacher who knows how to use a textbook." He supplements his lessons with computers and other technological aids for both remedial and enrichment activities. Figure 10–2 illustrates a typical schedule in his classroom.

Strategies Using Audio-Video Technology

Teachers have long used films, filmstrips, and audiotapes to supplement their classroom instruction. Many of these resources can be ordered through the media center located in the school. They can be used for whole class instruction, or they can be set up at a learning center so that individuals or groups of students may listen to tapes or watch a filmstrip on their own.

With the advent of video cameras, many new teaching strategies have emerged. Video discs used in conjunction with computers have produced the capability of employing interactive video for classroom use. An interactive format means that visual images stored on the video disc can be programmed to play on a television monitor. The order of the images can be completely controlled by the teacher or the students by typing commands on the computer. If teachers wish to teach students about recent historical events, they can obtain a videodisc of recorded speeches and newscasts in that time period. For example, as the teacher discusses President Truman, the monitor can display him speaking in public. When the teacher begins to describe Eisenhower, the monitor can be programmed to display a video recording of one of his speeches.

Video cameras provide the teacher with many exciting new strategies. Students' products and performances can be recorded by the teacher or an assistant for future evaluation purposes or to document that the event took place. Students can rehearse their presentations on videotape and watch the recording to see what they need to improve.

Another exciting possibility is to allow students to be camera operators themselves. As an oral history project, they can use video cameras to record their interviews with adults in their neighborhood who remember what it was like to live there many years ago. Students can also use the video camera to create news programs for other students. Jane Stevens, who teaches sixth grade in Arlington, Texas, uses video in this way (see the Perspective on page 240).

KEITH ANDERSON'S TEACHING AIDS PLAN

CLASS SIZE: 25 students

MATERIALS: five computers, tape player, television and VCR, headphones, overhead projector

TEACHER-DIRECTED LESSON: reading group—eight students

COMPUTER 1: two students: enrichment activity—math
Activity: speedway math disk No. A169—lesson 5

COMPUTER 2: two students: enrichment activity—language arts
Activity: writing narrative disk No. A776—lesson 2

COMPUTER 3: two students: remedial activity—math
Activity: subtraction puzzles disk No. A146—lesson 2

COMPUTER 4: two students: remedial activity—language arts
Activity: phonics prime time (vowels) disk No. 178—lesson 4

COMPUTER 5: one student: enrichment activity—reading comprehension
Activity: diagnostic prescriptive reading disk No. 6—inference

TAPE PLAYER: three students: remedial activity—language arts
Activity: Silver Burdett level 9—tape 6, side one; synonyms worksheet 6-1

TELEVISION AND VCR: three students: enrichment activity—language arts-science
Activity: tape 4, "Plants and Animals"
View the recording and prepare a group report on the life functions of all living things; discuss the difference between living and nonliving things.

OVERHEAD PROJECTOR: two students: enrichment activity—social studies
Activity: transparency on state names No. 13
Write the name of each state on the transparency.
Use green for southern states, red for midwestern states, and black for all others. Locate the state you live in and mark the capital with the correct symbol.

Your Own Repertoire of Teaching Strategies

With a repertoire of teaching strategies from which to choose, you can create a stimulating classroom that appeals to students from a wide range of backgrounds and with a variety of learning style preferences. You can be flexible and creative. When one teaching strategy does not work, you can select another and reteach the lesson. You can look forward to a year of varied experiences for yourself and your students.

The strategies described in this book are but the tip of the iceberg. Each one has dozens of variations, and there are many additional strategies that can be successfully employed to build a classroom environment that meets the needs of all

JANE STEVENS

Sixth-Grade Teacher, Dunn School, Arlington, Texas

USING VIDEO TECHNOLOGY
IN THE CLASSROOM

An important consideration for teachers when assisting students to become creative thinkers is to find the most effective vehicle possible. Lately, I've found that the video camera is just the vehicle needed to motivate my students.

It all started with a newspaper project. My students were writing news articles one day when I suggested that they try to write the same story as a news report such as those they see on TV. When the reports were ready, we arranged an area so that the students presenting them were facing the other class members. Each had to read his or her report employing the techniques of a TV newscaster. I provided the lead-in comments to move from one report to another. The students loved it! They immediately asked, "When can we do this again?"

For our second attempt, we decided to put our show on videotape so that we could critique the newscast and improve the "show." As the viewers watched, they filled out critique sheets with two columns headed "Strengths" and "Weaknesses." I provided areas for them to critique, such as careful reading while using eye contact, clear statements of main ideas, supporting details, and the use of facts rather than opinions.

For our next newscast, we added music and selected an anchorperson to take my role of providing introductions and lead-ins for each report.

Next, we added commercials, then weather. Soon the students were suggesting that we cover school happenings and grade-level news. They began to run interviews of school personnel as well.

When the principal was interviewed, she was so impressed that she asked us to take over the daily morning announcements. That was the beginning of K-DUN TV and the *Dunn-A-Hue Show*. The reporters soon suggested surveys to get students' opinions on various issues. They have planned special programs on hot news topics. They've added puppet shows, plays, excerpts from PTA meetings, and special music and sports events. As a result, we have made the news ourselves and been featured on Channel 5 (Fort Worth, Texas). One of our videos on the topic of how to treat a classmate with AIDS has been used throughout the state at AIDS education workshops. But most important, we are known as the heartbeat of our building.

It could be asked, "Isn't this a lot of work?" The answer, of course, is *yes*! But when I think of the benefits, it's worth it. My students are practicing problem solving, decision making, prioritizing, and time management, using their creative talents and working as part of a team, as well as using all the language arts skills. Daily I observe my sixth graders raising new questions and actively solving new problems in a way that develops fluency, flexibility, originality, and a great deal of elaboration.

---

of your students and creates new horizons and new interests that they did not have when they entered your classroom.

To continue to expand your repertoire, plan to conduct an active search for new ideas, methods, and learning activities. Consult your professors for sources of interesting learning materials. Talk to classroom teachers you admire and ask them for copies of their favorite ideas and activities. Read educational journals and magazines and clip out the best ideas. Begin now to build a file of interesting classroom materials that you can adapt and use some day.

Ask teachers or the secretary of the school you are visiting to share their catalogues of educational materials with you. Some catalogues contain unusually creative classroom materials. *Good Apple* is a catalogue of materials created by classroom teachers for other teachers to use. *Elementary Simulations* is a catalogue of simulation games published by Interact (mentioned earlier in the section on simulations). *Engine-Uity* is a catalogue of materials that teachers can use to set up learning centers on topics ranging from literature, history, and science to multidisciplinary themes. Most of the materials are organized around the framework of Bloom's Taxonomy. The *D.O.K.* catalogue is filled with materials that emphasize creative and critical thinking. *Creative Publications* contains many manipulative materials, as well as activity books geared toward problem solving in every subject area.

> *Creative Publications Catalogue* (math manipulatives and language arts
> activity books)
> Toll Free: 1-800-624-0822
> *Delta Publications* (science investigations)
> Toll Free: 1-800-258-1302
> *D.O.K. Publications* (thinking skills and problem solving)
> Toll Free: 1-800-458-7900
> *Elementary Simulations* by Interact
> Toll Free: 1-800-359-0961
> *Engine-Uity, Ltd.* (learning center and literature activities)
> 8900 N. Central No. 107, Phoenix, AZ 85020; 602-997-7144.
> *Good Apple* (Teacher-made materials in all subject areas)
> Toll Free: 1-800-435-7234
> *National Wildlife Federation Catalog*
> Toll Free: 1-800-432-6564
> *Project AIMS Catalog* (integrated math and science activities)
> P.O. Box 7766, Fresno, CA 93747; 209-291-1766
> Rigby Education, Inc. (Big Books and other whole language materials)
> Toll Free: 1-800-822-8661
> Minnesota Education Computer Consortium (MECC) (computer pro-
> grams with teaching instructions) 612-481-3500

OPPORTUNITIES FOR REFLECTION

▼ *Reflective Essay: Strategies I Prefer*

Which of the teaching strategies described in this chapter are you most likely to employ in your classroom? Why? How do they fit your own emerging style of teaching? Have you selected an adequate variety of strategies to motivate students with different learning styles and needs? Which strategies would you avoid using? Why?

▼ Classroom Visit: Teach a Lesson

Observe the variety of teaching strategies used in the class you are visiting. In addition to direct instruction, look for examples of student-centered strategies such as small-group discussion or problem solving, peer tutoring, and discovery learning. After describing an example of a strategy, describe how you would adapt or change it to fit your own style.

Arrange with the classroom teacher to let you plan and teach a lesson to a small group of students. Select your teaching strategies to fit the lesson and the needs of your students. You may be able to use more than one level of Bloom's Taxonomy in your lesson. Write a reflective evaluation of your lesson, its effects on the students, what they learned, and what you believe you could do to improve the lesson if you were to teach it again.

REFERENCES

ABELSON, H., & DISESSA, A. (1981). *Turtle geometry: The computer as a medium for exploring mathematics*. Cambridge, MA: MIT Press.

ANDERSON, R. (1977). The notion of schemata and the educational enterprise. In R. Anderson, R. Spiro, & W. Montague (Eds.), *Schooling and the acquisition of knowledge* (pp. 415–431). Hillsdale, NJ: Erlbaum.

AUSUBEL, D. P. (1960). The use of advance organizers in the learning and retention of meaningful verbal material. *Journal of Educational Psychology, 51*, 267–272.

BLOOM, B. (1974). An introduction to mastery learning theory. In J. H. Block (Ed.), *Schools, society and mastery learning* (pp. 12–21). New York: Holt, Rinehart & Winston.

BLOOM, B. (1984). The search for methods of group instruction as effective as one-to-one tutoring. *Educational Leadership, 41*(8), 4–17.

BLOOM, B., ENGLEHART, M., FURST, E., HILL, W., & KRATHWOHL, D. (1956). *Taxonomy of educational objectives: Cognitive domain*. New York: Longman.

BRANSFORD, J. (1983). Schema activation—schema acquisition. In R. Anderson, J. Osborn, & R. Tierney (Eds.), *Learning to read in American schools* (pp. 23–37). Hillsdale, NJ: Erlbaum.

CARROLL, J. (1963). A model of school learning. *Teachers College Record, 64*, 723–733.

CULLUM, A. (1967). *Push back the desks*. New York: Citation Press.

GAGNE, E. (1985). *The cognitive psychology of school learning*. Boston: Little, Brown.

HAWKINS, D. (1965). Messing about in science. *Science and Children, 2*(5), 5–9.

HUNTER, M. (1976). *Improved instruction*. El Segundo, CA: TIP Publications.

JOYCE, B., & WEIL, M. (1987). *Models of teaching* (3rd ed.). Englewood Cliffs, NJ: Prentice-Hall.

LEYSER, Y. (1982). Role playing in the classroom: A threat or a promise. *Contemporary Education, 53*, 70–74.

MOORE, D., MOORE, S., CUNNINGHAM, P., & CUNNINGHAM, J. (1986). *Developing readers and writers in the content areas*. New York: Longman.

PAPERT, S. (1980). *Mindstorms: Children, computers and powerful ideas*. New York: Basic Books.

PETERS, W. (1984). *A class divided: Then and now*. New Haven, CT: Yale University Press.

SHAFTEL, F., & SHAFTEL, G. *Role playing in the curriculum*. Englewood Cliffs, NJ: Prentice-Hall.

SILBERMAN, C. (Ed.). (1973). *The open classroom reader*. New York: Vintage Books.

SLAVIN, R. (1987). Cooperative learning and the cooperative school. *Educational Leadership*, 45(3), 7–13.

STALLINGS, J., & STIPEK, D. (1986). Research on early childhood and elementary school teaching programs. In M. Wittrock (Ed.), *Handbook of research on teaching* (3rd ed.) (pp. 727–753). New York: Macmillan.

TABA, H. (1967) *Teacher's handbook for elementary social studies*. Reading, MA: Addison-Wesley.

CHAPTER 11

Assessing Student Accomplishment

IT IS PERHAPS UNFORTUNATE that the chapters devoted to assessment of students' many and varied accomplishments are located at the end of this book. The implication of this physical placement is that assessment and evaluation take place at the end of the learning process, after all the planning and teaching have occurred.

Nothing could be further from the truth.

In order to be able to evaluate what students have achieved from a learning experience, the teacher must have fully thought out the assessment process prior to teaching the lesson. In fact, assessment methods are described frequently in earlier chapters of this book. In Chapter 3, which describes the processes teachers use to diagnose the needs of their students prior to teaching, many assessment devices are described. Cumulative files of information about students' past performance, standardized test scores describing levels of present achievement, and placement exams are all methods of assessing student accomplishment and are part of the reflective teacher's continuous process of evaluation.

In Chapter 4, long-term goals and outcome statements are described. These serve as the basis for later evaluation of what students gained from their school experience. Assessment of student accomplishment is primarily concerned with measuring how much students gained and comparing the actual gain with the original goal or outcome statement.

Chapters 5 and 6 describe the creation of learning objectives that specify what teachers *expect* their students to gain during short-term learning events such as a single lesson or a short sequence of lessons. To evaluate student accomplishment in these areas, the teacher must measure what students actually gained during the lesson and compare that gain with the criterion established for each objective.

Chapters 7 through 10 describe methods that teachers select for instructing students or facilitating their learning. These methods have an impact on the amount and type of accomplishment that students are able to achieve. Therefore, reflective teachers are continuously assessing student progress and achievement during every learning experience to verify that the teaching strategy they have selected is working or to alter it if they find that students are not accomplishing the objective for that lesson.

So, even though these final chapters on assessment and reporting on student achievement are located at the end of this book, you and I know that this is only a convenience. In order to genuinely understand what students have accomplished in a given school year, reflective teachers employ a systematic process of evaluation that includes observation, testing, collecting samples of students' typical work, and collecting portfolios of their best work. This process begins prior to the first day of school and goes on until the last dismissal bell rings.

ASSESSMENT TERMINOLOGY

The terms used in discussing student assessment can be confusing. This brief set of definitions is provided to make it easier to comprehend what each term in this text means.

First of all, there is a subtle difference between measurement, assessment, and evaluation. In this textbook, *measurement* is a broad term referring to the process of obtaining a number of correct responses or a raw score for a student on any type of assessment device. A *criterion* is a preestablished number or score that a teacher believes will demonstrate mastery of the planned objective (*criteria* is the plural form of *criterion*). The teacher makes an *assessment* by comparing the student's raw score with the criterion score and determining whether or not the student successfully accomplished the objective. *Evaluation,* in this text, is the reflective process of gathering objective and subjective data on a student and making a decision about how best to help that student succeed.

In this text, the term *student achievement* is used to describe the degree to which a student has demonstrated mastery of a subject on objective (usually paper-and-pencil) tests. *Student accomplishment* is meant to be a more inclusive term that indicates the degree to which a student has completed or demonstrated knowledge or skill on a wide variety of assessment devices, including tests, products, projects, oral presentations, performances, and creative works.

As described in Chapter 3, *criterion-referenced tests* are those created by teachers themselves in which the test items match the specific objectives they plan to teach. Scores on criterion-referenced tests can be used to assess how well students did in relation to the criterion for success on the planned objectives. In contrast, *norm-referenced tests* are written by professional test writers and are published widely. The items may or may not match the curriculum of the school. Scores on norm-referenced tests tell teachers how much a student achieved in relation to other students of the same age or grade throughout the country.

Many types of tests are used in an educational program. *Diagnostic tests* are used prior to teaching in order to inform the teacher about students' prior learning, especially to identify the gaps that need to be addressed. *Placement tests* are a form of diagnostic test that are used to help teachers make decisions about the difficulty level of material that will best match the student's present knowledge level.

A significant distinction exists between formative tests and summative tests. Although these two types of tests may look exactly alike, the difference between them is in the way they are used. *Formative tests* are used to measure the student's progress during a set of lessons or learning experiences so that the teacher can provide appropriate feedback and help the student correct errors in understanding or skill. They are *not* graded and are *not* used to make final judgments or evaluations of student achievement.

Summative tests are used at the end of a set of learning experiences in order to measure the progress made by a student over time. They *are* usually graded and *are* used to make final judgments or evaluations about student achievement.

Pretests are given prior to teaching a new unit or set of skills or knowledge. They are usually followed by *posttests* given directly after teaching the new set of skills. The comparison of posttest and pretest scores can be an important way for teachers to learn how much their students gained from a specific lesson, sequence of lessons, or unit of study. Pre- and posttests are often used in research to demonstrate gains students make under a certain set of conditions. Reflective teachers are likely to use pre- and posttests just as researchers do—as a means of gathering data about the value of various teaching strategies or sets of learning materials.

Nontest measures of student achievement and accomplishment also exist. These include informal observation, as well as student products, presentations, and portfolios. Teachers continuously use *informal observation* of their students' efforts and accomplishments. It may be planned or unplanned. Teachers may observe a single student or a group of students as they work together. While it is difficult to measure any specific achievement during an informal observation, the technique does provide subjective data that teachers need in order to understand the objective data gathered using other assessment devices.

In this text, a *student product* includes any form of written work, such as essays, stories, reports, poems, and plays that are handed in to be assessed and evaluated by the teacher. There are also a wide variety of student products that are not written but consist of completed works of art, music, models, machines, or other student-created items. A student product can be assessed by comparing it against a criterion or a set of criteria that fit that product type.

A *portfolio* denotes a collection of student products designed to show a progression of accomplishment from early undertakings to more recent and advanced efforts. By gathering a portfolio of students' work, teachers may assess the accomplishments made over time in a given type of endeavor. There may be portfolios of drawings, showing increasing attention to detail and craftsmanship, or portfolios of writing, showing growth in letter formation or use of grammatical conventions.

A *student performance* is a demonstration of effort and accomplishment that is presented orally to the public. It may be a speech given for classmates or a recital given for the entire school. It may be an individual effort or a group presentation such as a dramatization of a historical event. Student performances need to be captured on audio- or videotape for in-depth assessment and evaluation.

Objective measures implies that no matter who scores the assessment device, they will all get the same score. This occurs only on tests with items that have clear-cut right and wrong answers. *Subjective* measures are those that will be scored differently by different scorers, depending on their own interpretations and values. These include essays, artwork, and any other creative products or performances.

Reliability is related to objectivity. Reliable tests are those that consistently measure the same thing time after time. *Validity* means that a test is appropriate for the subject and contains items that will provide useful information about student achievement in that content area. Both test and nontest assessment devices should be constructed in such a way that reliability and validity are taken into account. When assessment devices are reliable and valid for their purpose, the information they provide can be used with confidence to make decisions about children's school experiences.

PUBLIC INTEREST IN STUDENT ACHIEVEMENT

Who cares about the accomplishments of students in elementary schools? Who wants to know the difference between achievement of students in the suburbs and students in the inner city? Why is so much energy, time, and money spent on assessment procedures in elementary education today? The answer is that we all care, and we all want to know at every level of society: national, state, local community, family, and individual.

At the national level, we care because we have seen signs that students educated in the United States are falling behind students from other industrialized nations. In 1983 the National Commission on Excellence in Education was commissioned to study American education. It reported:

> Our Nation is at risk. Our once unchallenged prominence in commerce,
> industry, science and technological innovation is being overtaken by competitors
> throughout the world. . . . What was unimaginable a generation ago has begun
> to occur—others are matching and surpassing our educational attainments. (p. 1)

The Commission, which wrote *A Nation at Risk*, recommended that academic tests be used to improve education by " (a) certify[ing] the student's credentials; (b) identify[ing] the need for remedial intervention; and (c) identify[ing] the opportunity for advanced work" (p. 28).

The National Assessment of Education Progress (NAEP) provides a measure of the academic achievement of students in the basic skills in elementary, junior high, and high schools. These statistics are not reported to students or their parents. They are collected for the purpose of comparing achievement of American students from year to year. Reports are made to the public and to policy makers about the level of achievement of various age groups, the changes over time, and the differences in achievement in gender and racial/ethnic groups. The NAEP uses the results of these tests to spot trends and to make forecasts and predictions about the future needs of American schools.

State governments are also vitally interested in assessing the achievement of students within their boundaries. As described in Chapter 4, each state government has established a state department of education that is responsible for providing guidance and standards to local school districts in the development of curriculum. The state departments are also responsible for holding school districts *accountable* for achieving the curriculum standards. *Minimum competency tests* are used by many state governments to determine whether districts are accomplishing the state guidelines.

Minimum competency tests are administered in schools by the classroom teachers on a specified date. Average scores are computed for various subjects and grade levels for each school district. In some states, these average scores are ranked and reported to the public in what is known as a *school district report card*. Districts with scores that are above the state mean are believed to be doing a better job of educating their students than are districts with scores below the mean. The purpose of this practice is to strengthen the feeling of accountability on the part of school district administrators.

In some school districts, administrators choose to rank and report the results of the test by schools. In this way, they hold the principal and faculty of each school accountable for the school's educational program.

There are many unanswered questions about the value of minimum competency tests and the practice of using the results to label schools and districts "poor," "good," "better," or "best." Some educators question whether the tests measure important student accomplishments or simply discrete, unconnected bits of knowledge. Others question whether the practice of reporting results is a valid measure of educational programming, since the socioeconomic status of each school is also believed to have an effect on test scores.

Standardized, norm-referenced tests of achievement in the basic skills are a fact of life in most school districts today, and teachers must learn how to interpret and use productively the information they provide. But at the same time that tests are gaining prominence in measuring and comparing achievement among school districts and states, they are also being severely criticized by many educators. Critics charge that testing takes too much time away from the curriculum. From 1 to 2 weeks of a 30-week school year may be given over to district, state, and national achievement testing.

Another criticism is that norm-referenced tests may measure only limited aspects of what the students have learned during the school year. Because they are written and distributed nationally by test publishers, the items on the tests are generic rather than specifically written to match what was taught in a particular school. Many items on a test may be unfamiliar to students because the material was not part of the curriculum of their school.

A further criticism of standardized tests is that they cause students to be labeled and categorized unfairly and unrealistically. There is great concern, for example, that generic achievement tests have a built-in bias against students who are members of racial minorities. Critics point to items, pictures, and language in early editions of such tests that were geared to the vocabulary and culture of the white middle class. While test manufacturers now employ test writers who represent various racial and ethnic minorities to develop fairer tests, the concern remains that students from minority groups may have less opportunity to learn the content of the tests, which causes them to earn unrealistically low scores.

Test results must be interpreted with caution and compared with other measures of student achievement. It is a serious breach of ethics when school districts misuse the data from standardized tests to classify students as learning disabled or gifted. Neither diagnosis can be made from the limited information derived from a generic test of basic skills. In fact, no serious educational decision should be made using only the data from standardized, norm-referenced tests of basic skills.

When test scores are overemphasized and generalizations are made about them, this practice is likely to damage students' self-concepts and may even create self-fulfilling prophecies (Gronlund & Linn, 1990, p. 472).

The emphasis given to standardized test scores varies from state to state and district to district. In some states and some districts, standardized achievement tests are given enormous weight in labeling children gifted or low achieving, in determining children's placement in special programs, and in determining who wins awards for merit. Reflective teachers who work in schools using these practices are likely to experience discomfort. It is important, then, to challenge such practices and encourage the use of a more balanced assessment and evaluation system.

In some states, school districts are encouraged to build evaluation systems that highlight the creative accomplishments of their students as being of equal or greater importance than tests of discrete skills. For example, the State of Illinois publishes curriculum guidelines in the form of outcome statements that describe achievement in terms of changes in behavior and productivity. For example, in the subject area of science, one of the four outcome statements is that "students will have a working knowledge of the principles of scientific research and their application in simple research projects" (Illinois State Board of Education, 1986, p. v).

The Illinois guidelines also provide specific objectives that must be attained by students in third, sixth, and tenth grades to demonstrate that they have accomplished each outcome. At the end of sixth grade, students in every school district in Illinois are expected to have worked in a laboratory group with other students; be able to distinguish between relevant and irrelevant information; convey accurately the findings and conclusions of their investigations; and organize their data into tables, charts, and graphs (p. 30).

Translated into action, this outcome statement and set of objectives holds elementary principals and teachers accountable for providing their students with laboratory experiences and opportunities to do scientific investigations and report their findings. No test of minimal competency can successfully evaluate an outcome statement of this type. Instead, each school district is expected to create a means of reporting how it has provided this experience and how well the students in the district have accomplished this outcome.

Similarly, the outcome statements in the State of California's Frameworks and Model Curriculum Guides call for the active construction of meaning in relation to the students themselves and their various cultures. School districts are encouraged to interpret the Frameworks in ways that are meaningful to their own communities. There has been a purposeful shift of emphasis from mastering basic skills to understanding concepts and ideas thoroughly. With this shift in curriculum emphasis has come a shift in the emphasis of assessment devices, as shown in the *English-Language Arts Model Curriculum Guide* (California State Department of Education, 1988):

> Guideline 21. Educators, recognizing the limitations of standardized and objective testing, augment the use of such testing and emphasize informal and subjective measures for diagnosis and assessment. (p. 31)

This guideline encourages school districts in California to be accountable to themselves and their local communities in the establishment of assessment procedures that measure student accomplishment. The state does provide representative informal and subjective assessment activities that districts can use for this purpose. In the area of reading and the language arts, for example, the California *Model Curriculum Guide* suggests these informal assessment techniques for primary students:

> Kindergarten through Grade Three
>> Each student reads aloud to the teacher on an individualized basis. The teacher determines the level of each student's decoding and comprehension skills by listening carefully and by asking appropriate questions.
>
> Grades Three through Six
>> After the entire class completes the reading of a work of fiction or nonfiction or a chapter in a social studies book, the students write at least two paragraphs in which they summarize the content of the literary work or the chapter in the book. Using predetermined and previously taught editing techniques, students work in read-around peer-group evaluating teams. . . . (pp. 31–32)

HOW TEACHERS SELECT AND USE METHODS OF ASSESSMENT

It is the responsibility of educators in state departments of education to create a balanced method of assessing whether students are meeting the state's standards. District administrators are responsible for creating a fair and useful collection of data about the achievement of students in the schools they serve. The principal of a single school provides guidance to classroom teachers in determining methods for evaluating the progress of the students in that school. But even with all of the direction and guidance provided by administrators and supervisors, there is still a great deal of leeway for individual classroom teachers in the area of student assessment.

Individual classroom teachers have varied philosophies of life and related curriculum orientations. Just as teachers' philosophies and curriculum orientations influence their methods of teaching, these values also greatly influence the types of assessment procedures teachers select and the weight they give to various measures of student accomplishment.

Teachers with an *R-A* conception of learning are likely to employ assessment methods that will reinforce their view that some students have the ability to learn, while others do not. They employ summative tests early and often, recording the results in their gradebooks as evidence of how each student's achievement matches the ability or IQ tests recorded in the student's cumulative file. Teachers with an R-A philosophy of education are, in many ways, very susceptible to the practice of making and carrying out self-fulfilling prophecies about their students.

Teachers with a *C-M* conception of learning are likely to employ many formative evaluation procedures in their effort to identify students' gaps in learning and cognitive processing errors. Through the application of a variety of formative evaluation strategies, these teachers provide the scaffolding necessary for students to achieve mastery and feel success in their classroom endeavors. If it has not been made obvious beforehand, it should be evident by now that the reflective teacher is likely to be one with a C-M view of teaching and learning. For the reflective teacher, evaluation is an integral part of the learning process.

Imagine that you are a teacher planning a unit on astronomy for your elementary classroom. You have gathered some very interesting learning materials, including filmstrips on the solor system, National Aeronautics and Space Administration (NASA) material on the space shuttles and telescopes, and many exciting books with vivid illustrations. You've planned a field trip to an observatory and invited an astronomer to visit the classroom. You have worked out a time line for several weeks' worth of individual and group investigations and projects.

But now it is time to think about evaluation. How will you know what the students have learned at the end of this unit? What do you expect them to learn? What techniques will you use to find out whether they have learned what you expect? What about the possibility that they may learn something different from what you expect or even that some children who become very actively engaged in the study may learn more than you expect? How will you know what they learned? How will you assign students science grades at the end of this unit? How will you communicate to the students' parents what each child has gained from it?

In the following sections, a variety of assessment devices will be described. Each one has many different uses and applications. Each one provides answers to different questions teachers have about evaluation. To illustrate how they compare and how they complement each other, each one will be applied to the astronomy unit described above.

Reflective teachers will consider each alternative and decide whether and how to use them in their own classrooms. Recognizing that this introductory text can provide only minimal information about each assessment method, the reflective teacher will want to search actively for more information about certain methods in order to fully understand their value and use before incorporating them into a program that affects children's lives.

Informal Observations

Teachers use informal observation intuitively from the first moment the students enter the classroom at the beginning of the term. They watch groups to see how students relate to each other; they watch individuals to spot patterns of behavior that are either unusually disruptive or extremely productive. In order to manage a classroom effectively, teachers with withitness are alert to observe the overt and covert actions of their students at all times.

Informal observations also have academic implications. Teachers who observe students while teaching a lesson are able to evaluate their understanding. Spotting a blank look, a nervous pencil tapping, or a grimace of discomfort on a student's face, the teacher can stop the lesson, check for understanding, and reteach the material in order to meet the needs of the students who didn't understand.

As students read aloud, primary teachers observe and listen for patterns of error in decoding words. They may also listen to the expression in the child's voice in order to determine whether the child is comprehending the material or simply saying words aloud. They listen for signs that indicate whether the student is interested or bored with the material. An additional tool in informal observation consists of asking the student pertinent questions to check for understanding and to comprehend the child's thought processes. This one-to-one interaction provides data and information not measurable on any paper-and-pencil test.

By observing the child read, asking a few questions, and comparing the results with those of other children of the same grade or age, the teacher is able to assess many things, including (1) the extent to which the child is able to use phonics and context clues to decode reading material, (2) the child's approximate reading level in terms of sight vocabulary, and (3) the child's comprehension level. In addition, the reflective teacher uses informal observation to gather information about the affective qualities of the child, including the confidence level, the child's interest in the subject or in reading itself, the amount of effort the child is willing to give to the task, and the expectations the child has about success or failure in the subject.

By observing as students write or by reading what they have written, teachers can gather similar data about children's writing abilities, interests, and expectations. As children work out unfamiliar math problems, teachers can observe who works quickly and who is struggling. They can then gather the struggling children together for an extra tutoring session.

In the astronomy unit, the teacher may observe as students take part in discussions to determine the extent to which various children understand the concepts. When the children visit the observatory, the teacher will watch them to learn about their interests in various aspects of the topic. When an astronomer visits the classroom, the teacher will listen to the students' questions to assess the depth of understanding they have achieved.

Informal observations are one of the most powerful assessment devices the teacher can use to gather new information about children's learning patterns and needs. Teachers may gather data about a child from academic and psychological tests, but in the end, it is informal observation that most teachers rely on in order to understand the test data and make a final evaluation about the appropriate placement or grade value of a child's work.

Mastery of Behavioral Objectives

In contrast to informal evaluations, which provide useful subjective information, behavioral objectives are relatively formal and provide useful objective data about what students have learned. Do not assume that teachers choose one or the other of these two devices. Many reflective teachers know that it is valuable to gather both objective and subjective data. They may choose behavioral objectives as a means of gathering hard data about what students have achieved during classroom learning experiences and compare those data with the subjective information they have gathered during their informal observations.

To plan an assessment system using behavioral objectives, it is necessary to begin before the lesson is taught. By preplanning a lesson with behavioral objectives, the teacher specifies the skills that students should be able to demonstrate at the conclusion of the lesson and the criterion for success. After each objective has been taught and students have had an opportunity to practice the new skill, there is a quiz or worksheet that calls on students to demonstrate that they have mastered the new skill and can perform it with few errors.

The teaching strategies that are most often used to help students master a series of objectives are direct instruction or mastery learning. When direct instruction of the whole class is used, each lesson planned by the teacher is based on one or more behavioral objectives with a prespecified criterion for success. The criterion for success is usually specified as a percentage or as a minimum number of correct responses. For example, the following behavioral objective specifies 80% (or 16 of the 20 possible items) as the acceptable demonstration of mastery of this objective:

> *Spelling Objective:* When the teacher reads the list of 20 spelling words aloud, students will write 80% of the words, using correct spelling and legible handwriting.

In the whole class method, teachers provide a period of direct instruction, and then students are given assignments of seatwork or homework that allows them to practice the new skills. A criterion-referenced test such as the weekly spelling test common in many elementary classrooms demonstrates whether the students have mastered the new skill. To record student achievement, teachers may write the percentage of correct responses that each student attained in a gradebook. These records are later used as the basis for computing report card grades (see Chapter 12).

Some teachers prefer to use mastery learning to motivate students to learn a sequence of skills. In mastery learning, individual students work through a series of learning experiences at their own pace and demonstrate mastery as they complete each objective. In this case, the daily or weekly measures of mastery are usually formative rather than summative, in that the teacher uses the information gained on the tests to provide helpful feedback and reteaching rather than as a record of achievement. Summative evaluations occur only at the end of a unit of study, when students are expected to demonstrate mastery of a whole sequence or unit of learning. These summative grades of unit tests are recorded and become the basis for determining the grades students have earned.

In the astronomy unit, the teacher may have written a number of objectives, such as these:

> After viewing the filmstrip on the solar system, the students will be able to match the picture of each planet with its name, with no more than one error.

> Students will be able to draw and label an illustration of the solar system, with the sun and nine planets in their respective orbits, with 100% accuracy.

Together these two objectives will inform the teacher whether students have learned the names, distinctive visual elements, and locations of the planets in the solar system. To determine whether the students have mastered this content, the teacher simply carries out the tasks described in the objectives after the students have had sufficient opportunity to learn the material. The teacher prepares a matching quiz with a column of nine names and another column of nine pictures of the planets. For those who do not achieve the criterion of eight correct answers, the teacher can provide a reteaching experience or require the students to do additional reading on their own. They can be retested until they achieve the criterion.

On another occasion, the teacher distributes blank paper and asks students to draw and label the solar system. From these two objectives and other like them, the teacher can begin to answer the question "How will I know what they have learned?" Also, the data gathered from this assessment system are more readily translated into letter grades than are the data from informal observations.

Criterion-Referenced Quizzes and Tests

Quizzes, such as the matching quiz described earlier, are frequently used in conjunction with behavioral objectives to determine whether students are successfully gaining each new skill or bit of knowledge in a unit of study. Quizzes are generally short, consisting of only a few questions or items, and are thought of as formative assessments, providing teachers with a way to know whether the students are learning the material day by day.

Tests, on the other hand, may be made up of many items and are generally thought of as summative assessments. They are often given at the end of a unit and contain a variety of items that measure students' achievement of content and skills that have been taught over a period of time.

In both cases, the term *criterion-referenced* refers directly to the criterion established for each behavioral objective. Each item on a criterion-referenced test should match a preestablished criterion. Criterion referencing provides objective data about material that all students in the class have had an equal opportunity to learn.

Objective tests may take a wide variety of forms. In the elementary curriculum, the most common are (1) matching, (2) true-false, (3) multiple-choice, and (4) short-answer or completion forms.

Matching items provide both the question and the response. Students have only to recognize the correct response for each item and draw a line to connect the two. These tests are created by writing the items in a column on one side of the paper and the responses in a different order on the other side. In terms of Bloom's Taxonomy, matching items are an excellent way of measuring knowledge-level objectives that require students to recognize correct responses.

To construct fair matching items, it is important that each right-hand response be clearly identified with only one item on the left. In our astronomy test, for example, it is necessary that the pictures of the planets contain clearly distinguishing visual elements so that only one picture looks like Mars. If several responses are vaguely correct, the reliability and therefore the objectivity of the test are diminished.

True-false items are also knowledge-level items, consisting of a statement that students must recognize as either true or false. These items are difficult to write, as they must be factual and objective in order to provide useful data. If items contain unsupported opinions or generalizations, the students must guess what the teacher intended.

For our astronomy unit, we might construct a quiz with statements such as these:

True False The sun orbits the Earth.
True False Venus is smaller than Jupiter.
True False Mars is closer to the sun than Neptune.

These items are reliable in that the correct responses are not likely to change in our lifetime. They are also valid because every item is an element that is directly related to our objective of teaching students about the physical characteristics of the solar system.

As examples of less reliable and less valid items, consider these:

True   False   Venus is a more interesting planet than Uranus.
True   False   The sun will never stop shining on the Earth.

Multiple-choice items also measure knowledge-level objectives because they call for recognition of a fact or idea on the part of the student. A multiple-choice item contains a question, problem, or unfinished statement followed by several responses. The directions tell the student to mark the one correct answer. While college admission tests may contain several near-right responses and students are expected to use reasoning to determine which one is best, elementary tests should probably be constructed with only one correct response. As with other objective measures, the reliability and validity of each item must be considered.

To fit the astronomy unit, two valid and reliable items are these:

1. Which planet is known as the *red planet?*
   A. Venus
   B. Orion
   C. Mars
   D. Jupiter
2. It would take longest to travel from Earth to
   A. Neptune.
   B. Mercury.
   C. Venus.
   D. Saturn.

Short-answer or *completion* items supply a question or an unfinished statement, and students are expected to supply a word, phrase, number, or symbol. These items are used primarily to test students' knowledge of specific facts and terminology. In our astronomy unit, two examples are these:

1. The planet Saturn has _____ rings around it.
2. Which planet has the most moons?

The advantage of these four types of objective items, which make up most criterion-referenced tests, is that they provide reliable measures of students' knowledge of the basic content of a subject. They can be written to match directly the criteria of the teacher's objectives for the lessons. They are also relatively easy to correct, and the scores are easily recorded and can be averaged together to provide the basis for report card grades.

The disadvantage of such items is that they measure only students' understanding of basic knowledge-level content and skills. They do not provide information about what students comprehend, how they would apply the knowledge they've gained, what they would create, or how they analyze and evaluate the ideas they've learned.

Essays

Essays have precisely the opposite advantages and disadvantages of criterion-referenced tests. They are subjective rather than objective. Two or more teachers rarely evaluate an essay the same way because each teacher has a unique set of criteria for a successful essay. They are also time consuming to read and mark.

On the other hand, essays provide teachers with an excellent means of knowing what students comprehend, how they would apply their new learning, and how they analyze and evaluate the ideas and concepts. Essays also provide students with opportunities to be creative by asking them to synthesize a number of previously unrelated notions into an original expression of their own. Essays can answer the question "How much more have they learned than what I taught in this unit?"

In form, essays may have either a restricted or an extended response. The *restricted essay* usually limits the topic with specific parameters and may even specify what must be included in the response. For example, in the astronomy unit, the teacher may want to assess whether students can describe the concept of outer space in their own words. This will provide information about how much students truly comprehend about the subject rather than what they simply remember. In the lesson plan, this aim can be written in the form of a behavioral objective with criteria for success:

> Students will be able to write a two-paragraph essay comparing the Earth's atmosphere with space and telling why humans cannot live in space without life support.

The essay's directions can be written as follows:

> In the first paragraph of the essay, describe how space differs from the Earth's atmosphere. Tell what is in space that is not in the atmosphere and what is in the atmosphere that is not in space.

> In the second paragraph, describe why humans can live in the Earth's atmosphere but cannot live in space without life support systems.

The directions are fairly explicit in terms of length and content. For these reasons, this form of essay is relatively objective. Two or more teachers are likely to look for similar elements when correcting the papers. This form is especially useful for assessing students' level of comprehension on a topic. It also provides an opportunity for students to demonstrate their ability to analyze the topic, but it limits their use of synthesis and evaluation.

The *extended-response essay* gives students more freedom to express ideas and opinions and to use synthesis-level thinking skills to transform knowledge into a creative new idea. In the astronomy unit, the teacher may hope that students will gain a sense of responsibility for the Earth after studying its place in the universe.

This affective goal for the unit may also be expressed as a series of problem-solving or expressive objectives. For example:

> At the end of the unit, students will write an essay entitled "The Big Blue Marble," in which they express their own hopes and fears for the future of the Earth. The essays will be edited, rewritten, illustrated, and hung up for parents to view on parent's night.

This extended-response essay calls on students to integrate all that they have learned in this unit and combine it with previous learning from geography and social studies units. Their individual experiences and outside readings are likely to affect their responses as well. Objectivity in marking this essay is very low. It is quite likely that teachers will view the responses very differently from each other. Nevertheless, within a single classroom, a teacher can state a set of criteria or expectations that can lead students to write a successful essay. In this instance, as stated in the objective, students will have an opportunity to receive critical feedback and make corrections on their essays before the final products are displayed.

Despite the lack of objectivity of extended-response essays, there is good reason to include them in an elementary educational program. They provide invaluable information about the creativity, values, philosophy, and maturity of our students. Moreover, they encourage students to become more creative and give them practice in making difficult judgments.

Oral Reports and Examinations

Like essays, *oral reports* can be restricted or unrestricted, depending on the type of assessment the teacher wants to generate. Examples of *restricted* oral reports include book reports in which students are expected to describe the main characters, the setting, the plot, and their favorite part of the story. In a restricted oral examination, teachers may ask questions that students must answer within specified parameters. In the astronomy unit, an oral examination may be scheduled for a certain day. Students are told to prepare for it by reading material supplied by NASA on America's space program. In the examination, the teacher asks questions taken from the reading material and students are expected to respond in their own words. For example:

> Tell how the astronauts prepared for weightlessness.
> Describe the food astronauts eat in space.

As the teacher listens to the students' responses, it is possible to make a judgment about whether their answers are right or wrong. It is also possible to assess whether the students have a poor, average, or unusually good understanding of the ideas they speak about. The teacher's evaluation of the students' responses can be recorded in some form, to be shared with each student later.

Unrestricted oral reports allow students more opportunities to speak about matters of great interest and importance to them. They encourage students to use their imagination to generate synthesis-level responses or to be persuasive about a matter of opinion or judgment. For example:

> Describe the space journey you'd like to take.
> Discuss what you think should be NASA's next big undertaking.

Debate is a form of oral examination in that it provides students with an opportunity to speak about a subject by learning a great deal of content and evidence for opinions prior to the event. During the debate, teachers can assess the students' energy and effort used in gathering information, as well as their understanding of the topic.

In evaluating oral presentations, teachers may write down comments as they listen, or they may videotape the presentations so that they can evaluate them more comprehensively later. Students may be involved in self-evaluation of their own efforts as well. They can view the videotapes and discuss with the teacher what they did well and what they need to improve.

Tests of Inquiry and Higher-Level Thinking Skills

It is possible to construct written or oral examinations designed to measure the higher-level thinking skills of analysis and evaluation, as well as the critical thinking skills of observation and inference and problem-solving strategies such as the creation and testing of hypotheses. These tests can be constructed as paper-and-pencil exams in which a situation or dilemma is presented and students are asked to respond to it in various ways. Such a test may consist of a passage to be read that describes a problem or dilemma. Maps, charts, graphs, or other forms of data might also be available on the test. The test items then consist of questions that allow the student to observe, infer, formulate a hypothesis, design methods of testing and hypothesis, and speculate about the possible outcome.

For example, in the astronomy unit, upper elementary or middle school students may be presented with a news article describing the failure of the Hubble Telescope to perform up to expectations. Diagrams of the telescope may be included, along with charts describing the expected and actual performances. The directions on the test would read:

> *Directions:* Imagine that you are a NASA scientist responsible for the deployment of the Hubble Telescope. When signals returning to Earth are not as strong and accurate as you expected them to be, what would you do? Put yourself in the shoes of this scientist. Answer these questions as a scientist would answer them.

> 1. List three observations about the way the telescope was constructed.
> 2. List three observations about the data in the charts.
> 3. Make two inferences about possible elements of the telescope that may have contributed to the problem.
> 4. Suggest a hypothesis about what may have gone wrong.
> 5. Describe what you'd do to find out whether your hypothesis is true.

This test may appear to be very difficult for elementary students, but its scoring does not depend on whether the students have knowledge about the actual problems with the telescope or other sophisticated engineering knowledge. The scoring would reflect the accuracy of their observations of the data presented to them and whether their inferences can be supported by their observations.

For intermediate children, a simpler test may focus on the orbit of the Earth around the sun and its relationship to the seasons of the year. A diagram of the Earth's orbit would be displayed, along with a chart on the dates of the four seasons in the Northern Hemisphere and questions such as these:

1. What do you *see* about the path the Earth takes around the sun?
2. What do you *see* on the chart about when seasons begin?
3. What connection do you think there is between the beginning of summer and the Earth's position in its orbit?
4. What other connections do you see?
5. What do you think the tilt of the Earth has to do with the seasons?

Even primary children can be tested for their inquiry skills, although it is probable that the tests will have to be oral rather than written. The teacher may ask students to observe a demonstration of the rotation of the Earth on its axis, using a flashlight on a beach ball in a dark room. After the demonstration, students can be asked to describe their observations, make inferences, and then respond to the unfinished statement, "What if . . . ?".

Checklists and Rating Scales

When teachers wish to assess students' products or presentations, they can tell the students their reactions in a conference or write comments on a piece of paper and give these comments to the students. These methods suffice for informing the students, in a general way, whether they have met the teacher's expectations, and they may be adequate for evaluating an unrestricted product or presentation.

When the criteria for a product or presentation have been prespecified by the teacher and there are several important elements that must be included, teachers may choose to create a *checklist* to use for notation when listening, for example, to a speech. This is frequently done when the objective is for students to use effective speaking skills in a presentation. In preparing the students for the speech, it is likely that the teacher will specify several important elements that the students should incorporate, such as maintaining eye contact with the audience, using appropriate volume to be heard by everyone in the room, and speaking rather than reading during the presentation. By preparing a simple checklist with these items on it, the teacher can quickly and accurately record whether or not the students used these skills in their presentations.

Checklists may be used to record mastery of many basic skills in the primary grades. Each item on the checklist can correspond directly to a behavioral objective. Together the items on a checklist provide an overview of a sequence of objectives. Kindergarten teachers frequently employ checklists to record the letter recognition of each pupil, letter by letter. Primary teachers use checklists to record mastery of basic math operations. Intermediate and middle school teachers may use checklists to record whether students have demonstrated fundamental research skills. In our astronomy unit, for example, the teacher may combine the goal of developing research and study skills with the goal of content mastery. To record the accomplishment of these skills, the teacher may use a checklist such as the one in Figure 11–1.

Checklists provide useful and efficient means of recording information about the accomplishments of individual students. They are also valuable during a student–teacher conference. Both teacher and student can quickly see what has been achieved and what still lies ahead. Checklists are also valuable when teachers confer with parents about the student's progress along a set of learning objectives.

Rating scales are used in circumstances similar to those of checklists. They provide additional information, however, in the form of a rating of how well the student achieved each element or skill on the list. They are used when it is useful to provide students with feedback that rates their performance on an objective. In the astronomy unit, for example, students' products may be turned in and evaluated by the teacher, using a rating scale of important elements. In many classrooms, teachers involve students in their own evaluation of products and the efforts expended in creating them. In Figure 11–2, a rating scale is structured so that both the student and the teacher rate the finished product.

Products of Individual Investigation and Research

The rating scale just described is used to evaluate the product of a student's independent research. In the elementary grades, a common method of assessing students' learning is to encourage them to do independent research on one aspect of a unit theme and to create a product that shows what they have learned. This method allows students to demonstrate their knowledge, comprehension, and all four of the higher-level thinking skills on a topic.

FIGURE 11–1
Astronomy Unit Checklist of Research and Study Skills

NAME _____ GRADE _____

This is a record of research and study skills demonstrated by this student. The teacher's initials and date indicate when the skill was successfully demonstrated.

Date	Initials	Skill Area
_____	_____	A. Located a book on astronomy in the card catalogue
_____	_____	B. Located a book on astronomy on the library shelves
_____	_____	C. Used the table of contents to find a topic
_____	_____	D. Used the index to find a subtopic
_____	_____	E. Orally interpreted a graph or chart
_____	_____	F. Took notes on a chapter in a book on astronomy
_____	_____	G. Summarized the chapter from notes
_____	_____	H. Wrote the bibliography for the book

FIGURE 11–2
Astronomy Unit Rating Scale of the Solar System Model

NAME _____GRADE _____		

To the Student: Please evaluate your own product, using the following scale:
O = OUTSTANDING; one of my best efforts
S = SATISFACTORY; I accomplished what I set out to do
N = NEEDS IMPROVEMENT; I need to revise and improve this element

Student's Rating	Skill Area	Teacher's Rating
_____	Did adequate research and information gathering	_____
_____	Elements of the model are accurate in shape	_____
_____	Elements of the model are accurate in scale (except for orbits of planets)	_____
_____	Labeling is accurate and legible	_____
_____	Legend is accurate and legible	_____
_____	Model is visually interesting and pleasing	_____

This assessment technique is appropriate for every area of the elementary curriculum. Students can do independent research or make an independent investigation in math, science, social studies, literature, music, or art. This method lends itself especially well to interdisciplinary units.

The strategy is for the teacher to introduce a unit or theme and provide some teacher-centered instruction on it at the outset. Readings may be assigned, and quizzes and worksheets may be used to assess the extent to which the student is developing a knowledge base about the topic. Essays or oral presentations may be assigned to assess whether students comprehend the main ideas and concepts of the topic. Finally, each student selects one aspect of the main topic on the basis of individual preference on interest and begins to research that subtopic independently. Each student decides on a final product that will demonstrate what has been learned and achieved during the independent study.

The types of products that might be created by students as a result of this type of investigation are limitless. Many elementary teachers prefer to plan their evaluations of student accomplishment to correspond to Bloom's Taxonomy. There are student products that are appropriate for learning objectives at all six levels. A sample of them can be found in Figure 11–3.

Evaluation of these student products may be accomplished by using a checklist or rating scale. Reflective teachers who wish to encourage critical thinking and reflectiveness among their students are also likely to involve the students in the evaluation of their own products. When students evaluate their work critically, they learn how to become more independent and responsible for revising and improving their work without the need for an outside evaluator.

Learning Contracts

A learning contract is a device that can be thought of both as a teaching strategy and as a means of assessment. The learning contract described in Chapter 10 listed

FIGURE 11–3
Student Products Related to Bloom's Taxonomy

Characteristics of Each Level	Products Associated with Each Level
Knowledge Level Can recognize and recall specific terms, facts, and symbols.	**Knowledge Level** Worksheet, Label a given diagram, Memorize poem or song, List, Quiz Recognition of math symbols, Spelling Bee, Response to Flashcard.
Comprehension Level Can understand the main idea of material heard, viewed, or read. Is able to interpret or summarize the ideas in their own words.	**Comprehension Level** Written paragraph or summary of main idea, Oral retelling of story, Use of math symbols and numbers in simple calculations, Report.
Application Level Is able to apply an abstract idea in a concrete situation, to solve a problem or relate it to prior experiences.	**Application Level** Diagram, Map, Model, Illustration, Analogy, Mental problem solving, Action plan, Teaches others, Diorama, Costume, Diary, Journal.
Analysis Level Can break down a concept or idea into its constituent parts. Is able to identify relationships among elements, cause and effect, similarities and differences.	**Analysis Level** Graph, Survey, Chart, Diagram, Report showing cause and effect, differences and similarities, comparisons and contrasts.
Synthesis Level Is able to put together elements in new and original ways. Creates patterns or structures that were not there before.	**Synthesis Level** Artwork, Story, Play, Skit, Poetry, Invention, Song, Composition, Game Collection, Hypothesis, Essay, Speech Videotape, Film, Computer program.
Evaluation Level Makes informed judgments about the value of ideas or materials. Uses standards and criteria to support opinions and views.	**Evaluation Level** Debate, Discussion, Recommendation, Letter to editor, Court trial, Panel, Chart showing hierarchies, rank order, or priorities.

FROM TAXONOMY OF EDUCATIONAL OBJECTIVES: The Classification of Educational Goals: HANDBOOK I: COGNITIVE DOMAIN. By Benjamin S. Bloom et al. Copyright © 1956. By Longman Publishing Group. Reprinted by permission of Longman Publishing Group.

several required activities and a number of options on the unit on westward expansion. Teachers using this strategy meet with individual students to agree on a suitable number and type of optional activities. The activities on the contract then provide the structure for daily learning experiences. When the unit is completed, the contract is used as the basis for assessing what each child has accomplished. Just as in adult life, students are held accountable for meeting the terms of their contracts. If they succeed, they can expect a positive evaluation. If they fail, they must explain why and describe what they will do to honor their contract.

Learning contracts can take several forms and can even be structured so that the student makes a contract to receive a certain grade for a specified amount of work. A point system can be employed to allow students to select from among options and earn the grade they desire. For example, in the astronomy unit, a learning contract with a built-in point system for earning a grade is shown in Figure 11–4.

Learning contracts also serve as the basis for recording accomplishments. In Figure 11–4, the parent is also required to sign the contract, indicating agreement to support the child's efforts. This strategy is a very efficient way to communicate with parents about the goals and expectations of the class. Later, during parent–teacher conferences, the parent can see the work that was accomplished. If a student did not complete the contract, the parent can see what was left undone.

Portfolio of Student Products

Portfolios are collections of work samples designed to illustrate a person's accomplishments in a talent area. Photographers collect portfolios of their best photos; artists collect their artwork; composers collect their compositions. In the elementary school, portfolios are used to document what a child has achieved in school. To use this technique, teachers collect samples of each student's work and put them in a file folder with that child's name on it. Some teachers collect many types of work in a single portfolio; others have writing portfolios that contain only writing samples, math portfolios filled with worksheets and tests, and others for other subject areas.

Teachers may collect only samples of a student's best work in a portfolio in order to demonstrate the maximum performance of that student. However, an argument can be made for the collection of samples of ordinary or typical work as well. These samples demonstrate how well the individual is performing on a day-to-day basis.

Portfolios may be kept for a long or short period of time. Many teachers collect writing samples in the first week of school and then periodically throughout the school year. In some cases, the teacher may assign a writing topic during the first week and again during the last week of school. When the two samples on the same topic are compared, the growth and development of the students' writing abilities are plain for everyone to see.

A short-term portfolio may be collected for the duration of a learning unit. For example, in the astronomy unit, all of the student's work, including quizzes, essays, pictures, and photos of the model solar system can be collected in a portfolio to document that student's accomplishment during the unit. If a contract was used during the unit, it will be included in the portfolio along with the work samples. Further recommendations for organizing and evaluating the contents of a portfolio are presented in Chapter 12.

Videotape Records

When the purpose of evaluation is to record the accomplishment of a student so that the work can be analyzed and evaluated more comprehensively later, a videotape is an

FIGURE 11–4
Sample Learning Contract

ASTRONOMY UNIT LEARNING CONTRACT

I, _____ , a student in the fifth grade at Otis School, do hereby contract to complete the following tasks during my investigation of the solar system.

Furthermore, I agree to complete these tasks by _____ .

I understand that I am agreeing to earn _____ points, which will earn a grade of _____ if my work is evaluated to be acceptable. I understand that the point values listed below are the maximum number that can be earned for each task and that fewer points may be awarded.

POINTS NEEDED TO EARN SPECIFIC GRADES

> 90 = A   > 80 = B   > 70 = C   > 60 = D   < 60 = F

_____	10 pts	Read Chapter 7 in the science text. Do exercises, pp. 145–146.
_____	10 pts	Matching quiz
_____	10 pts	True-false quiz
_____	10 pts	Multiple-choice quiz
_____	10 pts	Short-answer quiz
_____	15 pts	Drawing of the solar system, labeled correctly
_____	20 pts	Model of the solar system, labeled and scaled to size
_____	10 pts	Essay on Earth's atmosphere and outer space
_____	10 pts	Essay on "The Big Blue Marble"
_____	05 pts	per answer on NASA oral exam
_____	10 pts	Oral report on "A Space Journey I'd Like to Take"
_____	10 pts	Finished Checklist on Research Skills

Signed this day _____ 19 _____ at _____ School.

_____	_____
student signature	teacher signature
_____	_____
parent signature	witness signature

---

excellent way to capture and store a variety of learning events. Speeches can be videotaped easily. So can dramas, skits, presentations, and displays of students' products.

Videos are also excellent ways to communicate to parents about the accomplishments of a child or the entire class. They allow all interested parties to view the final products or performances of a unit of study. Teachers can store on tape a whole year's worth of accomplishments.

Video recordings also provide teachers with data they need to evaluate their own plans. By reviewing a video of a classroom learning event, reflective teachers are able to gain new understanding about what students need from their learning environment in order to be successful.

Cooperative Group Projects and Products

Many of the assessment methods described in this chapter can be adapted for cooperative groups. Evaluation of cooperative group efforts should include an assessment of a task that requires a group effort to complete and an assessment of individual efforts to ensure that each member of the group takes responsibility for doing personal reading and preparation.

As an illustration of how to adapt ordinary lessons and units to cooperative lessons and units, consider the astronomy unit. In adapting this unit for use by cooperative groups, each group can function as a study team, with directions to assist each other in reading and preparing for the quizzes. Group scores can be computed and recorded for each quiz at the same time that individual scores are recorded.

Rather than 30 individual models of the solar system, there will be 5 or 6 for each group in the class. The oral examination can be undertaken as a team effort, as proposed by Slavin's TGT model of cooperative learning. Essays and written reports can be combined as a group report.

The contract system works very well with cooperative groups. When it is used this way, there is one contract per group instead of per individual. Each group negotiates what they will accomplish together. Evaluations can include peer assessments of various tasks, with members of the group providing critical feedback for each other.

Conclusion

The assessment of student accomplishment is a complex and multifaceted undertaking. There is no one best way to assess what students have learned or accomplished in school. Some methods work better than others at various grade levels. Some work better than others with different individuals. This chapter has provided you with many different methods so that you can develop a repertoire of assessment devices to use as the basis for making judgments about the accomplishments of your students.

OPPORTUNITIES FOR REFLECTION

▼ Reflective Essay: Assessment in Your Class

What assessment devices are you most likely to use in your classroom? Why do you prefer them? What methods are you least likely to choose? Why?

▼ Classroom Visit: Assessment Methods

Ask the classroom teacher to discuss the methods he or she uses to assess learning in this classroom. Is one method used more often than others, or are a variety of methods used? Which methods are used that you would like to use in your own classroom? Which methods would you change?

REFERENCES

CALIFORNIA STATE DEPARTMENT OF EDUCATION. (1988). *English-language arts model curriculum guide*. Sacramento: Bureau of Publications Sales, P.O. Box 271, Sacramento, CA 95802-0271.

GRONLUND, N., & LINN, R. (1990). *Measurement and evaluation in teaching.* New York: Macmillan.

ILLINOIS STATE BOARD OF EDUCATION. (1986). *Illinois outcome statements and model learning objectives for biological and physical sciences*. Springfield, IL: State Board of Education.

NATIONAL COMMISSION ON EXCELLENCE IN EDUCATION. (1983). *A nation at risk: The imperative for educational reform*. Washington, D.C.: U.S. Government Printing Office.

CHAPTER 12

Recording and Grading Student Accomplishments

REPORT CARDS. These two words are likely to bring a number of memories filled with anxiety and a variety of other conflicting emotions to most people.

In your many years of schooling, you have probably received more than 50 report cards. You probably viewed many with relief and happiness and proudly displayed them to your parents; others may have caused torment and disbelief. On occasion, you may have questioned the teacher's fairness or integrity; you may have wondered whether the teacher really got to know you or understood the effort you put into your work. Perhaps you even approached a teacher and challenged the grade you received, showing evidence of why the assigned grade was unjustified.

Eight or 9 weeks into your first school year, you will be faced with the task of deciding on and recording report card grades for your students. For many first-year teachers, the responsibility is considered one of their most difficult challenges. Experienced teachers often report that the task doesn't seem to get easier as the years go by. In fact, many reflective teachers find that the more they know about grades and about children, the more difficult it is to sum up the work and efforts of a child in a single letter grade.

In Tracy Kidder's (1989) description of a year in a fifth-grade classroom entitled *Among Schoolchildren*, the teacher, Chris Zajac, takes a group of social studies tests home to grade:

> A stack of social studies tests lay before her on the table, slippery sheets of ditto paper, the questions in purple ink—fill in the blank questions that asked for definitions of terms such as "Tory." The test closed, as always, with an essay question; the children had to describe briefly a Famous Patriot. She stared at the stack of tests for a moment. "Do I want to?" she murmured to herself, and took the first test, Arabella's, off the pile. Chris's pen made a one-part scratching sound, inscribing red Cs down most of the page, and she began to smile.
>
> "84 = B," Chris wrote across the top of Arabella's test. . . . (pp. 72–73).

While Arabella's paper proves to be a pleasure to grade, Chris later encounters the test turned in by Jimmy:

> Chris stared at Jimmy's test. He had not tried to answer more than half the questions, and had not written an essay. Jimmy was the sleepiest boy Chris had encountered in years, also one of the stubbornest when it came to evading work that required thought. . . .
> Chris would explain an assignment. Jimmy would say, "I don't understand." Chris would explain again. Jimmy would say, "I don't understand." Of course, he was waiting for her to do it for him. . . .
> Chris stared at the window. Maybe tomorrow, she thought, she'd make Jimmy take this test again. She went back to the pile. (p. 76).

Still later in the evening:

> Chris sat down again at the table. Pedro's test lay on top of the pile. She read,
>
> Tory. Like a grup of sogrs.
>
> Chris placed her hand like a visor on her forehead. She stared at the blackened window across the room and slowly shook her head. "Poor kid."
> . . . He didn't often talk. He never misbehaved. He almost always tried to do his homework. It was as another teacher had said, "Poor Pedro. He works so hard to get an F." His situation had seemed intolerable to Chris the very first day when, after assigning some simple classwork, she stopped to look over Pedro's shoulder, and he looked up at her and asked, "Did I do good, Mrs. Zajac?" (pp. 79–80)
> "36 = F," Chris wrote on Pedro's social studies test. If she was not honest, she would never have the tangible evidence of progress or decline. (p. 85).

In carefully correcting and grading these tests, Chris Zajac is performing an important part of her job. She is holding students accountable for learning what they have been taught in her classroom. She is also providing them with feedback so that they can understand what they have accomplished and what they still need to work on. She is also contributing data to a growing record kept on each student so that assistance and special educational opportunities can be provided if necessary. But the task of grading is an arduous and time-consuming one, and the teacher may feel as emotional about giving grades to children as the children feel about receiving them.

VARIED PERSPECTIVES ON THE PURPOSE OF EVALUATION

As described in Chapter 11, many people want to know about student achievement in the elementary schools. Although the state and federal governments and school district administrators are interested in data about the average achievement levels of all students in a given grade, it is the child's parents and teachers who are most interested in the achievement of an individual child.

Teachers want to know what the child has gained from each learning event as a means of planning further experiences and as a measure of their own teaching methods. Parents want three very different types of information from an evaluation:

1. What has my child learned?
2. How well is my child doing in school?
3. What about my child's future? (Oakes & Lipton, 1990)

The question of what each child has learned focuses on an individual child. It does not ask for comparisons among children and assigns no value on the child's achievement. To evaluate what a child has learned, teachers select from a variety of assessment methods such as those described in Chapter 11. From informal observations, checklists of accomplishments, and data from tests and other assessment devices, it is possible to describe what a child knows about each subject in the curriculum and what skills the child has mastered. Compiling an accurate record of what each student has learned is an important part of the teacher's responsibility to the child and the parents. The record of what each child has achieved at each grade level is also valuable because it certifies whether the child has accomplished the expectations for that grade.

Reports of what a child has learned can be given through oral descriptions during a conference, accompanied by a portfolio of work samples, or it can be provided in written reports called *anecdotal records* that describe what the child has learned during a specific period of time. An anecdotal record might read:

In kindergarten, this child mastered letter recognition of all 26 capital letters of the alphabet. He has almost mastered the recognition of small letters, but at present he still confuses *b*, *d*, and *p*. He can give an example of a word that starts with each letter of the alphabet.

Another example:

Third Grade, Second Quarter Report:

Although she is still quite shy with other children, she has participated actively in her writing group. She writes full and complete sentences with interesting and detailed descriptions. She recently wrote a paragraph on dinosaurs and read it aloud to her group. They responded with much interest and enthusiasm to her vivid descriptions of various types of dinosaurs. She accepted suggestions from the group and incorporated their ideas into her revision of the work.

Such reports are valuable because they allow the parents to understand the objectives of the school and whether their child is achieving the intended learning outcomes. When parents understand the school's objectives, they are better able to join with school personnel in supporting their child's learning and affective development. Also, having accurate information about their child's achievements, failures, strengths, and weaknesses enables parents to give their child the support and encouragement he or she needs to be successful in school (Gronlund & Linn, 1990, p. 429).

School evaluation would be a relatively simple endeavor if it only concerned the question of how much each child has learned during a given period of time. Unfortunately, few parents are satisfied with that descriptive evaluation alone. Parents often ask teachers, "How is my child *doing* in school?" This question could mean "in relation to the curriculum" or "compared to his achievement at the beginning of the year." In response, teachers must be able to answer the question "How much of what I taught did this child learn?" (Oakes & Lipton, 1990, p. 136).

To answer this question accurately, the teacher must be able to compare the achievement of an individual child with a standard or criterion for success. This is the reason for the current strong interest in assessment by behavioral objectives. Each objective is written with a built-in criterion. Students who meet the criterion can be recorded to have passed or mastered the material. Students who do not meet the criterion are recorded to have failed or to be deficient in this learning task. Students who exceed the criterion can be reported to have excelled.

For example, consider the objective that students will apply recently learned math skills to calculate the answers to 100 problems, and the criterion for success is 90 out of 100 correct. If Joan gets 91 correct, she is reported to have met the criterion and passed. If Sam gets 74 correct, he is reported to have failed, and if Greg gets 98 correct, he is reported to have done excellent work.

A second way to interpret the question "How is my child doing?" reflects a strong parental interest in knowing how the child is doing *compared to others* of the same age or grade. This is the question that causes evaluations to become competitive in nature. In recording or reporting this information to parents, the teacher must not only tell how the child did in relation to the objective criterion, but also how the child's performance compared to those of others in the class.

Using the above example, imagine that out of the class of 30 students, 5 got scores of 95 or above, 15 got scores of 90 to 95, and 10 got scores below 90. Then the report on each child may contain the information that allows the parents to see how well the child is doing compared to the rest of the class. Joan met the criterion, but so did half the class, so her performance is reported to be near the mean or average. Sam got only 74 correct, but six other children made even more errors than he did. This means that Sam is in the bottom half of the class but above those who are in the bottom fifth. Greg, with his score of 98, was also the top scorer in the class, which may please his parents even more than knowing that he exceeded the criterion.

Standardized achievement test data can also be interpreted to inform parents where their child stands in relation to students in the same grade throughout the United States. In most elementary schools, the classroom teacher must be able to interpret the data from classroom events and achievement tests for the parents, so that they understand how well the child is doing compared to others at the same grade level.

The third question that parents ask in many school evaluations is "What about my child's future?" This really means, "What does the present performance tell us about this child's future?" In other words, "Is my child college material?" "Is it likely that my child will be able to earn a good living?" These questions call for more than simple descriptions or comparisons. The teacher is expected to be a forecaster, predicting the future achievements of the student based on the present school performance. This is not as difficult as it may seem, at least as far as the prediction of future success in school is concerned. Studies show that present performance in school is a fairly accurate predictor of future performance in school (Bloom, 1982).

Teachers are not usually required to speculate about future performance in their records or reports of student achievement. But many do so informally. They predict success or failure to other teachers in the school, as in "Oh, you have Greg this year? I had him last year. He's a straight A student." They may also offer conjectures to the parents, such as "If we don't get this kid's behavior straightened out now, I'm afraid he'll end up behind bars."

Teachers' predictions are often made as recommendations for special gifted or enrichment programs, college-bound or vocational curricula, and ability tracks when the child leaves the elementary school for junior and senior high school. These predictions may contribute to a self-fulfilling prophecy. It is certainly true that the students who are recommended for enriched educational opportunities are more likely to succeed in school than their classmates. But some reflective teachers wonder which comes first, the enriched opportunity or the success. They'd like to see how well average students would do if they were offered the enriched learning experiences that are available to students selected for elementary gifted programs.

PHILOSOPHIES UNDERLYING VARIOUS EVALUATION SYSTEMS

Reflective teachers struggle with many conflicting ideas, thoughts, and concerns when they confront existing evaluation systems. Prevailing systems seem highly related to the R-A view of teaching and learning, which is based on the assumption that students vary in ability and that they acquire learning by passively receiving knowledge from the teacher. From this assumption, it is logical to conclude that students should be evaluated by determining what they have learned and how this learning compares to that of other students of the same age. Categorizing and rank ordering of students is the next step, and is done by assigning letter grades to label their respective categories of ability. Teachers with this perspective can be overheard saying that "John is an A student, and Sally is a C student."

Teachers with a C-M view of teaching are often very uncomfortable with such statements. They recognize the complex mix of environmental, nutritional, genetic, and experiential factors that contribute to each child's success or lack of success in school. Moreover, according to their view of teaching and learning, it is the teachers responsibility to diagnose students' needs and then plan a series of learning experiences and the scaffolding necessary for each child to experience success. The competitive nature of letter grades contrasts sharply to this philosophy.

How Curriculum Orientations Influence Evaluation

In addition to having a general overarching philosophy of teaching and learning, each teacher may prefer one or more of the five curriculum orientations described in Chapter 4. Just as a teacher's curriculum orientation influences the learning activities that take place in that classroom, it also influences the assessment methods used to evaluate what children have learned and how well they have learned it. A teacher with only one strongly held curriculum orientation is likely to use similar methods of assessment day after day, in every subject of the curriculum. For example, a teacher with a strong academic rationalism orientation will use tests and restricted essays as the preferred method of evaluating student performance.

Students who do well on that type of assessment are likely to be perceived as being successful by that teacher. They will get A's in that class. Students who do less well on that type of assessment will get lower grades. The teacher will predict the students' future success based on this strongly held curriculum orientation. Teachers who do not know or understand the variations in curriculum orientations may assume that their own perspective is the only way, or the best way, to view schooling.

Many teachers have more than one curriculum orientation. They may combine several or have one orientation for one school subject and a different orientation for the arts or another academic area. These teachers are likely to select a variety of assessment devices because their vision of the curriculum is multifaceted. Students in their classrooms may do well on one type of assessment and poorly on another. This varied performance will be recorded and reported.

The purpose of describing how a teacher's curriculum orientation affects the types of assessment methods chosen and the evaluation is to allow you to begin to clarify your own curriculum orientation(s) and to help you see how your orientation(s) can influence your choice of assessment methods and your vision of how well a child is achieving in your classroom. It can also help you to interpret the judgments and recommendations about your students made by other teachers.

How Various Orientations Affect Teachers' Observations

Teachers with all curriculum orientations use informal observations as a means of evaluating what students know and what they need to know. Teachers oriented to the use of curriculum technology plan their curriculum with behavioral objectives. As they observe and listen to their students, they are assessing whether or not the student is reaching the criterion established for the lesson.

Academic rationalists are interested in assessing what has recently been termed *cultural literacy* (Hirsch, 1987). They assume that there is a body of traditional knowledge that all students should learn in school. As they listen to students discuss the content and ideas expressed in a classic text or literary work, they assess whether students have a mature understanding of the ideas or whether they require greater explication and perhaps a rereading of the text in order to gain the desirable degree of understanding.

Teachers with a social perspective plan a curriculum that emphasizes social awareness and responsibility. As they observe their students working, they are likely to be assessing the degree to which the students interact cooperatively or the extent to which a student is taking an active role in solving a social dilemma.

Teachers with a cognitive processes orientation emphasize the learning of processes over the mastery of content. As students work on problems, the teacher is likely to interrupt their independent practice to ask them to describe how they are attempting to solve the problem. As the students describe their thinking processes, the teacher assesses whether they are using an appropriate process. The teacher also makes a judgment about whether their thinking is efficient and likely to lead to a correct solution or whether the teacher should provide scaffolding that will lead to a more strategic problem-solving process.

Teachers with a personal relevance orientation emphasize the affective domain over the cognitive domain. They are interested in helping students develop self-esteem and interest in learning. Their observations monitor student interest and engagement in the learning events.

How Curriculum Orientations Relate to Test Construction

Teachers with all five curriculum orientations are likely to use occasional short-answer quizzes and tests. However, academic rationalists and curriculum technologists are likely to use more of them than teachers with the other three orientations.

The type of tests used by curriculum technologists has been fairly well described in the section on mastery of learning objectives in Chapter 11. These teachers create both formative and summative quizzes and tests that are designed, item by item, to be related to their preplanned behavioral objectives.

Academic rationalists are likely to use summative tests to assess whether their students have gained knowledge about the identity of the world's great thinkers and the contributions each has made to our culture. For example, tests that ask students to match the author with an idea or a title would be created by a teacher with an academic rationalist orientation.

Teachers with a cognitive processing orientation are likely to use tests in which students solve problems. They are also likely to ask students to show their work rather than simply provide an answer. This is because these teachers are primarily concerned with assessing how students think, and they can evaluate that more accurately if they can understand the steps used by the student in thinking through a problem.

Teachers with a social perspective design tests to assess whether their students are able to understand and solve difficult social problems. Tests and quizzes would likely consist of some short-answer items designed to test the student's knowledge base on each subject, but most items would probably ask students to apply this knowledge to social concerns.

Teachers with a personal relevance orientation may include a few short-answer knowledge base questions, but most items would require students to apply the new information to their own lives or give their opinions about the ideas they've read. It is also likely that these teachers would write the test in such a way that students are free to choose to answer some items and omit others in which they are less interested. Directions for tests given by this type of teacher usually include "Choose three of the five questions."

How Curriclum Orientations Affect the Selection and Use of Other Assessment Devices

Aside from informal observations and tests, teachers with a curriculum technology orientation are likely to use checklists and rating scales describing the mastery of skills. They are less likely to use essays, as these are less objective than a curriculum technologist prefers. They may use learning contracts, but these would resemble checklists of skills and would simply be used as a reminder to students of where they are in the sequence of objectives that must be mastered. They are very unlikely to use tests of inquiry, creative products, or performances as a means of evaluating student progress. Portfolios of student products would contain primarily worksheets, formative tests, and summative tests.

Academic rationalists emphasize the assessment of students' knowledge and comprehension of a large body of content in classic literature and subject areas. They are quite likely to use essays as a means of assessing the students' comprehension of historically valued information, principles, and works of art and literature that make up the bulk of their curriculum. Oral presentations and debates are also likely to be employed for the same reason. They are less likely to use checklists and rating scales, since these typically emphasize skills rather than content. The portfolios kept by academic rationalists would contain mainly tests and essays.

In contrast, teachers with a cognitive processes orientation are more interested in process than content. When they evaluate essays, they are more likely to look for evidence of the students' application of ideas, research skills, and hypothesis testing than for learning of the content itself. Oral presentations would also be evaluated more on process than on content. Tests of inquiry are likely to be used more frequently than objective tests, since these teachers believe in teaching students how to use inquiry and critical thinking skills to gain knowledge. Individual creative products and performances are likely to be assigned and evaluated with an emphasis on how well the students are progressing in processing information through the use of research, investigations, experiments, and reporting of findings. Portfolios are likely to contain "before" and "after" work samples and a variety of students' products to demonstrate how each student's skill in cognitive processing is growing and developing over time.

Teachers with a social perspective are likely to emphasize cooperative group projects and products over individual ones. Group learning contracts may be employed to assess cooperative efforts. In assessing individual work, these teachers are likely to use many expressive essays and oral presentations on social topics and problems to evaluate the extent to which each individual is growing in awareness of social needs and taking responsibility for creating solutions. Tests of inquiry into social concerns are also likely to be given. Portfolios are likely to contain the aforementioned essays, as well as letters to the editor, political cartoons, and other work that shows evidence of social awareness and concern.

Teachers with a personal relevance orientation are most likely to use learning contracts with many options for self-selection as a measure of student accomplishment. These teachers believe that it is important to match the interests and individual needs of students with the topic being learned, and that self-selection encourages intrinsic interest and motivation in completing school assignments. Essays are likely to be open-ended and expressive in nature. Students are encouraged to create individual products and performances, and these are likely to be prized by the teacher as evidence of student acccomplishment and achievement. Portfolios of creative efforts and videotapes of performances are likely to be used to display students' accomplishment to others.

Conventional methods of assessing students' accomplishments have stressed the use of objective tests and content-oriented essays. That is probably due to the strong orientation toward academic rationalism that was the basis of the first schools in the United States and exerts a strong influence up to the present day. The second major orientation in this country is curriculum technology, which also stresses the use of objective tests and checklists.

Although Dewey exhibited a combined orientation toward cognitive processing, social perspectives, and personal relevance, his influence did not fundamentally change the orientation of school personnel in the early twentieth century. Since the 1960s, these three orientations have grown in strength, number, and influence. When you enter the teaching profession, you will see and hear evidence of all five orientations any time that teachers meet to discuss curriculum concerns. You will also see and hear the philosophies of all five orientations being debated when teachers get together to discuss how to assess student learning. It will serve you well to clarify which of these orientations you hold so that you can assert your own views on the appropriate assessment methods to use to evaluate the accomplishments of your students.

METHODS OF REPORTING STUDENT ACCOMPLISHMENT

Due to the time-consuming task of correcting students' work and the complexities of the evaluation processes described above, it is easy to see why school personnel have resorted to a form of shorthand to record and report student progress. Most teachers have too many students and too little time to hold discussions with each child's parents or write extensive narratives of each child's learning on a regular basis. Schools use standardized shorthand methods known as *grades* and *test scores* to communicate with parents, future teachers, college admission personnel, and future employers (Oakes & Lipton, 1990, p. 152).

The practice of awarding letter grades as measures of individual achievement has been part of the American educational scene for many decades. In the 1960s and 1970s, personnel in some school districts attempted to replace conventional report cards with detailed anecdotal records describing what each student had accomplished in each subject area during the course or term. But these attempts to change the prevailing evaluation system met with opposition from parents, who insisted on a return to the letter grade system with which they themselves had grown up. Parents were not satisfied with a description of their own child's achievements. They wanted to know how their child compared with other children. They expressed concern that these records would not be accepted at the most prestigious colleges.

In response to these debates, school boards and administrators in most school districts arrived at a compromise. While they reestablished the letter grade report cards for the intermediate and upper elementary grades, they retained the use of anecdotal report cards for the primary grades. This is the prevailing practice today. That means that if you are planning to teach at the primary grades (kindergarten through the second or third grade), you will be expected to write anecdotal report cards describing and documenting what each child in your classroom has learned. If you are planning to teach at the intermediate grades (second or third grade through sixth grade) or in the middle school (fifth through eighth grade) or at a junior high school (sixth or seventh grade through eighth or ninth grade), you will be expected to compute letter grades every quarter for the students' report cards.

Combining Evaluation Data

There is no formula that beginning teachers can learn from experienced teachers to guide them in selecting appropriate assessment devices and combining the data into a rationale for a grade. That is because no two teachers have the same philosophy or combination of curriculum orientations. Consider what would happen, for example, if Mary, an experienced teacher who holds an R-A view of learning and a strong academic rationalist curriculum orientation, tells Pam, a beginning teacher with a C-M view of learning and a mix of curriculum orientations, how to compute grades for report cards. Their conversation might sound like this:

PAM: Mary, can you tell me how to figure my report card grades?

MARY: Sure. Here are the tests I use. They are fill-in-the-blank and short essay items. I use a straight percentage to figure my grades. Ninety percent and above is an A, eighty is a B, and so on. Then, for report cards, I just average the results of the tests.

PAM: But how do you count in projects like the models my students made of the Indian villages during colonial times?

MARY: I don't count those at all, except maybe for extra credit. If a student is on the borderline, I might give him the higher grade if he did a nice project.

PAM: Well, then what do you do about students who try very hard but don't do well on the tests?

MARY: I just give then what they earn. That's what grades are supposed to do—communicate whether students learned what we taught them.

PAM: But what if they cooperated very well with their groups and helped to put on a great dramatic skit about the Pilgrims and the Indians but still did not retain the facts and dates on these tests? How can I give those students a flunking grade?

MARY: That's easy. You don't need to do so many of those *extra* projects. They just confuse you and the students. Spend more time on reading, recitation, and worksheets, and they'll do better on the tests. Grades are supposed to reflect knowledge of content, not fluff like group projects, models, and plays.

Pam is likely to come away from this exchange discouraged and more confused than ever. Mary makes it sound so easy. She seems to have an efficient system for deciding on grades, but it just does not seem to fit Pam's curriculum or her philosophy that every child can accomplish something valuable in school, although not all children can be expected to learn in the same way or accomplish the same goals. In an attempt to gather more useful information, Pam may consult a second experienced teacher named Tom, who is known for his creative projects and highly interactive relationships with his students. "I like the way he teaches," Pam thinks. "Perhaps his system of grading will work for me too."

PAM: Can you tell me how you figure your report card grades?

TOM: Oh, I wish you hadn't asked me that. It's not something I feel very sure about.

PAM: But you've been teaching for several years. How have you figured your grades up to now?

TOM: Well, I mostly go with student effort. If a student is willing to work and takes an active part in our class projects, I give her an A.

PAM: What kinds of tests do you give? How do you record what students have learned?

TOM: That's why I wish you hadn't asked. I use my gradebook for attendance only. If I had to show evidence of why a child got a certain grade, I'd be in trouble.

PAM: Well, don't you have to show that kind of data to the parents during the conferences?

TOM: So far, I've avoided it. They're usually so happy with the high grades their kids are getting that they don't ask me for too many details.

If you are like Pam, you are probably not satisfied with either of these explanations. You probably feel a need for answers to such questions as these:

1. What should be included in a letter grade?
2. How should achievement data be combined in assigning letter grades?
3. What frame of reference should be used in grading?
4. How should the distribution of grades be determined? (Gronlund & Linn, 1990, p. 437)

Gronlund and Linn's (1990) textbook *Measurement and Evaluation in Teaching* is an excellent resource for teachers who want to know more about this important subject than can be presented in this text. A brief summary of their response to each of these questions follows.

What Should Be Included in a Letter Grade?

Traditionally, there are five letter grades (A, B, C, D, F), although some schools reduce this number to three (E = excellent, S = satisfactory, U = unsatisfactory). According to Gronlund and Linn, letter grades are efficient systems for communicating student achievement to both parents and students when they are used for evaluation of academic achievement only. When extraneous factors such as behavior and effort are combined with achievement data, letter grades lose their meaning. For example, if effort and achievement are combined in the teacher's mind, a grade of C may mean excellent achievement combined with little or no effort, or it could mean excellent effort combined with very low achievement, or it could mean a moderate amount of effort and achievement. Therefore, the first recommendation is to use separate systems for communicating student behavior and effort, and to compute the letter grades on achievement data alone.

Secondly, "if letter grades are to serve as valid indicators of achievement, they must be based on valid measures of achievement" (Gronlund & Linn, 1990, p. 437). This means the assessment devices selected or created by the teacher need to fit the objectives of the learning experience.

The emphasis given to tests, essays, ratings, and other measures of achievement should be guided by the types of objectives that were planned and covered in the course or term. The more important the objective in the curriculum, the greater weight it should receive in the final grade.

Teachers with various curriculum orientations are likely to establish different objectives for their classrooms or give varying weights to the same type of item. This variation among teachers cannot be eliminated. But each teacher must be able to define the learning objectives established for the subject area and to base the letter grade on a reasonable combination of all these objectives.

Combining data is difficult because various assessment measures are often different from each other. Some tests may contain 100 items, while others may contain only 25. If two measures are not equivalent, the grades on each should be given different weights.

For example, if a student receives an A on the 100-item test and a C on the 25-item test, what grade does he deserve when the two items are combined? The average of an A and a C is typically a B, but that is valid only if the tests were equivalent. In this case, the 100-item test is worth four times as much as the 25-item test. That can be taken into account in at least two ways. One way is to multiply the value of the 100-item test times four when combining it with the 25-item test. That means that it is worth four As. Four As and one C will compute to a final grade of A.

What Frame of Reference Should Be Used in Grading?

Gronlund and Linn suggest that three typical frames of reference are used in grading decisions:

1. Performance in relation to other groups (relative grading)
2. Performance in relation to prespecified standards (absolute grading)
3. Performance in relation to learning ability or amount of improvement (p. 439)

Relative grading involves determining grades by comparing one student's achievement with the achievement of the other members of the class. An individual's grade is influenced by both the individual's performance and the performance of the group. A student is likely to receive a better grade in a low-achieving group than in a high-achieving group.

Absolute grading is the method of establishing a standard for mastery and awarding grades according to the extent of mastery each student achieves. The most common system of this type used in elementary schools is the percentage system.

The system of grading performance *in relation to learning ability* or amount of improvement is used fairly widely in elementary schools, but, as employed, it is seldom a reliable assessment. Reliable measures of growth or improvement are difficult to achieve with or without tests. Teachers may use the system in order to motivate low-achieving students, but Gronlund and Linn believe that the available measures are so undependable that achievement should be reported using one of the other two frames of reference and that improvement should be reported as a secondary or supplemental grade.

How Should the Distribution of Grades Be Determined?

Relative grading has become known as *grading on the curve*. That is because it was developed to coincide with the normal curve of distribution, but this is not a reasonable possibility in a group the size of a single class. Instead, Gronlund and Linn suggest that a reasonable distribution may be in the following ranges:

A = 10 to 20% of the pupils
B = 20 to 30% of the pupils
C = 30 to 50% of the pupils
D = 10 to 20% of the pupils
F = 0 to 10% of the pupils
(pp. 441–442)

These ranges are not scientifically determined, but they represent a general target for this type of grading. Final decisions regarding the actual distribution should take into account the school's philosophy, the population served, and the purpose of the grades. One element that distinguishes this distribution from the normal curve is that it does not require some children to fail because they are at the bottom of the distribution.

Using an absolute grading system, Gronlund and Linn recommend the following distribution ranges:

A = 95 to 100% correct
B = 85 to   94% correct
C = 75 to   84% correct
D = 65 to   74% correct
F = below 65% correct
(p. 443)

Elementary teachers may prefer to alter these ranges in order to create more opportunities to earn the highest grade. With absolute grading systems such as this, the distribution of grades is not dependent on the achievement of others. If all pupils demonstrate a high level of mastery, they can all receive high grades. Gronlund and Linn argue that whether students pass or fail a course should depend not on their ranking within the class but on their absolute level of learning. If all low-ranking students have mastered the material sufficiently, they should all pass (p. 442).

A Grading System That Encourages Success

A major reason for failure in elementary schools is that often the students do not know what they are expected to do in order to succeed. In some classrooms, the teacher's expectations may be vague and unclear. The students know only that they are supposed to work hard and do well on all the classwork and tests that come their way. But some children may not be good at guessing what the teacher's real priorities are. This may be because the teacher has not sorted out these priorities either.

No two grading systems are alike. Teachers have different expectations due to their philosophies and views of how students learn. They have widely different priorities because of their curriculum orientations. They also have many other personality traits, interests, and values that influence their expectations for their students.

How can students be expected to adapt to so many different teachers with such a variety of expectations? It appears that most children can and do adapt if they are informed clearly and precisely about what the expectations are in each class. On entering a class for the first time, students want to know what the rules and expectations are in *this* class. Just as a clear statement of behavior rules and procedures is important, so is a clear statement of how to get a good grade on each project, paper, or test.

To be able to describe clearly to your students what you expect, it is essential that you first clarify your expectations for yourself. A synthesis of research on effective evaluation suggests that you are most likely to clarify your own expectations and communicate them effectively to your students if you use the following steps for each subject area that you are grading:

1. Plan a set of educational objectives.
2. Decide which objectives are most important. Plan how you will weight them when you combine their data.
3. Plan learning experiences for each objective.
4. Select a suitable assessment device to measure the students' accomplishments for each objective.
5. Create a clear criterion for success for each objective that is also appropriate for the assessment device you selected.
6. At the beginning of each learning event, *inform students* about
   a. the goal or purpose of the learning activity.
   b. the criterion for success.
   c. what you will be looking for when you correct their work and precisely how you will *score* their work.
   d. what they may do if their first attempt is not acceptable.
7. When you correct and mark students' work, provide adequate feedback on what was done correctly and what needs to be improved. Give suggestions for improvement. Encourage students to confer with you about how to improve their work.
8. Well before report card grades are due, *inform students* about
   a. what work will count toward the report card grade.
   b. what work will be given the greatest weight for the report card.
   c. what they may do to improve their work for a higher grade.
9. When report cards are distributed, have a conference with each child and explain the reason for each grade. Describe the good work that resulted in good grades and describe the unacceptable work that resulted in poor grades. Help the student see how to make improvements in the unacceptable work during the next term.

While some of these nine steps are commonly used in elementary classrooms, many are not. Most teachers do plan learning objectives, but many do not consider which ones are most important. Often teachers treat all objectives as if they are equal, at least on paper. They may have priorities, but these priorities are not well communicated to their students. Few teachers have clarified the weight they plan to give to each type of work and each objective. This situation was illustrated by Pam's dilemma. She had carefully planned a stimulating set of learning activities but had given no thought to how she would combine and weight the outcomes until the last moment.

Another rarity in elementary classrooms is the practice of telling students how each piece of work will be scored and graded. Some teachers, exemplified by Tom, don't appear to know what they are really looking for in student work, apart from enthusiasm and participation. Others may have a much clearer understanding of this issue, but they do not believe that students need to know their conclusions.

Teachers with a C-M view of the teaching and learning processes believe otherwise. Rather than keeping the evaluation process a mystery, these teachers believe strongly that students *need to know* exactly how to succeed and what is expected of them. If they know these things, then they can learn to take an active role in monitoring and evaluating their own work. One of the cognitive processes that these teachers want students to learn is known as *metacognition,* the capacity to monitor and regulate their own work. They plan learning activities that promote independence and personal responsibility. They are also likely to organize their evaluation system around the principle of helping students gain more control over the quality of their work (Anderson, 1989, p. 92).

Informing students of exactly what is expected, how each piece of work will be scored and graded, and how various assignments and assessments will be weighted in determining the final grade gives students the information they need in order to regulate their own work. With this knowledge, they can make well-informed decisions about how much time and energy to spend on each assignment or task. They can learn to recognize when they should revise and improve a piece of work before turning it in or when to revise their work further after the first attempt.

Teachers who plan their evaluation systems to assist students in the development of metacognition need to recognize that the capacity for self-regulation entails the use of a complex set of cognitive processes, such as recognition of whether they comprehend an idea or whether the learning strategy they are using is appropriate. The development of metacognition takes time. It also takes many learning experiences in which it is used and practiced by children. In the elementary grades, students need a great deal of scaffolding to help them gain these skills. Clear statements of what is expected and how to succeed, examples of what a good piece of work contains and what a poor piece of work looks like, precise and detailed feedback, and suggestions for improvement are all scaffolds that students need at this age.

An Illustration of a C-M Evaluation System

Imagine that all the sixth-grade teachers in an elementary school join together to plan a 9-week interdisciplinary unit on people and their environment. The cognitive goal of the unit is to inform students about the present dangers to the natural environment. The affective goal is to create in each student a sense of responsibility for the environment. The psychomotor goal stresses how to live in the environment, using it wisely.

The primary learning activities of this unit will include 4 weeks devoted to developing a knowledge base and understanding the basic concepts related to environmental concerns. Readings will be assigned, discussions planned, guest lecturers invited, and films ordered. During the entire fifth week, the whole group is scheduled to live at an outdoor education site learning how to use natural products, how to test for environmental hazards, and to create artwork and write poems, stories, essays, and dramas about the relationship of people to their environment. During the final 4 weeks, students will work in cooperative groups to investigate one environmental problem and present their findings and solutions to their peers in a science exhibit at the conclusion of the unit.

The primary objectives of this unit, with the criteria for success italicized in each, are listed below. The number of asterisks (*) next to each objective indicates the importance of that objective and the weight that will be given to its product in the final determination of grades.

Knowledge-Level Objective

*1. On a matching test, students will be able to *identify 7 out of 10 sites* of environmental pollution and connect them with the type of hazard that exists at that site.

Grade equivalents: A = 10 correct
                    B = 9 correct
                    C = 8 correct
                    D = 7 correct
                    F = less than 7 correct

Comprehension-Level Objective

*2. On a short-answer test, students will be able to write the definitions of *10 terms* related to the environment, *with no more than two errors.*

Grade equivalents: A = 10 correct
                    B = 9 correct
                    C = 8 correct
                    D = 7 correct
                    F = less than 7 correct

Application-Level Objectives

**3. Students will conduct *two tests* for water and air pollution during the outdoor education experience. They will write laboratory reports worth *10 points each* that include their observations, hypotheses, tests, and the results of their tests.

Grade equivalents: A = 20 points
                    B = 18 points
                    C = 16 points
                    D = 14 points
                    F = less than 14 points

*4. Students will demonstrate that they can find food and create a safe shelter in the natural environment. They will *identify at least 10 edi-*

ble foods, for 0.5 point each, and draw a picture, worth 5 points, of the shelter they would create out of natural materials.

Grade equivalents: A = 10 points
        B = 9 points
        C = 8 points
        D = 7 points
        F = less than 7 points

Analysis-Level Objective

*5. Students will create a chart showing cause and effect or a comparison between environmentally safe and hazardous practices for their cooperative group display at the science fair. The chart will contain *at least 10 comparison or cause-and-effect elements*.

Grade equivalents: A = 10 or more points
        B = 9 points
        C = 8 points
        D = less than 7 points
        F = not done or not handed in

Synthesis-Level Objective

*6. Students will create a song, poem, story, essay, play, or skit to read aloud or perform at an assembly during the outdoor education week. Each work will contain a description of how people interact with nature and stress the importance of good ecology. *Criteria: Each work will receive 0, 1, or 2 points for each of the following three elements: Fits Topic, Clarity, Interest, Length, and Originality.*

Grade equivalents: A = 9–10 points
        B = 7–8 points
        C = 5–6 points
        D = 3–4 points
        F = not done or not handed in

Evaluation-Level Objective

***7. Students will write a three-page essay giving their opinions of the most serious concern related to the environment. The essay will contain *at least five elements* as supporting evidence for this evaluation and will suggest *at least three ways* people can solve the problem and alleviate the hazard. *Criteria: 1 point for each element stated above. In addition, each essay will receive 0, 1, or 2 points for each of the following elements: Clarity and Originality, for a total of 12 points.*

Grade equivalents: A = 10 points
        B = 8 points
        C = 6 points
        D = 4 points
        F = not done or not handed in

Note that these seven assessment methods have a total of 10 asterisks. That means that each asterisk symbolizes a value worth 10% of the final grade. Most objectives are each worth 10%; the set of experiments is worth 20%; and the final essay is worth 30% of the final grade. The teachers planned the unit this way so that they could easily weigh the value of each assessment in determining the students' final grades for the unit. They plan to distribute a list of all the requirements, with their criteria for grades and the weight of each grade, to the students on the first day of the unit so that the students will know at the outset what is expected of them and how they can succeed.

When they correct each of the seven assignments, the teachers plan to provide adequate feedback in their written comments or in a conference with the students so that they know what they did that was successful and what did not meet the criteria. Then the students will have 1 week to make revisions and improvements on all assignments except the two objective tests if they wish to raise their grades.

At the end of the unit, the grades may be recorded in the teacher's gradebook, as shown in Figure 12–1.

Computation of Grades

The computation of the final grades for the unit is shown in Figure 12–2. It involves a straightforward computation of an average grade by awarding numerical equivalents to each letter grade, multiplying each grade by its weighted value, adding the seven items, and dividing the total score by 10. Note that although there are seven items, the average score is computed by a factor of 10 in order to take into account the greater weight placed on two of the items.

An alternative method for computing grades is to award points for each assessment product, add up the points, and compare the total to a predetermined scale. In this unit, each of the seven assessments could be assigned a certain point value. Refer back to the objectives with their point values. Notice that objectives 1, 2, 4, 5, and 6 are each worth 10 points. Objective 3, which is considered to be twice as important as the others, has a point count that is also double in value. Only objective 7 must be weighted to reflect its relative value. The logical method for calculating a student's total points for the unit, then, is to record the raw score or points in the gradebook, multiplying objective 7 by 3 before recording it. This

FIGURE 12–1

Teacher's Gradebook Showing the Grades Recorded for the Objectives of the People and Their Environment Unit

Name of Student	Graded Objectives						
	*1	*2	**3	*4	*5	*6	***7
Jane	A	B	B	A	C	A	B
Bill	B	C	A	B	C	C	B
Gary	D	C	A	C	B	F	C

Note: Assignments and weights shown by *.

FIGURE 12-2
Teacher's Computations of Grades for the People and Their Environment Unit

Name	*1	*2	**3	*4	*5	*6	***7	Final Grade
			Value of Grade (×) Weight (*)					
Jane	A	B	B	A	C	A	A	
	4×1	3×1	3×2	4×1	2×1	4×1	4×3	
								35/10 =
	4	+ 3	+ 6	+ 4	+ 2	+ 4	+ 12	3.5 = A
Bill	B	C	A	B	C	C	B	
	3×1	2×1	4×2	3×1	2×1	2×1	3×3	
								29/10 =
	3	+ 2	+ 8	+ 3	+ 2	+ 2	+ 9	2.9 = B
Gary	D	C	A	C	B	F	C	
	1×1	2×1	4×2	2×1	3×1	0×1	2×3	
								22/10 =
	1	+ 2	+ 8	+ 2	+ 3	+ 0	+ 6	2.2 = C

Values of Grades for Computation Purposes

A = 4.0   B = 3.0   C = 2.0   D = 1.0   F = 0.0

Final Grade Point Averages Equivalent to Final Letter Grade

A = 3.5–4.0   B = 2.5–3.4   C = 1.5–2.4   D = 0.5–1.4   F = 0.0–0.4

produces a total of 100 points for all the assessments in the unit. Using 10% increments, the grades can be assigned as follows:

A = >90 points
B = >80 points
C = >70 points
D = >60 points
F = <60 points

The rationale for using this system instead of the first one is that it diminishes the focus on grades during the unit itself. Rather than receiving a C on a paper, the student receives a certain number of points. With appropriate critical feedback, students may be able to revise their first attempts to earn more points. When students are allowed and encouraged to revise and return their work, they are able to monitor their own progress. By keeping track of how many points they have earned to date, they can decide for themselves whether they need to revise and return their work for additional points. Deadlines for revisions, such as 1 week after receiving the corrected paper, can be used to hold students accountable for timely efforts on their own behalf. This system fits very well with the R-A philosophy of encouraging students to use metacognitive skills in evaluating and taking control of their own school achievements.

Whatever method you choose for determining grades, after they are computed they are recorded in the children's cumulative folder and on the report cards that are sent home to parents. Intermediate report cards are likely to use letter grades to sum up the student's achievement in each academic subject. Some report cards, such as the one in Figure 12–3, may also provide checklists of subskills beneath the letter grade as a means of explaining to parents how the letter grade was determined. Because few report cards have categories for interdisciplinary units such as the one on people and their environment, it is likely that the teachers in this example would record the grade for this unit under Science or Social Studies and explain in an accompanying note what the grade represents.

Within this unit, many learning experiences are planned, but only these seven products will be assessed as a means of determining a final grade. The teachers who created this unit are very proud of the way these assessments evaluate learning at all six levels of Bloom's Taxonomy. They are also pleased that the assessments allow students with different learning styles to demonstrate what they have learned.

They have agreed that they will inform students of exactly what is expected at each stage of the learning process. During the first 4 weeks, when the students are reading and doing assignments to establish a knowledge base, the teachers will inform them of the nature of the two objective tests and provide them with samples of the items on the test.

When the classes go to the outdoor education site, the teachers will inform the students which activities are to be graded and how much each grade is worth. They will provide examples of well-written lab reports and will demonstrate the difference between a creative writing product that fits the topic and has clarity and originality, and one that misses the topic and lacks clarity and originality (for example, one that borrows heavily from an existing nursery rhyme or song).

Back in the classroom, as students begin their individual investigations, the teachers will show examples of well-researched charts and give examples of evaluation essays that contain all important elements. At all stages of the evaluation process, the teachers will encourage their students to revise and return their first attempts so that they can experience the good feeling of being in control of their own success in school.

Writing Anecdotal Records

In most school districts, teachers are responsible for writing three or four report cards per year. These contain descriptions of each student's current level of accomplishment in each of the major areas of the curriculum, plus a summary of the child's work habits and social adjustment to school and peers. In the primary grades, report cards usually consist of either anecdotal records or checklists of skills rather than letter grades. Some school districts may use both (see Figures 12–4 and 12–5).

FIGURE 12–3
Intermediate Report Card

Name _____

Explanation of Marks

A—Excellent Progress
B—Very Good Progress
C—Satisfactory Progress
D—Minimal Progress
U—Unsatisfactory Progress

Sub Skills

/ / Meeting expectations
/ √ / Needs Improvement
/ + / Exceeding Expectations

Level of Materials

1—Above Grade Level
2—At Grade Level
3—Below Grade Level

GENERAL STUDY SKILLS

Listens Attentively
Is Prepared for Class
Works Independently
Completes Work on Time
Uses Time Well
Cooperates in Group Work
Follows Directions
Works Accurately
Uses Assignment Notebook
Works Neatly

PERSONAL AND SOCIAL GROWTH

Accepts & Respects Authority
Practices Self Control
Respects Rights, Opinions
 and Property of Others
Assumes Responsibility
 for Own Actions

LANGUAGE ARTS

READING

Level of Materials
Effort
Comprehends What is Read
Understands Vocabulary
Uses Word Analysis Skills
Applies Reference/Study Skills
Reads for Pleasure

WRITING

Effort
Organizes Ideas
Uses Correct Grammar
Uses Proper Mechanics
Proofreads
Expresses Ideas

SPELLING

Effort
Applies Spelling Skills
Knows Assigned Words

HANDWRITING

Effort
Legibility

SPEAKING

Expresses Ideas Clearly
Uses Correct Grammar
Projects Voice

MATHEMATICS

Level of Materials
Effort
Knows Basic Facts (+,-,x,÷)
Understands Concepts
Computes Accurately
Uses Problem Solving Strategies
Understands Geometry

SCIENCE

Effort
Understands Concepts
Draws Conclusions
Makes Observations and
 Comparisons
Participates in Activities

SOCIAL STUDIES

Effort
Understands Concepts
Applies Graph, Chart and
 Map Skills
Is Aware of Current Events
Participates in Activities

From Glenview School District No. 34, Glenview, Illinois. Reprinted with permission.

FIGURE 12-4
Primary Report Card (Checklist of Skills)

Name: _____ Year: _____

School: _____ Teacher: _____

The marks on this page reflect your child's performance. If your child is working significantly above or below grade level, that information is noted in the comment sections.

Explanation of Marks

+ - applies appropriate grade level skills on consistent basis

√ - has been introduced to skills

| - needs further practice on appropriate grade level skills

No mark indicates that your child has not been introduced to this skill at the present time.

READING

	1	2	3
has concept of word			
identifies consonant sounds			
recognizes sight words			
uses pictures and context clues			
recognizes word family patterns			
applies phonic skills to attack new words			
recognizes long and short vowels			
comprehends material read			
can retell story in sequence			
predicts outcomes			

LANGUAGE ARTS

	1	2	3
expresses thoughts orally			
writes words			
writes sentences			
writes stories			
spelling			
handwriting			
recognizes capitalization			
recognizes punctuation			

MATHEMATICS

	1	2	3
sorts and classifies			
identifies patterns			
demonstrates concept of number			
recognizes numbers			
writes numbers in sequence			
addition			
subtraction			
uses problem solving strategies			
place value			
time			
money			
graphing			

SCIENCE

Present Unit

	1	2	3
participates in activities			
understands concepts			

SOCIAL STUDIES

Present Unit

	1	2	3
participates in activities			
understands concepts			

+ - indicates appropriate behavior

√ - indicates need for improvement in this area

CITIZENSHIP AND WORK HABITS

	1	2	3
has positive attitude			
practices self-control			
assumes responsibility			
respects rules			
respects property/materials			
respects people			
uses good manners			
cooperates with others			
puts forth effort			
has pride in schoolwork			
listens attentively			
follows directions			
uses organizational skills			
makes good use of time			
completes assignments on time			
works well independently			
works well in group activities			

From Glenview School District No. 34, Glenview, Illinois. Reprinted with permission.

FIGURE 12–5
Primary Report Card (Anecdotal Record)

Date: _____   **Name:** _____

COMMENTS ON READING DEVELOPMENT

COMMENTS ON SCIENCE/SOCIAL STUDIES

COMMENTS ON LANGUAGE ARTS DEVELOPMENT

COMMENTS ON PERSONAL AND SOCIAL SKILLS

COMMENTS ON MATHEMATICS DEVELOPMENT

COMMENTS ON STUDY SKILLS

SUGGESTIONS

From Glenview School District No. 34, Glenview, Illinois. Reprinted with permission.

The advantage of this double format is that it allows the teachers to describe and report their direct observations of a student's actual behaviors and accomplishments with sufficient detail so that parents clearly understand the student's strengths and deficiencies. This is especially useful for such skill areas as listening, speaking, writing, study habits, social skills, and interests (Gronlund & Linn, 1990).

In the upper elementary grades, anecdotal records are used less often in report cards. But when a concern about a student arises, the teacher's daily observations of the child's work habits or social interactions can be important sources of data to help parents or school personnel understand the particular needs and strengths of the child. These observations may be augmented by the use of written anecdotal records of what the teacher observes. For example, if a child comes to school late, appears tired, and has difficulty sitting still at her desk, the teacher may want to document these observations by keeping a short anecdotal record for a week, recording how late the child is every morning, and describing episodes of falling asleep or inattentiveness. When this written record is shown to the parents, it is more likely to enlist their cooperation with the teacher in seeking answers to the problem than if the teacher simply reports orally that the child is "always late and too tired to work."

To be used to their best advantage, anecdotal records should be limited to observations of specific skills, social problems, or behavioral concerns. If a teacher sets out to record every behavior and event in a child's school day, the process will become too tiring and difficult to be feasible. Instead, when a student is exhibiting a particular behavior or deficiency in a skill area, the teacher can focus on daily descriptions of that one area and succeed in producing a useful document.

The major limitation or disadvantage of the anecdotal record is the tendency of teachers to project their own value judgments into the description of a child's behavior or accomplishment. This is due, in part, to the tendency to observe what fits one's preconceived notions. "For example, they will tend to notice more desirable qualities in those pupils they like best and more undesirable qualities in those they like least" (Gronlund & Linn, 1990, p. 380). The recommended way to avoid this tendency is to keep descriptions of observed incidents separate from your interpretation. First, state exactly what happened in nonjudgmental words. Then, if you wish to add your interpretation of the event, do so in a separate paragraph and label it as such (Gronlund & Linn, 1990, pp. 381–382).

In general, a single observation is seldom as meaningful as a series of events in understanding a student's behavior. Therefore, anecdotal records should contain brief descriptions of related incidents over a period of time to provide a reliable picture of a student's behavior.

Organizing Portfolios to Document Accomplishments

Portfolios are among the newest methods of documenting student accomplishment. They provide an excellent source of data when accompanied by an anecdotal record. As mentioned in Chapter 11, they may contain work samples in one subject area alone or reflect the student's work across the entire curriculum. Teachers who tend to think of the curriculum as a number of separate subjects are likely to use separate portfolios of work, while teachers who think of the curriculum as multidimensional are likely to include all relevant work samples in one portfolio. Some teachers may create portfolio categories such as *verbal work, technical work,* and *artistic work.*

When portfolios are meant to be used to document student accomplishment, they must be organized in such a way that they reveal the development of a skill or the growing understanding of a set of ideas. Three collection strategies that are likely to demonstrate growth and change are what Wolf (1989) calls "biographies of works, a range of works and reflections" (p. 37).

The biography of a work consists of several drafts of a work, showing the student's initial conception of the project, the first attempts, and the final product. By collecting these items, the teacher is able to document the growth and development that has occurred for this student. Wolf further recommends that after this collection is complete, the teacher may ask the student to reexamine all stages of the work and reflect on the process and the products from beginning to end. The student's reflection may be done in writing or captured on audiotape (and later transcribed on paper) and should then be included in the portfolio itself. This self-evaluation is valuable in helping the student develop metacognitive abilities that can then be applied to future projects.

Wolf suggests that teachers should collect a range of works, meaning a diverse collection, consisting of journals, essays, poems, drawings, charts, graphs, letters, tests, and samples of daily work. When they use the portfolios as a basis for a parent–teacher conference, this range will allow the teacher to discuss and document many different aspects of the child's school accomplishments.

Primary teachers must take responsibility for collecting and filing all items in students' portfolios. In the upper grades, however, students may be asked to keep their own. The teacher may suggest items to be included, and the student may decide on others. At the end of the unit on people and the environment, for example, each student may have a portfolio containing the tests, lab reports, essays, creative writing, and charts they created for the unit.

At the end of a unit or term, the teacher can collect the portfolios, examine them, ask for reflections on certain items or sets of items, and arrange the materials in chronological order in preparation for a parent–teacher conference. Many times teachers ask students to create covers for their portfolios, which are then displayed during parent open house visits or conferences.

Portfolios of student work are an excellent way to communicate with parents about a student's accomplishments. When the parent and teacher look at the writing samples together, they can both understand the child's strengths and weaknesses at a glance. When a parent sees the signed contract and the completed work, both parent and teacher view the same evidence to support the resulting grades.

Involving Students in Evaluation Procedures

For C-M teachers, the natural extension of the teaching process is the interactive evaluation process that encourages students to become active evaluators of their own efforts and products. The current writing programs organized around periodic student–teacher conferences and the grouping of children who edit each other's work are excellent examples of this type of evaluation. In classrooms that feature writing programs, the role of the teacher in evaluation is to confer with the students about their current writing projects and to ask questions that engage the students in analyzing what they have written.

Teachers may use open-ended questions designed to gather information on what the child has intended to do in a piece of writing. When the teacher has a sufficient understanding of the student's goal, teacher and student may begin to zero in on ways to improve the quality of the writing so that it more nearly matches the child's purpose. This may mean correcting the mechanics of the writing so that it can be understood by others, or it may mean guiding the student to rethink the way a passage is written and to consider new ways of stating the ideas.

The editing groups used in such writing programs encourage students to learn how to listen to and respect the work being created by their peers. Students in a group, typically, each read aloud from a current piece of writing and then answer questions on the content from the other students in the group. Through this type of interactive evaluation, students may learn how to work cooperatively, accept critical feedback, and write better at the same time.

This interactive evaluation system can be used in other parts of the elementary curriculum as well. "What did you learn?" should form the core of the classroom evaluation. The more often this question is asked, the easier it is for students to identify and receive the help they need. It is a question children can learn to ask themselves (Oakes & Lipton, 1990, p. 132).

Interactive evaluation procedures are the benchmark of the C-M teaching philosophy. The purpose of the R-A evaluation system is simply to sum up and communicate what each student has gained and how the achievement of one student relates to those of the others in the class. But a C-M evaluation system is designed to breed success and enhance students' metacognitive capacities. It is as much a part of the *learning process* as it is a part of the assessment process. In fact, the long-term goals of C-M teachers are likely to emphasize the development of independence, self-responsibility, self-discipline, and self-evaluation as important affective goals of education. These goals are achieved through the development of metacognitive processes as children learn to understand how to succeed in any learning environment.

OPPORTUNITIES FOR REFLECTION

▼ Reflective Essay: What Grades Mean to You

Did you get good grades in elementary school? Do you believe that the grades you received were an accurate reflection of your effort and achievement? How will you determine the grades in your classroom?

▼ Classroom Visit: Ask to View the Classroom Teacher's Gradebook

What system does this teacher use for recording grades? Are there elements of this system that seem useful to you? Does the teacher use an absolute or a relative frame of reference? Which would you use? Do the students in this class appear to understand the teacher's grading policies and expectations? What would you do to improve their understanding?

REFERENCES

ANDERSON, L. (1989). Learners and learning. In M. Reynolds (Ed.), *Knowledge base for the beginning teacher (KBBT)* (pp. 85–104). New York: Pergamon Press.

ATTEA, W. (n.d.). *Student progress report handbook.* Glenview, IL: Glenview Public School District No. 34.

BLOOM, B. (1982). *Human characteristics and school learning.* New York: McGraw-Hill.

EISNER, E. (1985). *Educational imagination* (2nd ed.). New York: Macmillan.

GRONLUND, N., & LINN, R. (1990). *Measurement and evaluation in teaching.* New York: Macmillan.

HIRSCH, E. (1987). *Cultural literacy: What every American needs to know.* Boston: Houghton Mifflin.

KIDDER, T. (1989). *Among schoolchildren.* Boston: Houghton Mifflin.

OAKES, J., & LIPTON, M. (1990). *Making the best of schools.* New Haven, CT: Yale University Press.

WOLF, D. (1989). Portfolio assessment: Sampling student work. *Educational Leadership, 46*(7), 35–39.

CHAPTER 13

Reflective Teachers and the School Community

AT THE BEGINNING of Chapter 1, Lori Shoults described the many thoughts, feelings, and decisions she had to make on her first day of teaching. In the week prior to that first day, Lori spent a lot of time in her classroom setting up bulletin boards and learning centers. As she worked that week, many of her new students and their parents who had come to the school for registration stopped by her classroom to see the "new teacher." Some stood outside her door, looking in quietly until she approached them and introduced herself. Others came into the room and looked around, exclaiming over the brightly decorated walls. The children were all interested in trying to discern whether the new teacher was "nice" and whether they thought they would be happy in her class.

Their visits, before the first day of school had even arrived, alerted Lori to the fact that she had more than the needs of 28 students to consider. She also had to be aware of and concerned with the needs of their parents.

Some parents of primary children may be especially reluctant to see the beginning of school because, for them, it marks an end to an important phase in their lives. For 5 years, they've had complete jurisdiction over the lives of their children. Now they recognize that the teacher may have almost as much influence over their children as they have. I have observed the parent of a first grader, for example, standing outside the school after dropping off the child and saying tearfully, "But we've had lunch together every day of his life."

For the majority of mothers, many of whom work outside the home and whose children have gone to day care centers and preschools, this leavetaking may not be so abrupt, but it is still a significant event in their own lives, as well as those of their children. Many mothers feel a strong interest in, and responsibility for, determining whether this particular classroom is a healthy and welcoming environment for their children. For this reason, they are likely to come to school, on one pretext or another, in the first days of school, just to see for themselves that their children are in good hands.

Beginning teachers may feel somewhat overwhelmed by these visits. All their available energy has gone into planning the curriculum, moving furniture and decorating the classroom, and meeting and becoming acquainted with the other teachers in the school. When a parent suddenly shows up, unannounced, it can be unsettling, especially if the parent wants to ask questions when the students are present. When this occurs, it is necessary for the teacher to suggest, politely but assertively, another time for this impromptu conference: "I'm sorry, Mrs. Jones, but all my attention is needed in the class right now. Would you prefer to talk about this after school or tomorrow morning at 8:15?"

Throughout the school year, there are many occasions where the teacher is expected to communicate with parents, either singly or in large groups. In addition, many classroom teachers invite parents to become involved in the life of the classroom. This chapter will describe some methods of establishing a manageable and mutually beneficial two-way communication pattern with parents and other members of the community.

TWO-WAY COMMUNICATION WITH PARENTS

Fall Open House

When parents come to visit the classroom early in the year, one method of deflecting their concerns is to state that they will be able to have many of their questions answered within a few weeks at the annual Fall Open House (sometimes called *Back to School Night*). This event is planned especially for that purpose in many school districts.

The Fall Open House is usually held on an evening in late September. To prepare for the event, teachers are asked to be ready to describe their goals for the year and give an overall picture of the school's curriculum at that grade level. The event usually begins in the school auditorium or other large meeting room, where the principal welcomes everyone to the school and describes the important events that the entire school has planned for the coming year. The teachers are introduced, with special attention given to presenting any new teachers on the faculty. At the conclusion of this general meeting, the teachers are released to go to their classrooms and make themselves ready for the Open House. After a few minutes, the visitors are dismissed from the general meeting to find their children's classroom.

When the parents assemble in the classroom, the teacher makes a short presentation to the entire group, describing what is planned for the year. A time for questions of interest to the entire group is also likely to occur. Because most school districts intend the Fall Open House to be a time for general discussions of goals and curriculum, there is no planned opportunity for individual parents to ask teachers for specific information about their own child's achievement or behavior. If parents approach the teacher and begin to discuss personal concerns, it is expected that the teacher will suggest an alternative time and place for an individual conference.

Parent–Teacher Conferences

Conferences between individual parents and teachers vary greatly in purpose. Some are used primarily for the diagnosis of a problem or concern, while others are set up to report to the parents about a child's progress in school. Diagnostic conferences were described in Chapter 3, but will be discussed briefly in this context as well, since they are such a valuable means of evaluation.

If either the teacher or the parent has a serious concern about a child, one or the other may arrange a conference in the first weeks of school. When teachers, for example, observe unusually aggressive, passive, depressed, or antisocial behavior in a child, they are wise to call home immediately and set up a conference right away to gain information about the nature of the child's problem. This is especially true when a child's behavior disrupts other students in the class.

Setting up a conference sends an important signal to a student who is exhibiting unusual or unacceptable behavior. It tells the student that the teacher is withit and is going to take action to correct the problem rather than let it go. It allows the teacher to seek information about the underlying reasons for the observed behavior. In a conference of this type, it is recommended that the student attend with the parents in order to gain a better understanding of the adults' view of the behavior.

When the conference takes place, the teacher should describe the behavior and, if possible, supplement the oral description with written anecdotal reports of examples of the behavior. The teacher should express concern about the behavior and then ask both the student and the parents to explain why it is occurring.

"Students usually cannot explain fully why they act as they do, and teachers should not expect them to. If the students had such insight, they probably would not be behaving symptomatically in the first place. Instead, the hope is that clues or helpful information will emerge from the discussion" (Good and Brophy, 1987, p. 293).

When the parents discuss their own views of the child's problem, the teacher may gain significant insight by learning about the home environment. For example, the parents may agree that they have observed the same behavior at home and that it seems to be related to a crisis the family is dealing with, such as a death, divorce, lost job, or move. When the teacher, the child, and the parents confront this matter together, they can begin to put together a workable plan to help support the student during this difficult period and, at the same time, help the child gain awareness about the effects of the behavior on others.

Conferences don't always result in such harmonious cooperation. Parents may not present much useful information. On occasion, they may become very defensive or resentful of the suggestion that their child's behavior is unacceptable. In their family, this behavior may be okay. For example, a fifth-grade teacher was alarmed to see a boy walk into her class on the first day of school with a T-shirt that read "Born to Raise Hell!" True to the message on the shirt, the child fought with other children at least once a day. When the parents were called in for a conference and the teacher described this behavior to them, the father replied, "So what? I tell my kids not to let anyone get the best of them." From the words and the father's tone of voice, the teacher learned that fighting was an acceptable behavior in that family. No happy resolution was discovered in this conference, but it did give the teacher some additional insight into the source and the depth of the boy's difficulties in social interactions with his peers.

Conferences designed for reporting on student progress rather than for diagnostic purposes usually take place in the late fall to coincide with the end of the first marking period and the first report card. In many districts, the parents are asked to come to the school for a conference with the teacher shortly after report cards are sent home. This gives the parents an opportunity to look at the report card and think about the questions and concerns they may want to raise at the conference. Some school districts require parents to come to the school to pick up the child's report card and have a conference with the teacher. In this case, the teacher explains the grades and observations to the parent as the parent views the report card for the first time. This second strategy is used primarily to make sure that parents do attend the conference.

Report card conferences are generally approximately 15 to 30 minutes in length. They may be offered during the day and at night so that parents who work during the day may choose a night conference. Usually 1 or 2 school days are used for the fall conferences. In some school districts, the entire process is repeated in the spring. A schedule of 30 conferences over a period of 1 or 2 days is a very tiring experience for most teachers. They may find that conference days are more exhausting than regular teaching days. This is due primarily to the tension caused by the teachers' recognition that they are responsible for the smooth flow of conversation and information. When this feeling of responsibility is multiplied by a factor of 30 in a few short days, it is easy to see how draining it can be.

To minimize the tension, it is extremely important that teachers plan each conference very carefully. Prior to the event, reflective teachers often write a page of notes about each student, highlighting the accomplishments and the matters of concern that the teacher wants to discuss with the parents.

In addition to planning what you want to say about each child, it is recommended that you make a general plan on how to conduct your conferences. The primary purpose of the report card conferences is to inform the parents about the child's progress in your class. But the conference is also designed to elicit information from the parents that may help you to help the child. The parents may also have concerns that they wish to discuss. To accomplish all of these things in one brief conference is very difficult. To do so, you must act as the timekeeper and allot a reasonable amount of time to each purpose. The parent will not be concerned about going overtime, but you will because you will be aware that the next set of parents is waiting outside the door for their appointment with you.

Gronlund and Linn (1990) suggest that you consider the following elements when planning your conferences:

1. Make plans for each conference. For each child, make a list of the points you want to cover and the questions you want to ask.
2. Begin the conference in a positive manner. Making a positive statement about the child, such as "Betty really enjoys helping others," or "Derek is an expert on dinosaurs," is likely to create a cooperative and friendly atmosphere.
3. Present the student's strong points before describing areas needing improvement. Present samples of work and focus on what the child can do and what he or she still has to learn.
4. Encourage parents to participate and share information. You must be willing to listen as well as talk. They may have questions and con-

cerns about the school and about their child's behavior that need to be brought out into the open before constructive, cooperative action can take place.

5. Plan a course of action cooperatively. Guide the discussion toward a series of steps that can be taken by the teacher and the parents to assist the child. At the end of the conference, review these steps with the parents.

6. End the conference with a positive comment. Thank the parents for coming and say something positive about the student such as, "Erik has a good sense of humor and I enjoy having him in my class" (pp. 445–446).

The regularly scheduled report card conferences may be the only times you will meet with the parents of most of your students. But for others, those whose behavior or learning problems are quite serious, it is necessary to continue to contact the parents by telephone or in follow-up conferences in order to monitor whether the cooperative plan of action is being implemented and what effects it is having.

Effective two-way communication with parents is essential for assisting students with severe problems. In working with children whose behavior interferes with their learning in school, an excellent resource for both teachers and parents is Rimm's (1986) *The Underachievement Syndrome: Causes and Cures*. This book describes many of the most feared behavior problems that teachers must face: hyperactivity, passiveness, perfectionism, rebellion, bullying, and manipulative behaviors. Rimm believes that these behaviors cause children to achieve much less than they are capable of achieving in school. In her studies of underachievement, she has discovered that most of these behaviors were learned by children in response to some elements of their home environment. Changing the behavior takes a concerted effort by the parents to isolate the causes and create new procedures to help children learn healthier, more productive behavior patterns that can lead to success.

Often it is the teacher who spots the self-defeating behavior. Parents have been living with the child for so long that they may not see that the child's behavior is unusual, and they may not be able to recognize how it affects the child's school achievement. Some examples of home situations that may lead to underachievement are the following:

▼ *The Overwelcome Child:* Although it has long been recognized that an unwelcome or rejected child is likely to have problems in life, it is also likely that excessive attention can cause achievement and emotional problems. When parents overprotect and overindulge, the child may develop a pattern of not taking initiative and of waiting for others to do the child's bidding.

▼ *Early Health Problems:* When a child is born with allergies, birth defects, or other handicaps and parents respond by investing themselves almost totally in the child's well-being, a set of behaviors similar to that of the overwelcome child can develop.

▼ *Particular Sibling Combinations:* Birth order and sibling rivalry affect all children, but some combinations may be particularly damaging to a child's achievement. A student who is the sibling of a child who has severe health problems or is considered to be extremely gifted may feel left out or inadequate in comparison to the sibling. This can lead to the development of attention-getting behavior patterns such as clowning or mischief making, which may prevent the child from achieving fully.

▼ *Specific Marital Problems:* A single parent may develop a very close relationship with the child as a result of seeing the child as the only purpose for living. The parent may treat the child more like a spouse or a partner than a child, thus giving the child too much power. The child may learn to expect power and is not willing to give it up to conform to the requirements of the school (Rimm, 1990, pp. 24–32).

These are four of the many possible situations that can cause children to develop behaviors that may prevent them from achieving well in school. When a teacher spots a child who is exhibiting overly dependent or overly aggressive behaviors, it is important to confer with the child's parents, to report the problem, and to learn how the behavior first developed and how the parents are responding to it. The first step toward a positive behavior change is for the teacher to describe and give examples of the behavior and the effects it has on the child's achievement. The parents may deny that the behavior exists or that it is serious, but if the teacher is successful in establishing a cooperative two-way dialogue with the parents, this may lead to new insights for all of them.

If parents do acknowledge the behavior, the next step is for you to describe the changes you plan to make at school to support the development of new, more positive behavior patterns and to suggest modifications that the parents may make at home. Together with the parents, set some reasonable goals for the child in terms of both behaviors and grades. Discuss methods of helping the child reach these goals, and agree on a plan that fits the child and the situation. Then specify the ways that you plan to continue your communication with the parents about your joint goals and plan of action, such as daily reports (Figure 13–1), weekly reports (Figure 13–2), or frequent telephone conferences (Rimm, 1986, p. 168).

Rimm cautions that children will not change their behavior just because the adults in their lives want them to do so. The child must want to break the underachieving patterns and substitute for them behaviors that lead to success. Both the teacher and the parents must also confer with the child, describing the behaviors and their effects in words the child can understand and accept. When the teacher, parent, and child all have the same goal and are working together on a plan of action tailored to fit the needs of the child, it is quite possible that the child will succeed.

Independent contracts are also useful support systems for helping children change behavior. A contract can specify work that is to be done, with deadlines and expectations for success. It can be used to specify behavioral expectations as well. When the teacher negotiates the contract with the child ahead of time, there is an intrinsic incentive to complete it—after all, the child helped to create it and decide what would be required. A sense of ownership is likely to increase the likelihood of the contract being fulfilled.

FIGURE 13–1
Daily Evaluation Form

```
STUDENT                    TEACHER
NAME_____      NAME_____      DATE_____

Assignments Completed: _____ All _____ Most _____ Half _____ Less than Half

Quality of general class work: _____ Excellent _____ Satisfactory
                               _____ Fair         _____ Unsatisfactory

Behavior:  _____ Excellent _____ Satisfactory _____ Fair
           _____ Unsatisfactory

Comments: _____
_____
_____
_____

Thank you very much for your help.
```

From *The Underachievement Syndrome: Causes and Cures* (p. 172) by S. Rimm, 1986. Watertown, WI: Apple. Copyright 1986 by Apple. Reprinted by permission.

Additional extrinsic incentives may be employed if the teacher believes that these are useful in a given circumstance. Either the parents can provide the rewards, such as the new bicycle in Figure 13–3, or the teacher can provide rewards in exchange for earning points for successful completion of items on the contract.

FIGURE 13–2
Weekly Evaluation Form

```
STUDENT                    TEACHER
NAME_____      NAME_____      DATE_____

Subject: _____

Approximate grade for week: _____

Assignments Completed: _____ All _____ Most _____ Half _____ Less than Half

Behavior:  _____ Excellent _____ Satisfactory _____ Fair
           _____ Unsatisfactory

Comments and missing assignments: _____
_____
_____
_____
```

From *The Underachievement Syndrome: Causes and Cures* (p. 173) by S. Rimm, 1986. Watertown, WI: Apple. Copyright 1986 by Apple. Reprinted by permission.

FIGURE 13–3
Sample Study Plan Contract

Troy, his mom, dad, and Mrs. Norbert agree that Troy will spend at least one hour each day, five days a week, studying and doing his homework independently at his desk in his room. He will do this before he watches TV and there will be no radio, stereo, or TV on in his room during study time. After his work is complete his dad will review his materials and together award him points which Troy will save up toward the purchase of a bicycle. Troy's mom and dad will not remind him to study and he will take the initiative independently. This agreement may be changed only by mutual agreement of the undersigned.

Troy
Mom
Dad
Teacher

From *The Underachievement Syndrome: Causes and Cures* (p. 211) by S. Rimm, 1986. Watertown, WI: Apple. Copyright 1986 by Apple. Reprinted by permission.

This contract exemplifies the type of plan that may be created as a result of a successful parent–teacher conference. In this case, the behavior observed by the teacher was that the child was not turning in homework. Alerting the parents to this concern resulted in a discussion of the probable causes. The parents were able to accept the reality of the problem and its negative consequences for their child's achievement. They were also able to suggest that the major cause might be the fact that the child and his family watch a great deal of television, beginning right after school and continuing up to bedtime. When the teacher alerted the parents to the problem, they expressed a willingness to do their part to help change the child's behavior, and together they drafted this contract. Daily reports can be written by the teacher for a while to inform parents whether the homework is actually being turned in. Knowing that these daily reports will be written is likely to help all parties remember the commitment they have made.

One final caution about conducting parent–teacher conferences: Occasionally, participants in the conference may reveal a family problem that is unusual and extremely serious. Revelations of extreme poverty, desertion, or physical or sexual abuse can be made to a teacher by the student or the parents in a desperate attempt to get help. If this happens, the classroom teacher is well advised not to try to deal with this problem alone. If this happens to you, ask the parent to allow you to discuss this matter with the social services personnel in the school, and immediately contact the principal, school psychologist, social worker, and other members of the crisis team to assist in the matter.

Teaching in a Multicultural Community

When the language, culture, and values of the parents match those of the teachers in the child's school, communication is likely to be relatively clear and agreements not too difficult to achieve. When the culture of the child's home differs significantly from the culture of the teacher, the teacher must be especially willing to listen as well as talk during parent–teacher conferences.

Prior to the *Brown v. Board of Education* Supreme Court decision in 1954, children who were racially different from the white majority were often segregated in separate (and inferior) schools. Since that time, federal mandates have required school systems to integrate both the student bodies and the faculties of their schools. But federal laws have not been able to mitigate the subtler forms of racism that still exist in some educational settings.

Although America is known as a nation of immigrants, a melting pot of cultures, there has also been a traditionally accepted cultural norm that mirrors the philosophy of the white Anglo-Saxon majority. Other cultures have been known as *minority cultures*. The prevailing belief is that children from minority cultures must be taught the language and habits of the majority. Researchers have found that "to the extent that the home culture's practices and values are not acknowledged or incorporated by the school, parents may find that they are not able to support children in their academic pursuits even when it is their fervent wish to do so" (Florio-Ruane, 1989, p. 169).

Reflective teachers are aware that their own values and expectations may vary considerably from those of the families in their school community. But rather than assume that the children and their parents should be taught to mimic the language, behavior, and norms of the teacher's own culture, reflective teachers strive to gain a better understanding of the various cultures that make up the school community and to celebrate these differences by incorporating them into the curriculum.

In parent–teacher conferences, the reflective teacher is likely to ask with great interest about the home environment and the cultural values of the parents as a means of gaining a better understanding of the various cultures and conveying respect to the parents. When parents sense this respect from the teacher, they are more likely to return it and to feel that the teacher shares their own concerns for their child. It may be necessary for the teacher to be especially encouraging to parents of other cultures, urging them to share their own concerns and ask questions. People from many cultures were not raised to ask questions of teachers and may be very reluctant to do so. But if the teacher encourages them to ask questions or make suggestions for the child's benefit, they may feel comfortable enough to do so. This two-way communication and mutual understanding can lead to a more productive arrangement to work together to support the child's achievement at home and at school.

The needs of children and their parents who have emigrated to the United States from other countries are especially important, as First (1988) found when she interviewed them:

> Immigrant children and adolescents, many of whom have survived wars, political oppression, and economic deprivation, find that their problems are not over when they enter American schools. Confronted with hatred, prejudice, and violence in U.S. schools, many newcomers are left asking what they have done to deserve such treatment. One Vietnamese student spoke for many when he said, "I like school here. But I wish there would be more friendships among immigrants and American students." (p. 210)

A Spanish child revealed the following:

> I came upon a world unknown to me, a language I did not understand, and a
> school administration which made ugly faces at me every time I spoke Spanish.
> Many teachers referred to us as animals. Believe me, maintaining a half-decent
> image of yourself wasn't an easy thing. . . . I had enough strength of character to
> withstand the many school personnel who tried to destroy my motivation. But
> many of my classmates didn't make it. (p. 210)

The classroom teacher must demonstrate a willingness to assist culturally
different children and their parents as they make the difficult transition from one land
to another. One of the best ways to accomplish this is to show sensitivity and respect
for the cultures of all the children in the class. Each year, the teacher may plan a
special unit of study on the contributions of the cultures represented by the members
of the class. The parents of the students can be invited to participate in the learning
experience by visiting the classroom to show and tell the children about the crafts and
food of their countries. They can teach the children the songs and games of their
homelands. First (1988) believes that when teachers involve the parents in the education of their children, they send a powerful message that the school cares about
them (p. 210).

Visits to Students' Homes

When the teacher cares sufficiently about understanding the home and cultural
environments of their students, one way to seek information is to visit the children
and their families in their homes. This may be done by sending home a newsletter
early in the year, with the announcement that the teacher would enjoy meeting the
parents and seeing the children in their homes, and that invitations to do so will be
gladly received. This allows the parents to invite the teacher when it is a good time
for them.

The visit will probably take place after school or during the evening meal.
No agendas need to be established for such a visit; in fact, doing so would be
counterproductive. The visit is not a structured parent–teacher conference at all. It
is simply an opportunity for the teacher to understand more fully the conditions
under which the child lives. As the teacher shares the family's meal, looks at their
photographs, and hears some of their stories, it greatly enhances the feeling of the
child and the parents that they are respected members of the school community.

On occasion, it may become necessary for school personnel to make a more
structured visit with an agenda. This may occur if a child is having extremely serious
problems and is referred for special services and a psychological evaluation. In that
case, the school social worker or psychologist may visit the home to determine what
factor in the home environment may be causing the child's problems.

Newsletters and Notes

Many elementary teachers communicate with parents by sending home handwritten
notes describing a particular behavior or accomplishment of their child. In some
classrooms, a note from the teacher signifies only bad news that is sent home when
the teacher wants to describe an incident or pattern of misbehavior, a poor test result,

or excessive tardiness. More recently, many reflective teachers have considered how to use the note home to encourage good behavior and reward achievement. Many teachers now send home notes describing a special accomplishment, an improvement in classwork, or an act of friendliness or generosity by the child.

To ensure that all children benefit from this system, the teacher may send a note of good news home to the parents of a certain number of children per week until every child has had one. Others prefer not to use a schedule, but send a note whenever they observe a child doing something especially well. Without a schedule, however, it is important that teachers be careful not to favor some children over others.

In some classrooms, teachers prepare and send home classroom newsletters describing the important events planned for that week or month. The newsletter may contain items describing completed projects and new ones just getting underway. In the newsletter, the teacher can request parent volunteers for various projects and write notes of appreciation to parents who have recently helped out in some way.

In primary classrooms, the teacher generally takes full responsibility for creating the newsletter. But in intermediate and upper elementary classrooms, many teachers allow students to help write the items. They may use a computer program designed for creating newspaperlike formats. In this case, the production of the newsletter becomes more than just a method of communicating with parents. It becomes an enriching learning experience as well.

Parent Support of Educational Activities

If teachers are able to communicate the classroom goals for that year of school and to supply parents with regular newsletters or other reports of student progress, this increases the likelihood that the parents will support the school's educational goals at home.

Parents can support their child's education and increase the chances for the child's success in school if they understand what they can do to help and are capable of giving that help at home. Becker and Epstein (1982) report that teachers vary considerably in what they ask parents to do to support their children's education. This variation seems to be linked to the different expectations teachers have about what parents are capable of and willing to do. When asked what they request parents to do to support the child's achievement in school, many teachers have reported that they ask parents to read aloud to their children or allow the child to read aloud to them. To support this request, many teachers said that they were willing to loan school books and other materials to parents to use at home.

Many teachers have also reported that they frequently ask parents to take their children to the library. Many also suggest that parents ask their children what they did that day in school and discuss it with them. Teachers also occasionally suggest activities and games that can be used at home to support the educational goals of the class (Becker & Epstein, 1982).

Many parents welcome the opportunity to support their children in school-related activities. Teachers who regularly report to parents on classroom events and ask parents to participate by doing parallel activities in the home are likely to develop very productive two-way relationships with parents that can increase the child's self-esteem and achievement and, at the same time, add to the teacher's understanding of the student's home environment.

Telephone Calls

The telephone provides an important link between school and home. Teachers often call students' homes for the same reasons as they write notes. Some use a phone call to report a child's misbehavior and poor achievement in order to enlist the support and assistance of parents in correcting the problem. Other teachers try to call students' homes to report both positive and negative news. They may make their first call to report a problem or concern and follow up several days later with a second phone call to report that the student is making progress in solving the problem.

Teachers are often on the receiving end of telephone calls from students' homes as well. Parents may call to clarify something about an assignment or an announcement that they cannot understand from their child's description. If parents hear confusing stories about something that happened during the school day, they may call the teacher to find out what really occurred. Responding to these calls in an open and informative manner promotes a positive pattern of communication between home and school.

Occasionally, parents call in anger or frustration. They may disagree with the contents of the curriculum, the way a test was graded, or the way a classroom incident was handled. When a teacher receives one of these calls, it is very easy to become defensive and angry too. Dealing effectively with these calls takes mature, well-developed communication skills. It is difficult, but very important, to listen empathetically to what the parent says. Even when the instinctive reaction of most teachers is to break into the parent's statements and present their own side of the situation, it is more productive if the teacher's initial responses encourage the parent to describe the problem in more detail and express personal feelings.

After the parent has had an opportunity to describe fully the reason for the phone call, the teacher's side of the story can be presented in a quiet, nonthreatening, and nondefensive way. In a situation such as this, the teacher has the responsibility for attempting to resolve the conflict and creating a mutually acceptable solution.

For example, suppose that there is a fight in the classroom during the day and John is punched in the face by Dean, a much stronger boy. Because his lip is bleeding, the teacher decides to send John to the nurse. She then tries to talk to Dean to find out what prompted the fight. Dean claims he was provoked by John's name calling, and many children in the class support that claim. When John returns from the nurse, the teacher tells him that both he and Dean will have to stay in during recess for fighting. John seethes with anger for the rest of the day.

After school, the teacher is called to the phone to find John's very angry parent on the other end. "Why did you keep my son in for recess when he got hit by that bully? And why didn't you call me immediately when he got hit? Do you know he was bleeding? I'm going to come in right now and talk to your principal about this matter, and you will be sorry you treated my son this way!"

The instinctive reaction for most teachers is to jump in and explain after the first few words are spoken. If the parent continues to question the teacher's judgment, the teacher may soon feel as angry as the parent does. But reflective teachers recognize that there are going to be days like this in a classroom with 30 children and only 1 adult. They will try to keep their own feelings under control and say something to soothe the parent's hurt pride and upset feelings.

"I'm glad you called, Mrs. Jones. I can understand how you feel. Tell me how John's lip is now." This type of comment will help the teacher gather information and gain time to formulate a good response. Not all such problems can be readily resolved. It may be that the teacher and the parent will continue to have different points of view no matter how much they discuss it. If that is the case, it is necessary to acknowledge it and end the conversation with a comment such as "I recognize how you feel about this situation. I'm sorry John got hurt today, and I'll do my best to see that he is not involved in any more fights this year."

The key point of this section is expressed in the phrase "reflective teachers recognize that there are going to be days like this." There are days like this in every school year. There are incidents in which values clash and feelings are hurt. The beginning teacher may be shocked the first time this happens and overreact by feeling angry, guilty, or defensive. If possible, when incidents such as these occur in your classroom, remember that every teacher experiences conflict. Conflict is unavoidable in this career, and the first step in learning how to handle it is learning to expect and accept it as part of the job.

Spring Open House and Other Special Events

In the fall, the purpose of most conferences and open house events is to allow parents and teachers to get to know each other, communicate their goals for their children (students), and make plans for accomplishing these goals. As the year goes by, the purpose of most meetings between parents and teachers is for the teacher to demonstrate to the parents how these goals are being met.

Many classroom teachers invite parents frequently, perhaps as often as once a month, to attend exhibits, plays, assemblies, or other occasions for students to display what they are learning and what they have accomplished. Some of these events may be schoolwide assemblies, such as Thanksgiving plays and feasts, Christmas pageants, midwinter cultural fairs, and spring open houses in which collections of student work are displayed throughout the school.

Individual teachers may also invite the parents of their own students to school to view the performances or an exhibit of products resulting from a unit of study. These events are usually highly prized by students and parents, and are an excellent way for the teacher to interact and communicate continually with parents.

Consider, though, how some parents might feel if they attend a spring open house and find that their own child's work is not displayed. In some competitive classrooms, teachers tend to display only the papers with "100%" written across the top. For those children who rarely get perfect papers, this can be a very discouraging experience; for their parents, it is likely to be equally discouraging. If classroom displays include examples of students' work, it is important to display the best works of all students in approximately equal numbers.

To avoid creating a competitive environment, you may wish to display students' work inside their portfolios on their desks, so that parents can view the work done by their children alone. General classroom displays can consist of group projects and murals so that every child and parent can take equal pride in the classroom.

COMMUNITY INVOLVEMENT IN CLASSROOM ACTIVITIES

Parents as Volunteers

Parents volunteer to do many things in schools to benefit their own children and the larger community. Many parents enjoy being members of an all-school organization known as the *Parent Teacher Association (PTA)* or *Parent Teacher Organization (PTO)*. These organizations have regularly scheduled meetings and yearly fund-raising events to serve the needs of the school. In most cases, parents do the greatest part of the work on the committees, although teachers are usually represented as well.

In many schools, parents are encouraged to volunteer their time during the school day to assist teachers in educational or extracurricular programs. Parents can serve as coaches, assistant coaches, or referees for some sports events, such as all-school field day events. They often serve as helpers on class field trips, accompanying the class on the bus ride and throughout the day. Usually, teachers ask each adult to be responsible for a small group of children during the trip, reducing the adult:child ratio from 28:1 to 4:1 or 5:1.

In the classroom, many primary teachers invite parent volunteers to serve as assistants in the reading/language arts program. A parent can work with one small group, while the teacher works with another or with the rest of the class. In this way, parents can serve many important functions. They can read aloud to a group of children or listen to an individual or a small group of children read aloud to them. Parents can write the words as a child dictates a story or edit a piece of writing done by a child. Parents can listen to book reports and keep records of the number and types of books read by each child.

With the advent of computers in the classroom, many teachers enjoy having parents who are knowledgeable about computers volunteer to work with groups of children as they learn to operate a computer or to monitor students' progress as they work with tutorial or problem-solving computer programs.

During individualized math or spelling programs, or those structured on a mastery learning model, parents can serve as assistants who correct formative tests and provide feedback to students. They can also help to organize the large amounts of paperwork, filing, and record keeping that often accompany individualized instructional programs.

There are many benefits to having parents volunteer to work in your classroom, and often there are knowledgeable and experienced parents who enjoy this type of work. There are many parents who have interrupted their own careers during their child-raising years and who enjoy having a regular volunteer job to look forward to.

Not all teachers, however, enjoy having parent volunteers in their classrooms. Some teachers are reluctant to have parents view the ups and downs that occur in any school day. Other teachers are not comfortable with parent volunteers because the teacher must be ready with activities and materials whenever the parent arrives. For some teachers, this is a burden that outweighs the benefit of having the extra help. It is true that working with parent volunteers means greater responsibility for the teacher, who must manage the other adults as well as the students in the class.

Whether you wish to use parents as volunteers in your classroom is one of those issues that you will need to reflect on, considering the benefits against the costs. One of the best ways to gather information about the efficacy of this practice in your classroom is to try it out with one subject area and a knowledgeable, experienced parent volunteer in order to find out if it is a system you want to employ.

To increase the likelihood that the practice will work in your classroom, it is important that you and the parent volunteer discuss in advance what you expect the parent to do and agree on the times the parent will visit. Usually parents do only routine tasks or monitor students as they work on a program that is planned by you and your co-workers. When these matters are clarified, you will probably find the volunteer effort to be very productive, allowing you to reduce the amount of time you spend on routine tasks.

Community Resources

Parents with special interests, abilities, careers, and accomplishments can also enrich your program by visiting to speak to the class about their specialties. A unit on community helpers can certainly benefit from the visits of parents who are nurses, police officers, fire fighters, and others who perform community services. Parents who are manufacturers or waste haulers can provide input during a unit on ecology. When the class is studying economics, parents who work as merchants can describe the theory of supply and demand to the class.

During the first parent–teacher conference in the fall, you may be able to discover what talents your parents possess and create a community resource file to draw on throughout the year. In some schools these files are kept schoolwide, and parents listed in the file are happy to come to any classroom in the school to share their knowledge and experience with the children. The file may also contain the names of adults in the community who are not parents of children attending the school but who are willing to visit as a service to the community.

Moral Education Programs

The interaction between home and school becomes more complex and controversial when the school's objective changes from supporting the child's academic development to supporting the child's moral development. Nevertheless, schools in the 1990s and the twenty-first century are likely to be at the center of a growing concern over the need for greater emphasis on moral education. This concern has grown out of an awareness that schools must take more responsibility for countering the influence of drugs, violence on television and other media, the fragmentation of the family, and the publicity about questionable ethical practices in business and industry (ASCD, 1988, p. 4).

A panel of educators met in the summer of 1988 to discuss the schools' role in teaching values. They agreed that due to the enormous temptations and distractions facing children today, the schools must take an active role in teaching children about the nature of right and wrong. While the panel recognized that the increasing social, religious, and ethnic diversity of the schools makes it difficult to agree on one set of values, there are a few common themes that appear in almost every culture. The panel recommends that schools develop community-supported programs centering on at least four themes: *justice, altruism, diligence,* and *respect for human dignity.*

Lickona (1988) recommends that each school recruit local parents to serve on a school–parent support group to (1) arrive at a consensus on the moral values most important to that community and (2) write a moral education curriculum that will be taught at school and in the home at the same time (p. 36).

Mary Ellen Saterlie (1988), a school administrator in Baltimore, Maryland, illustrates how such a parent–school partnership can be formed and what it can produce. She describes the Baltimore public schools' experience, in which school administrators created a community task force to participate in an open dialogue on community values. They purposely invited people with very different religious and political beliefs to serve on the task force. After extensive reading and debate, the task force was able to agree on a "common core" of values appropriate for a democratic and pluralistic society. They are:

> compassion, courtesy, critical inquiry, due process, equality of opportunity, freedom of thought and action, honesty, human worth and dignity, integrity, justice, knowledge, loyalty, objectivity, order, patriotism, rational consent, reasoned argument, respect for others' rights, responsible citizenship, rule of law, self-respect, tolerance, and truth. (pp. 46–47)

Following the identification of these community-acknowledged values, the task force wrote outcome statements for the development of these moral values. Their report was then discussed and ratified by the Board of Education. The PTA developed a brochure on the values education program, which they distributed to all parents in the system.

The method of implementation of this program allowed each of the 148 schools in the district to appoint its own values committee, which was encouraged to select certain of the task force–identified values to emphasize in its own school projects. This encouraged a creative response from most schools. Some addressed additional values such as computer ethics or academic honesty, as well as those identified by the task force. The Baltimore model linked parents, schools, and the community in a unified examination of moral and ethical issues in order to "strengthen the character of our students, which in turn will contribute to strengthening our free society" (p. 47).

As a beginning teacher, you may find that your school district is taking similar measures, and you may wish to become an active part of the task force that identifies the moral values of your community and creates school programs to educate students in these values. If you find that your school district has not yet considered such a challenge, perhaps you can be the one who initiates the idea. It is issues such as this that are initiated and supported by reflective individuals who are committed to searching for solutions to the ever-widening gap between those who show little respect for moral principles and those who prize and uphold them.

THE REFLECTIVE TEACHER AS A MEMBER OF THE EDUCATIONAL COMMUNITY

Teacher Empowerment

The focus of the current research on educational reform and the restructuring of schools centers on the teacher, indicating why the role of the teacher is growing in responsibility and respect. Some use the term *teacher empowerment* to describe the new role of the teacher. Teachers are gaining power by showing a growing willingness to take responsibility for all aspects of planning, teaching, and evaluation.

Prior to the 1990s, teachers were viewed by many as the weak links in the educational system. The publishers of elementary textbooks, for example, seemed to assume that the role of the teacher was simply a technical one, and in many school districts, teachers were encouraged or required simply to follow the texts, workbooks, and elaborately detailed teacher's manuals, without much opportunity to exercise creativity or judgment.

During the 1980s considerable lip service was paid to creating excellence in the schools, but at the same time, many states established restrictive mandates and required extensive new assessment procedures that purported to raise the achievement level of students in the basic skills but, in reality, caused many teachers simply to teach to the test.

In contrast, in the 1990s, there is growing evidence that this is a time of change and school improvement from the bottom up. "A survey last year by the National Governor's Association found that 21 states offered school districts the chance to apply for waivers to impeding regulations as part of their restructuring initiatives, and several others were considering doing so" (O'Neil, 1990).

State curricula such as the California Frameworks are designed to encourage classroom teachers to generate creative learning experiences that fit the needs of their own students. They are challenging textbook publishers to provide materials that enhance, rather than limit, teachers' use of a variety of instructional strategies. School districts are being restructured to encourage teachers to contribute innovative proposals for change. Methods of assessing student achievement have changed in several states, including Connecticut, California, and Vermont, where portfolios are replacing multiple-choice tests (O'Neill, 1990, p. 9). These methods of assessment empower teachers to make more and better choices about how to meet the needs of their students and design school programs that encourage success.

Teacher empowerment means that teachers have more opportunities to make choices and decisions, a necessary ingredient for reflectiveness. For without the right and responsibility to make decisions, reflecting on the way to improve one's teaching and improve the lives of one's students would be fruitless.

Teachers Mentoring Each Other

One of the most exhilarating changes in teaching today are the opportunities that classroom teachers have to take part in the education and support of college and university students and beginning teachers. In Glenview, Illinois, for example, many classroom teachers have contributed to the development of an innovative teacher education program in which De Paul University students are hired as teacher interns at the same time that they take their methods courses in education. The classroom teachers work with university personnel in designing and teaching these methods courses, many of which take place in the school itself. These teachers enjoy the sense of collegiality that they share with each other, the university teachers, and the students. It gives them a sense of passing on the best of what they know to the next generation of teachers.

A few years ago, only the school principal was responsible for observing and evaluating teachers' classroom performance. But in many school systems today, teachers are sharing their own perspectives with each other as part of the evaluation process. Experienced classroom teachers, sometimes called *coaches* or *mentor teachers*, observe less experienced teachers as they work with children in their classrooms. Afterward, the two teachers discuss the observed classroom events. This practice allows the mentor teacher to provide critical feedback and to share personal knowledge with colleagues. It also encourages the beginning teachers to reflect on what they do, the effects of their actions, and decisions and ways to improve their teaching.

Conclusions

At the center of all of this change is the teacher, and the growing power, responsibility, and respect the teacher has earned. Porter and Brophy (1988) report that since the early 1970s there has been a surge of activity in research on teaching. Much of it has been predicated on a deceptively simple thesis: Effective school learning requires good teaching, and good teachers are those who exercise good judgment in constructing the education of their students (p. 74). In other words, as described in Chapter 1 of this text, good teachers are those who use reflective thinking, based on moral principles, in making judgments about classroom events. There is a strong, undeniable link between *reflective* and *effective* teachers.

As discussed in Chapter 2, research shows that the most effective teachers are good classroom managers. This management skill grows directly out of reflective, empathetic, and democratic leadership from the first day of school. As shown in Chapter 3, the role of the teacher includes the responsibility for making accurate diagnoses, which occurs when teachers use formal and informal sources of information as a means of making reflective judgments about appropriate placements of students in the curriculum so that they can achieve success.

Throughout the research on effective teaching and effective schools, the attribute of *teacher clarity* surfaces again and again. "Effective teachers are clear about what they intend to accomplish through their instruction, and they keep these goals in mind both in designing instruction and in communicating its purposes to the students" (Porter & Brophy, 1988, p. 81). Clarity of goal setting requires the reflective planning practices described in Chapter 4.

It is also becoming apparent that it is very effective to combine or integrate subjects into multidisciplinary units of study, as described in Chapters 5 and 6. Rather than being textbook technicians, reflective teachers prefer to create their own learning experiences, either individually or with teammates. They frequently focus on interesting themes or topics in which students use and develop their reading, writing, and research skills as they gain new knowledge about a wide variety of subjects.

Another common element identified throughout the literature on effective teaching is that effective teachers create learning experiences in which students are not simply passive recipients of fact-based knowledge; instead, they teach their students how to use many *cognitive processes,* how to organize information in new ways, and how to solve problems for themselves. It takes a reflective teacher with a C-M view of learning to recognize and select the appropriate teaching strategies that will engage students in active learning, as described in Chapters 7, 8, 9, and 10.

Reflective teachers are willing to use a variety of assessment techniques, such as those described in Chapter 11, rather than rely on one objective method. This is an especially effective practice because it allows students with a variety of learning styles to demonstrate their accomplishments and experience success. Effective teachers are also talented at providing students with useful, timely, and detailed *critical feedback* so that students know what is expected and what they must do in order to succeed. But we now know that simply being a good evaluator is not enough; the most effective teachers are those, described in Chapter 12, who cause their students to take an active role in the evaluation of their own learning by teaching them how to apply *metacognitive strategies* in order to become independent and self-reliant, able to monitor and regulate their own learning.

In addition to their responsibilities to their students, effective teachers are able to communicate well with the parents and other members of the school community in order to support the moral development of students.

The role of the teacher in the educational community is changing. Teaching shows considerable promise of becoming a highly respected profession in the United States during the twenty-first century. This is largely due to the efforts of reflective teachers who are asking the important questions about how they can improve classroom events and children's lives. Alone or in collaboration, reflective teachers are seeking out new alternatives and selecting the ones they believe might improve their teaching. They are taking responsibility for evaluating their classroom practices by gathering data from their own observations and from the current research and knowledge base on teaching and learning. They are disseminating what works for them in faculty meetings, workshops, conferences, and articles in professional journals.

Elementary classroom teachers, such as Ginny Bailey in Carpentersville, Illinois, Tim Curbo in San Francisco, California, Jane Stevens in Arlington, Texas, and Jean Malvaso-Zingaro in Rochester, New York, are wonderful examples of what this profession can become if new teachers like you are willing to take the risks and the responsibility they take. If you are like Ginny, you will view yourself as a learner throughout your teaching career. If you are like Tim, you will take initiative for seeking out new and better ways of teaching. If you are like Jane, you will reflect deeply about what works and what doesn't work in your classroom. If you are like Jean, you will show caring and take responsibility for meeting the emotional and cognitive needs of your students. If you are willing to do these things, you will contribute to the profession of teaching and win the respect of teachers like these four, as well as of the entire educational community.

OPPORTUNITIES FOR REFLECTION

▼ Reflective Essay: Teacher Empowerment

Are you a person who is comfortable or uncomfortable with decision-making power? If you work in a school district that encourages teachers to take responsibility for many important decisions, will you welcome this as an opportunity or look on it as a burden? Would you prefer to make decisions about your own classroom independently, or would you rather share the power and the responsibility with your teammates?

▼ Classroom Visit: Teacher Empowerment

In your observations of this classroom and school over the past several weeks, what have you noticed about the decision-making power? Does the power reside completely in the hands of school administrators, or is it shared? What are some examples of teacher empowerment that you have observed? Ask your cooperating teacher to discuss the changes in teacher power that have occurred in the past few years. What are the major impediments to teacher empowerment in this school or district?

REFERENCES

ASSOCIATION OF SUPERVISION AND CURRICULUM DEVELOPMENT (ASCD). (1988). Moral education in the life of the school. *Educational Leadership, 45*(8), 4–8.

BECKER, H., & EPSTEIN, J. (1982). Parent involvement: A survey of teacher practices. *Elementary School Journal, 83*, 85–102.

FIRST, J. (1988). Immigrant students in U.S. public schools: Challenges with solutions. *Phi Delta Kappan, 70*(3), 205–210.

FLORIO–RUANE, S. (1989). Social organization of classes and schools. In M. Reynolds (Ed.), *Knowledge base for beginning teachers* (pp. 163–172). Oxford: Pergamon Press.

GOOD, T., & BROPHY, J. (1987). *Looking in classrooms* (4th ed). New York: Harper & Row.

GRONLUND, N., & LINN, R. (1990). *Measurement and evaluation in teaching*. New York: Macmillan.

LICKONA, T. (1988). How parents and schools can work together to raise moral children. *Educational Leadership, 45*(8), 36–38.

OAKES, J., & LIPMAN, M. (1990). *Making the best of schools*. New Haven, CT: Yale University Press.

O'NEIL, J. (1990). Piecing together the restructuring puzzle. *Educational Leadership, 47*(7), 4–10.

PORTER, A., & BROPHY, J. (1988). Synthesis of research on good teaching. *Educational Leadership, 45*, 74–85.

RIMM, S. (1986). *The underachievement syndrome: Causes and cures*. Watertown, WI: Apple.

SATERLIE, M. (1988) Developing a community consensus for teaching values. *Educational Leadership, 45*(8), 44–47.

ABOUT THE AUTHOR

SINCE THE LATE 1960s, the author has been a successful teacher from Head Start to graduate school. In her view, the term *successful teacher* means that her students experienced success. In her classrooms, students gained self-esteem and the ability to express themselves. They were motivated to set high goals for themselves and to engage in challenging learning activities with interest and enthusiasm.

For 7 years, she specialized in teaching and coordinating gifted programs, but found that her moral principles were in daily conflict with some of the prevailing practices in gifted education. She was especially troubled by the effects of labeling a small quota of children "gifted," which then led to the unwitting label of "not gifted" for the rest of the school population. She turned her attention to creating school programs that encouraged critical and creative thinking for all students. These ideas are expressed in a book she co-authored with Joan Smutny, entitled, *A Thoughtful Overview of Gifted Education*.

A turning point in her life came in 1984, when she initiated a meeting with Benjamin S. Bloom that resulted in the opportunity to work under his guidance on her Ph.D. at Northwestern University. Since completing this degree in 1986, she has been immersed in teacher education programs at De Paul University, where she teaches courses in elementary education, communication skills, curriculum planning, and instructional strategies to develop critical and creative thinking.

Her future plans include an ethnographic study of unusually reflective teachers who use a set of moral principles to guide the decisions they make in schools. This book is designed to assist novice teachers in clarifying their own moral principles and establishing patterns of reflective thinking as they enter the profession of teaching.

Judy Eby